SEPOY GENERALS.

THE DUKE OF WELLINGTON.

SEPOY GENERALS

WELLINGTON TO ROBERTS

BY

G. W. FORREST, C.I.E.
EX-DIRECTOR OF RECORDS, GOVERNMENT OF INDIA

Lancer * New Delhi * Olympia Fields IL
www.lancerpublishers.com

Published in the United States

by Lancer Publishers,
a division of Lancer Inter Consult, Inc.
19900 Governors Drive, Suite 104
Olympia Fields IL 60461

Published in India

by Lancer Publishers & Distributors
2/42 (B), Sarvapriya Vihar,
New Delhi-110016

First published 1901

Printed and bound in India.

ISBN: 0-9815378-0-4   978-0-9815378-0-1

Online Military Bookshop
www.lancerpublishers.com

PREFACE.

THIS book contains some of the biographical studies which were written while their author was employed in examining the ancient records in the archives at Bombay, Madras, and Calcutta, and each essay is in a measure the result of his work as Director of Records to the Government of India. They are now, after many years, recast and republished in trust that they will have their use in reminding Englishmen by what thoughts and actions our empire is made and held together. The Peninsular war and Waterloo campaign have cast into the shade the Mahratta campaign and the victory of Assaye; but the knowledge Wellington acquired in the Mahratta campaign of the details of the business of war, and the experience he gained in the fine art of reconciling conflicting interests among his subordinates and allies, carried the "Sepoy General," as he was contemptuously called by his great antagonist, through the toils and difficulties which beset his path in the Peninsula. He did not display a cooler and more indomitable resolution during the crowning action of his life than he did at

Assaye. His hardly won victories entitle him to a foremost rank among the great captains who established the military supremacy of England throughout India, and a study of the authoritative records of his administration shows that he was almost the first of the race of soldier-statesmen who by their wisdom, their sympathy, and their sense of an inviolable justice have bestowed permanence and stability on our great and illustrious dependency.

The story of Wellington's Indian career is told mainly from his despatches and letters published in the first two volumes of Colonel Gurwood's work, and the *'Supplementary Despatches,'* edited by his son. These have been collated with the letters and State Papers preserved in the Bombay Record Office. When the Indian despatches were in the course of publication, thirty years after Assaye, the Duke said to Lady Salisbury: "I have just been reading them over, and was surprised to find them so good—they are as good as I could write now. They show the same attention to details—to the pursuit of all the means, however small, that could promote success." The despatches of a general, however, cannot tell the whole tale, and materials for it have also been collected from Jackson and Scott's *'Military Life of Field-Marshal Duke of Wellington.'* Lushington's *'Life and Services of General Lord Harris'*; *'Notes Relative to the late Transactions in the Mahratta Empire'*; *'The Despatches, Minutes, and Correspondence of the Marquess Wellesley, during*

his Administration in India,' by Montgomery Martin;
Wilks's *'Historical Sketches of the South of India'*;
Beatson's *'View of the Origin and Conduct of the War
with Tippoo Sultaun'*; *'The Military Reminiscences of
Colonel James Welsh'*; and Major David Price's *'Memoirs
of the Early Life and Services of a Field Officer,'* present
us with many dramatic incidents of which the writers
were eyewitnesses.

Sir Thomas Munro, like Wellington, took as a soldier-
statesman an important part in the settlement of Southern
India. The sketch of his career is mainly based on his
Life by G. R. Gleig, and the selections from his Minutes
edited by Sir A. T. Arbuthnot. In his diary, February 15,
1830, the Hon. Mountstuart Elphinstone, no mean judge,
writes: "I have begun Sir T. Munro's Life, and am quite
enchanted with it. It cannot fail to delight even those
who had previously no interest in the subject. It is almost
all made up of his own letters, which have fortunately
been preserved, and which show that his judgment and
sagacity at nineteen were as superior to those of ordinary
people as they were to those of his contemporaries when
his reputation was more extensive. They also most
fortunately disclose the many accomplishments which
were concealed by his modesty, and that delicacy of taste
and tenderness of feeling which lay hid under his plain
and somewhat stern demeanour." It was that delicacy of
taste and tenderness of feeling which won the hearts of
the natives, and gained for Munro the proud title of "the

father of the people." His administration in Baramahal is
a vivid exemplification of the personal rule which created
our Indian Empire. Munro, Metcalfe, Elphinstone,
Jonathan Duncan, Thomason, knew the people, and by
their sympathy and frankness gained their confidence.
At this time, when there is a tendency to exaggerate the
importance of material progress, it is well to remember
the wise words of Mountstuart Elphinstone: "It is not
enough to give new laws or even good courts. You must
take the people along with you, and give them a share in
your feelings, which can only be done by sharing theirs."
Munro's success as an administrator has overshadowed
his fame as a soldier. But as a commander in the field
he showed in the subjugation of the Southern Mahratta
country both spirit and fertility of resource. To Munro
Wellington wrote: "As you are a judge of a military
operation, and as I am desirous of having your opinion on
my side, I am about to give you an account of the battle
of Assye" (Assaye).

The sketch of Sir David Baird, one of the most thorough
soldiers that ever devoted their lives to the service of
their country, was written at the time when a fresh
Indian expedition to Egypt led to an examination of the
records relating to the last expedition, which had long
been forgotten. A cautious use has been made of Theodore
Hook's 'Life of Sir David Baird,' a book of considerable
literary merit marred by the unfair spirit in which it is

written. How the body of Tippoo Sultan was found hidden beneath a heap of slain is told in a letter which has never before been printed.

The career of Herbert Edwardes is recorded in 'A Year on the Punjab Frontier,' one of the most fascinating books in our English, and in the Memoirs written by his widow. Englishmen, however, cannot too often wander with Edwardes through the fair and fertile valley of Bunnu which he subjugated without firing a shot, or keep pace with him in his brilliant march to Multan. Lady Edwardes kindly sent the author some important letters relating to the originating and negotiating of the two treaties with Afghanistan.

The story of Napier's various campaigns, from Corunna to Meeanee, is told in his own words. History has endorsed Sir William Napier's fine summary of his brother's rule over Sind: "He left a united regenerated people rejoicing in a rising civilisation, the work of his beneficent genius." Sufficient justice, however, has never been done to the hard and splendid work he did as Commander-in-Chief in India. The details of his administration are now given from the old warrior's impetuous speeches, his general orders, and his caustic criticisms on the verdicts of the courts-martial which came before him for final judgment. His disquisitions display the qualities of his administrative talent, and must always prove invaluable to the military reader.

The example set by Charles Napier of carrying out inspections with thoroughness, of minutely inspecting barracks to see that the soldier was lodged in comfort, of striving to the utmost to increase the welfare of the soldier and the sepoy, has been followed ,by his illustrious successors–Napier of Magdala, Sir Donald Stewart, Earl Roberts, and Sir William Lockhart.

The memoirs of Donald Stewart and Lockhart were printed in 'Blackwood's Magazine' under the title of "Two Great Soldiers."

The sketch of Lord Roberts' career was written before he left India, and printed on the day of his departure, which was generally supposed to mark the date of the close of his active military life. It has now been entirely recast. The account of his services in the Indian Mutiny is based on official records and contemporary literature. The story of the Afghan campaign is mainly told from his own despatches, which the author has examined more closely than is common, as he was at one time asked to edit the official history of the war. The scheme had to be relinquished, as the editing of the State Papers relating to the Mutiny was considered to be a work of a more pressing nature. The account of Lord Roberts' South African campaign is also mainly based on his own despatches, and what the Duke of Wellington said of his Indian despatches is applicable to them: "They show the same attention to details–to the pursuit of all the means, however small, that could promote success."

The earnest endeavour of the author has been to record not only the heroism of the British soldier but also the gallantry of the Sepoy. To the courage shown in brilliant attack, the patience and coolness in danger, of the British soldier we owe our victories from Plassey to Assaye. Of them it was well said, "They may be private, but they never are common soldiers"–a phrase worthy of the gallant Napiers. But it must be remembered that a handful of Englishmen could never have conquered India if we had not been assisted by the bravery and devotion of the native armies of Bengal, Bombay, and Madras. It was the first battalion of the light regiment of Madras infantry which was the favourite corps of the Duke of Wellington. They were with him on every service, and the men of the regiment used to call themselves "*Wellesley ka Pultan*" (Wellesley's Regiment); and at Assaye, which made us masters of India, they proved themselves worthy of the proud title. A staff officer after the battle saw some Muhammadans engaged in a funeral and inquired who they were burying. "We are going to put three brothers into one grave," said one of the party. The officer began to express his regret and offer some consolation to the survivors, when he was interrupted by one of the men. "There is no occasion," he said, "for such, feelings or expressions; these men" (pointing to the dead bodies) "were sepoys; they have died in the performance of their duties; the Government they have served will protect their children, who will soon fill the ranks they have occupied."

Buried in the old records and memoirs of the day are to be found many examples of the patient endurance of privation and fatigue and the splendid valour of our native troops. The noble fall of such men as Hussain Khan (p. 70) and Subahdar Ally Khan (p. 88) shows the undaunted courage of " those glorious sepoys, who have so often fought side by side with their European officers, striving with them even unto their death."

GEORGE W. FORREST.

THE KNOWLE,
BRENCHLEY, KENT, *October* 1901.

CONTENTS.

PORTRAITS.

THE DUKE OF WELLINGTON.

THREE months before the opening of the nineteenth century the Governor-General of India, the Marquess Wellesley, writes to Mr Addington, " My brother Arthur has distinguished himself most brilliantly." This brother, Colonel Arthur Wesley, had landed with his regiment, the 33rd, at Calcutta on the 17th of February 1797. He was then twenty-eight years of age, and a brother officer describes him "as a little above the middle height, well limbed and muscular, with little encumbrance of flesh beyond that which gives shape and manliness to the outlines of the figure; an erect carriage; a countenance strongly patrician, both in feature, profile, and expression; and an appearance remarkable and distinguished: few could approach him on any duty, or any subject requiring his serious attention, without being sensible of something strange and penetrating in his clear light eye." [1] When Colonel Arthur Wesley arrived at Calcutta Sir John Shore (Lord Teignmouth) was Governor-General, and the first interview between them was at a levee. As the young colonel retired, Sir John, turning round

[1] *The Military Memoirs of the Duke of Wellington,* by Major Moyle Sherer, vol. i. pp. 50, 51.

to his aides-de-camp, exclaimed, "If Colonel Wesley should ever have the opportunity of distinguishing himself, he will do it, and greatly." To Sir John Shore Colonel Wesley brought a letter of introduction from his illustrious predecessor, the Marquess of Cornwallis, who was colonel of the 33rd. It was short and to the point :-

DEAR SIR,–I beg leave to introduce to you Col. Wesley, who is lieut.-col. of my regiment: he is a sensible man and a good officer, and will, I have no doubt, conduct himself in a manner to merit your approbation." [1]

The young colonel was a frequent guest at Government House, and the Governor-General used to say that he never had found in any man such a union of strong sense and boyish playfulness. Forty years after the Duke of Wellington wrote to the son, "His lordship received and always treated me with great kindness and consideration." [2]

Colonel Wesley arrived in India prepared for his work. He not only knew how to handle his men and the internal economy of his regiment, but also he had studied with close attention the higher problems of his profession, and had gained in the Low Countries some experience of war and its requirements.[3] Thirty years after he said: "I believe I owe most of my success to the attention I always paid to the inferior part of tactics as a regimental officer. There were few men in the army

---

[1] He became colonel on the 3rd of May 1796.

[2] *Life of Lord Teignmouth,* by his son, Lord Teignmouth, vol. i. p. 424.

[3] When Earl Stanhope observed to him that his previous experience and trial of war in the Dutch campaign must have been very useful to him in India, he answered, "why, I learnt what one ought not to do, and that is always something."—*Notes of Conversation with the Duke of Wellington,* by Philip Henry, 5th Earl of Stanhope, p. 182.

who knew these details better than I did; it is the I foundation of all military knowledge. When you are sure that you know the power of your troops, and the way to handle them, you are able to give your mind altogether to the greater considerations which the presence of the enemy forces upon you." Colonel Shawe, a great friend of Wellington's, told Croker that in the Duke's early residence in India, and before he was in command, his critical study of his profession afforded a marked contrast to the general habits of that time and country. Shawe also added another early anecdote. " The Duke inherits his father's musical taste, and used to play very well, and rather too much, on the violin. Some circumstances occurred which made him reflect that this was not a soldierly accomplishment, and took up too much of his time and thoughts, and he burned his fiddles, and never played again. About the same time he gave up the habit of card-playing." [1]

Colonel Wesley's military attainments soon became known, and he had not been three months in the country when he was consulted on a project for establishing light artillery. His letter on the subject, dated Fort William, 11th April 1797, is characteristic, and though his remarks upon the artillery question are now out of date, and there is no longer any very great difficulty in procuring horses, his remark on the question of cost when it is necessary to provide for military efficiency should not be forgotten. He writes: "The only objection to light artillery is the scarcity of horses in India. I put the expense out of the question, as, if the establishment is necessary, the expense of it is not to be considered." He suggested that a beginning

---

[1] *The Croker Papers,* vol. i. p. 337.

should be made on a small scale. His reputation as a good officer led to his being selected for an important command. England being at war with Spain, the Governor-General, acting under instructions from home, determined to send out an expedition for an attack upon the Spanish settlement of Manilla, and the 33rd was one of the regiments selected to compose the expeditionary force despatched for this purpose from the Bengal Presidency. On the 17th of April Wesley wrote to his brother, the Earl of Mornington: "Since my last an expedition to Manilla has been talked of, upon which I am to go, and, I believe, to have the command of the corps furnished by this settlement. It was proposed by Mr Spike, the Deputy-Governor, to give me the chief command of the expedition; but I desired the person who communicated his wishes to me to decline it in my name, and to propose Doyle. If anything should prevent Doyle from accepting it in case they offer it to him, and they should afterwards offer it to me, I intend to accept of it; taking the chance that the large force they intend to send, the known pusillanimity of the enemy, and my exertions will compensate in some degree for my want of experience." [1] A month later he writes to his brother: "–is determined to send–as commander-in-chief, notwithstanding the entreaties of his friends and the orders of his superiors. He does so without fear of failure, although he knows his incapacity, and says he sends with him a good adjutant-general and a good quartermaster and a good army. But he is mistaken if he supposes that a good high-spirited army can be kept in order by other means than by the abilities and firmness of the commander-in-chief." [1]

---

[1] *Supplementary Despatches of the Duke of Wellington,* vol. i. p. 4.

Colonel Wesley submitted a "Memorandum on the Expedition against the Spanish Islands" to the Governor-General. It was the first of a series of State papers which is one of the greatest facts in English letters. He urges strongly that the first step should be the destruction of the Dutch colony of Batavia in the island of Java, "a town surrounded by a slight brick wall which has no defence." "It has on the eastern side of it a citadel which stands close to the hay, but which, however, is not within shot of the artillery ground. There are no guns mounted on the land side of the citadel. In the rear of the town, at some distance, are two redoubts; while, however, as I am informed, there are no guns. But even if the place were strong and in good order, as the Dutch have but few troops nearer than Sheribou, which is at the distance of forty miles at least, they could not stand against the attack which would be made upon them by surprise." [2] He discusses the climate and the best season for operations with the marvellous fulness of knowledge and accuracy which distinguished all he wrote.

On the 12th of July Colonel Wesley wrote to his brother: "The destruction of Batavia would ruin the Dutch, but it awakes question whether it would be right completely to annihilate them, and it is probably that consideration which has prevented us from

---

[1.] Sir Herbert Maxwell writes: "He [Wesley] observes that in the appointing a commander-in-chief to the expedition the Governor-General 'does so without fear of failure.'" Wesley does not observe, and he never meant the Governor-General. It was Lord Hobart, Governor of Madras, who appointed—notwithstanding the orders of his superior, the Governor-General. Wesley in his letter adds: "He has lately quarrelled with General Harris upon the subject of the disposal of the patronage of the army upon the coast." Lord Hobart quarrelled with General Harris, the commander-in-chief of the coast or Madras army.

[2.] *Supplementary Despatches,* vol. i. p, 4.

attacking them. Mauritius ought to be taken. As long as
the French have an establishment there Great Britain
cannot call herself safe in India." [1] In August the Bengal
troops under Colonel Wesley set sail. Before embarking he
issued regimental orders for men on board ship, which, as
high military experts state, are well worth studying even
now. From the Company's ship *Heroine* he wrote a warm
remonstrance to the Governor-General regarding an order
he had received that "in cases of coming to action the troops
will be under the command of the captain of the ship." "I
embarked with this regiment, a step which, however attached
I may be to the king's service, I would have sooner quitted it
than have taken, had I known that matter was to be arranged
as I find it is." He added, "However, sir, uncomfortable as I
feel it embarking under such circumstances, I shall do
everything in my power, and shall make those under me
do everything in their power, to forward the service." [2]
Sir John Shore returned a private answer to the letter,
expressing regret at the inadvertence which he had
committed, and adding a hope that the revocation of the
order would reach the ships before their departure. "No
man," he writes, "can be more impressed than I am with
a sense of the zeal, alacrity, and spirit shown by yourself,
and the officers and men of your regiment; and I had
flattered myself with the pleasing expectation of having,
as far as depended upon me, done everything in my power
to render this service agreeable to you." [3] In the month
of September the troops from Bengal under Wesley met

[1] *Supplementary Despatches,* vol. i. p. 12.

[2] Ibid., p. 22.

[3] Ibid., p. 23.

the contingent from Madras at Paulo Penang; but they got no farther, as Lord Hobart, the Governor of Fort St George, apprehensive of the designs of Tippoo Sultaun, exercised the discretionary powers intrusted to him and recalled the expedition. Colonel Wesley accordingly returned with his regiment to Bengal. While at Penang he wrote a paper on the advantages of our occupying the island, dealing thoroughly not only with its military defences, but also with commerce, future government, and taxation. Soon after returning he wrote a Memorandum on Bengal, and discusses roads, markets, foreign trade of India, East and West India sugars, necessity for naval defence of Britain, with equal ease and knowledge. Whatever may now be thought of the economic soundness of some of his statements, it must be remembered that in 1797 he argued as a general proposition in favour of breaking through the Company's monopoly of trade in India.

In the cold weather of that year Colonel Wesley paid a visit to Madras to meet Lord Hobart, the Governor, who was about to depart for Europe. It was a new country, and he spent his time in an examination of the military establishments of that Presidency and in making frequent excursions along its borders in order to study the topography of the hills. The time, he knew, might at any moment come when an English army would have to penetrate them. The intrigues and military movements of Tippoo Sultaun had attracted the attention of the Government, and grave apprehensions were entertained of his design and power. Colonel Wesley made a tour through the newly-acquired district of Barahmahal, and found that Colonel Read had made a fine road through that wild region, studded with formidable forts, by Ryaccotta to the outlet on the Bangalore side. The information he gathered during his tour enabled him to write the following year his Memorandum on Barahmahal, when war with the Sultan of Mysore was imminent. After a stay of two months Wesley left Madras and returned to Calcutta.

Soon after his departure from Madras his brother Richard, Lord Mornington, the brilliant scholar and great statesman who has stamped the name of Marquess Wellesley upon the pages of the history of our Indian Empire, landed at that port. The same day the French frigate *La Preneuse,* with the ambassadors which Tippoo had sent to the French Governor-General of the Mauritius and the French troops levied for his service, arrived at Mangalore, a port of the Sultan of Mysore on the Malabar coast. Since the treaty of Seringapatam (1792) the destruction of the British power in India had formed the favourite and unremitting object of Tippoo's hopes and exertions. His haughty mind could never be reconciled to the sacrifices which he had been compelled to make for the purchase of peace. On one occasion in his *durbar* he declared "that a nice sense of honour should be the predominant feature in the sense of a king, and that one who had suffered misfortunes from the superiority of his enemies should never be appeased until he had obtained ample revenge. That, for his part, he should every day seek the most likely means for effecting the ruin of his enemies, and that his mind was principally occupied in the contemplation of this object. The means I have taken," he added, "to keep in remembrance the misfortunes I experienced six years ago from the malice of my enemies are to discontinue sleeping on a cotton bed and to make use of a cloth one; when I can victorious I shall resume the bed of cotton." His eagerness to recover his lost dominions urged him to pursue a systematic course of intrigue against the British power among all the native states, and this he conducted with great skill and perseverance. By the treaty of Seringapatam his power had been considerably reduced, but it had not been sufficiently curtailed to render him incapable of deranging the balance which it was the policy of that treaty to establish between the native states. His dominion was still extensive, he was master of the highland plateau of Mysore, and he had a sea-coast and ports. His army was well equipped and sufficiently well mounted to turn the scale in a contest between any two states. At the same moment that he concluded the peace of Seringapatam Tippoo resumed his intrigues with the French Government, and began his secret negotiations with the Courts of Poona and Hyderabad. To detach them from the English Government was a prime necessity. He promised the Court of Hyderabad never to trouble them in any way and to shield them from the Mahrattas. But the Nizam, who placed every reliance on the good faith and sincerity of the British Government, would not trust Tippoo, and refused to make an alliance with him on any terms. The Mahrattas, however, regarded the extension of our influence and our connection with the Nizam with characteristic jealousy. They advanced their reliance on Tippoo as a counterpoise to our increased power. A war with the Nizam, with Tippoo as a powerful ally, would diminish that power and give them a great augmentation of wealth and predominance. The seeds of quarrel were soon found. An old demand for *chouth* was revived. Tippoo assembled an army and threatened to come forward as an ally of the Mahrattas. The Nizam earnestly solicited the interference of the English, but Sir John Shore, who had succeeded Lord Cornwallis as Governor-General, unwisely and ungenerously refused any aid. He did not think loss of prestige could be placed "in competition with the greater evils likely to attend a war with the Mahrattas and Tippoo Sultan." It required the genius and courage of the great Proconsul to revive among the native princes a reliance on our faith and dread of our arms. And he had to fight with Tippoo and the Mahrattas. Nana Fadnavis, the able and all-powerful Prime Minister of the Peshwa, pressed the claims of his master. The demands of the Mahratta envoy were treated with scorn. Both sides prepared for war. On the 12th of March 1795 the Nizam's army was totally defeated, and a few days afterwards he consented to the humiliating terms on which alone the Mahrattas would make peace.

After staying a fortnight at Madras Lord Mornington embarked for Calcutta, and arrived on the 17th of May at the capital of his realm. It was at the foot of the letter to Mr Lushington at Madras, stating that "Lord M. arrived here the day before yesterday, and was in good health," that Colonel Wesley first signed himself Arthur Wellesley, his family having adopted the ancient spelling of their name. Four days after, having reached the seat of Government, Lord Mornington informed the Peshwa that he had taken over charge of the affairs of the Honourable Company, and added, "I am happy in the present opportunity of assuring you that it will always be my study to cultivate and improve the harmony subsisting between the two states, to establish the utmost degree of individual friendship and attachment with you, and to maintain the Company's reputation, and seek the confidence of all the princes and chiefs of Hindustan, by a strict attention to the principle of justice and good faith and adherence to engagements." The native chiefs, however, had lost their old belief in our adherence to engagements, by Sir John Shore's refusal to aid the Nizam in the hour of need. After his defeat at Kharla that sovereign, incensed by the absolute neutrality of the Governor-General, disbanded the English who had been attached to him and increased the forces under the command of M. Raymond, a French soldier of fortune. At the time when Lord Mornington assumed office the very existence of the British Empire in India was threatened with grave danger. Tippoo, the Nizam, and Sindia were all under French influence, and their armies chiefly officered by Frenchmen. The Nizam's forces, under M. Raymond, were 15,000 strong, with an efficient park of artillery. Sindia's forces, under De Borgne, were at least 40,000 men, in the highest state of discipline and efficiency, supported by more than 400 guns. A Jacobin club had been organised at Seringapatam. It was not beyond the bounds of probability that the French commanders might unite to strike a deadly blow at the power of the English in the East. Lord Mornington therefore determined to destroy the chance of a federation. By a stroke of daring and genius he had the French force at Hyderabad disbanded, and a corps of British troops, paid by the Nizam, officered by Europeans, substituted for it. Lord Mornington was desirous of concluding a similar treaty with the Peshwa, and having a British detachment stationed at Poona. He wrote to the Governor of Bombay that he had authorised the Resident at the Court of the Peshwa to apply to him for a military force to be marched directly to Poona: "We are fully aware of the objections even to a temporary diminution of the force on your establishment, but when we acquaint you that the permanent security of the British possessions in India is essentially concerned in the measures which we are now concerting with the Courts of Poona and Hyderabad, and that the success of those measures will become impracticable unless the force which may be required by Colonel Palmer shall reach Poona with all possible expedition, we are confident that you will not suffer so important an arrangement to be frustrated by any difficulty which is not absolutely insuperable." The Peshwa, however, at the instigation of Nana Fadnavis, rejected the treaty, but gave a solemn assurance of his fidelity to existing engagements. Lord Mornington felt that the time had now come when some decisive action must be taken against Tippoo, who had actively pursued his endeavours to negotiate foreign alliances.

On the 8th of June 1798 there was published in a newspaper at Calcutta a proclamation issued by Mr Malartie, the Governor-General of the Isle of France. It was dated the 30th of January, and stated that an embassy had arrived at the Isle of France with letters from Tippoo Sultaun, addressed not only to the Government of that island but also to the Executive Directory of France.

[1.] He desires to form an offensive and defensive alliance with the French, and proposes to maintain at his charge, as long as the war shall last in India, the troops which may be sent to him.

[2.] He promises to furnish every necessary for carrying on the war, wine and brandy excepted, with which he is wholly unprovided.

[3.] He declares that he has made every preparation to receive the succours which may be sent him, and that on the arrival of troops the commanders and officers will find everything necessary for making a war, to which Europeans are but little accustomed.

[4.] In a word, he only waits the moment when the French shall come to his assistance, to declare war against the English, whom he ardently desires to expel from India.

The Governor-General received the first regular authentication of the proclamation in a despatch from Lord Macartney of 28th March from the Cape of Good Hope. At the same time several persons arrived at Calcutta who had been present in the Isle of France at the time the proclamation was issued. It could now no longer be doubted that the proclamation actually had been issued by the Governor-General of the Isle of France. Lord Mornington resolved on instant war. On the 25th of June he wrote a minute stating his reasons why Mysore should be invaded, and he issued orders for the armies on the coast to be assembled without delay. He sent the minute to Colonel Wellesley, who returned it on the 28th of June with some masterly observations. He admitted that the cause of war was sufficient, but held that the moment was inopportune. We had a long and expensive war in Europe, our allies were not ready to assist even as they did in the last war with Tippoo, and the Company's "resources in this country were not in flourishing condition." "In my opinion," he concludes, "if it be possible to adopt a line of conduct which would not lead immediately to war, provided it can be done with honour, which I think indispensable in this Government, it

ought to be adopted. . . . Let the proclamation be sent to
Tippoo, with the demand that he should explain it and the
landing of troops. Don't give him reason to suppose that we
imagine he has concluded an alliance with the object stated
in the proclamation; and finding he has derived so little
benefit from the alliance, there is every probability that he
will deny the whole, and be glad of an opportunity of getting
out of the scrape. In the meanwhile we shall believe as much
as we please, and shall be prepared against all events."

The opinion of his brother being supported by a report
from the Madras Government, stating that it would be
fully six months before they could equip an army and place
it in the field, Lord Mornington, "with pain and regret,"
postponed the declaration of war. In order to strengthen
the Madras army and hasten its equipment for the field, he
sent there Colonel Wellesley with the 33rd. On the 13th of
August Arthur Wellesley writes from the ship *Fitzwilliam* to
his brother Henry, then private secretary to the Governor-
General: "The ship struck this morning at about five upon
what is called Sangor Reef, and remained fast until about
one, when she was got off, I may almost say, by the bodily
strength of the soldiers of the 33rd. She struck with
great violence several times in almost every minute, and
now leaks much. . . . If the weather had not been more
moderate than it is usually, we must all have been lost." [1]
With the delectable flavour of satire so often found lurking
in his despatches, he adds: "Tell—that I conceive it to be
very inconsistent with the principles of the Christian
religion to give people bad water when he had notice of

[1] *Supplementary Despatches*, vol. i. p. 84.,

the probability that it would be so. We have, however, let it almost loose. You may likewise say that a Gentile could not have done worse than give us a bottle of good rum by way of muster, and fill the casks with the worst I ever saw. I have written to him a public letter on the subject."

The next day he added a postscript: "The pilot did not leave us last night, and I did not therefore close this letter. The ship leaks less than I at first imagined, and we have fine weather and every prospect of a favourable passage."

The ship, however, took three weeks in sailing from the mouth of the Hooghly to Fort St George. On the 15th of September Colonel Wellesley wrote to Lord Mornington: "I arrived here the day before yesterday, and should have written yesterday, only that I had not an opportunity of seeing those persons about whom you had given me instructions." [1] He adds: "I have had a long conversation with General Harris. He has kept me in Fort St George for orders, as he says, to co-operate with him in keeping Lord Clive [2] in the right road. I think that we shall succeed in that object. He has already stated his determination to enter into no discussion with your Government." It was not with Lord Clive but his advisers that Colonel Wellesley had to contend. He describes him as "a mild, moderate man, remarkably reserved, having a bad delivery, and apparently a heavy understanding. He certainly has been unaccustomed to consider questions of the magnitude of that now before

---

[1] *Supplementary Despatches,* vol. i. p. 85.
[2] Governor of Madras. His Lordship arrived from England on the 21st of August 1798 and replaced Lieut.-General Harris, who had been acting Governor from February 1798.

him, but I doubt whether he is so dull as he appears or as people here imagine he is." Lord Clive had, like his father, the victor of Plassey, the appearance of a man of heavy understanding, but Colonel Wellesley soon discovered that he had inherited some of his father's capacity for government. Writing to his brother Harry on the 19th of October, he says: "Lord C. opens his mind to me very freely upon all subjects. I give him my opinion, and talk as I would to M. The truth is, he does not want talents, but he is very diffident of himself; and now that he has begun to find out there is no conjuration in transacting the business of Government, he improves daily, takes more upon himself, and will very shortly have less confidence and reliance than he must have at present upon the opinion and abilities of those who have long done the business of the country."

With regard to the great question of peace or war the soldier continued to urge on his brother the desirability of peace. On the 19th of September he wrote to him :—

I am very anxious to hear of the conclusion of your negotiations with the Peshwa and the Nizam, that you may make your proposition, whatever it may be, to Tippoo as soon as possible, and that he may see that you are not bent upon annihilating. He is well aware of the bad consequences which resulted in the last war from his suffering us to make our preparations at our leisure and to attack him; and you may depend upon it that if he is not convinced that we do not mean to go to war, he will endeavour to strike the first blow at the time I have mentioned (close of the monsoon) to the southward of the Cauvery. Our great strength, to which all addition will have been made by the re-establishment of our allies and the total failure of his allies the French, will induce him to grasp at any favourable opportunity which a moderate proposition from you will give him of

settling this difference. This is no new opinion of mine; I held it
before, and never departed from it, and from what I have seen and
heard since my arrival here, I am more than ever convinced that
the proposition, whatever it may be, ought to be made without loss
of time." [1]

He did not know that the Governor-General was at that
moment desirous of sending him to Hyderabad to conduct the
business there to its issue, and that he should afterwards be
the bearer of his propositions to Tippoo, but the refusal of the
Sultan to receive an ambassador prevented the mission.

Colonel Wellesley remained at Fort St George, keeping
Lord Clive to the right road and pushing on the preparations
for collecting the infinite wants of an army in the field. But
he writes to his brother Henry,[2] then private secretary to
the Governor-General, that "if the army takes the field I
shall not much like to be kept in Fort St George"; and with a
soldier's eye for the commissariat, he asks him to send him
"some Bengal sheep, some potatoes, some smoked hams, and
rounds of beef." Always alive to social influence, he adds,
"I hope that Mornington has been introduced to the ladies
of Calcutta, and that you give dinners frequently." On the
26th September he informs the Governor-General that "all
accounts and intercepted letters tend to prove the hostile
intentions of Tippoo, and therefore nothing ought to induce
them to relax our preparations. I have recommended that the
battering train should be sent forward to Arnee or Vellore
at least; that some general plan of operations should be
determined upon; and that the grain and other stores should

---

[1] *Supplementary Despatches*, vol. i. p. 89
[2] Afterwards Lord Cowley.

be placed upon the line which it may be intended to take."[1] But "that cursed institution," the Military Board, caused a delay in sending the train, and after a month had passed he writes to his brother: "I have gained a complete victory. The battering train is to go off to Vellore immediately. They are at this moment getting it out of the fort. If I can only get intelligence of what is going on, I shall be more than equal to the Military Board. I am, however, heartily sick of the business, and wish I was anywhere else. It is reported here that De Meuron is desirous of leaving Ceylon: if there be no war, would it not be possible to send me there? I don't wish that this should be mentioned to M." [2] Though heartily sick of the business, he continued to labour hard in procuring bullocks, in filling the depots with munitions of war and provisions. He brought to the administrative transactions of war the dry judgment, the calm temper, and the power of detail which distinguishes the eminent man of business, and enables him to surmount all obstacles. On the 9th of November he writes to his brother Henry: "The battering train is arrived at Vellore: it got there even sooner than we expected if the weather had held up. The second division crossed the Palas on the 5th. There are accounts of Tippoo's preparations, which we certainly had reason to expect. However, we are as forward as he can be, and I don't fear him."

Hitherto no direct communication had been made by the Governor-General to Tippoo regarding his knowledge of the proceedings of his ambassadors at the Isle of France, and no remonstrance or explanation had been offered or demanded on either side. But the day drew

---

[1.] *Supplementary Despatches,* vol. i. p. 97.

[2.] Ibid., p. 118.

near when Lord Wellesley would have to assert the supreme ascendancy of the English in India, and events in Europe hastened its approach. Tippoo's ambassadors had brought back an offensive alliance with the French. On the 18th of October Lord Wellesley received a despatch of the Secret Committee of the Court of Directors dated the 18th of June, "and forwarded overland," informing him that a very large armament of ships, troops, and stores had sailed on the 19th of May from Toulon. "Although the ultimate object of this armament has not been ascertained, it is not improbable, from many circumstances that have transpired and from the spirit of daring adventure by which the French have been actuated during the present war, that its destination may be for India, either (having first taken possession of Egypt) by way of the Red Sea or Bussora." [1] Their empire in the East, they add, has ever been an object of jealousy to the French, and they "would risk a great deal, and even adopt measures of a most enterprising and uncommon nature, for the chance of reducing, if not annihilating, the British power and consequence in that part of the world. To effect this without the aid and previous concert of one of the Indian Powers seems almost impossible, and would scarcely be attempted. In the present situation of India, Tippoo appears to be the fittest instrument to be employed in the furtherance of such ambitious projects." With regard to the proclamation issued at the Mauritius, if the Governor-General had not already adopted the necessary measures for bringing Tippoo to a satisfactory explanation he should immediately take the proper steps for so doing. "And should you judge, either from

[1] *Despatches of the Marquess Wellesley,* vol. i. p. 61.

his answers or from the steps he is taking, that his designs are such as the French proclamation represents, and that he is making preparations to act hostilely against us, we think it will be more advisable not to wait for such an attack, but to take the most immediate and most decisive measures to carry into our enemy's country." [1] The same day that Wellesley got the sanction of his masters to demand satisfaction from Tippoo he received a confirmation of the reports of the progress of the French arms in Egypt. He at once wrote to Hyderabad to hasten the disarmament of the French army, to Madras to quicken the military preparations, and he took steps to increase the strength of the fleet on the Malabar coast. On the 22nd of October the French army at Hyderabad was disarmed. "On the 31st of October," Mornington writes to Henry Dundas, "we learnt the satisfactory intelligence of the glorious victory at Beker, which I immediately announced by a circular letter to the Princes of India, not omitting Sultan Tippoo." There is a fine touch of sardonic humour in the close of his letter to Tippoo: "Confident from the union and attachment subsisting between us that this intelligence will afford you sincere satisfaction, I could not deny myself the pleasure of communicating it." The Governor-General considered that, owing to the destruction of the French fleet in Egypt and of the French army in the Deccan, a favourable opportunity had come for opening a negotiation with Tippoo. On the 8th of November he wrote him a studiously courteous letter, informing the Sultan of his knowledge of the nature of his intercourse with the French nation, and proposing to him to receive Major Doveton, "who will explain to you more fully and

[1] *Despatches of the Marquess Wellesley,* vol. i. p. 342.

particularly the sole means which appear to myself, and to the Allies of the Company, to be effectual for the salutary purpose of removing all distrust and suspicion, and of establishing peace and good understanding on the most durable foundations." Tippoo, whose fierce and intractable temper was fast driving him into war, sent no answer. On the 10th of December Lord Mornington again wrote to him, informing him of his intention to proceed to Fort St George, and again urging him to receive Major Doveton. On Christmas Day Lord Mornington embarked on board his Majesty's ship *La Sybella,* and arrived at Fort St George on the last day of the month. Meanwhile Colonel Wellesley, who had strongly urged him to come to Madras, had gone to command the troops collected at Arnee, and was directing with all his energy the preparations for a campaign. He found, according to a well-established English custom, every necessary arrangement incomplete. There was very little grain, there were no bullocks to carry it; the fortresses, which ought to have been stored with provisions, were empty. Night and day he laboured to supply these deficiencies, and when General Harris arrived in camp on the 29th of January, he praised him for the state of his division and for "his judicious and masterly arrangements in respect of supplies." On that very day Colonel Wellesley, in answer to a request made by his brother Henry, wrote to Lord Mornington as "to the propriety and utility of your joining the army and accompanying it during the campaign." "All I can say on the subject is," was his frank comment, "that if I were in General Harris's situation, and you joined the army, I should quit it." On the 2nd of February Lord Mornington replied: "Nothing has given me more pleasure

that to hear from all quarters such unqualified com-
mendations of your arrangements in your late command.
I wish to God the whole were under your direction; but
even as it is, I think our success is certain. I entirely
concur in your opinion respecting the impropriety of my
taking the field to the army; my judgment was always the
same as yours, but certain persons made such a clamour
on the subject that I wished to know how you thought of
it." War with Tippoo was inevitable, though to the last
Colonel Wellesley strove to avert it by negotiations. Upon
Lord Mornington's arrival at Madras a letter from Tippoo
was delivered to him in which the Sultan gave a ludicrous
version of the history of his embassy to the Isle of France.
It was a mercantile adventure on a vessel of two masts,
on the return of which a few Frenchmen had taken their
passage to India. To some of them he had given service, but
others had departed from his dominions. "But the French,"
he observes, "who are full of deceit, have perhaps taken
advantage of the departure of the ship to put about reports
with a view to ruffle the minds of both Governments." He
evaded the proposition of opening a negotiation: "A first and
permanent observance of existing treaties is necessary, and
these, under the favour of God, daily acquire new strength
and improvement by means of amicable correspondence.
Continue to allow me the pleasure of your correspondence,
making me happy by accounts of your health." On the 9th
of January the Governor-General answered Tippoo's letter.
He recapitulated at some length the grounds of complaint
enumerated in his first letter, and detailed the whole of the
Sultan's hostile proceedings. He renewed the proposition of

opening a negotiation: "I once more call upon your Highness, in the most serious and solemn manner, to assent to the admission of Major Doveton, as a measure which I am confident would be productive of the most lasting advantage to all parties. I trust that your Highness will favour me with a friendly letter in reply to this, and I most earnestly request that your reply may not be deferred for more than one day after this letter shall reach your presence: dangerous consequences result from the delay of arduous affairs." [1] January passed, and no reply having been received from Tippoo, Lord Mornington on the 3rd of February commanded General Harris to enter Mysore territory and to march on Seringapatam. On the same day he issued orders to Lieut.-General Stuart, commanding the Bombay army, to co-operate in the attack on Tippoo's capital by advancing simultaneously on it from Cannannore, a town on the Malabar coast about one hundred miles south-west of Seringapatam. The army of the Nizam had in the meantime moved from Hyderabad and arrived about twenty miles north of Vellore. On the 11th General Harris moved forward from Vellore, and on the 18th effected a junction with the Nizam's force. It consisted of 6000 foot under Colonel Roberts and Captain Malcolm, and 10,000 horse– "which," says Wellesley, "they call 25,000"– under Meer Allum. It was now reinforced by the 33rd Regiment, and the general command of the British forces serving with it was given to Colonel Wellesley.

On the 10th of February the long-expected letter from Tippoo reached the Governor-General. He acknowledged the receipt of his two friendly letters, and informed him that, *"being frequently disposed to make excursions and*

[1] *Despatches of the Marquess Wellesley,* vol. i. p. 394.

hunt, I am accordingly proceeding upon a hunting excursion.
You will be pleased to despatch Major Doveton (about whose
coming your friendly pen has repeatedly written) slightly
attended." On the 14th February Lord Mornington wrote to
his brother:—

FORT ST GEORGE, 14*th February* 1799.

MY DEAR ARTHUR, –I recommend the letter which I received
yesterday from Tippoo, and which General Harris will
communicate to you, to your particular attention; and I wish
to know whether you think it requires any change of system.
In order to judge of this point you must read the whole of my
correspondence with Tippoo (now at headquarters), and my
orders to General Harris of the 3rd instant, connected with my
declaration to the Allies. Tippoo's silence was evidently designed
for the great purpose of gaining time; his present compliance
with my repeated request is founded on the same principle.
If Doveton were now to be sent to Tippoo, the Allies would no
longer be cordial, and we could not properly avail ourselves of
the defection of any of Tippoo's subjects: even if Doveton were
to be sent, the army must march to Seringapatam, otherwise
we have the whole game in Tippoo's hands. You will observe
that my letter of the 9th January demanded an answer from
the Sultan within the space of one day, for the express purpose
of precluding procrastination.

Send me your opinion on the whole subject as soon as possible.
I conclude that Henry is on his return, and therefore I have not
sent him any of his letters.–Yours, ever most affectionately,

MORNINGTON.

Arthur Wellesley replied: "My opinion is that you
ought to send Doveton to Tippoo immediately, and give
him notice at the same time that you intend to march
an army into his country in order to enforce the propositions which you will make to him." [1] The objection

---

[1] *Supplementary Despatches,* vol. i. p. 193.

as to there being a risk of the safety of Doveton's person he curtly dismissed: "But I put that out of the question, as, if the measure be a good one in other respects, there is no more reason for not risking Doveton's person than there is for not risking that of any private soldier." He considered the propriety of sending Doveton "immediately depends upon our chances of success. If we are certain that we shall succeed, there is no necessity for it; although, as I said before, there is no objection to it, and it will not in any way diminish our means of carrying on the war." But he was not sanguine of success: "I am really apprehensive that the best that can happen to us is to have a fair prospect of making the siege of Seringapatam in the next season instead of in this. Others, however, are of a different opinion; particularly those at headquarters still believe that we shall succeed in one campaign." The Governor-General, however, feeling certain that Tippoo's grand object would be to gain time till he could see what was going on in Egypt and Europe and the season of the year would render it almost impossible to move the army, wrote to him on the 22nd of February as follows:—

Your long silence on this most important and pressing occasion compelled me to adopt the resolution of ordering the British forces to advance in concert with the armies of the Allied Powers. You are not ignorant that the period of the season rendered the advance of the army absolutely necessary to the common security of the Allies. This movement of the army is to be imputed entirely to your repeated rejection of my amicable proposal of sending an ambassador to your presence. Under the present circumstances, to send Major Doveton to you would not be attended with those advantages which would have resulted from his mission at a proper season.

The Allies, however, retaining an anxious desire to effect

an adjustment with you, Lieut.-General Harris, commander of
the British troops, has been empowered to receive any embassy
which you shall despatch to him. Lieut.-General Harris will also
authorise such persons as he may think proper to concert, in
communication with your ambassadors, a new treaty of friendship
with your Highness, founded on such conditions as appear to the
Allies to be indispensably necessary to the establishment of a
secure and permanent peace.[1]

General Harris was ordered to forward this letter to the
Sultan on the day on which the army under his command
crossed the frontier. He was at the same time to issue the
declaration "of the Right Honourable the Governor-General
in Council on behalf of the Honourable East India Company
and the Allies of the said Company, their Highnesses the
Nizam and the Peshwa." It was a simple, frank, and explicit
proclamation, showing the provocations received from
Tippoo and the fruitless efforts made to induce him to make
proper reparation and satisfaction.

On the 6th of March "the Grand Army," as it was called,
crossed the frontier, and General Harris despatched to
Tippoo the Governor-General's letter. The Sultan, on
hearing that the British army was approaching his
territory, exclaimed: "All my decisions must now be
desperate. I am but losing precious time in waiting for their
ambassador, while they are closing in upon me on either
side. I will march and strike a decisive blow." Leaving a
small force to watch the main army struggling through
the valleys and passes to gain the plateau, he made a
rapid dash at the Bombay army, which had marched from
Cannannore on the 21st of February, and had, four days

[1] *Despatches of the Marquess Wellesley,* vol. i. p. 453.

later, reached the summit of the Pondicherrum Pass. "The scenery around would, indeed, bear a parallel with some of the noblest parks in England, studded as it then was with verdant and beautifully wooded knolls, and shut in at intervals by the deep shade of the surrounding forests." [1] On the 2nd of March it took post at Sedapore, having about eight miles to the front a brigade of native infantry under Colonel Montressor stationed at Seediseir, a lofty hill, sheer below which lies the tableland of Mysore. On the 6th of March an extensive encampment was seen forming below, and among the tents was one of green with several flags displayed. It was Tippoo's. Early next morning several massive columns were seen advancing along the open ground towards the kopje, and about two o'clock there commenced a vigorous attack with a discharge of rockets, and in numbers vastly superior they rushed forward with unexpected daringness to within twenty or thirty yards of our bayonets.

"At this perilous crisis, through some negligence on the part of the bombardier on duty, it was discovered that in the 12-pounder field-piece, planted to secure the road, the cartridge had been rammed home, shot foremost; and it occupied some time before this alarming blunder could be rectified, by extracting the shot: the artillerymen and lascars (native artillerymen) being drawn up in front of the gun, with the enemy close upon them, while the perplexing operation was going on." [2]

While the attack was thus proceeding in front, a large body of the enemy penetrated to the rear of the hill,

---

[1] *Memoirs of the Early Life and Services of a Field Officer on the Retired List of the Indian Army,* p. 365.
[2] Ibid., p. 373.

and taking its defenders by surprise, killed Captain Sholl and many of his sepoys.[1] The isolated brigade of brave sepoys, attacked both in front and rear, defended itself for several hours with the utmost gallantry against four times its numbers. They were exhausted by fatigue, and their supply of ammunition was nearly at an end, when "three distinct and tremendous rolling volleys of musketry, pealing through the woods, announced to us in the rear that our soldiers were in the midst of the enemy." Surprised at the sudden appearance of the Europeans, and astonished at the deadly effect of their fire, they endeavoured to escape in different directions into the jungle on either side; "being tumbled headlong in masses, under the bayonets of the soldiers, into the ravines, by which in some places their retreat was intercepted." The European force, consisting of the 77th and part of the 75th Foot under General

---

[1.] "Captain Sholl was possibly wounded early in the business, and in the dispersion of his people had managed to creep to the side of the river hard by the jungle, where he lay down to slake that burning thirst incidental to the wounded. Here he was soon discovered by the enemy, who, according to custom, immediately struck off his head; and together with the epaulettes, which they tore off his shoulders, conveyed it to the Sultan as the earliest trophy of success. In this mutilated state, at all events, was the body of my poor friend discovered a few days afterwards."—*Price's Memoirs*, p. 374. "The situation of Lieutenant Rebenack of the Engineers, and nephew to Colonel Sartorius, was extremely singular and critical. He was on duty at the Pioneers' working station, in the rear of the post, superintending the preparation of gabions and fascines, some of the former being of extraordinary size. Into one of these, set upright, when the conflict was raging round him, and he was left without defence, he contrived to introduce himself; and there remained seated, as he said himself, from nearly ten in the morning until two in the afternoon. What his feeling must have been during a crisis so appalling it would not be difficult to conceive, nor the joyous revolution that must have succeeded to this protracted agony of suspense when he heard the triumphant roar of musketry which announced the sure approach of deliverance."

Stuart himself, reached the advanced front without further resistance. Tippoo retreated to his camp, and on the 11th of March returned to Seringapatam. On the 14th he moved from his capital to meet the Grand Army.

On the 27th of March, when the British army was approaching its encamping ground near Malavelly, Tippoo, who was posted on high ground, opened a distant cannonade. The advanced pickets were attacked by the enemy, and more troops being sent to their aid, a general action began. The British troops under General Harris formed the right, and the Nizam's contingent under Colonel Wellesley the left. The right having deployed into line, began to advance under a steady fire of artillery. "An interval between two brigades, caused by the nature of the ground, seemed to present an opportunity for an effort of cavalry, which the Sultan himself directed and accompanied till in the very act to charge. The charge was prepared with deliberate coolness, and executed with great spirit; it was purposely directed against the Europeans, and, although many horsemen fell on the bayonets, was completely repelled without causing the slightest disorder in the ranks, and the advance of the line being continued in a direction outflanking the enemy's left, the Sultan's guns began soon afterwards to be withdrawn from the heights." [1]

Meanwhile Colonel Wellesley, having formed his forces in echelon of battalions, moved forward to turn the enemy's right, supported by a brigade of cavalry under Colonel Floyd; "the English centre being entirely exposed and Colonel Floyd being

[1] *Historical Sketches of the South of India,* by Lieut.-Colonel Mark Wilks, vol. ii. p. 351.

prepared to act with either attack as circumstances might require." [1] Two thousand of Tippoo's best infantry advanced with great steadiness, and when within sixty yards of the 33rd their musketry opened. The British soldiers, replying with a volley, gave a loud cheer and charged the advancing line. They stood out for a moment, and then Floyd rode into their broken ranks and completed the rout with great slaughter. Thus ended Wellesley's first Indian battle. Writing to his brother, he states that Tippoo's troops behaved better than they had ever been known to behave. "His infantry advanced, and almost stood the charge of bayonets of the 33rd, and his cavalry rode at General Baird's European Brigade. He did not support them as he ought, having drawn off his guns at the moment he made his attack, and even pushed forwards these troops to cover the retreat of his guns. This is the cause of the total destruction of the troops he left behind him, without loss to us, and of the panic with which we have reason to believe all his troops are now affected." [2]

On the 5th of April the British army took up its ground opposite the west face of the fort of Seringapatam, at the distance of 3500 yards, the left being to the river Cauvery, while Wellesley with his division was encamped to the extreme right. Along the whole front of the British position ran a watercourse. Passing along the low ground bordering the river on our left, it was directed straight upon the fortress; but on arriving within 1700 yards of the walls it

---

[1] *Historical Sketches of the South of India,* by Lieut.-Colonel Mark Wilks, vol. ii. p. 351.

[2] To the Earl of Mornington, camp two miles west of Seringapatam, 5th April 1799. *Supplementary Despatches,* vol. i. p. 208.

turned suddenly to the eastward, or right, and, describing a
winding course, reached the village of Sultaun-pettah.
All the strong points of this winding aqueduct were held
by Mysorean troops, and in front of it were some ruined
villages and rocky eminences which afforded facilities to
the Sultan's troops to annoy the camp with rockets and
occasion some disquietude for the safety of the park of
artillery stores. It was therefore imperative to dislodge
the enemy from these retreats without delay. On the
day the enemy encamped before the fortress one column
under Colonel Shawe was ordered to attack a ruined
village in front of the centre of the British position, while
another under Colonel Wellesley was directed to drive the
enemy from a grove of cocoa-trees and bamboos situated
to the left of the village of Sultaun-pettah. As Colonel
Wellesley's instructions were not sufficiently explicit he
wrote to General Harris :—

I do not know where you mean the post to be established, and
I shall therefore be obliged to you if you will do me the favour to
meet me this afternoon in front of the lines and show it to me.
In the meantime I will order my battalions to be in readiness.

Upon looking at the tope as I came in just now, it appeared to me
that when you get possession of the bank of the *nullah* you have
the tope as a matter of course, as the latter is in the rear of the
former. However, you are the best judge, and I shall be ready.[1]

Soon after sunset the two columns set forth. Shawe
seized the village without firing a shot; Wellesley,
marching over broken ground; reached the edge of the
nullah, and his advanced-guard crossed it. No sooner
had they entered the grove than they were met by a hot
fire of musketry and rockets. The intensest darkness,

---

[1] *Despatches of the Duke of Wellington*, vol. i. p. 23.

the almost impenetrable jungle of shrubs, the unexpected impediment of a succession of deep trenches dug through the betel-shrubs, the uncertainty of the enemy's position, threw our soldiers into confusion, and they retired in disorder across the aqueduct. Colonel Wellesley, not being able to find the post which it was desirable he should occupy, was obliged to desist from the attack, and the enemy having retired from their position, returned to the camp to report the failure to the Commander-in-Chief. General Harris in his private diary states: "Near 12 Colonel Wellesley came to my tent in a good deal of agitation, to say he had not carried the tope. It proved that the 33rd, with which he attacked, got into confusion and could not be formed, which was a great pity, as it must be particularly unpleasant to him. Altogether, circumstances considered, we got off very well." He also mentions that General Baird made the same night an expedition against the enemy's horse and "missed the road coming back, although one would have thought it impossible; no wonder night attacks so often fail." [1] Wellesley never refrained from night attempts because of their perilous nature, but during the remainder of his long military career he objected to such attacks where the force and position of the enemy were unknown. On the 18th of April he wrote to the Governor-General: "I got a slight twitch on the knee, from which I have

---

[1] Alison's statement that "the young officer proceeded at midnight to the general's tent, at first much agitated, but finding General Harris not yet awake, he threw himself on the table of the tent and *fell asleep*-a fact, in such a moment, singularly characteristic of the imperturbable character of the future hero of Torres Vedras," is mere fable, as Mr Lushington states (*The Life and Services of General Lord Harris, G.C.B.,* by The Right Hon. T. R. Lushington, p. 294).

felt no inconvenience, on the night of the 5th and I have come to a determination, when in my power, never to suffer an attack to be made by night upon an enemy who is prepared and strongly posted, and whose posts have not been reconnoitred by daylight." [1]

As the fire of the enemy continued heavily during the night, General Harris determined that next morning he would make a more vigorous and extended attack to drive the enemy from their whole line of outposts. [2] Colonel Wellesley was again to command the attack on the Sultaun-pettah tope. Colonel Shawe was to advance at the same time from the ruined village which he occupied, and to dislodge the enemy from the aqueduct; and Colonel Wallace, with the grenadiers of the 14th and two companies of sepoys, was to attack a village on the enemy's right flank. Early next morning the troops destined for the attack were assembled. General Harris was on the spot on horseback, and several officers of rank, including General Baird, were present as spectators. But Wellesley, whom Harris had ordered to command, was absent. As the day advanced the commander-in-chief became impatient and apprehensive that the favourable moment for the attack would be lost by further delay, and he directed General Baird to take the command and proceed to the attack.

I made no reply [Sir David Baird says], but drew my sword, and, turning my horse, I rode towards the column. I had not moved many paces when General Harris called me back and said, "I think, upon reflection, that we must wait a little longer for Colonel Wellesley."

[1.] *Supplementary Despatches,* vol. i. p. 209.
[2.] Lieut.-General Harris to the Earl of Mornington, Camp before Scringapatam, 7th April 1799.

I then expressed to General Harris, in the hearing of all around
us, my great satisfaction at this determination, because I felt
that it could not fail to be painful and mortifying to Colonel
Wellesley if any other person was employed to complete the
operation which he had begun. [1]

Colonel Wellesley appeared a few moments afterwards,
having by an omission in the adjutant-general's office been
only just then warned for duty. He instantly took command
of the troops, and at nine o'clock, with the Scotch Brigade and
two battalions of sepoys with four guns, advanced against
the Sultaun-pettah tope, from which the enemy fired under
cover of the bank of the aqueduct. [2] Their fire was returned,
and as the corps advanced parties were thrown out to turn
their flank. The enemy, shaken by the fire of the artillery and
threatened in flank, were thrown into confusion and retired in all

---

[1] From the account given by Sir David Baird himself, only the year
before he died, to Colonel Meyrick Shawe of the circumstances which
took place on the morning of the 6th April 1799 (*The Life and Services
of General Lord Harris, G.C.B.,'* p. 298). Alison states: "General Harris
next morning drew out the troops for a second attack, and offered
the command to General Baird, but that generous officer suggested
that Colonel Wellesley should be again intrusted with the command.
But for the elevation of mind which prompted both General Harris
and General Baird to overlook this casual failure and intrust the next
attack to the defeated officer, the fate of the world might have been
different and the star of the future conqueror of Napoleon extinguished
in an obscure nocturnal encounter in an Indian watercourse." General
Baird's statement proves Alison's account to be eloquent fiction.
Alison's authority was Colonel Gerrard, but the colonel only repeated
a story current in the camp at the time. Beatson and Wilks make no
mention of the incident in their account of the war. Colonel Gurwood
doubts the accuracy of the story (*Despatches of the Duke of Wellington,*
vol. i. p. 25 note).

[2] *A View of the Origin and Conduct of the War with Tippoo Sultan,*
by Lieut.-Colonel Alexander Beatson, p. 91. Major Basil Jackson and
Captain C. Rochfort Scott, in *'The Military Life of Field-Marshal the
Duke of Wellington,'* state he advanced with a strong force.

haste.[1] At the same moment Colonel Shawe sallied forth from the ruined village and forced the aqueduct, and Colonel Wallace seized the village on the right. Colonel Barry Close, the adjutant-general of the army, who accompanied Wellesley, hastened to General Harris's tent with the announcement, "It has been done in high style and without loss."

On the 4th of May Seringapatam was taken by assault, but to Colonel Wellesley was assigned only the command of the reserves in the trenches. He, however, entered the fortress immediately after the assault, says Colonel Gurwood, "and was one of the few present when Tippoo Sultan's body, still warm, was discovered in the sally-port gateway." [2] The next day he was appointed governor of the captured city by General Harris. General Baird, who led the assault, remonstrated against being superseded by a junior, but Wellesley was the fit person for the post. On the 24th of January 1831 the Duke of Wellington wrote to Crokcr :—

My Dear Croker,—I have received your note, and shall he happy to see you on the day that you have fixed.

I have often heard of Sir D. Baird's dissatisfaction on my appointment to take the command at Seringapatam, where he had commanded the successful storm of the town, on which I was not employed, having been appointed to command the reserve

---

[1.] *A View of the Origin and Conduct of the War with Tippoo Sultan,* by Lieut.-Colonel Alexander Beatson, p. 91. Possession of the tope was therefore eventually obtained, without a direct attack upon it, and nearly in the manner suggested by Colonel Wellesley in his note to General Harris, when he said that by gaining "possession of the bank of the nullah you have the tope as *a matter of course, as the latter is in the rear of the former".* (*The Military Life of Field-Marshal the Duke of Wellington,* by Major Basil Jackson and Captain C. Rochfort Scott, vol. ii. p.34),

[2.] See Baird, *Post,* p. 250, note.

in the trenches. Of course I had nothing, I could have nothing, to say to the selection of myself, as I was in the trenches, or rather in the town, when I received the order to take command of it, and instructions to endeavour to restore order.

Baird was a gallant, hard-headed, lion-hearted officer; but he had no talent, no tact; had strong prejudices against the natives; and he was peculiarly disqualified from his manner, habits, &c., and it was supposed his temper, for the management of them. He had been Tippoo's prisoner for years. He had a strong feeling of the bad usage which he had received during his captivity; and it was not impossible that the knowledge of this feeling might have induced Lord Harris, and those who advise his Lordship, to lay him aside. However, of course I never inquired the reason of his appointment, or of Baird's being laid aside.

There were many other candidates besides Baird and myself, all senior to me, some to Baird. But I must say that I was the fit person to be selected. I had commanded the Nizam's army during the campaign, and had given universal satisfaction. I was liked by the natives. It is certainly true that this command offered me the opportunities for distinction, and thus opened the road to fame, which poor Baird always thought was, by the same act, closed to him. Notwithstanding this, he and I were always on the best terms, and I don't believe that there was any man who rejoiced more sincerely than he did in my ulterior success.—Believe me, ever yours most sincerely,

WELLINGTON.[1]

[1.] Lord Harris wrote to Lord Mornington, June 28, 1799: "Ill-intentioned people talk nonsense, I hear, of your brother's appointment to command in Seringapatam; but I can defend it on principles most militarily correct, if it were worth while to attend to the words of the idle. Colonel Wellesley was the next officer to relieve Baird, who had requested to be relieved. So little did I think of any particular person at the time, that Roberts (Colonel) was named by Turing (Major Deputy Adjutant-General) as next for duty, and agreed to by me, when Turing corrected himself and said Colonel Wellesley was next. 'Then let him go,' was my answer. He was afterwards permanently appointed by me from my thinking him more equal to the particular kind of duty than any other officer in the army."

In two months from the commencement of the campaign the powerful kingdom that had been created by the courage and genius of Hyder, and sustained by the determination and vigour of Tippoo his son, was destroyed. The speedy success of the operations was largely due to Colonel Wellesley. He held only a subordinate military command; but the reorganisations of the army departments, which rendered a rapid advance possible, were the result of his clear and commanding intellect, and the discipline and efficiency of the troops of his energy and skill as a commander. Harris launched the Grand Army against Tippoo, and, as Wellington said, "conducted the details of the victorious army which he commanded in Mysore," but it was the master-mind of Wellington that prepared it for its work. As governor of Seringapatam, an office needing equal labour and delicacy, he exhibited the same firmness and sagacity that he had shown in the business of war. On entering the fortress he took vigorous steps to put down plunderers. He wrote to General Harris at midnight, "I wish you would send the provost here and put him under my orders. Until some of the plunderers are hanged it is in vain to expect to stop the plunder." A few hours later he wrote: "Things are better than they were, but they are still very bad, and until the provost executes three or four people it is impossible to expect order, or indeed safety. There are at this moment sepoys and soldiers belonging to every native regiment in your camp and General Stuart's in the town." Four of the plunderers were hanged. On the 6th he says: "Plunder is stopped, the fires are all extinguished, and the inhabitants are returning to their houses fast. I am now employed in burying the dead, which I hope will be completed this day, particularly if you send me all the pioneers." [1] That day Tippoo was taken to the splendid mausoleum of his father, and two companies of English grenadiers preceded the body. His personal attendants carried the bier, and it was followed by his second son on horseback, attended by the chief officer and nobles on foot. Two companies of British soldiers closed the sad procession. As it wound its way through the city the *kazi* chanted some verses from the *Koran*, which were taken up by the mourners, and the people who lined the streets prostrated themselves before the earthly remains of their late monarch. On reaching the gate of the mausoleum the grenadiers formed a street and presented arms to the body of their fallen foe as it passed. By the side of his father they laid him, and when the last rites had been performed peals of thunder rent the air and flashes of lightning lit the sky. It was a fitting close to the stormy career of Tippoo Sultaun.

Owing to the severe punishment meted out to plunderers and the personal activity of Colonel Wellesley, who himself placed safeguards over the houses of the principal inhabitants, order and confidence were soon restored. "The inhabitants who had quitted the town during the night of the storm, and had slept in the open fields, returned quietly to their houses and occupations. In a few days the bazaars were stored with all sorts of provisions and merchandise, for which there was a ready and advantageous sale. The main street of Seringapatam, three days after the fort was taken, was so much crowded as to be almost impassable, and exhibited more the appearance of a fair than that of a town just taken by assault."

[1] *Despatches of the Duke of Wellington*, vol. i. pp. 27, 28.

Not only was order restored in the capital, but Wellesley's effectual measures of reconciliation swiftly restored tranquillity in the country and paved the way to the establishment of a final arrangement. He used every means to conciliate the adherents of the late Sultan and win the confidence of the Mohammedan population. The tombs of Hyder Ali and Tippoo were covered with rich cloths at the Company's expense, and the establishment of *moulahs* to offer up prayers was kept up as formerly.[1] The walls of Tippoo's palace were covered with paintings of Colonel Baird's defeat. It was urged on the English commander to efface these mementoes of a great disaster. He refused to entertain the suggestion, and had one which was damaged repaired at his private expense.

Four days after the capture of the city Colonel Wellesley wrote to the Governor-General, "The question respecting what is to be done with the Mysore empire at the present moment is certainly a most important one,"[2] and he suggested a scheme which he considered would be safe, creditable, and not likely to lead us into new wars. The family of Tippoo and the great soldiers in his service might be provided for by suitable *jaghires*. The remainder of the territory (after deducting these grants of lands) to be divided into three parts, either equal or otherwise, and taken by each of the Allies. "We must have Seringapatam and a safe communication with it from the Carnatic, likewise the sea-coast." Lord Mornington determined, as his brother advised, to allot certain shares of territory to the English and their Allies,

---

[1] *A Journey from Madras through the Countries of Mysore, Canara, and Malabar,* by Francis Buchanan, p. 74.

[2] *Supplementary Despatches,* vol. i. p. 212.

and to reconstitute the remainder into a state under the old Hindu reigning family whom Hyder Ali had expelled. "It would have been more grateful to my mind," he wrote to the Honourable Court of Directors (securing a munificent provision for the ancient family of Mysore), "to have restored that of Tippoo Sultan to the throne, if such a restoration could have been accomplished without exposing Mysore to the perpetual hazard of internal commotion and foreign war, and without endangering the stability of the internal settlement of your interests and those of your Allies in this quarter." On the 4th of June the Governor-General issued a special commission appointing Lieut.-General Harris, the Honourable Colonel Wellesley, the Honourable Henry Wellesley, Lieut.-Colonel William Kirkpatrick, and Lieut.-Colonel Barry Close, Commissioners of Mysore. They assembled at Seringapatam on the 8th of June, and their first act was to make provision for the principal surviving officers and chiefs of the late Sultan and for the families of those slain in the campaign. Many of the chiefs were restored to the trusts and places they had held under Tippoo. The four sons of Tippoo were removed to the fortress of Vellore. Then Colonel Wellesley paid a visit to the young rajah, whom he found, with others of his family, in a condition of poverty and humiliation which excited the strongest emotions of compassion. Shortly before the siege the whole family had been stripped of even the poorest ornaments, and the young rajah, a child of four, from bad treatment was so sickly that his death was soon expected. It was determined to fix the residence of the rajah in the ancient town of Mysore. Tippoo had razed the city and removed the stones of the palace and temples to a neighbouring height, and thither the young rajah and his family were conducted with fitting honours.

On the 30th of June he was formally placed on the *musnud* (throne) by Colonel Wellesley and General Harris, assisted by Meer Allum, the representative of the Nizam. Purneah, Tippoo's Brahmin Finance Minister, a man of eminent talents and integrity, was appointed his Highness's *dewan* (prime minister). Colonel Close, whom Wellesley described as the ablest man in the Company's army, was appointed to be Resident at his Court. The settlement of the Partition Treaty of Mysore and the subsidiary treaty between the Company and the Rajah of Mysore brought the labours of the commission to a close. The Company secured by the Partition Treaty an uninterrupted tract of territory from the coast of Coromandel to that of Malabar, together with the entire sea-coast of the kingdom of Mysore and the base of all the Eastern, Western, and Southern Ghauts. "To these I thought it necessary to add," writes the Marquess, "the forts and posts forming the heads of all the passes above the Ghauts and the tableland." Thus in a few months the Madras Presidency grew from a few scattered districts into the great country known by that name, comprising almost the whole of Southern India. The Nizam received a large increase of territory, revenue, and power; together with several fortresses, tending greatly to secure the tranquillity of his dominions. To the Peshwa was offered a large portion of the Mysore kingdom, but he refused to accept the position of a subsidised and protected ally, and the territory was divided between the English and the Nizam.

On the 11th of September the following appeared in

Army Orders: "The commander-in-chief being about to proceed to the Presidency, in obedience to the orders of the Governor-General in Council, appoints Colonel the Hon. A. Wellesley to command the troops serving above the Ghauts." The civil administration of the new kingdom of Mysore and the territories acquired by us was also assigned to Colonel Wellesley. It was a trust of great delicacy and importance, and it was performed with marvellous tact and sympathy. He proceeded at once to visit the different districts, and made himself thoroughly acquainted with their topography and their resources, and the feelings and prejudices of the inhabitants. He reorganised the civil and military establishments, and replaced the most intelligent and experienced of Tippoo's officers in their former posts. To prevent the disbanded soldiers from combining in marauding bands he ordered that every horse in Mysore should be registered, and that no horseman should be allowed to travel through the country without a passport. The speedy and quiet settlement of the centre part of the territories of Tippoo ensued. The inhabitants returned to their villages and rejoiced at their escape from the blighting sway of the Mohammedan usurpers. But it was no easy task to make peace on the border; the newly annexed districts of Wynad and Malabar, which had defied the power of Hyder and Tippoo, were not disposed to brook the dominion of a new master. Wide tracts, consisting of mountain and jungle, had to be reduced, rock-fortresses to be taken, and robber chiefs subdued. Wellesley's letters bear testimony to the foresight with which he forestalled the designs of his foes, the skill with which his combinations were planned, and the vigour with which they were executed. It was a work which, however, always demands time and patience to accomplish. On the 7th of May he wrote to Munro :—

I think that upon the whole we are not in the most thriving condition in this country. Polygars,[1] Nairns,[2] and Moplahs[3] in arms on all sides of us; an army full of disaffection and discontent, amounting to Lord knows what on the frontier, which increases as it advances, like a snowball in snow. To oppose this we have nothing that ought to be taken from the necessary garrisons, and the corps we have in them are incomplete in men and without officers. If we go to war in earnest, however (and if we take the field at all it ought to be in earnest), I will collect everything that can be brought together from all sides, and we ought not to quit the field so long as there is a discontented or unsubdued Polygar in the country.

Towards the end of the month Mr Webbe, secretary to the Government of Madras, wrote to Wellesley: "You are to pursue Dhundia Waugh wherever you may find him, and to hang him on the first tree. For this purpose you will receive immediate authority to enter the Mahratta frontier." Dhundia Waugh was a Mahratta freebooter who, after committing depredations

---

[1.] Pálegára, corruptly Polygar, Polligar, a petty chieftain. In the south of India, especially in Karnata, the Poligar, or Polygar, of early writers, occupying chiefly tracts of hill and forest, subject to pay tribute and service to the paramount state, but seldom paying either, and more or less independent, subsisting in a great measure by plunder. On the subjugation of the country most of the Palegars were dispossessed, some were pensioned, and a few were allowed to retain some of their villages at a quit-rent: these have now subsided into peaceable landholders (*Glossary of Indian Terms*, by Wilson).

[2.] Náyar, commonly Nair, or Nayr, name of the ruling caste in Malabar, professing to be *Sudras*, but bearing arms and exercising sovereignty.

[3.] *Mapilla*, commonly *Moplah*, or *Moplay*, a native of Malabar, a descendant of the Arabs who first settled in Malabar (*Glossary of Indian Terms*, by Wilson). See *Hobson-Jobson*, by Yule and Burnell.

on the territories of Tippoo, fell into that monarch's hands, was compelled to conform to the Mohammedan faith, and was afterwards employed in his military service. Detecting him in some treachery, or suspecting his fidelity, Tippoo had him confined in irons at Seringapatam. After the storming of that fortress he was let loose by the victors, again became a freebooter, and laid the rich country of Beddenore under severe contributions, which he exacted with the most unrelenting cruelty. Two detachments were sent in quest of him, but he made his escape into Mahratta country, which his pursuers had strict orders not to enter. But Dhundia had killed a famous Mahratta and defeated a Mahratta force, and the Peshwa, after some difficulty, gave the English permission to attack him in his territory.

Colonel Wellesley promptly took the field and put his troops in motion from various points in order to concentrate at Hurryhur, the frontier station on the Toombuddra. On the 14th of June he arrived there, and found, owing to the bursting of the south-west monsoon, the river so swollen that it could be passed only in boats. None had been collected. He managed, however, to secure a few, and by the 16th he sent over a regiment of cavalry and a battalion of infantry with four guns. On the 24th of June all his troops had crossed, and were busy till the 2nd of July in clearing the country of Dhundia's cavalry. Then he pushed for the river Werdah, and having crossed it, built a redoubt, as well for the protection of the boats as to secure the communication with the rear. Information having now reached him that Dhundia was advancing to give battle, Wellesley moved on and took possession of the town of Savanore.

Dhundia, though he approached within a few miles of the British position and closely reconnoitred, did not venture to attack. On the contrary, he marched rapidly northward, and Wellesley following, took on the 26th of July the fort of Dummul. Four days later he writes to Colonel Barry Close : "I surprised his camp at three o'clock in the evening with the cavalry, and we drove into the river or destroyed everybody that was in it, took an elephant, several camels, bullocks, horses innumerable, families, women and children, &c., &c. The guns were gone over, and we made an attempt to dismount them by a fire from this side; but it was getting dark, my infantry was fatigued by the length of the march, we lost a man or two, I saw plainly that we should not succeed, and I therefore withdrew my guns to my camp." In a postscript he adds: "I have just returned from the river, and have got the guns, six in number. I made the Europeans swim over to seize a boat. The fort was evacuated." [1] The boats and guns were given to the body of Mahrattas, who had joined him in order to be avenged upon Dhundia for the murder of their chief. The orders were given to advance again, but it was no easy task to catch the dexterous Mahratta, who knew the country and had the sympathy of the people. On August the 7th Wellesley writes to Munro: "I arrived here on the 5th. Dhundia had gone even to the sources of the Malpoorba, where he passed, and his baggage is following him. Colonel Stevenson is after them, and will cut off part of the tail, I hope. I have halted here in the neighbourhood of a bamboo-jungle to make boats, which I must have on the river in order to keep up communication with my rear." [2]

---

[1] *Despatches of the Duke of Wellington,* vol. i. p. 153.
[2] Ibid., p. 160.

The tail was not cut off. On the 16th of August Wellesley writes: "A detachment from Stevenson's corps followed his track, and the road was covered with dead camels, bullocks, and people, but we got nothing." Through dense jungles and over swollen rivers the weary chase continued. On the 1st of September 1800 Wellesley wrote to Munro: "Unfortunately the Malpoorba fell on the 24th, and Dhundia crossed it on that night and the next day at a ford a little above the junction with the Kistna. Lieut.-Colonel Capper was then at this place; and although I had desired the Mahrattas to push on for the very place at which Dhundia passed, and Colonel Capper entreated them to attend to the orders I had given them, and promised to follow with all expedition, they would not move from the camp. If they had occupied that place Dhundia could not have passed there; he must have returned to look for another ford higher up the river, and would then have fallen into my hands. He is gone towards the Nizam's country." He adds, "I have crossed the river, and I am going to the Nizam's country." Eleven days later he wrote :—

CAMP AT NEPULPURVY, 11*th Sept*. 1800.

MY DEAR MUNRO,–I have the pleasure to inform you that I gained a complete victory yesterday, in an action with Dhundia's army, in which he was killed. His body was recognised, and was brought in on a gun attached to the 19th Dragoons.

After I had crossed the Malpoorba, it appeared to me very clear that if I pressed upon the "King of the two Worlds," with my whole force on the northern side of the *Dooab*, his majesty would either cross the Toombuddra with the aid of the Patan chiefs, and would then enter Mysore, or he would return into Savanore, and play the devil with my peaceable communications. I therefore determined at all events to prevent his majesty from putting those designs in execution, and I marched with my army to Kanagherry. I sent Stevenson towards Deodroog, and along the Kistna, to prevent him from sending his guns and baggage to the ally, the Rajah of Soorapoor; and I pushed forward the whole of the Mahratta and Mogul cavalry in one body, between Stevenson's corps and mine.

I marched from Kanagherry on the 8th, left my infantry at Nowley, and proceeded on with the cavalry only, and I arrived here on the 9th–the infantry at Chinnoor, about fifteen miles in my rear.

The "King of the World" broke up on the 9th from Mudgherry, about twenty-five miles on this side of Raichore, and proceeded towards the Kistna; but he saw Colonel Stevenson's camp, returned immediately, and encamped on that evening about nine miles from hence, between this place and Bunnoo. I had early intelligence of his situation, but the night was so bad and my horses so much fatigued that I could not move.

After a most anxious night I marched in the morning, and met "the King of the World" with his army, about 5000 horse, at a village called Conahgull, about six miles from hence. He had not known of my being so near him in the night,–had thought that I was at Chinnoor, and was marching to the westward, with an intention of passing between the Mahratta and Mogul cavalry and me. He drew up, however, in a very strong position as soon as he perceived me, and "the victorious army" stood for some time with apparent firmness. I charged them with the 9th and the 25th Dragoons,[1] and 1st and 2nd regiments of cavalry, and drove them before me till they dispersed, and were scattered over the face of the country. I then returned and attacked the royal camp, and got possession of elephants, camels, baggage, &c., which were still upon the ground. The Mogul and Mahratta cavalry came up about eleven o'clock, and they have been employed ever since in the pursuit and destruction of the scattered fragments of "the victorious army."

Thus has ended this warfare; and I shall commence my march

---

[1] Afterwards the 22nd Light Dragoons.

in a day or two towards my own country. An honest *killedar* [1] of Chinnoor had written to the "King of the World," by a regular *tappal* [2] established for the purpose of giving him intelligence, that I was to be at Nowly on the 8th, at Chinnoor on the 9th. His majesty was misled by this information, and was nearer me than he expected. The honest *killedar* did all he could to detain me at Chinnoor, but I was not to be prevailed upon to stop; and even went so far as to threaten to hang a great man sent to show me the road, who manifested an inclination to show me a good road to a different place. My own and the Mahratta cavalry afterwards prevented any communication between his majesty and the *killedar*.

The *binjarry* [3] (bags) must be filled, notwithstanding the conclusion of the war, as I imagine that I shall have to carry on one in Malabar–Believe me, yours most sincerely,

ARTHUR WELLESLEY.

Fifteen years later Arthur Wellesley conquered one who had a better right to the title which the Mahratta freebooter had assumed, "King of the World." It was, however, in the campaign against Dhundia that he first revealed the qualities, decision and boldness tempered by prudence, which bore him from the Rock of Lisbon to the shores of Garonne. After Dhundia was slain, Arthur Wellesley showed the kindness and generosity which marked him as a man. In Dhundia's camp his little son was found and rescued by the Colonel, who took him in his charge, and when he quitted India left some hundreds of pounds to be expended on the boy, of whom he was often mindful in after-years.

After the short but brilliant operation againt Dhundia, Colonel Wellesley remained in Mahratta territory, watching

---

[1] Governor of a fort.

[2] Post.

[3] *Brinjarries*, grain-dealers who supply remote villages now, and the armies in old days, with rice and grain loaded in bags on bullocks,

the proceedings of Sindia, who had made himself master of the powers and resources of the Peshwa. He did not return to Seringapatam till the end of November, and on the 2nd of December he was ordered by the Governor-General, now Marquess Wellesley, to assume the command of certain forces to be assembled at Trincomalee. In May, when the Dhundia trouble was reaching a serious crisis, Colonel Wellesley had received a letter from Lord Mornington offering to join him with Admiral Rainier in the command of an expedition destined against the island of Batavia. The Governor-General wrote: "The King has given me power of selecting the persons who are to conduct this expedition; and I have thought it, on every ground, most expedient to place the principal conduct of the equipment and negotiations in the hands of Admiral Rainier. It will be necessary to join a military officer in the commission with him, and a conscientious sense of duty induces me to think that you are the most fit person to be selected for that service, provided you can safely be spared from Mysore for the period of the expedition, which I imagine may be four or five months, but probably cannot be longer." [1]

Lord Mornington proceeded to point out the contingent advantages of the command. The warehouses at Batavia contained property to a very large amount, and "the expedition will be very advantageous to the naval and military commanders." The Governor-General, however, stipulated that he should postpone any decision on the subject " until you have ascertained that Lord Clive can substitute in your present command, during your absence, a person completely satisfactory to him in every respect. For this purpose I

[1] *Despatches of the Duke of Wellington,* vol. i. p. 103.

request you to write privately to Lord Clive and act according to his wishes."

Colonel Wellesley accordingly wrote to Lord Clive, and the Governor of Madras replied: "I have long felt, and still feel, that you fill, with singular advantage to our own country as well as to Mysore, a situation in which, for the prosperous settlement of our new acquisitions, integrity and vigilance of conduct are indispensable; and in which your acquired knowledge and experience, especially in the event of actual operations, must give you the advantage over other men, and in which I should find it not only difficult but impossible to replace you to my satisfaction." [1] Colonel Wellesley promptly determined to refuse the offer of the command of a campaign which promised wealth and glory, in order to remain and conduct a small operation against a horde of freebooters in a remote corner of India. He wrote to his brother that if the Government of Poona was inclined to give up Dhundia or co-operate with us in his destruction it might be possible for him to go to Batavia. "If they should not, matters here will take a very serious turn, and no prospect of advantage or of credit to be gained shall induce me to quit this country." [2] The path of duty led to glory. The campaign against Dhundia proved his eminent fitness for the conduct of Indian warfare, and suggested and justified his selection for the delicate task of restoring the Peshwa, which ultimately led to Assaye.

On the 19th of December 1800 Colonel Wellesley, having selected his staff, sailed for Trincomalee to take

---

[1] *Despatches of the Duke of Wellington,* vol. i. p. 106.
[2] Ibid., p. 207.

command of the force assembled at that port. In November the Governor-General had informed him that, in consequence of the state of the war in Europe, and of the strength of the French Power in Egypt, he had determined to suspend the intended expedition against Batavia. The force about to be assembled at Trincomalee was to be applied to either of the following objects if required: "(1) To proceed up the Red Sea in order to co-operate with the British force which may be employed in Egypt from the side of the Mediterranean. (2) To proceed to any point which the French may menace in India, especially on the western side of the peninsula. (3) Intelligence which I have received has satisfied me that a blow might now be struck, with every prospect of success, against the Isle of France. If the state of my accounts from Europe and Egypt should leave me at liberty to make such an attempt at the close of the month of December, my anxious wish is that you should proceed, on or about the 25th of December, from Trincomalee direct to the Isle of France." [1] A short time before the Marquess Wellesley had written to Vice-Admiral Sir Roger Curtis, commanding his Majesty's Squadron at the Cape of Good Hope: "It appears highly probable, with a view to all her objects in Egypt and India, that France may endeavour, at an early season, to throw a reinforcement into the Isle of France. Recent information leads me to believe that such a design is entertained by the enemy. Its success would certainly aggravate in a great degree the danger of our Indian Empire." He wrote to Henry Dundas, then Foreign Secretary, on the 25th of October: "The reduction of Mauritius would indeed destroy the present

---

[1] *Despatches of the Marquess Wellesley,* vol. ii. p. 414.

resort and haunt of the most formidable forces of piracy in these seas." [1]

On reaching Trincomalee, Colonel Wellesley proceeded at once to make an arrangement for the proposed expedition. He paid his wonted attention to the commissariat. The governor of Ceylon proposed that it should sail without certain requisite stores, in hopes of their being despatched afterwards. Colonel Wellesley wrote: "Articles of provision are not to be trifled with or left to chance; and there is nothing more clear than that the subsistence of the troops must be certain upon the proposed service, or the service must be relinquished." After having been a month at Trincomalee, Colonel Wellesley wrote to Lord Mornington that "he had received no tidings of the admiral," and inferred that the attack upon the Mauritius had been postponed. The admiral was willing enough to act against Batavia, because the reduction of Batavia had been suggested some time previously by the King. But he could not take specific orders from the Governor-General, and he declined to risk his Majesty's fleet on any enterprise which had not received the sanction of his Majesty's Government. As the admiral remained obdurate, the destination of the expedition had to be changed to Batavia, and General Baird was appointed to command it. Before the news of the change reached Trincomalee Colonel Wellesley had left it with the troops, owing to a despatch from Dundas to the Marquess Wellesley, dated Downing Street, 6th October 1800, having been sent to him from Madras. It informed the Governor-General "that Sir Ralph Abercromby had received his Majesty's order to proceed up the Mediterranean, and by

---

[1] *Despatches of the Marquess Wellesley,* vol. ii. pp. 402-414.

an attack on Alexandria, and the coast, to co-operate with the Turkish army, assembling in Syria, in whatever plan may be concerted with them for expelling the French from Egypt; and that it is thought expedient that a force should also be sent from India to act in such manner as may appear conducive to that essential object from the side of the Red Sea: with this view, Captain Sir Home Popham, with a proper squadron, will be immediately sent into that sea, taking with him a regiment from the Cape." The Foreign Secretary proceeded to state: "I have thought it right to send a copy of this despatch to the Governments of Madras and Bombay. I have directed the two Presidencies to proceed in making those preparations without delay, and even to carry these orders into execution without waiting for your lordship's directions, if they are ready in other respects." [1]

Colonel Wellesley considered he was justified in carrying out these orders without waiting for the Governor-General's decision. A month must elapse before he could hear from Calcutta. Though apprehensive of his brother's displeasure, he determined to act on his own responsibility, and in February (1801) he sailed with the troops for Bombay. At Cape Comorin he received the notification of Sir David Baird's appointment to the command. He was very sore at what he considered to be a supersession, and bitterly complained of it. But he had no substantial ground for complaint. The Marquess Wellesley had stated in a letter, dated the 3rd of March, "The extent of the force rendered it necessary to appoint a general officer to the chief command." He added: "You will, however, exercise your judgment upon the

---

[1] *Despatches of the Marquess Wellcsley,* vol. ii. p. 436.

propriety of desiring leave to return to Mysore; and if you should entertain any great anxiety on that subject, I shall not attempt to obstruct your wishes, nor shall I feel any sentiment of unkindness upon the transaction; but my decided opinion is, that you will but satisfy the call upon your public duty, and maintain the reputation of your public spirit, by serving cheerfully and zealously in your present condition." Colonel Wellesley yielded to his brother's wish, and consented to retain command under General Baird. On his arrival at Bombay he laboured with unwearied zeal in the task of completing the reorganisation and equipment of the troops. His health had been affected by his recent campaign, but he did not allow it to relax his zeal or affect his energy, and so effectually did he labour for the departure of the expedition, that when General Baird arrived on the 30th of March he found most of the transports ready to put out to sea, and before three days elapsed six of them sailed under Colonel Beresford with sealed orders. On the morning of the 6th of April General Baird left Bombay, but, owing to an attack of illness, Colonel Wellesley could not accompany him. On the 31st of March he wrote to his brother: "When I wrote to you on the 25th, I was in hopes that I should be able to sail the next day, but on that night I was seized with a fever which has lasted ever since, and of which I have not yet recovered." On the 9th of April he wrote to Baird: "I have had no fever since I saw you; but I am sorry to say that the breaking-out of which I complained is worse than it was; and it has become so bad as to induce Mr Scott to order me to begin a course of nitric baths, and this remedy, exclusive of the disease itself, is sufficient to induce me to be desirous to wait at least rather longer than the *Susannah* will, if not to give over all thoughts of joining you." [1] The *Susannah* sailed on the appointed day and was lost with all hands in the Red Sea. Wellesley adds :–

I do this, I assure you, with reluctance, notwithstanding I think it very probable that I shall soon hear of your being recalled; however, considering that circumstances, and the bad state of my body and the remedy which I am obliged to use, I should be mad if I were to think of going at this moment.

As I am writing upon this subject, I will freely acknowledge that my regret at being prevented from accompanying you has been greatly increased by the kind, candid, and handsome manner in which you have behaved towards me, and I will confess as freely, not only that I did not expect such treatment, but that my wishes before you arrived regarding going upon the expedition were directly the reverse of what they are at this moment.

I need not enter further into this subject than to entreat you will not attribute my stay to any other motive than that to which I have above assigned it; and to inform you that as I know what has been said and expected by the world in general, I propose, as well for my own credit as yours, to make known to my friends as to yours not only the distinguished manner in which you have behaved towards me, but the causes which have prevented my demonstrating my gratitude, by giving you every assistance in the arduous service you have to conduct. I shall stay here as long as the season will permit, and then I propose to go round to Madras; and if I cannot get well, I believe I must try a cold climate. [2]

[1.] " 'But, sir, were not you very ill at the time of the expedition to the Red Sea?'

"Yes, but I was not confined to my bed. What I had then was the Malabar itch–a much worse kind of itch than ours–it would not yield to brimstone. I caught it on shipboard at Madras–in a man's bed that was given up to me. Dr Scott, the same who invented nitric acid, cured me at last by baths of that nitric acid; and they were so strong that the towels which dried me on coming out were quite burnt.' " —*Notes of Conversations with the Duke of Wellington,* by Philip Henry, fifth Earl Stanhope, p. 103.

[2.] *Despatches of the Duke of Wellington,* vol. i. p. 246.

A memorandum upon "The Operations in the Red Sea" accompanied the letter. It exhibits extraordinary knowledge of the topography, condition, and resources of a country then little known; it discusses the situation, prospects, and intentions of the French, and the policy to be observed towards the natives.

On the 12th of May 1801 Arthur Wellesley wrote from Seringapatam: "I arrived here on the 7th, since which day I have had a slight return of fever. I have again recovered, however, and I hope that this attack will be the last." Writing to his brother Henry he said, "I found your friend Mrs Stevenson, who had been with difficulty restrained from turning the house out of doors and windows during the time I was absent"; but he wrote to her husband, who had been ruling the provinces during his absence: "I hope that you and she will make use of my house, &c., &c., as long as it may be convenient to you." He at once took measures to render the city less unhealthy, and strenuous were his efforts to improve the health and comfort of the troops. But the fever hung about him, and he wrote to his brother Henry: "I have some thoughts of going home in the next winter if I don't see some prospect of being actively employed in India. I do everything I can to lose all thoughts of what has happened; but everybody that I see and speak to is of the same opinion that I have always held on it." [1] Against "quitting this hateful country Henry strenuously argued, pointing out, "The war on the Continent is now at an end, so that unless Bonaparte chooses to invade us there is little or no prospect of any active service in Europe." India was the

[1] *Supplementary Despatches,* vol. ii. p. 409.

only country in which there was a possibility of his being actively employed. "Whenever you are a Major-General you are certain of being upon the staff in India; and although you care less about money than any man I ever met with, I cannot help observing that in this respect your situation is more advantageous than it could be in any other part of the world." [1] The brother wisely added, "For God's sake try to forget what has happened." So Wellesley stayed. For nearly two years he governed Mysore, and he regained composure and serenity in labour. He frequently visited the different districts, and made himself thoroughly acquainted with their topography and resources. To convert Mysore into a tranquil and prosperous province he constructed roads, and to make it healthy he improved the drainage and constructed other sanitary works. The details of his administration as revealed in his letters to his subordinates are instructive, because they exhibit the qualities which made him a great administrator. Imaginative power stamps both his civil as well as his military career. The genius of a great administrator is not so imposing as that of a great general, but is perhaps equally rare, and needs the same peculiar combination of qualities. A great administrator, like a great general, must be able to see the other side of a hill. He must think not only of the day but also of the morrow; he does not only what he must but what he wants. [2]

The plans which the creative intellect of Wellesley supplied were matured with clearness and decision, and carried out in the most subordinate detail by the

---

[1] *Supplementary Despatches,* vol. ii. p. 409.

[2] *Biographical Studies,* by Walter Bagehot, p. 128.

force and strength of his character. He was always eager
to extirpate abuses, but he was reluctant to attach blame
without the most convincing proof of culpability. His letters
to the various officers under him reveal thoughtfulness, a
disposition to oblige, a readiness to forward the interests
of those whom he considered deserving of reward. Like all
genuine men, he was an object of special attraction to the
natives. They said, owing to the interest he took in their
wellbeing, their habits and customs, that he must be a
Company's officer. And no higher compliment was ever paid
to the old officers of the East India Company. The system
of forced labour he considered unbearable, and his words
should be borne in mind by every young officer who makes
a tour in an Indian district: "It must be abolished entirely,
or so arranged and modified as to render it certain that
the unfortunate people employed as coolies are paid, are
not carried farther than their usual stage, and are not ill-
treated." To evil-doers he was a hard, stern man. But he
was always just. He put down with a strong and vigorous
hand the disturbances in Canara and Malabar. He hunted
out rebels, and step by step he crushed rebellion. Then
he occupied posts which would lay the country so open
to our troops as to secure the military command of every
part of it. He was willing to execute summarily obstinate
rebels, and in order to disarm the people he had to permit
provisionally semi-military rule in Malabar; but he writes:
"I acknowledge, however, that I long for the return of the civil
government. Although a soldier myself, I am not an advocate
for placing extensive civil powers in the hands of soldiers
merely because they are of the military profession, and I have

always opposed the idea excepting in cases of necessity. The case of Malabar is one of these, which I regret exceedingly; but I hope that the necessity will not be of great duration." He would not consent to the establishment of martial law in a greater degree than was absolutely necessary. In answer to the request made "to allow the full operation of martial law" [1] in Malabar and Canara he writes :–

I am fully aware that the military gentlemen in Malabar are exceedingly anxious to establish what they call military law. Before I should consent to the subversion of one system of law and to the establishment of another I should be glad to know what the new law was to be; and I have never procured from any of these gentlemen yet a definition of their own idea of military law. I understand military law to be the law of the sword, and in well-regulated and disciplined armies to be the will of the general.

I should not wish to have the trouble of managing a country like Malabar myself, and I acknowledge that I should not think it very proper to commit the management of that province (by the establishment of military law) to any other officer under my orders. [2]

Wellington read the consequences of events and the motives of men with singular penetration, and no crisis ever took him entirely by surprise. In September 1801 he found time amidst his multifarious civil and military duties to write a memorandum upon operations in the Mahratta territory,[3] "for the benefit of those in whose hands may be placed the conduct of the operations of the army, in case of such a war as I have supposed we may expect." He discusses with his wonted accuracy the seasons, the nature of the country, its roads, its products, and its means of defence.

[1] *Supplementary Despatches,* vol. ii. p. 293.
[2] Ibid., p 262.
[3] *Despatches of the Duke of Wellington,* vol. i. p. 295.

"The season at which it is most convenient," he states, "to commence a campaign with the Mahrattas is that at which the rivers which take their rise in the Western Ghauts fill." The Mahratta army was principally composed of cavalry, and their plan of operation against a British army would be to endeavour to cut off its communication with its rear and to impede the junction of its supplies from the Mysore country. "As the rivers are not fordable, as there are no bridges and no means of passing them except by basket-boats, which it is difficult, and might be rendered impossible, to procure, the fulness of the river operates as a barrier." The British army would experience no inconvenience or delay "if good pontoons were provided and a bridge were thrown across each river for the passage of the army. The communication might afterwards be kept up by means of the common basket-boats." Having detailed his observations on the Mahratta territory with a view to operations within it, Wellesley states those he would recommend: "The first object in any Mahratta campaign commenced in the season which I think most favourable to a British army would be to push the enemy across the Kistna, and to establish ourselves firmly on that river as a barrier from which we could advance to their capital, or to such other ulterior objects as might be held out." The army would then cross the Toombuddra at Hurryhur, and the next object would be to get possession of Darwar, the only place not liable to be taken easily by assault. He, however, describes a method by which it might be taken by *coup de main*. A year after the minute was written Holkar defeated the army of the Peshwa at Poona, and on the 30th of October 1802 the Governor of Bombay received a letter from Baji Rao, the Peshwa, that he had sought an "asylum" on British territory.[1] On the last day of the year (1801) was signed the treaty of Bassein, by which the English engaged to restore the Peshwa to power on condition of his becoming a subsidiary prince.

Owing to the state of Mahratta affairs a strong force had assembled on the north-west frontier of Mysore. On the 8th of February 1803 Wellesley, who had become Major-General by seniority on 29th April 1802, and a Major-General on the staff of the Madras establishment on the 28th of November, left Seringapatam with his division to join it. On his way, at Hurryhur, he heard that a strong detachment was to enter Mahrattan territory and proceed to Poona. He wrote to General Stuart:

If you should take command of it [the detachment] yourself, I hope you will do me the favour to allow me to accompany you in any capacity whatever. All that we know of the country and its inhabitants, in a military point of view, was learned when I was in it; and I should do everything in my power to make myself useful to you. If you should not think proper to take command of this detachment yourself, in consideration of the information which I have had opportunities of gaining of that country and its inhabitants, and the communications which I have constantly held with its chiefs, should you be pleased to entrust it to me, I shall be infinitely gratified, and shall do everything in my power to forward your views. [2]

On the 9th of March General Wellesley with a mixed force, European and native, slightly exceeding 10,000

---

[1] Selection from the Letters, Despatches, and other State Papers preserved in the Bombay Secretariat (Mahratta Series), edited by George W. Forrest, p. 55.

[2] *Despatches of the Duke of Wellington*, vol. i. p. 338.

men, marched from Hurryhur, crossed the Toombuddra on the 12th, and reached the Kistna on the last day of the month. The detachment included his own Mysore troops, who had been long prepared and well equipped for any service. Speed was of vital importance, and the army marched quickly because it consisted of disciplined troops and the General had himself attended to every detail. He had won the respect and confidence of the turbulent Mahratta chiefs by the way he had conducted the campaign against Dhundia, and almost all in the vicinity of his route joined with their forces and accompanied him to Poona. He conciliated the inhabitants by preventing with a strong hand all plunder and excess. On the 18th of April he heard that Amrut Rao, the adopted brother of the Peshwa, who had been appointed Viceroy by Holkar, intended to take Poona.

In consequence of this information [he writes] I marched last night [19th April] with the cavalry and a battalion, and arrived here this day at about two, and the town is safe. . . I was detained about six hours in getting the cavalry guns through the Bhore-ghaut, in consequence of which I imagine that Amrut Rao received intelligence of my march in such time as to enable him to depart this morning before I arrived.

The infantry will be here on the day after to-morrow, and on the next day I shall move towards the Ghauts.

We have marched sixty miles since yesterday morning.'

Lord Wellesley wrote with just pride: "It is a circumstance equally honourable to the British character and propitious to the British interests in that quarter of India, that the first effects of the British influence in the Mahratta dominions should have been displayed

---

[1.] Despatches of the Duke of Wellington, vol. i. p. 403.

in rescuing the capital of the empire from impending ruin, and its inhabitants from violence and rapine."

On the 27th of April General Wellesley set forth towards the Ghauts, but after marching fourteen miles he had to halt because "I found that my march from Poona created great alarm, that several of the principal inhabitants were leaving the place, and that the ladies of the Peshwa, who had been desired by his Highness to come down from Sevaghur this day, were afraid to venture in. I have therefore sent back all the Mahratta horse, and I shall remain here. I have sent the cattle farther up the valley to graze." [1] He adds: "It is reported that Holkar has entered the Nizam's country near Dowlutabad and Aurungabad, and that he is about to attack those places. I have therefore ordered Colonel Stevenson to make a movement to the northward, and even to go to their support if he should find Holkar has already attacked either of them." The General occupied his time until the arrival of the Peshwa in riding to Poona to supervise the preparations which were being made for his march to protect the territory of the Nizam. He was wroth at being informed that the wheels for which he asked from Bombay could not be ready till the middle of June: "I have made forty wheels since I arrived at Poona, and I could march to-morrow if I could get the iron which I required from Bombay." He informs the governor, "I have made it a rule that I never will allow abuses to interfere with the service," and "there must be both abuse and neglect in the department of the commissary of stores, otherwise he must have been able to make wheels at least as soon as my departments, and to send the iron required." On the 27th

---

[1.] *Despatches of the Duke of Wellington,* vol. i, p. 417.

of April the Peshwa, attended by Colonel Close and escorted by a division of more than 2000 men, left Bassein. On the 9th of May Wellesley writes: "You will have heard that the Peshwa is now in a village about nine miles from Poona, where I imagine he will remain till a lucky day for entering the city will arrive." On the 13th of May the lucky day arrived, and the Peshwa entered his capital escorted by a numerous train of the principal chiefs of the Mahratta empire, and remounted the *musnud* with all due ceremony. On the 15th of May General Wellesley wrote: "I saw the Peshwa last night according to his appointment. . . . In the course of the conversation his Highness showed much quickness and ability, and I observed that he appeared particularly anxious to perform all the stipulations of the treaty, of course at the smallest expense to himself."[1] He, however, soon gauged the character of Baji Rao—a treacherous, worthless creature, endowed with showy accomplishments and a good address.

Neither Sindia nor Holkar, nor any of the great Mahratta chiefs, could tolerate the Peshwa having signed away the Mahratta independence. Baji Rao they despised, and they were willing to usurp his power, but the reverence for the office had not departed. A strong love for the old hereditary office was the spirit which animated all the Mahrattas. Mahadji Sindia, when sovereign of Hindustan, took pride in carrying the Peshwa's slippers. "This is my occupation," he said; "it was that of my father." The restoration of the Peshwa by British bayonets wounded the national pride. But it was of vital importance to the English empire that there should be a settled government at Poona. We were

---

[1.] *Despatches of the Duke of Wellington,* vol. i. p. 450.

now bound by treaty to protect the territories of Mysore and of the Nizam, and this could only be done by obtaining a commanding influence at the capital of the Deccan. Sindia and Holkar had made the territories of the Pcshwa their theatre of war, and laid them waste. Want alone might compel their troops to invade the more fertile lands of their neighbours. As long as Sindia kept an army in the Deccan we must have a strong force to watch him. The Duke of Wellington wrote: "The most expensive article in India is an army in the field; and the most useless is one destined to act upon the defensive." [1]

The first result of the restoration of the Peshwa was the flight of Holkar from Poona. There was a momentary gleam of hope that order would be restored to the land without war. The southern chiefs paid their obeisance to the Peshwa. The Resident at the Court of Sindia read to Daulat Rao the chief text of the treaty of Bassein. He owned it contained nothing to which he could object; but both Daulat Rao Sindia and the Raja of Berar refused to acquiesce in the proposal "that the former should immediately recross the Narbada with his army, and the latter return to Nagpur." General Wellesley was now invested by the Governor-General with full powers to make peace or declare war. He wrote to the Resident at the Court of Poona "to inform Sindia and the Raja of Berar that, consistently with the principles and uniform practice of the British Government, I am perfectly ready to attend to their interests, and to enter into negotiation with them upon objects by which they may suppose their interests

[1] Selection from the *Letters, Despatches, and other State Papers preserved in the Bombay Secretariat* (Mahratta Series), edited by George, W. Forrest, p. xxxiii.

to be affected. But they must first withdraw their troops
from the position which they have taken up on the Nizam's
frontier, and return to their usual stations in Hindustan
and Berar respectively; and on my part I will withdraw
the Company's troops to their usual stations." Sindia and
Bhonsla replied, "that the armies now assembled here, and
those of the English Government and of the Nizam, shall
commence their return upon the same date, and that each
of the armies shall arrive at their usual stations on a date
previously settled; that is, that the army of the English and
of the Nizam now encamped near Aurungabad, the army of
the English encamped near the Kistna, and you also with
your army, shall all march towards their stations on the
same date that the armies move from this encampment; and
on the same date that all those different armies reach their
respective stations at Madras, Seringapatam, and Bombay,
Sindia and myself will reach Barhanpore."

This proposition at first sight seems fair, but the absurdity
of the last condition is apparent when we remember that
the distance from Ahmednagar, where General Wellesley
was then encamped, to Madras was more than 1000 miles,
to Seringapatam more than 500, and to Bombay more
than 300; but Barhanpore was only distant about 50 miles
from the Nizam's frontier. General Wellesley's answer was
eminently characteristic of the man. It was frank and firm.

Your Highness will recollect [he wrote] that the British
Government did not threaten to commence hostilities against
you; but you threatened to commence hostilities against the
British Government and its Allies; and when called on to explain
your intentions, you declared it was doubtful whether there
would be peace or war; and, in conformity with your threats and

your declared doubts, you assembled a large army in a station contiguous to the Nizam's frontier. On this ground I called upon you to withdraw the army to its usual station, if your subsequent pacific declarations were sincere, but, instead of complying with this reasonable requisition, you propose that I should withdraw the troops which are intended to defend the territories of our Allies against your designs; and that you and the Rajah of Berar should be suffered to remain with your troops assembled in readiness to take advantage of their absence. This proposition is unreasonable and inadmissible, and you must stand the consequences of the measures which I find myself compelled to adopt in order to repel your aggression. I offered you peace on terms of equality, and honourable to all parties; and you have chosen war, and are responsible for all consequences.

On the 8th of August General Wellesley marched to the vicinity of Ahmednagar, and saw the *petta* (suburb) and fort lined with men whose arms glittered in the sun, whilst another body of troops was encamped outside between them. "The *petta* was a very large and regular native town, surrounded by a wall of stone and mud above eighteen feet high, and very neatly built, with small bastions at every hundred yards, but no rampart to the curtains, the wall being rounded off at the top, and scarcely broad enough for a man to stand upon." [1] The General, reconnoitring from a small elevated spot within long gunshot, directed the leaders where they were to fix their ladders; "but unaware that there was no rampart, we were ordered to escalade the curtains without breaching. The fort lay on our right hand, and the *petta* in front within gunshot of each other." The first column was ordered to attempt a long curtain to the extreme left. "The ladders were speedily planted and the assault made; but each man, as he ascended, fell

[1] *Military Reminiscences,* by Colonel James Welsh, vol. i. p. 156.

hurled from the top of the wall. This unequal struggle lasted about ten minutes, when they desisted with the loss of about fifteen killed and fifty wounded." The third party, consisting of the flank companies of the 74th and the 1st battalion 3rd Regiment, under the command of Captain Vesey, advanced under a fire from the heavy guns of the fort, reached the curtain, and planted the only two scaling-ladders with which they were furnished. "Such a rush was made at first that one ladder broke down with our gallant leader and several men, and we were forced to work hard with the other. Captain Vesey was then a very stout and heavy man; but what impediment short of death can arrest a soldier at such a crisis? He was soon in the bastion surrounded by men determined to carry everything before them. Our two European companies had all scrambled up, and about 150 or 200 of the 3rd, when a cannon-shot smashed our last ladder and broke the thigh of my *subahdar*." [1]

The party, dashing down, scoured the streets near the wall till they arrived at a gate marked for the centre attack. A loud peal of cannon and musketry from without answered the second party under Colonel Wallace, "and some of my men opened the gate whilst they were battering at it from the outside." The two parties united, and after a brisk and gallant contest were masters of the *petta*. Our loss in killed and wounded was 160 men. A Mahratta chief who was in camp with a body of horse wrote to his friends at Poona: "These English are a strange people, and their General a wonderful man; they came here in the morning, looked at the *petta* wall, walked over it, killed all the garrison, and returned to breakfast! What can withstand them?"

---

[1] *Military Reminiscences*, by Colonel James Welsh, vol. i. p. 158.

The first man killed at the storming of the *petta* was Captain Duncan Grant of the 78th Highlanders. He "was a young officer of great promise; with an uncommonly fine form and great personal strength, he possessed a kind and affectionate disposition, a liberality of soul, and a flow of spirit which endeared him to every one who had the happiness of knowing him."

Captain Browne, who commanded the grenadiers, and had the pipers attached to his company, was much older than any man in the corps, having been unfortunate in promotion. He had been a brother subaltern with Wellesley. As an Englishman he did not mix much with his comrades. Immediately before starting for Ahmednagar Grant gave a party in his tent, and sent for Browne's piper. The next day Browne at parade remonstrated with Grant for having sent for the piper without a previous application to him. Grant replied "that he did not conceive such an application necessary, and that he should send for the man again whenever he pleased." Captain Browne, with great solemnity, exclaimed, "Sir, you are a boy, and nobody but a boy would tell me so." Grant sent a challenge. They met and fired together; and Browne was shot dead.

"Poor Grant was placed in arrest, and seemed deeply to lament the mischief he had done. When riding by my side on the march he suddenly seized my hand with energy and pressed it without uttering a word, then rode off, and, unarmed as he was, rushed up the first to the top of the ladder, from which he fell a lifeless corpse! It is scarcely necessary to say that, being in arrest, he had no business to be in the way of danger this day; but his mind was tortured with remorse, and his high spirits led him to the very post he would have chosen, at the head of men by whom he was greatly beloved." [1]

Among the brave men who fell that day was Hussain Khan, a native officer of the 3rd, who had been raised at once to that rank by bringing 200 recruits. He was therefore eyed with considerable jealousy by the other native officers. Fully aware of the feeling, he was most zealous in the performance of every duty, and often asked Captain Welsh, who commanded his company, to keep an eye upon him in action and report his conduct accordingly. When they were approaching Ahmednagar he again reminded him of his promise.

"But being suddenly called to lead the corps, by my commanding officer putting himself at the head of the Europeans, we were separated by some distance. I had, however, scarcely reached the top of the ladder when I heard a voice behind me calling out, "Oh, sir, remember your promise!" and looking round, I perceived my little friend at my heels, he having contrived to scramble through the crowd in his eagerness to perform some signal service. The words were scarcely spoken before a cannon-shot from the fort fractured his thigh and broke the ladder. I got off, but he fell, and was carried into the hospital, where he died a few days afterwards." [2]

On the 9th General Wellesley reconnoitred the ground in the neighbourhood of the fort. At dusk he seized a position within 400 yards of it, on which in the course of the night a battery was constructed for four guns. At daylight it opened and fired with such effect as to induce the governor to desire that "we

---

[1] *Military Reminiscences,* by Colonel James Welsh, vol. i. p.160.
[2] Ibid., p. 162.

should cease firing in order that he might send a person to trial for his surrender." "In my answer I told him that I should not cease firing till I should have taken the fort or he should have surrendered it."[1] On the morning of the 12th of August, "when our ammunition was running short and the 12-lb. shot nearly all expended, the General granted them terms, and our corps (3rd Regiment), then in the trenches, moved and took possession with a company of the 78th.[2] The garrison marched out with the honours of war. "One of the terms on which the *killedar* capitulated was that he and his garrison should have their private property. Major-General Wellesley is convinced that there is no good soldier in this detachment who would infringe this capitulation, and he is determined that it shall not be infringed, and he will punish with the utmost severity any person that may be found plundering in the fort of Ahmednagar."

The capture of the fort, then considered one of the strongest in India, secured Wellesley's line of advance, and supplied him with a useful depot.

Leaving a garrison in it, he marched northward on the 18th of August; and six days later his army crossed the Godavery by means of wicker boats made by the troops themselves from the neighbouring jungle. Moving forward, and marching rapidly, as was his wont, he arrived at Aurungabad on the 29th of August. Here he heard that Sindia and the Rajah of Berar had entered the Nizam's territory with an army of horse only, and had passed Colonel Stevenson, who, with a force of 7000 men, was watching the Agunta Pass. The next day General Wellesley marched southwards towards

---

[1] To the Governor-General, Camp at Ahmednagar, 12th August 1803.

[2] *Military Reminiscences,* by Colonel James Welsh, vol. i. p. 163.

the Godavery, having received intelligence that the enemy intended to march in that direction, to cross the river, and go forward to Hyderabad. But the enemy were quite undecided as to their plans of operation. On hearing of the movement of the English forces they countermarched in a northerly direction. They wished to cross the Godavery, as it was fordable, and to make a dash to the southward, "although it is certain they do not like my position upon that river and my readiness to cross with them. They know that the river must rise again, and they do not like to be cut off from their own country and all assistance." If they should march upon the Nizam's capital, he intended to reinforce Poona and move to Hyderabad with the remainder of his corps. If they did not, he should endeavour to bring them to an action on this side of the river. "As I have before me such active operations," Wellesley writes to Malcolm, "you will be glad to hear that I never was in such marching trim. I marched the other day 23 miles in 7½ hours; and all our marches are now made at the rate of 3½ miles an hour." Colonel Stevenson made several attempts to bring the enemy in action, but in vain. General Wellesley himself had to remain stationary till the convoys of grain which he expected reached him. On the 18th of September the last of them arrived, and on the 25th he was enabled to move forwards towards the enemy, who had been joined by his regular infantry and heavy guns. On the 21st General Wellesley and Colonel Stevenson had a conference, at which they concerted a plan to attack the enemy on the morning of the 24th. It was deemed expedient "to separate their forces, because both corps could not pass through the same defiles in one day; secondly, because it was to be apprehended that if we left open one of the roads through these hills, the enemy might have passed to the southward while we were going to the northward, and then the action would have been delayed, or probably avoided altogether." [1] On the 23rd the two forces advanced against the combined armies of Sindia and the Rajah of Berar, Colonel Stevenson's division marching about eight miles on the left of Wellington. "As usual," writes Wellesley, "we depended for our intelligence of the enemy's position on the common *hurcarrahs* [2] of the country. Their horses were so numerous that without an army their frontier could not be reconnoitred by a European officer; and even the *hurcarrahs* in our own service, who are accustomed to examine and report positions, cannot be employed here, as, being natives of the country, they are as well known as any European." [3]

The messengers reported the enemy to be at Bokerdun. "Their right was at Bokerdun, which was the principal place in their position, and gave the name to the district in which they were encamped; but their left, in which was their infantry which I was to attack, was at Assaye, about six or eight miles from Bokerdun."

Wellesley directed his march so as to be within twelve or fourteen miles of their army at Bokerdun on the 23rd. He was going through a hilly tract of country, and, as he states to Munro, he could get no certain information

---

[1] To Lieut. -Colonel Munro,1st November 1803. See *Munro,* p. 84.

[2] *Hurcarrahs,* messengers. Earl Roberts writes: "On that occasion his dispositions are certainly open to criticism. His knowledge of the enemy's movements was so defective that he came upon the Mahratta army a day sooner than he expected, and before he had been joined by the larger portion of his force, which was under Colonel Stevenson's command."—*The Rise of Wellington,* by Field-Marshal Earl Roberts, V.C., K.G., p. 40.

[3] Letter from General Wellesley, November 1, 1803.

from the natives, and for his knowledge of the country he was dependent on foreign scouts; he could not venture to reconnoitre without his whole force, and when he reached his encampment at Naulniah he found he was not more than six miles from Bokerdun. He was then informed that the enemy's cavalry had marched, and the infantry were about to follow, but were still on the ground. His troops had already marched fourteen miles, but believing the report to be true, he resolved to continue the march and attack the enemy's infantry. He apprised Colonel Stevenson of his determination, and desired him to move forward. Leaving the baggage at Naulniah under the protection of a battalion of sepoys and 400 men taken from the native corps, General Wellesley ordered an immediate advance. Taking the 19th Dragoons and three regiments of the regular native cavalry, he hastened on to reconnoitre. On reaching some rising ground he saw not only the infantry but also the combined army of the confederates before him. Thirty thousand horses in one magnificent mass crowded the right; a dense array of infantry, powerfully supported by artillery, formed the centre and left. Along their front flowed the seemingly impassable Kaitna between high and rugged banks, which received its tributary the Juah a short distance beyond the enemy's left. It was a formidable position, defended by 10,000 disciplined infantry, thousands of horse, and 100 cannon. Wellesley's whole force numbered only 4500 British troops (of which one regiment of cavalry and two of infantry were Europeans), and 5000 Mysore and Mahratta horse, with 18 guns. News at this time was brought to him that the Mahratta horse intended to descend to the enemy the moment the battle began.[1] But Wellesley determined to fight at once. Mountstuart Elphinstone, who accompanied him as Political Assistant, relates how the General after the engagement vindicated himself from the charge of rashness. "Had I not attacked them," he said, "I must have been surrounded by the superior cavalry of the enemy, my troops must have been starved, and I should have nothing left but to hang myself to these tent poles."[2]

Wellesley immediately formed his plan. While reconnoitring he noticed two villages, Peepulgaum and Warooge, one on each bank of the river, and beyond the left flank of the enemy, which appeared unguarded; and on the assumption that where villages exist on opposite banks of a river there is generally a passage between them, he directed a flank march for the purpose of crossing there and turning the enemy's left flank.[3] The narrow delta between the Kaitna and its northern affluent the Juah gave sufficient space for Wellesley to employ his small force (while the *nullahs* or river-beds on either side secured his flanks); but the space was so confined as to restrict the enemy from bringing his

[1] Grant Duff's *History of the Mahrattas.*

[2] Selections from the Minutes of the Honourable Mountstuart Elphinstone, with an Introductory Memoir, edited by George W. Forrest, p. 10.

[3] January 23, 1834.– "After dinner we talked of India. The Duke gave an account of his attack at Assayc and of his acting on the conclusion that there must be a ford at a particular point of the river, because he there saw two villages on opposite sides of it. 'That,' he added, 'is commonsense. And when one is strongly intent on an object, commonsense will usually direct one to the right means.' "–*Notes of Conversations with the Duke of Wellington, 1831-1851,* by Philip Henry, fifth Earl of Stanhope, p. 48, and *post,* p. 182.

Speaking to Croker in 1825, Wellington stated: "I immediately said to myself that men could not have built two villages so close to one another on opposite sides of a stream without some habitual means of communication, either by boats or a ford–most probably the later." –*The Croker Papers,* vol, i. p. 353.

immense superiority of numbers into action, and the decisive struggle was therefore limited to almost equal numbers of the two forces. The attack on the left also gave a real advantage: inasmuch as the enemy's lines of retreat lay to his left rear, he would have run much risk of being cut away from it, and in that case might be driven in the direction towards which Colonel Stevenson's force was coming up; and in a case of a less decisive success the enemy would at least be taken in flank on his line of retreat, and he would have to cross the Juah river, an operation in which he might find difficulty in carrying off his guns.

About 3 P.M. Wellesley, placing himself at the head of the line, marched his little column diagonally towards the unguarded ford at Peepulgaum, near the junction of the two ravines. Small pickets of infantry led, the British cavalry followed in rear, and the Mahratta and Mysore cavalry supporting them on the right flank protected the ford against Sindia's cavalry. A large body of the enemy's horse having crossed the river, threatened an attack, but they were deterred by the bold front of the British cavalry and their supporters. For a length of time the enemy did not see the advance of the British infantry or discover their object.[1] "When they did discover it, they altered their position, and threw their left up to Assaye; but in more than one line." The first line extended from the Kaitna across to the village of Assaye upon the Juah river. The second line was formed nearly at right angles to the rear of the enemy's front line,

---

[1] "Luckily they did not occupy the ford at Peepulgaum; if they had, I must have gone lower down, and possibly I should have been obliged to make a road across the river, which would have taken so much time that I should not have had day enough for the attack."–*Memorandum on the Battle of Assaye.*

with its left towards the village of Assaye and its rear to the Juah river, along the bank of which it extended in a westerly direction from the village of Assaye.[1] On catching sight of the marching column the enemy commenced a cannonade, but the distance was great and they did little execution. However, when the column approached the ford, the enemy got the range and smote it with a terrific fire, "which galled us much." The Highlanders plunging in middle deep, crossed the stream, and after much driving and tugging the bullocks got the guns across. Wellesley's first intention was to attack the enemy's left flank and rear, and to throw his right up to Assaye.

When I saw that they had got their left to Assaye I altered my plan, and determined to manoeuvre by my left, and push the enemy upon the *nullah*, knowing that the village of Assaye must fall when the right should be beat. Orders were given accordingly. The column was drawn up in three lines. The first consisted of the advanced pickets to the right, two battalions of sepoys, and his Majesty's 78th Regiment; and the second of his Majesty's 74th Regiment and two battalions of sepoys; and the third of his Majesty's 19th Dragoons with three regiments of native cavalry.[2] During these formations we lost numbers of officers and men, as the enemy fired mostly grape and chain shot. The village of Assaye was on our right: the pickets were

---

[1.] Lieutenant (afterwards Sir Colin) Campbell, who was Wellesley's brigade-major, in a letter written at the time states: "We were detained by our guns for a little time at the *nullah*, and when we crossed we were obliged to bring our right shoulder to attack their left flank. The enemy upon this were obliged to change their front, which they (did with the greatest regularity and precision."

[2.] "The Peshwa's and the Mysore cavalry occupied the ground beyond, or to the southward of the Kaitna river, on the left flank of the British troops, and kept in check a large body of the enemy's cavalry, which had followed General Wellesley's route from the right of their own position."–*Notes Relative to the late Transactions in the Mahratta Empire*, Fort William, December 15, 1803, p. 58.

ordered not to go near it, as there appeared to be some infantry in it, and, in advancing, on no account to incline towards it.

The order of battle being formed, the last instructions given, Wellesley ordered the line to advance at a quick pace, without firing a shot, but to trust all to the bayonet.

This order was received with cheers and instantly obeyed. It was soon perceived, however, that the leading battalion, composed of the pickets, had diverged from the line of direction, which made it necessary to halt the whole front line. This was a critical moment. The troops had got to the summit of a swell of the ground which had previously sheltered their advance; and the enemy, believing that the halt proceeded from timidity, redoubled their efforts, firing chain-shot and every missile they could bring to bear on the line. General Wellesley, dreading the influence of this momentary halt on the ardour of the troops, rode up in front of a native battalion, and, taking off his hat, cheered them in their own language, and gave the word to advance again. This was also received with cheers, and instantly put in execution. When the 78th was within 150 yards of the enemy they advanced to quick time and charged. At this instant some European officers in the service of the enemy were observed to mount their horses and fly. The infantry, thus deserted by their officers, broke and fled with such speed that few were overtaken by the bayonet; but the gunners held firm to their guns; many were bayoneted in the act of loading, and none gave way till closed upon by the bayonet. [1]

Having captured the guns of the first line, the Highlanders and sepoys made a rush for those in the second line and quickly drove the enemy from them. "But many of the artillery who pretended to be dead, when we

---

[1] *Stewart's Sketches of the Highlanders,* vol. ii. p. 193.

passed on to the second line of guns turned the guns we
had taken upon us, which obliged us to return and again
drive them from them.[1] The General himself led the 78th
Regiment and the 7th Native Cavalry, and in the course of
the operation had a horse shot under him."

At this time things were not going well on the right. The
officer commanding the pickets, instead of keeping out of
shot from Assaye as he had been ordered, led directly upon
it. A tremendous fusillade from the village, supported by
continuous showers of grape, checked their advance. " Major
Swinton, 74th Regiment, went to the pickets and asked them
why they did not move on. On his return to his regiment he
found that numbers of his officers and men had fallen. He
immediately moved forward. At this period the cannonade
was truly tremendous. A milk-hedge in their front, which
they had to pass to come at the enemy's guns, threw them
into a little confusion; but they still pushed forward, and
had taken possession of many of their guns when the second
line, which opened on them, obliged them to retire from
what they had so dearly purchased." [2] The gallant band left
half its number on the field. Men fell by the dozen. A body
of Mahratta horse, stealing round the enclosures of Assaye,
charged and broke their diminished ranks. A supreme
moment! Then Maxwell's men heard, "Forward and charge!"
"It was taken up in an instant. Through the broken ranks of
the 74th the 19th Dragoons, followed by the native cavalry,
rode, and breaking on the Mahratta horse, swift as
the stormwind, drove them with great slaughter into the
river. Pressing forward through a hurricane of grape and

---

[1] Letter from Lieutenant (afterwards Sir Colin) Campbell.
[2] Ibid.

musketry, they rode into the batteries on the enemy's left. "General Wellesley at the same time threw the 78th forward on their right to move down on the enemy, who still kept their position at Assaye." The splendid charge of the Dragoons and the irresistible sweep of the Highlanders decided the day. The enemy's line gave way in all directions, and were driven into the Juah ravine with great slaughter at the point of the bayonet. The British cavalry, crossing in hot haste, cut in among their broken infantry, and charged them along the bank with great effect. But, as the General states, the cavalry, having lost horses and men, and been separated, was not in a fit state to continue the pursuit, "and thus make the victory more complete than it was." Ninety-eight guns and seven stands of colours, however, became the spoil of the victors. The victory was bought at a heavy price in killed and wounded. Twenty European officers, 175 European soldiers, and 230 native soldiers were killed; and 30 European officers, 412 European soldiers, and 696 native soldiers were wounded, comprising about a third of the troops engaged. "Out of 19 officers (of the 74th) 11 were killed and 6 wounded, and out of 569 men and officers exactly 400 have been returned killed and wounded." [1] One company was almost annihilated. It went into action with an officer and fifty men, and in the evening four of the rank and file were all that survived that bloody day. The enemy left 1200 dead on the ground, and at least 4000 wounded lay scattered over the field. Their loss was principally among

[1] Letter from the Honourable Mountstuart Elphinstone, Camp near the village of Assaye, 25th September 1803. 'Selections from the Minutes of the Honourable Mountstuart Elphinstone,' by George W. Forrest, p. 15.

the artillery and infantry. The artillery-men served their guns well and stood by them to the last. "Sindia's infantry," writes Wellesley, "behaved well; they were driven from their guns only by the bayonet, and some of the corps retreated in great order and formed again." The British soldier behaved as he always does behave. There is no finer incident in our annals than the steady advance of the infantry at Assaye, under a most destructive fire, against a body of infantry far superior in number, and no finer feat of arms than the charge of the 19th Dragoons. The General was worthy of his men. He was in the thick of the action the whole time, and had, as has been noted, a horse killed under him.[1] Mountstuart Elphinstone writes: "It is nothing to say of him that he exposed himself on all occasions, and behaved with perfect indifference in the hottest fires (for I did not see a European do otherwise, nor do I believe people ever do); but in the most anxious and important moments he gave his orders as clearly and coolly as if he had been inspecting a corps or manoeuvring at a review." On the

---

[1.] Writing to his brother Henry, the General says: "I lost two horses— Diomed (Colonel Aston's horse, who has carried me in so many campaigns) piked, and another horse shot under me. Almost all the staff had their horses either killed or wounded, or were struck in some place or other." Writing to Malcolm on the 26th of September 1803, the General says: "The bay horse was shot under me, and Diomed was kicked, so that I am not sufficiently mounted. Will you let me have the grey arab? I must also request you to get for me two good saddles and bridles." Diomed, whether "piked" or "kicked," was lost at Assaye. "I was this morning astonished," Malcolm wrote from Sindia's lines on the 3rd of February, "at the might of old Diomed, whom you lost at Assaye. I, however, concealed my pleasure till by hard bargaining I had got him in my stable for 250 rupees. The fellow gave me your Gibson's bit into the bargain. The old horse is in sad condition, but he shall be treated like a prince till I have the pleasure of restoring him to you" (*Life and Correspondence of Major-General Sir John Malcolm,* by John William Kaye, vol. i. p. 233).

25th of September General Wellesley announced to the governor of Bombay in a few simple words the victory of Assaye, which made us masters of India :–

CAMP, *Sept. 25th*, 1803.

SIR,—I attacked the united Armies of D. R. Sindiah & the Rajah of Berar with my division on the 23rd, and the result of the action which ensued was that they were compleatly defeated with the loss of 90 pieces of cannon which I have taken. I have suffered a great loss of Officers and Men.

I inclose a copy of my letter to the Govr.-General, in which I have given him a detailed account of the events which led to and occurred in the Action.

I have the Honor to be, Sir, with great respect, Your most obedient and faithful Honourable Servant,

ARTHUR WELLESLEY.

JON^N. DUNCAN, Esq.

The day after the battle of Assaye Colonel Stevenson joined General Wellesley, and was immediately despatched in pursuit of Sindia beyond the Tapti. The capture of the famous fortress of Asurgarh deprived that chief of his last stronghold in Khandesh. The Rajah of Berar turned towards his own dominions, and was followed by both corps of the British army. Sindia, now thoroughly disheartened, sent an envoy for peace, and on the 7th of November he was escorted into camp. "He was richly dressed and well mounted, and had an elephant, two camels, and many led horses, escorted by ninety of his master's best cavalry."[1] The Brahmins deemed the next day to be auspicious for a visit to the English Commander. Four o'clock in the afternoon was the hour fixed for the reception, "and

---

[1.] *Military Reminiscences,* by Colonel James Welsh, vol. i. p. 185.

many of us, in the best uniforms that a year's wet, dust, and sunning could afford, met at the General's tent." But that hour was proscribed by the Brahmins, and at sunset "every officer who could command a change or a tolerably clean suit" assembled, and the procession set forth to meet the envoy.

Having passed at a canter to the Mahratta lines on our left, and there meeting the *vakeel*, who with his friends had dismounted to receive the General, we all alighted, when a *gulleh-millow*, or hugging scene, commenced among the great folks, which lasted some minutes, after which the ambassador and General Wellesley again mounted, followed by the rest, and the cavalcade returned by torchlight to headquarters, where the band of his Majesty's 78th Regiment and company were drawn up, who saluted the *vakeel* as he dismounted. The General's tent, a large square, single-poled, of about thirty feet, although half the officers had retired, could hardly retain the genteel crowd which remained. Taking a particular interest in such scenes, I contrived to get close to the General's chair. He first handed the *vakeel* in, and seated him on his right hand, and Gokliah, our head ally, on his left, and so on with the rest according to their rank. A silver salver with betel was then brought in, which the General distributed with his own hand to all the seven natives on his right and left entitled to such compliment. He then gave them rich dresses and shawls, and lastly presented the *vakeel* in particular with two superb jewels and a rich gold chain, which were immediately fastened round his turban, and several more beautiful shawls and dresses were added to this donation, during which time the band of the 78th played "God save the King" and several other tunes. The great men conversed on common topics till the last present, when the *vakeel* told General Wellesley, in very good Hindustani, that "the Maharajah, his master, wished for nothing so ardently as his friendship and amity," and rising to take leave, was conducted to the door by the General. A great concourse having assembled at the entrance, it was with difficulty the guard could make way for a very large

elephant and beautiful horse to be brought up and presented
to the *vakeel*,who, mounted on a superb white charger most
richly caparisoned, galloped off in great style, followed by his
presents and escort; and thus ended the first visit. [1]

Owing to Sindia's envoy not being properly accredited
by his master, it was not till the 22nd of November that
suspension of hostilities was granted by General Wellesley
on condition that Sindia's force should move to the eastward,
but "I positively refused to suspend hostilities against
the Rajah of Berar." By leaving the Rajah of Berar out of
the arrangement the confederacy became dissolved, and
Wellesley was able to direct his whole force against that
chief. With this view he put his army in motion to co-operate
with Colonel Stevenson, whose column he had directed upon
the stupendous mountain-fortress of Gawilgurh in the Berar
territory. Stevenson was old and broken in health, and the
deputy adjutant, in the letter conveying the order that he
was to commence the siege on arrival, and carry it on with
the utmost celerity and activity, stated: "The General begs
that you will not risk your life in the arduous undertaking of
the siege of Gawilgurh, if you do not find your strength equal
to conducting the operations of it. And if you find yourself
too weak for that, he will change situations with you for
the period of the siege, by his joining the subsidiary forces,
while you take the command of this division." [2] The gallant
old soldier refused to exchange.

On the 25th of November Wellesley descended the
Rajoora Ghauts, and on the morning of the 29th November

---

[1] *Military Reminiscences,* by Colonel James Welsh, vol. i. pp. 185, 186.
[2] *Despatches of the Duke of Wellington,* vol. ii. pp. 875, 876.

his division, each man having sixty rounds of ammunition, marched for Parterly. "After advancing eight miles on the road a cloud of dust was observed a few miles off on the left flank, and we concluded, as it proved to be, that it was Colonel Stevenson's force moving for the same object, though no one but the General knew what that object was."[1] Although the General had been separated from Colonel Stevenson for several months at a distance of hundreds of miles, he had maintained constant communication with him by the foot-messengers who then carried the post. Rattle in hand to scare away the wild beasts, they traversed enormous distances, running at the rate of five or six miles an hour. Wellesley, on seeing the dust on his left flank, desired an officer near him to ride off to Colonel Stevenson and tell him to move to a particular village, which he pointed out, and that there he should have further orders. "But," said the officer, "what am I to do if it should not be Colonel Stevenson?" " 'Why, then,' I answered, 'you are mounted on a d—d good horse, and you have eyes in your head, and you must ride off as hard as you can.' "[2]

"Passing through a beautiful country," writes Colonel Welsh, "full of game, we even amused ourselves as usual in hunting and shooting on the right flank the whole way, until, after a march of ten miles, we found our camp colours at a stand, and Colonel Stevenson likewise pitched on our left."[3] The armies of the two chiefs had decamped, and from a ruined tower

[1] *Military Reminiscences,* by Colonel James Welsh, vol. i. p. 189.
[2] "The Mahrattas near me were much surprised at my message. 'How,' they said, 'can you possibly tell Colonel Stevenson's dust from anybody else's dust?' "–*Notes of Conversations with the Duke of Wellington, 1851,* by Philip Henry, fifth Earl of Stanhope, p. 181.
[3] *Military Reminiscences,* by Colonel James Welsh, vol. i. p. 189.

Wellesley saw a confused mass, which he concluded to be their armies on the march. He determined not to pursue the retreating foe. The day was hot, the men had marched ten miles, and it was two o'clock when the order was given for them to form and rest on their arms. The infantry, however, had hardly halted when torrents of horse plunged out and engaged with the Mysore cavalry. They rapidly increased in numbers, and Wellesley led the pickets of the infantry to support the cavalry and take up the ground of encampment. He had reached to within six miles of the place at which he intended to encamp, when, getting on a knoll, he saw a long line of infantry and cavalry and artillery regularly drawn up on a vast plain. " There will be time to take these guns before night," he exclaimed, and before night closed in thirty-eight of those guns and all their ammunition had been captured.

The General galloped back and straightway ordered the troops to advance with the guns. Himself at their head, they marched in single column "through a country so thickly covered with high grain that we could see nothing in our front for the first three miles." After emerging from the walled village of Sersooley they reached a vast plain much intersected by water-courses. On the farther side, straight in front, in a grove of mango-trees, was the village of Argaum. In front of it was drawn up in a straight line extending five miles the enemy's army. Sindia's heavy body of cavalry was on the right, next which stood the Berar Rajah's infantry and fifty guns, flanked on his left by his cavalry. A swarm of light horse hovered on the right. Directly in front of the village Wellesley formed his force in two lines, "the infantry in the first, the cavalry in the second and supporting the right, and the Mogul and Mysore cavalry on the left, nearly parallel to that of the enemy: with the right rather advanced, in order to press upon the enemy's left." The village was the only entrance to the plain, and on it the enemy's batteries were planted. At the first glimpse of our troops forming they opened fire. "A European officer, three native officers, and forty sepoys," says Welsh, "were knocked down by the cannon-shot." Three entire native battalions, who had behaved so admirably at Assaye under Wellesley, broke and ran away. He rushed personally into the vortex, rallied these broken battalions, and again led them up. But valuable time was lost. The Indian day is short, and it was about half-past four when the General gave the order for the infantry to leave their guns and advance. "It was a splendid sight," says an eyewitness, "to see such a line advancing as on a field-day; but the pause when the enemy's guns ceased firing, and they advanced in front of them, was an awful one. The Arabs, a very imposing body, singled out our two European regiments; and when we arrived within about sixty yards, after a round of grape which knocked down ten of our men and about as many in each of the European regiments, they advanced and charged us with tremendous shouts. Our three corps were at this time considerably in front of the rest of the line, and a struggle ensued, in which we killed about 600 of these Arabs, and one corps alone took eight standards." [1] The rest of the line coming up, the enemy abandoned their guns and fled. The General led the British cavalry to the charge. "Not more than twenty minutes' sun remained," he writes to his brother; "but the moon was bright, and the horse pursued

---

[1] *Military Reminiscences,* by Colonel James Welsh, vol. i. pp. 190, 191.

the fugitives for some miles." "If we had had daylight an hour more," he adds, "not a man would have escaped." The routed enemy left on the field thirty-eight guns and immense quantities of ammunition and stores. "The field of battle was strewn with arms, and about 1000 sun-dial turbans, like those worn by the Bengal army, and twenty or thirty standards fell into our hands." The battle of Argaum was a memorable and fine bit of work. "The troops were under arms and I on horseback," the General says, "from six in the morning till twelve at night." The British loss only amounted to 46 killed and about 300 wounded.Eleven British officers and three native officers were among the wounded. And of all that went down that day there was no braver and better soldier than Subahdar Ally Khan. He was far advanced in life, and so diminutive in person that his officers used to call him the little cock-sparrow.

In action he was the life and soul of those around him, and in devoted affection to the service he had no superior. The whole of the flesh and sinews of the higher part of both thighs being torn away by a large shot, he fell and could not rise again ; but as soon as the action was over, he requested his attendants to carry him after us, that his dear European comrades might see him die. We had halted on the field, upwards of a mile in front of where he fell, when he arrived, and spoke to us with a firm voice and most affectionate manner; recounted his services, and bade us all adieu. We endeavoured to encourage him, by asserting that his wound was not mortal, and that he would yet recover. He said he felt assured of the contrary, but he was not afraid of death; he had often braved it in the discharge of his duty; and only regretted that he should not be permitted to render further services to his honourable masters. He died shortly afterwards. [1]

---

[1] *Military Reminiscences,* by Colonel James Welsh, vol. i. pp. 193, 194.

After the victory of Argaum no time was lost in commencing the siege of Gawilgurh, a strong fortress which stands at an elevation of 3500 feet on a spur of the ranges which divide the waters of the Tapti from those of the Poorna. "It is detached on all points from the range except the north. The other faces are very steep, and the rock is scarped in many places. The works are erected round the top of the hill, which is flattish. There are no works below. The fort has three gates, one in the south face, with a road leading to it up a promontory or root of the hill (or neck or nose, whatever it is called). It has another gate to the west, or north-west, which I have not seen, and which I understand has been built up, and another to the north. The approach to the north is over moderately waving ground, and on that side the fort is no stronger than if it stood on a plain. But this ground is not to be got at without crossing the range of hills on which the fort stands." On the 5th General Wellesley marched over a very rich plain to Ellichpoor, some twelve miles to the south-east of the fortress. On the 7th Colonel Stevenson, who had equipped his corps for the siege, proceeded into the mountains, and Wellesley marched his division towards the southern face of Gawilgurh. The heavy ordnance and stores were dragged by hand over mountains and through ravines by roads which the troops had to make for themselves. "There is a good custom of beating drums and playing the 'Grenadiers' March,' " writes Elphinstone, "while the sepoys are dragging the guns up the Ghauts."[1] It was no light task getting them over the boulders. "Here we found

[1] *Life of the Honourable Mountstuart Elphinstone,* by Sir T. E. Colebrooke, Bart., M.P., vol. i. p. 94.

our own 12-pounder sticking. It had got into such a position that if it moved forward the nave of the wheel came against a tree. The people, however, put stones under the wheel, so that when the sepoys gave a general pull the bullocks moved forward, and the elephants pushed, the wheels rose over the stones, and the carriage leant to the other side, so that the nave was clear of the tree. I could not have thought the getting a gun over a stone was so interesting." On the 10th of December Wellesley and his staff rode through much wild and picturesque country till they got to a beautiful valley where Stevenson's headquarters' line and a brigade were encamped. But the colonel was not there. After clambering up a very steep hill and riding over rather steep swells of ground for a mile or more, they met him, accompanied by his troopers and three companies of sepoys. "There was steep rising ground between us and the fort," Elphinstone says, "behind which we were quite concealed. We dismounted and ascended the rising ground, where from behind some stones the whole north side of the fort suddenly appeared. There was something of surprise and grandeur in this. The wall with battlements, the fort with tents, mosques, and other buildings, all burst on our view at once. Between the fort and us on the right some houses were burning, and some of the enemy, who had set them on fire, were still there. They were very near; we had not time to look carefully at the fort. I did not like to look long for fear of drawing a fire on the General." [1] As it did not appear distinctly whether there was a chasm or interruption between them and the

---

[1] *Life of the Honourable Mountstuart Elphinstone,* by Sir T. E. Colebrooke, Bart., M. P., vol. i. p. 96.

fort, the party proceeded to the place where the burning houses stood. Wellesley was satisfied that there was no interruption. "In going off the General rode to rising, round to take a look at the fort, and all his troops rode after him. We thought it would draw a fire, but did not. As we went off the fort began firing, but without effect."

On returning to his camp the General found a vakeel from the Berar Rajah. "The interview lasted several hours, but led to nothing." On the 12th, at night, Colonel Stevenson erected two batteries in front of the north face, while General Wellesley, upon the side of a mountain that looked on the south defence, constructed another battery with a view to breach the wall near the south gate. The troops worked hard at it, and cleared a road to it; but notwithstanding the utmost exertions of the men, they could not move the iron battering guns above a few hundred yards from the bottom, so steep and rugged was the ascent. "I was just relieved," writes Colonel Welsh, "from working by a fresh party, and enjoying a few moments' rest in some clean straw, when the officer commanding the working party came up to Colonel Wallace and reported that it was impossible to get the heavy guns up to the battery. The colonel, who was brigadier of the trenches, exclaimed, 'Impossible! Hoot, mon! it must be done! I've got the order in my pocket!'"[1] But it could not be done. The iron guns were abandoned and covered with leaves, and two brass twelves and two howitzers substituted "in the mock battery, for a breaching one it never was." On the night of the 14th a wide breach in the front wall and two good breaches in a higher wall behind became practicable. At ten next morning

[1] *Military Reminiscences,* by Colonel James Welsh, vol. i. p. 196.

the signal for assault was given. "Our advance was silent, deliberate, and even solemn." On reaching the breach the storming party halted, and "at the forlorn-hope a sergeant's party ran up, then we followed, ran down, and darted at the second breach, and leaped down into the second place." The enemy retreated down a narrow valley to the north-west gate, where they met a detachment which had been sent by the General to attack it. "The 94th pressed behind, firing from above, and a terrible slaughter took place." [1] The storming party endeavoured to push on, when, to their astonishment, they found they had only gained a separate hill, and that the fort lay behind a deep valley, beyond which appeared a double wall and strong gates. The British soldiers rushed across the valley and began steadily to climb the steep hill which formed the first wall. The enemy kept up a hot fire from their works. At last the first wall was got over and the first gate opened. Scaling-ladders were brought, and got up the hill and applied to the second wall. Captain Campbell with the light infantry of the 94th escaladed it, opened the gate for the storming party, and soon after the union was hoisted in the highest part of the fort. "The number of our killed and wounded," writes Elphinstone, "is 53 Europeans and 100 sepoys, or thereabouts. That of the enemy is immense. They are fine, tall, handsome Hindustanis. Beni Sung, their commander, is among the slain. His body, with that of the *killedar* or governor of the fort, was found amidst a heap of slain near the gateway. These two men, of good Rajput families, had determined to die in defence of

---

[1] *Life of the Honourable Mountstuart Elphinstone,* by Sir T. E. Colebrooke, Bart., M.P., vol. i. p. 96.

their trust; and, according to the custom of their country, to save their wives and daughters from destruction, by putting them to death before they went out to meet their own. From some cause unknown to us, this was but imperfectly performed; of twelve or fourteen women, but three, I think, were dead when our men discovered them; and three or four more lay bleeding, having received two or three cuts or stabs with a knife or dagger. Probably these Rajputs intrusted this shocking duty to hands more humane than their own. General Wellesley visited them, and ordered every respect and care to be given them." [1]

The capture of the strong mountain fortress following the victory of Argaum and the annihilation of Sindia's disciplined infantry at Laswaree by General Lake crushed the hopes of the Mahratta confederates, and negotiations were now opened in earnest. Two days after the capture of Gawilgurh a treaty was signed by General Wellesley on one part and the envoy of the Rajah of Berar on the other. The rajah was allowed eight days to refuse or confirm it. On the sixth day it was returned ratified. At three o'clock that afternoon "our light companies arrived at the General's tent to await the arrival of Sindia's *dewan,* who made his appearance in great state about five, attended by the General, Major Malcolm, and all the English officers off duty, and followed by state elephants, camels, horses, &c., and 200 of his master's chosen cavalry as an escort. We saluted him with presented arms and

---

[1] Journal of Major-General Sir Jasper Nicholls, K.C.B. *The Military Life of Field-Marshal the Duke of Wellington* by Major Basil Jackson and Captain C. Rochfort Scott, vol. i. pp. 195, 196.

the 'Grenadiers' March,' the park also resounding its shouts
of welcome." Thus arrived at the tent, the envoy dismounted.
"A decrepit old Brahmin, whose nose and chin almost met
each other, and dressed in a coarse white cloth, without a
single ornament, yet the prime minister and chief ruler of a
most extensive kingdom, stood before our astonished eyes."
He was conducted into the pavilion by the General and the
Political Agent, Major Malcolm, and seated between them.
"I looked in vain," writes an eye-witness, "for indications in
his old countenance of that superior and intelligent mind
he was known to possess. He said little and appeared very
grave; some thought him sulky." [1] The Mahratta chief who
closely attended on him asked the General in the envoy's
name "whether he would attend to his mission." "I shall be
happy to confer with him to-morrow," replied the General.
"Do you march to-morrow?" the envoy asked. "Yes." "In what
direction?" "I never tell anybody when or where I intend
to march." The envoy said it was near sunset and it would
be unlucky to stay beyond it, when the General "gave them
their leave in the usual manner, and we mounted to conduct
our great men a part of the way." It was dark before the
General and his escort reached the encampment of the
vakeel of Berar, "in whose tent there was a carpet spread

---

[1] *Military Reminiscences,* by Colonel James Welsh, vol. i. p. 200.
Malcolm said of him that he never saw a man with such a face for the
game of brag. From that time Wattel Punt was known by the name of
"Old Brag" in the British camp; and years afterwards, when Malcolm
met General Wellesley, then the Duke of Wellington, in Europe, and
the conversation one day turned upon the characters of the great men
of France, the latter, when questioned regarding Talleyrand, replied
that he was a good deal like "Old Brag," but not as clever (*Life and
Correspondence of Major-General Sir John Malcolm,* vol. i. p. 241).

upon the floor, upon which we all squatted like a company of tailors." Wattel Punt observing that Major Malcolm used many Persian words in his Hindustani, asked him if he knew Persian. "A reply in the affirmative produced a very pretty stanza in that language, which appeared to me most apposite, expressive of the General's kindness to him." He then added in Hindustani, for the General's ear, that his having succeeded in making a peace would give him a consequence with his master which he could not otherwise have ever hoped to acquire. "The General as kindly and readily replied that he had by his conduct throughout well merited his approbation and that of his master, and that whoever acted his part with integrity and diligence could not fail to meet with a just reward." [1] So the General and the envoy parted on the best of terms.

At the conference in the General's tent next day the question of peace and the conditions on which the English Government would consent to make it were fully discussed, and the discussion gave good promise of a speedy and satisfactory conclusion. On the 30th of December General Wellesley wrote to the Governor-General, "I have the honour to inform your Excellency that I have this day concluded with the vakeels of Dowlat Rao Sindia and signed a treaty of peace, copies of which in the English, Persian, and Mahratta languages I have the honour to enclose." The treaty with Sindia was immediately ratified by the Governor-General. "It is," wrote Lord Wellesley in a private letter, "a glorious and brilliant termination to the war, and equal to the lustre of the campaign." [2]

[1.] *Military Reminiscences,* by Colonel James Welsh, vol. i. p. 201.
[2.] *Despatches of the Duke of Wellington,* vol. ii. p. 933.

By the war the English Government were certainly left
in a glorious situation. "They are," wrote General Wellesley,
"the sovereigns of a great part of India, the protectors of
the principal Powers, and the mediators, by treaty, of the
disputes of all. The sovereignty they possess is greater,
and is settled upon more permanent foundations, than any
before known in India. All it wants is the popularity which,
from the nature of the institutions and the justice of the
proceedings of the Government, it is likely to obtain, and
which it must obtain after a short period of tranquillity
shall have given the people time and opportunity to feel the
security and happiness which they enjoy."

The war had come to a brilliant termination. But much
hard work remained to be done in dispersing the strong band
of marauders who infested the country. The native princes
were unable to protect their subjects from these formidable
banditti. "The Nizam's servants, who," Wellesley writes, "at
the commencement of the campaign drove us away from
their forts and refused to allow us to purchase grain in their
country, now press me by dozens of letters in a day to move
to their assistance, otherwise they will be destroyed." The
Peshwa's government, he adds, is at present only a name.
"His Highness has not settled even the country along the
Beemah five miles from Poona. It is at this moment a dreary
waste overrun by thieves." The task which Wellesley had to
undertake was no light one, for the country was difficult, the
roads nearly impassable, the guides untrustworthy, and his
allies, "like true Mahrattas," gave the freebooters information.
"The Nizam's rascals in this country," he writes, "have given
me false intelligence of the practicability of the Ghauts, and

I am in consequence a little thrown out in pursuit of the thieves." After sundry chases his efforts were crowned with success. On the 2nd of February 1804 news reached him that a formidable band of freebooters, amounting to about 50,000 men, were committing depredations about eighty miles from his camp. He determined to surprise them by making forced marches.

On the morning of the 4th he started with the British cavalry, the 74th Regiment, the 1st battalion 8th Regiment, and 500 men belonging to the other native corps in his camp, and the Mysore and Mahratta cavalry. On his arrival at the encamping ground at Perinda, after a march of twenty miles, he learnt that the enemy were not farther from him than twenty-four miles. He therefore marched again at night with the intention of attacking their camp at daylight.

Unfortunately the road was very bad, and we did not arrive till nine in the morning. The enemy had received intelligence of our approach, and I am sorry to say that I have every reason to believe that they received it from persons in my own camp: their camp was struck, and they had begun their march to their rear when I arrived. I followed them, however, with the British cavalry in one column, acting upon the right of their rear, while the Mysore and Mahratta cavalry, under Bislnapah Pundit, Goklah, and Appal Dessaye, pursued the centre and left. The enemy formed a large body of cavalry, apparently with an intention to recover the retreat of their guns and baggage, which were falling into our hands, and I formed the British cavalry into two lines to attack them. I followed them in this order from height to height, as long as I could see any of them collected. In this advance some horse and infantry were cut up, and the whole of the enemy's guns, ammunition, bazaars, and baggage fell into our hands.[1]

---

[1] *Despatches of the Duke of Wellington,* vol. ii. p. 1023.

Though the chiefs escaped, the result of the day was the complete defeat of the freebooters, who were the terror of the country and were daily increasing in numbers. "I do not think," General Wellesley wrote, "that they will venture, or indeed that they can collect again, as they have lost everything which could enable them to subsist when collected. The troops bear with the utmost cheerfulness the extraordinary fatigue of this short but active expedition. The infantry, under Major Swinton of the 74th Regiment, arrived at the point of attack at the same time with the cavalry; but, from the nature of the action, they could not co-operate further in it than by moving into the enemy's former camp, which they did with great regularity." This was Wellington's last service in the field in India, and he often referred to it as the greatest march he ever made. Thirty years after the event he said to Croker:–

I once marched in India seventy miles in what I may call one march–it was after Assaye–to the borders of the Nizam's territory, against a body of predatory natives, whom by this extraordinary march I surprised in their camp. I moved one morning about four o'clock, and marched till noon, when I had rest till about eight in the evening, by which time I had marched twenty-five miles; at eight we moved again, and did not stop till about twelve mid-day, when I was in the enemy's camp, distant seventy miles from my first point; and these were not computed miles, nor am I talking by guess, for the whole march was measured by the wheel. I had five regiments, two European and three native, and two regiments of regular cavalry, in all about 5000 men, with a large body of native irregular horse.

What sort of troops were these native horse? What would they be like in Europe?

About equal to the Cossacks. I had before Assaye made

another forced march which saved Poona; but it was not so far, hardly sixty miles, and I took more time to do it, but it was a surprising march; but this was with cavalry alone.[1]

Leaving his division, "who had been marching since February 1803, and who since the battle of Assaye in September have not halted more than one day in any one place, excepting during the siege of Gawilgurh," to enjoy a long rest, General Wellesley proceeded to Poona, where the conduct of the Peshwa gave grave cause for anxiety. "Since he signed the treaty of Bassein," writes Wellesley, "he has done no one thing that has been desired, either with a view to forward his own interest or the views of the alliance or the common safety during the war." By the treaty the English bound themselves to defend Baji Rao against external foes, and to protect him from rebels. From the day of his restoration the Peshwa made use of them in endeavouring to establish his authority over his own powerful feudatories, and he attempted to employ them in gratifying his revenge. "The Peshwa is callous to everything but money and revenge. He will call upon

---

[1] *Croker's Correspondence and Diaries,* vol. ii. p. 232.
Three years before he said to Earl Stanhope: "The most surprising march, I believe, ever made was one of mine in India—seventy-two miles from five one morning to twelve the next, and all fair marching; nor could there be any mistake as to distance, for in India we always marched with measuring wheels. The country was not very flat—a few hills, but, however, no ghaut or mountain pass to get over."—*Notes on Conversations with the Duke of Wellington, 1831-1851,* by Philip Henry, fifth Earl of Stanhope.
Colonel Welsh, writing in 1830, states, "Our common marches were between twenty and thirty miles a-day, and on the 6th of February, when we came up with the enemy's camp at ten o'clock, we had marched fifty-four miles in the last twenty-four hours." *Military Reminiscences,* by Colonel James Welsh, p. 204.

the British Government to gratify the latter passion, but
he will make no sacrifices unless to procure money." After
many conferences with the Peshwa and his ministers, he
managed gradually to secure from the Court an unwilling
acquiescence to his endeavours to maintain peace.

"I observed to Munkaiser that in my opinion it would be
much better for his Highness, after seven years of difficulty
and civil wars, in the course of which nearly every man
in the empire had at some time or other been opposed to
his government and armies, to endeavour, by pardon and
conciliation, to settle his government and country, than to
enter on any system of revenge so extensive as that proposed,
and so dangerous and so imprudent."

On the 6th of March General Wellesley wrote to
Jonathan Duncan, Governor of Bombay, "Mr Webbe and
I leave this place for Bombay to-morrow; and, wind and
weather permitting, I hope to dine with you on the 10th,
provided the boats are at Panwell when I arrive there." The
governor's yacht met him at Panwell, and "on approaching
the harbour a salute of fifteen guns was fired from the
Elphinstone Indiaman, and the compliment was repeated on
the hon. General's landing; while the whole of the troops in
garrison formed a street from the dockyard, through which
the General passed, to Government House." An address
was presented him from 120 British inhabitants of "the
settlement," congratulating him "on the glorious and happy
termination of one of the most decisive, brilliant, and rapid
campaigns ever known in the annals of British India — a
campaign in which he had personally borne so conspicuous
a share, and proved himself at its close equally great in

the Cabinet as in the field." His answer was dignified and modest :–

The approbation of this settlement is a distinction which will afford a permanent source of gratification to my mind, and I receive it with a high sense of respect, the honour conveyed to me by your address.

The events which preceded the war are of a nature to demonstrate the justice of our cause; while the forbearance with which the British Government refrained from the contest is calculated to manifest that the efficient state of our military equipment was directed to the preservation of peace, and consistent with the principles of our defensive policy. The comprehensive plan of operations for the conduct of the war was equalled by the extent of our resources, and supported by the concentrated power of the empire. The conflict in which the British armies were in consequence engaged presented a theatre capable of displaying at once the most splendid objects of military glory, and substantial proofs of the pervading wisdom of the British councils. To be engaged in such a scene was an object worthy of the highest ambition; and the contingencies which placed a division of the army under my command enabled me to appreciate the permanent causes of our success and power in the established discipline of our troops, in the general union of zeal for the public interests, in the uniform effects of our consolidated strength, in the commanding influence of our national reputation in India.

Under the effects of certain causes the troops under my command were able to give that support which they were destined by the Governor-General to afford to the operations of the commander-in-chief. And while the Grand Army, under his Excellency's immediate command, decided the war in Hindustan by the most rapid career of brilliant victories, the army of the Deccan, emulating that noble example, contributed to elevate the fame and power of Great Britain in India to a height unrivalled in the annals of Asia.[1]

[1.] *Despatches of the Duke of Wellington,* vol. ii. p, 1096.

Honours now poured thick upon him. While at Poona he received a letter from the officers who served under his immediate command with the division of the army in the Deccan, stating their desire to present him with a pledge of their respect and esteem; "and to express the high idea they possess of the gallantry and enterprise that so eminently distinguish you, they request your acceptance of a golden vase of the value of 2000 guineas, on which it is proposed to record the principal event that was decisive of the campaign in the Deccan." The General replied:–

To Lieut.-Colonel Wallace, &c., and Officers of the Division of the Army in the Deccan.

CAMP AT POONA, 4*th March* 1804.

I have had the honour of receiving your letter of the 1st inst., in which you have announced your intention to present to me a most handsome pledge of your respect and esteem, which shall commemorate the great victory which you gained over the enemy. Be assured, gentlemen, that I shall never lose the recollection of the events of the last year, or of the officers and troops by means of whose ability, zeal, disciplined bravery, they have in a great measure been brought about in this part of India; but it is highly gratifying to me to be certain that the conduct of the operations of the war has met with the approbation, and has gained for me the esteem, of the officers under my command." [1]

He had been only a few days at Bombay when he received through the Governor-General a resolution passed at a meeting of the British inhabitants of Calcutta held on the 21st February 1804– "That a sword of the value of £1000 be presented to Major-General the Hon. A. Wellesley, in the name

---

[1] *Despatches of the Duke of Wellington*, vol. ii. p. 1078.

of the British inhabitants of this settlement, as a testimony of the sense which they entertain of the services rendered by him to the East India Company and to the country."

During his residence at Bombay Wellesley carried on an unwearied correspondence with the Governor-General and his agents at the native Courts regarding the two treaties he had made. In their negotiations he had engaged in no selfish match of state-craft, but he had striven as an honest soldier and statesman for the best interests of both parties and the maintenance of peace. The Governor-General was inclined to interpret the precise meaning of two hastily constructed and ambiguous treaties by the strict letter of international law, and to make arrangements consistent with justice, but not with generosity. The soldier was afraid that a too exacting interpretation of the treaties might lead to a renewal of war. If it were renewed he would enter upon it with zeal and ardour, having no doubt of success. "But," he added, "however I may be pleased with the prospect of that success, as far as I am concerned I should prefer the continuance of peace for the public and for you." He considered the renewal of war to be the greatest misfortune that could occur. "In the eyes of those who are to judge of your conduct, it would efface the glory of the last war and of your whole administration."

The main contention was about the fort of Gwalior. Sindia had executed the treaty under the hope that by the words of the treaty Gwalior, which had belonged to him before the war, would be restored to him on the conclusion of peace. The Governor-General, by a not wholly inadmissible interpretation of the letter of the treaty, declared that justice did not require us to surrender the fort, while sound policy imperatively called upon us to keep it out of Sindia's hands. The General considered that "the argument is on our side"; but he wrote to Malcolm: "I would sacrifice Gwalior, or every frontier of India, ten times over, in order to preserve our credit for scrupulous good faith, and the advantages and honour we gained by the late war and the late peace; and we must not fritter them away in arguments drawn from overstrained principles of the laws of nations, which are not understood in this country. What brought me through many difficulties in the war and the negotiations of peace? The British good faith, and nothing else." [1]

The Governor-General believed that "the peace which has been concluded comprehends every object of the war with every practicable security for the continuance of tranquillity." General Wellesley did not hold the same opinion. He had lived with the Mahrattas, negotiated treaties with them, and no man had a better knowledge of their character. He wrote to his brother Henry, "In truth I consider the peace to be by no means secure." The war had ended in the discomfiture but not the ruin of the two Mahratta Powers, who were still left at the head of very considerable states. Sindia had been much gratified by the manner in which the treaty was negotiated; by which, after he had been humbled to the dust, his pride wounded, and his power destroyed, he was raised to a degree of power greater than that possessed by any other prince in India. But if by the arrangements consequent to the treaty he was to be deprived of a larger portion of territory which he imagined he should hold, those favourable feelings and dispositions of Sindia's mind must be effaced by one

[1] *Despatches of the Duke of Wellington,* vol. ii. p. 1106.

which operates most strongly upon every native—viz., wounded pride. "We must not depend," writes Wellesley, "on Sindia's sense of his interests, although we may have found him and his ministers to know them well. None of the native princes are guided by a sense of their permanent interest, even as they understand it themselves, but in every instance by their passions, of which the strongest is pride."[1] General Wellesley regarded Sindia as the most formidable of the three confederates, and his attitude towards the English was both haughty and insolent. "If Sindia," he writes to his brother Henry, "should not be satisfied, and should take advantage of the state of our affairs to attack us again, the Rajah of Berar, who is equally dissatisfied, will likewise enter into the war." The Governor-General and the commander-in-chief thought that as Holkar had not entered into the strife before Assaye, he would not now provoke a conflict with the British power strengthened by the results of the campaign. They knew not that his troops were actually on the march to join the confederates when the news of Assaye arrested their progress. After the battle of Laswaree he had made up his mind to enter the field against Lake. The commander-in-chief, acting under the Governor-General's instructions, began to negotiate with Holkar. Much correspondence ensued between them. But Holkar had no intention that Mahratta supremacy should perish without another struggle, and he too determined to stagger humanity. He wrote that in the event of war, although unable to oppose the British artillery in the field, "countries of many hundred *coss* [miles] should be overrun,

---

[1] *Supplementary Despatches,* vol. iv. p. 357.

plundered, and burnt; the commander-in-chief should not have leisure to breathe for a moment; and calamities would fall on lacs of human beings in continued war by the attacks of his army, which overwhelms like the waves of the sea." On the 16th of April 1804 the Governor-General issued orders to the commander-in-chief and Major-General Wellesley to commence hostile operations against Holkar both on the north and the south, and he announced his intention of giving back the possessions of Holkar to the native chiefs from whom they had been taken. The promise was a fine stroke of policy. Sindia was delighted, and he pledged his word to promote the war with his utmost exertions. On receiving his instructions to co-operate with General Lake, Wellesley augmented the force in Guzerat by three battalions of native infantry, and instructed Colonel Murray to begin the march as soon as may be practicable against Holkar's possessions in Malwa. But from the Deccan he could afford little help to General Lake. A famine raged in the land. At Ahmednagar fifty deaths occurred daily from want of food. The despatch of Wellesley, dated 11th April 1804, lays down the fundamental principles to be adopted in solving the most difficult problem in Indian administration. Donations of food and money he considered "a very defective mode" of providing against the effects of famine. "It is liable to abuses in all parts of the world, but particularly in India."

Those who suffer from famine [he writes] may be divided into two classes–those who can, and those who cannot, work. In the latter class may be included old persons, children, and sick women, who, from their former situation in life, have been unaccustomed to labour, and are weakened by the effects of famine. The former–viz., those of both sexes who can work—

ought to be employed by the public, and in the course of this letter I shall point out the work on which I should wish that they might be employed, and in what manner paid. The latter– viz., those who cannot work–ought to be taken into hospital and fed, and receive medical aid and medicine at the expense of the public. According to this mode of proceeding, subsistence will be provided for all; the public will receive some benefit from the expense which will be incurred; and, above all, it will be certain that no able-bodied person will apply for relief unless he should be willing to work for his subsistence; that none will apply who are able to work, and who are not real objects of charity; and that none will come to Ahmednuggur for the purpose of partaking of the food which must be procured by their labour, or to obtain which they must submit to the restraint of hospital.[1]

On the 18th of May General Wellesley quitted Bombay. At Panwell the same day he saw the widow of Nana Fadnavis, and had a long conversation with her regarding her future residence. "She had a Moorish woman interpreter, and as I heard her give orders to her interpreter in the Moorish language, and receive her reports in the same, I must consider the conversation of first authority." [2] Wellesley discovered, as all those who have come in contact with them know, the ability and strength of character of a Mahratta woman. Wellesley said that he had heard that she wished to go to Poona, "and I told her

---

[1] *Despatches of the Duke of Wellington,* vol. ii. p. 1140.

[2] Moorish woman was the old way of speaking of a Hindustani woman. The widow's mother-tongue was Mahratti, but she spoke Hindustani for Wellesley to understand. The writer in the 'Calcutta Review' on Wellington in India states, "Notwithstanding his seven years of residence in India, General Wellesley does not appear to have been sufficiently acquainted even with lingua fiauca Hindustani to converse with it." Wellington would not have considered "the conversation of first authority" if he had not understood Hindustani. At Assaye and Argaum he adressed the sepoys in the vulgar tongue.

that if that was her wish I would take her there with me, and
would see her settled in honour and security." The widow of
the late prime minister, however, declined to set out with
him, and she would not go to Poona unless five of her most
intimate attendants were to be in security as to their lives,
their persons, and their property. "She also said her pension
was not sufficient." Wellesley writes to Colonel Close, the
Resident: "Upon the whole, I am convinced that she will not
come to Poona; but it is as well to prevail upon the Peshwa to
allow us to engage for the security of the five persons, at all
events, and to promise an increase of pension, if she would
reside at Poona, and possibly she may be prevailed upon
to comply." He gallantly adds, "She is very fair and very
handsome, and well deserving to be the object of a treaty."

On the 22nd of May Wellesley rejoined the army near Poona,
and was busy supplying it with clothing and equipments ready
for the field when instructions reached him that as it appeared
to the Governor-General that the war with Holkar could not be
conducted with advantage during the rains, the British troops
in the field were to withdraw into cantonments. The Governor-
General further commanded the General to proceed to Fort
William "for the purpose of communicating with me and with
the commander-in-chief upon the various and important
political and military questions now depending in India, and
bearing an intimate relation to your political commission and
political command."

On the 20th of June Wellesley wrote to Webbe, now
Resident at the Court of Sindia: "I fear that Sindia will
not like my going away, but you must tell him that the

Governor-General has ordered me to Bengal, and that I had arranged everything for the campaign before I had gone off. . . . I go by Seringapatam in order to see Purnea, and by Madras to see General Stuart, as I am not quite prepared to speak upon the military affairs of Fort St George without knowing his opinion.[1] No man was more loyal to his chiefs than Arthur Wellesley. On the 24th of June General Wellesley resigned the political and military powers vested in him by the Governor-General, and immediately commenced his march for Mysore. As he proceeded through the Southern Mahratta country the chiefs came to meet him. He had won the hearts of the wild Mahratta lairds by his kindness and courtesy, and their respect by his integrity and sagacity. These qualities have caused the descendants of these warriors to cherish the memory of Arthur Wellesley. Seventy years after a Mahratta chief showed the present writer with pride a short note written to his father by Wellesley Sahib. On the 11th of July Wellesley writes, "Bappojee Sindia, the *killedar* of Dharwar, met me outside of his fort on the morning of the 7th and invited me to an entertainment within it." Wellesley went, much to the surprise of every one, even the *killedar* himself, who, in remarking afterwards that he had not taken advantage of it, said, "For I am still a Mahratta." On the 15th of July Wellesley reached Seringapatam, and the native inhabitants welcomed his return with the following address:–

We, the native inhabitants of Seringapatam, have reposed for five auspicious years under the shadow of your protection. We have felt, even during your absence in the midst of battle and of victory, that your care for our prosperity

[1] *Despatches of the Duke of Wellington,* vol. ii. p. 1273.

had been extended to us in as ample a manner as if no other object had occupied your mind.

We are preparing to perform in our several castes the duties of thanksgiving and of sacrifice to the preserving God, who has brought you back in safety, and we present ourselves in person to express our joy.

As your labours have been crowned with victory so may your repose be graced with honours. May you long continue personally to dispense to us that full stream of security and happiness which we first received with wonder, and continue to enjoy with gratitude, and, when greater affairs shall call you from us, may the God of all castes and nations deign to hear with favour our humble and constant prayers for your health, your glory, and your happiness.[1]

Towards the end of July Wellesley proceeded to Madras, and after a brief stay embarked for Calcutta. On the 1st of August the following general orders by his Excellency the most noble the Governor-General and Captain-General were published in a Calcutta Gazette extraordinary:–

In honour of the eminent services of Major-General the Hon. Arthur Wellesley, in the command of the forces in the Deccan during the late memorable and glorious campaign, and as a testimony of respect to the gallant officers and troops who, under the command of Major-General Wellesley, have contributed to the splendid success of the war against the Mahratta confederates, the Governor-General will proceed down the river to meet Major-General Wellesley, and to conduct that distinguished officer publicly to the Presidency of Fort William. The usual salute to be fired when the Doonamookee yacht, with the Governor-General on board, shall pass Fort William in proceeding down the river, and also on her return.

---

[1] *Despatches of the Duke of Wellington,* vol. ii. p. 1281.

Early on the morning of the 12th Lord Wellesley attended by the officers of his suite, embarked on board his yacht and proceeded down the river to meet his brother. At six P.M. the Governor-General, accompanied by Major-General Wellesley and the officers of the Governor-General's staff, landed at the GovernorGeneral's ghaut.

The Governor-General was received by Major-General Cameron and the staff of the garrisons of Fort William; all the principal civil officers of the Government and the principal European inhabitants of Calcutta had also assembled to congratulate Major-General Wellesley on his arrival; a vast concourse of natives was present on this occasion.

A street of troops was formed from the Governor-General's ghaut to the north front of the Government House, through which the Governor-General's carriages, with the Governor-General, the Hon. Major-General Wellesley, the Hon. Chief-Justice, Sir George Barlow, Mr Udny, Major-General Dowdeswell, and the Governor-General's suite, proceeded to the Government House; the Governor-General was received with the usual honours as he passed the different corps.

On the arrival of Major-General Wellesley at the Government House a salute of the thirteen guns was fired from Fort William, and in the evening the Hon. the Chief justice, the members of Council, and all the principal civil and military officers of the Presidency dined at Government House. [1]

General Wellesley took advantage of his freedom from the laborious duties of office to write several State Papers for the Governor-General. His observations on the policy of the Treaty of Bassein, in reply to Lord Castlereagh's strictures, possess precision and dignity, and form a model of what a State Paper ought to be. It is a State document written by one more anxious to advance solid arguments than use striking expressions,

[1] *Supplementary Despatches,* vol, iv. p. 671.

and it displays in a conspicuous degree the great merit which Wellington possessed of being able to marshal his facts so as to seize and express the main point. The "Memorandum on the Treaty of Bassein" remains the best historical summary of the events of the period, and gives the most clear conception of the entangled web which the Marquess Wellesley had to unravel. At Calcutta General Wellesley also wrote memoranda on the freebooter system in India, and on the system of regulating the supplies for an army. He was busy drawing up a paper on the operations against Holkar when news reached the capital of Monson's retreat. Rashness and incompetency on the part of our generals had brought disaster to our arms. In May, when Holkar's stronghold, Rampura, had been taken, and he had retreated south, General Wellesley urged Lake to continue his pursuit of Holkar, even although he should have no hopes of bringing him into action. "If he does this, I have not a doubt but that the business will soon be over." But he did not follow his advice. Thinking it highly improbable that any force would bring Holkar to action, the commander-in-chief retired to Cawnpore, and left Monson with five battalions of native infantry, some artillery, and about 4000 irregular horse, to form such a disposition of his forces as to obstruct the return of Holkar. After the departure of the commander-in-chief Monson advanced through the Mokundra Pass to a point considerably beyond that where he was instructed to remain, and on the 7th of July he received the alarming intelligence that Holkar with his whole force was about to cross the river Chumbul. He also heard that Colonel Murray, who was advancing from Guzerat, and with whom he daily hoped to open communication, had fallen back. He wrote to Lord Lake that he intended to attack the Mahrattas while crossing the river, but he changed his mind and determined to fall back. It was a fatal decision. The periodical rains had set in with great violence; the soil, consisting of soft black mould, became knee-deep in mud, the bullocks could not drag their loads, and the baggage and guns had soon to be abandoned. The troops had no shelter from the pouring rain, nor any food but what they could find in the deserted villages which were contiguous to their route. "The rain it raineth every day: "if it held up for a few hours, it came down more sharply than ever after each interval. "The country," writes one who was present, "was so completely overflown that the only objects to be seen were distant scattered villages, which in these parts are built on high grounds, but sometimes at so great a distance that dry land was nearly out of sight; and the troops were dispersed, and passing by single files over such places as promised to be less deep. Fifteen elephants and an additional number of camels of the detachment were left stuck in the slough." Swollen rivers had to be crossed. "The only mode that could be resorted to for getting the troops across was by making rafts of such wood as could be got from the roofs of the houses in the neighbouring villages, and by making the elephants swim to and fro with as many men as they could carry at a time. But a dreadful scene of confusion and disaster ensued; rafts crowded with men went down before they reached the opposite bank; and when the elephants became tired from swimming across so often, they frequently in the midst of the stream shook all who were on their backs into the river, most or all of whom perished." [1]

[1.] *A Historical Account of the Rise and Progress of the Bengal Native Infantry,* by Captain Williams, Appendix H.

The Meenahs–freebooters who inhabited the neighbouring hills–often came in disguise "and offered to conduct the rafts, and when they got them into the middle of the stream, they, as if by accident, let the rafts down to where their friends were lying in ambush, who immediately rushed out and murdered the people for the sake of the plunder and booty." At the passage of the Banas river on the 24th August three battalions and the only gun left having been sent across the stream, the enemy suddenly assailed by a heavy fire the rearguard, consisting of one battalion. Major Sinclair charged the enemy's guns. Just as he was planting the British colours on them he received a shot in the knee which brought him and the colours to the ground. The enemy, on seeing him fall, came down like a whirlwind of sand, and the sepoys, faint, worn out, and broken by the nature of the ground, fell back. Plunging at every step into the clayey soil saturated with rain, they slowly made their way to the ford. Many rushed forth to meet assured death by contending with a multitude. The jemadar of the regiment stalked slowly along with a stand of colours in one hand and defending himself with the other "until he reached the bank of the river, into which he plunged, but sank with the colours to rise no more." [1] The Mahratta guns opened with grape, and so unrelenting and strong was the fire that few reached the ford unwounded. They entered the stream, the Mahratta horse dashed in after them, and its current was crimsoned with the blood of the fugitives.

---

[1] *A Historical Account of the Rise and Progress of the Bengal Native Infantry,* by Captain Williams, Appendix H. " The colours of the native battalions, of which there are two stands with each corps, as in his Majesty's service, a union and a regimental colour, are always carried by native commissioned officers."

Throughout the day Monson displayed unshaken resolution and bravery. He thrice led his handful of infantry to the attack, and was the last man to cross. He was wounded, and all his staff killed or drowned except his major of brigade.

The three battalions, harassed at every step by the enemy, marched thirty-six miles to the town of Kooshalghur. The enemy surrounded it with 20,000 horse, some battalions of infantry, and twenty-five pieces of cannon. To defend it was impossible. At half-past 8 P.M. on the night of the 26th the detachment moved out of the town with the least possible noise and formed a square outside of the gateway. In this formation they marched past the Mahratta camp before they were discovered. The enemy's guns opened, but did them little harm, as they were laid for the gate. Their cavalry charged the rear, "but were as often repulsed by the steady and brave 2nd Battalion 21st Regiment." [1]

The last remaining gun of the force, a howitzer, had, however, to be spiked and abandoned. The sepoys, living on a few ounces of hard grain which they had not time to cook, marched on till sunset the next day (27th August), when they reached the ruins of an old fort in Hindown. Here Monson rested his men for some hours. 'At 1 P.M. they again steadily and silently set forth in the same formation. At dawn they left some ravines, with the men rather straggling, and entering a wide plain, found the Mahratta cavalry, some 14,000 in number, formed up in

---

[1] Narrative of the Retreat of the Detachment under the Command of Brigadier-General Monson, including a period of fifty-four days, from the 8th July, when it first commenced, until the 30th August 1804, when the Remains of the Detachment arrived at Agra, on the banks of the Jumna.

front and on either side of them. The men had hardly closed up when the enemy charged them on all sides with the greatest impetuosity, but they were foiled by the courage and discipline of the sepoys. "Not a musket was fired until the enemy was within a few paces, when many of them fell close to the ranks, and a few individuals finished their career within the square. When the dust and smoke cleared away the men cheered their officers on the result of this determined effort on the part of the enemy, and hoped they would repeat their attempt." [1]

After halting for about two hours, expecting another attack, the square was re-formed and the march resumed. After crossing a *nullah* at a ford full of quicksands the detachment halted in a ravine beyond it, having chosen a position secure against any cavalry charge. The enemy, however, brought up some guns, and planting them on an eminence on the opposite bank of the streamlet, opened a murderous fire. The detachment was obliged again to get into motion. Exposed to the enemy's fire in the rear and the musketry of the bandits who lined the high ground on the left, they made their way through the Biana Pass, "and from its being so narrow and steep and full of ravines the men straggled very much and never again got into any kind of order, and from this period there was a final separation of the detachment, every one making the best of their way." On the 30th of August a crowd of footsore half-starved sepoys streamed into the fort at Agra. "I have lost," wrote Lake, "five battalions and six companies, the flower of the army, and how they are to be replaced at this day God only knows.

---

[1] *A Historical Account of the Rise and Progress of the Bengal Native Infantry,* by Captain Williams, p. 303.

I have to lament the loss of some of the finest young men and most promising in the army."

A disaster was, as General Wellesley warned his brother it would be, fatal to the Governor-General's position. But the courage and lofty mind of the great Proconsul proved itself in the hour of trial and defeat. He wrote to the commander-in-chief: "I fear my poor friend Monson is gone. Whatever may have been his fate, or whatever the result of his misfortune to my own fame, I will endeavour to shield his character from obloquy, nor will I attempt the mean purpose of sacrificing his reputation to mine." In a long letter written on the 12th of September to his friend, Colonel Wallace, Arthur Wellesley deduces "some important lessons from this campaign: first, that a corps should never be employed on a service for which it is not fully equal; secondly, that in all military operations we should take care to be sure of plenty of provisions; thirdly, that British troops should never depend on native allies for supplies, which should be purchased by British officers, or, if purchased by natives, ought to be seen before the troops are exposed in a situation in which they may want the supplies; fourthly, that any fort which can support the operations of an army ought to be filled with provisions and stores in case of need; fifthly, that any river which is likely to be full in the rains ought to have a post and boats in it." He adds: "In respect to the operations of a corps in the situation of Monson's, they must be decided and quick; and in all retreats it must be recollected that they are safe and easy in proportion to the number of attacks made by the retreating corps. But attention to the foregoing observations will, I hope, prevent a British corps from retreating." Sir Robert Peel, in speaking of the Duke of Wellington, said that he considered him the most powerful writer in the English language, and that the letter upon Colonel Monson's retreat was the best military letter he had ever read, and quoted the line from Horace—

"Scribendi recte sapere est et principium et fons."

Napier after the battle of Meeanee wrote: "The Duke's letter on the retreat of Colonel Monson decided me never to retire before an Indian army. If I have done wrong abstractedly (for success, like charity, covers sins), the great master led me into it; but my own conviction is that I have done right, and that my admiration of him and study of his words and deeds, as the great rules of war, have caused this victory." [1]

The Governor-General gave General Lake the opportunity of asking for the services of General Wellesley, but the commander-in-chief desired that the latter should return to the Deccan. On the 14th of November General Wellesley set sail for Madras, and seven days later he wrote from Fort St George to Colonel Close at Poona: "I have just time to write a few lines to inform you that I arrived here this day, and that I propose to leave as soon as the bearers can be posted for me. I shall go to Seringapatam, and thence either by the route of Darwar or Meritch to Poona; or if I should find the country not in tranquillity, I shall go to Mangalore and thence by sea to Bombay. I shall be with you about Christmas, by one route or another." On the 30th of November he reached Seringapatam. Passing by Arcot, he paid a visit to his old friends" the 19th Dragoons and the

---

[1] *Despatches of the Duke of Wellington,* vol. ii. p. 1311.

4th Regiment of Native Cavalry, which had been sent into the Carnatic. "I sent them into the Carnatic," General Wellesley writes, "because I was aware that they required rest, and I knew that the men had not seen their families since the corps marched with the Grand Army to Seringapatam in February 1799." His kind-heartedness comes out in many ways in his Indian letters. From Seringapatam he wrote to Major Campbell: "General Stuart was always kind to me. . . . I therefore trust to you to let me know, if you should think that I can render you, or Major Munro, or any of General Stuart's friends, the smallest service." On the 11th of December he writes: "I have been detained here these last two days by something very like a fever and ague; but I still hope it is only an increased attack of the rheumatism. I received yesterday the accounts of the successes of General Lake and General Fraser, and I must sincerely congratulate you upon them. I am rather of opinion that these successes will render it unnecessary for me to go north-ward." At the beginning of 1805, all signs of danger having disappeared, the slow fever confirmed his determination to return to England. He was told that the command of the Bombay forces would be offered to him, and on the 15th of January he writes to Sir John Cradock,[1] who had succeeded General Stuart as commander-in-chief of the Madras army: "It may be true that I have overrated my chances of employment in Europe, and have not given sufficient weight to the advantages of the situation which you say is to be offered to my acceptance. In respect to the latter, however, I believe that my opinion is not incorrect, and I have determined not to accept if it should

[1] Afterwards Lord Howden.

be offered." [1] He adds: "You think about my staying in India like a man who has just come out, and I like one who has been here for seven years involved in perpetual troubles. I acknowledge that I am anxious to a degree which I cannot express to see my friends again; and even if I were certain that I should not be employed in England at all, there is no situation in India which would induce me to stay here. I am not rich in comparison with other people, but very much so in comparison with my former situation, and quite sufficiently so for my own wants."

On the 1st of February he wrote to Lord William Bentinck, governor of Madras: "From the tenor of the letter which I received yesterday it appears that the Governor-General is of opinion that it is not necessary that I should return into the Deccan, and he intends to leave it to my own option to go to England or not as I may think proper. I shall therefore certainly return to England." The same day he wrote to an agent regarding a passage: "I am not very particular about accommodation, . . . and I don't care a great deal about the price. I should prefer, however, either half a round-house or the starboard side of a great cabin; and I don't much care who the captain is or what the ship." On the 15th of February General Wellesley, having obtained leave of absence, arrived at Fort St George. The following day the English mail arrived at Madras with letters of September 4, 1804, and the 'London Gazette,' Whitehall, 1st September, notifying that "the King has been pleased to nominate and appoint Major-General the Hon. A. Wellesley to be one of the Knights Companions of the most hon. Order of the Bath." But a higher honour

[1.] *Supplementary Despatches,* vol. iv. p. 483.

had been bestowed on him. On the 27th of September the General wrote to his brother :–

I enclose copies of letters which I received yesterday in a box containing the insignia of the Order of the Bath. This box was kicking about the *Lord Keath,* which arrived here ten days ago, and was brought on shore by a passenger who went to the ship by accident to look for his own luggage, and he informed me yesterday that he had got it.

It was very unlucky that I did not receive it when the ship came in, as it proves to me that Sir John Cradock had no right to invest me with the Order of the Bath, which he did soon after the account arrived, stating that it had been conferred upon me, and I should have been invested by your order in a manner more consistent with the intentions of the Secretary of State. However, there is no remedy for what has passed; and it now only remains that you should authorise Sir John Cradock to invest me with the Order of the Bath, antedating the authority, and then the proceeding will be regular. If you should not approve of this mode of proceeding, which appears to me to be the best, I request you to let me know it by the first overland despatch, as well as by sea; as in that case I suppose I must go through all the ceremonies in England.[1]

One of the letters enclosed in the box was from the Earl Camden, dated Downing Street, 30th August 1804:—

His Majesty has been greatly pleased, as a mark of his royal approbation of your eminent and brilliant services, and in order that he may immediately evince his sense of the same, to direct that you should be created an extra Knight Companion of the most hon. Order of the Bath; and that your nomination and investiture should not wait for a succession to a regular vacancy therein, I have the honour to transmit to you by the King's commands the proper insignia of that Order, which you will herewith receive, together with a dispensation for wearing the same.

---

[1] *Supplementary Despatches,* vol. iv. p. 496.

I have also the honour to transmit to you the statutes of the Order of the Bath, together with a copy of my letter to the Marquis Wellesley, signifying his Majesty's commands that his lordship should perform the ceremony of investing you with the insignia of that Order.

Allow me, sir, to offer you my most sincere congratulations on a distinction so highly merited.

When it was announced that Sir Arthur Wellesley was about to quit India addresses poured in from Europeans and Asiatics, from the soldiers he had led to victory and the subject races he had governed with equity and justice. The officers of his own regiment, the 33rd, sent him an address, in which they wrote:–

Although by the changes in the service many of the officers have not individually experienced the peculiar advantages of having served under your personal superintendence, yet the benefits which have resulted to the whole corps by having had you at its head will be long felt; and it must ever remain a source of pride to the 33rd Regiment, that the person who has so eminently distinguished himself in every branch of the public service intrusted to him, and who has been so deservedly honoured by our most gracious sovereign, was the commanding officer of the 33rd Regiment.

The officers of the division of the army commanded by him also forwarded an address, in which they stated:—

Participating with the army at large in admiration of those exalted talents and splendid achievements which have been so recently distinguished by our gracious sovereign, we are desirous of offering to you the tribute of our particular respect and gratitude for that consideration and justice in command which has made obedience a pleasure, and for that frank condescension in the private intercourse of life which it is our pride individually to acknowledge.

With these sentiments of public reverence and individual attachment deeply impressed on our minds, our regret on the occasion of your departure is mixed with a humble hope that we are not to consider this important branch of the British Empire to be finally deprived of your eminent qualifications.

But in whatever quarter of the globe further honours or distinctions shall await you, our sincerest good wishes will constantly follow your career; and we now beg you to accept our most respectful but cordial farewell.

The native inhabitants of Seringapatam also forwarded a last testimony of their—

gratitude for the tranquillity, security, and happiness we have enjoyed under your auspicious protection... Respect for the brilliant exploit you have achieved, which strengthened the foundation of that tranquillity, and reverence for your benevolence and affability, glow all at once in our hearts with such force that we are unable to find language sufficient to express our feelings and regret on the occasion of your departure. We pray to God to grant you health and a safe and pleasant voyage to Europe; but we earnestly hope, and look with anxiety, for the period of your speedy return to this country, once more to extend and uphold that protection over us which your extensive knowledge of our customs and manners is so capable of affording.

Wellesley's answers to the addresses are written in a passionless and formal style, expressive of a strong mind under control, but his letters on the eve of his departure are distinguished by their human feeling and gratitude. He wrote to Malcolm, "I cannot express to you how much distressed I am at going away and parting with my friends in this country." During his last week he wrote farewells to the friends who had served him loyally and toiled for him with enthusiasm, and he put forward the claims of all who had rendered good and faithful service. He brought to the special notice of the commander-in-chief the names of many officers who had served with distinction in the Mahratta campaign. But Wellesley did not keep his expressions of approval and gratitude for his European comrades only. He named a large number of Mahratta and Mysore officers whose services he considered should be recognised by pecuniary rewards or grants of lands. He wrote to the adjutant-general begging leave to lay before the commander-in-chief the case of a native officer in the 18th battalion 8th regiment, now a pensioner, in the hope that his Excellency will see some grounds for recommending that this *subahdar* may have as a pension the full pay of his rank and class instead of the half-pay to which only he is entitled.

"It appears by his certificate that he has served the Company forty years, and that he was a *subahdar* of the first class. He was also a man of good character, and well connected in his corps, and five of his relations, commissioned and non-commissioned officers in the battalion, were killed in the battle of Assaye, wherein he also received the wounds which have occasioned his being transferred to the non-effective establishment."

The soldier was also mindful of the great lieutenants who had aided him in his civil and political work. He recorded his high sense of the services rendered by Major Kirkpatrick, the Resident at Hyderabad, and Mountstuart Elphinstone, the Resident at Nagpore; and he recommended that Major Wilk, the eminent historian, who had been acting as Resident in Mysore, should be given the pay of the appointment as Resident, and confirmed in it when it became vacant. "The *Dewan*," he wrote, "and all the principal people of that country, have the highest respect and regard for him." To

Purneah, the *Dewan,* the first of the illustrious line of native statesmen who have done so much to consolidate our Indian Empire by their able management of a great feudatory state, he wrote a letter charged with chivalrous sympathy and noble appreciation.

Every principle of gratitude [he wrote], for many acts of personal kindness to myself, and a strong sense of the public benefits which have been derived from your administration, render me anxious for its continuance and for its increasing prosperity, and in every situation in which I may be placed, you may depend upon it that I shall not fail to bear testimony of my sense of your merits upon every occasion that may offer, so that I shall suffer no opportunity to pass by which I may think favourable for rendering you service. As a testimony of my sense of the benefits which the public have derived from your administration, of my sincere regard, and of my gratitude for many acts of personal kindness and attention, I request your acceptance of my picture.

He added–

Let the prosperity of the country be your great object; protect the *ryots* and traders, and allow no man, whether vested with authority or otherwise, to oppress them with impunity; do justice to every man.[1]

The words addressed to a native statesman may well be taken to heart by those who hold the destinies of India in their hands. India will be ours as long as the toiling millions are content. They have no dream of national independence or political rights, but they ask that their social customs may be respected, their interests may be protected, and their claims and disputes be settled by good administrators of the law.

[1] *Despatches of the Duke of Wellington,* vol. ii. p. 1437.

The letter to Purneah was the last of the memorable series of public papers written by him during his residence in India. Admirably clear and simple, sometimes warmed to a fine heat by earnestness and indignation, they will always remain to the Indian administrator and soldier a treasury of military and political knowledge. On the 9th of March General Wellesley notified in a general order to the troops his resignation of the command in the Deccan:–

In the course of the period of time which has elapsed since Major-General Wellesley was appointed to a command of the division of this army various services have been performed by the troops, and great difficulties have been surmounted, with a steadiness and perseverance which have seldom been surpassed. Upon every occasion, whether in garrison or in the field, the Major-General has had reason to be satisfied with their conduct, and he once more returns them his thanks, and assures them that he shall never forget their services, or cease to feel a lively interest in whatever may concern them.

He earnestly recommends to the officers of the army never to lose sight of the general principles of the military service, to preserve the discipline of the troops, and to encourage in their respective corps the spirit and sentiments of gentlemen and of soldiers as the most certain road to the attainment of everything that is great in their profession.[1]

On the 10th of March, after eight years of splendid labour, Sir Arthur Wellesley embarked for England on board the *Trident* man-of-war. The Peninsular war and Waterloo have cast into the shade the Mahratta campaign and the victory of Assaye; but the knowledge he acquired in the Mahratta campaign of the details of the business of war, and the experience he gained in the fine art of reconciling conflicting interests among

---

[1.] *Despatches of the Duke of Wellington,* vol. ii. p. 145.

his subordinates and allies, carried the "Sepoy General," as he was contemptuously called by his great antagonist, through the toils and difficulties which beset his path in the Peninsula. He did not display a cooler and more indomitable resolution during the crowning action of his life than he did at Assaye. His hardly won victories entitle him to a foremost rank among the great captains who established the military supremacy of England throughout India, and a study of the authoritative records of his administration shows that he was almost the first of the race of soldier-statesmen who by their wisdom, their sympathy, and their sense of an inviolable justice have bestowed permanence and stability on our great and illustrious dependency.

SIR CHARLES NAPIER.

MORE than sixty years have elapsed since the Life of Charles Napier was written by his brother. It is in four volumes–too long for this busy twentieth century; and the pleasure of reading it is marred by William Napier's fierce and wild commentary on Outram and John Jacob. Yet these four volumes contain the heroic tale of the exploits of a great soldier and a man of genius. He is allowed to tell his story in his own words, by means of his copious journals, and Charles Napier wrote with the vigour that he fought. "A wayward life of adventure," he himself calls it, "a good romance it would make; full of incidents by flood and field, stories of love and of war, and ship-wrecks of all kinds."

On the 10th of August 1782 Charles Napier was born at Whitehall; romance and genius held conspicuous places in his lineage. On his father's side he was descended from the Lord of Logarithms. On his mother's side he was sixth in descent from Henry of Navarre. All lovers of Joshua Reynolds are familiar with Sarah Lennox, the peerless beauty of her day. "Lady Sarah," writes Walpole, "was more beautiful than you can conceive. No Magdalen by Correggio

SIR CHARLES NAPIER.

was half so lovely and expressive." She was in the full glow of her youthful beauty when the monarch fell in love with her making hay in front of Holland House. "He sighed and he longed, but he rode away from her," writes Thackeray. After an unhappy first marriage she became the wife of the Hon. George Napier and the mother of the most illustrious family of warriors that ever graced the roll of the British army. For her those rugged soldiers, who were always at war with the world, had the deepest love and veneration. The tenor of his correspondence speaks for the depth of Charles Napier's affection for his mother. Seventeen years after her death, when in the heart of the Sindian desert, he writes: "I dreamed of my beloved mother; her beauteous face smiled upon me! Am I going to meet her very soon? Well, we shall all meet again, unless this dreadful work of war sends me to hell, which is not improbable."

At the age of twelve Charles Napier obtained a commission in the Duke of Wellington's regiment, the 33rd, but was soon transferred to the 89th, then forming part of an army assembling at Netley camp under Lord Moira. "His father was assistant quartermaster-general to that force, and the boy was taken there: thus without joining his regiment he was early initiated in the ways of soldiers, by which his natural genius for war was quickened." When the camp broke up for foreign service he was sent back to Ireland and exchanged into the 4th Regiment; but instead of joining, was placed with his brother at a large school in Celbridge, a small town on the Liffey ten miles from Dublin, where his father had settled. Four years later (1799) Napier was appointed *aide-de-camp* to Sir James Duff, commanding the Limerick district, who transferred an old friendship for the father to the son. At the close of 1800 he resigned his staff situation on obtaining a commission in the 95th, a rifle corps which was being formed by a selection of men and officers throughout the army. He joined it at Blackington, and now found, as his brother tells us, the greatest secret of war is discipline, and never forgot it: he discovered, also, that to know soldiers requires experience, and is a most important part of war. He also realised that no officer can be successful who does not know the science of his profession, and he set to work vigorously to study the theory and history of war. "I quit the mess," he writes in November 1801, "at five o'clock, and from that to ten o'clock gives me five hours' more reading. There is a billiard-table; but feeling a grievous fondness for it, and fearing to be drawn into play for money, I have not touched a cue lately." The peace of Amiens, now being negotiated, alarmed him for his future destiny.

"About this peace! As charming for England as it is ruinous for her soldiers. What can one do? My plan is to wait for a few months, and see what Powers continue at war; then exchange with George to half-pay and get into some foreign service. As to remaining an English full-pay lieutenant for ten or twelve years! not for the universe! Sometimes my thought is to sell my commission and purchase one in Germany or elsewhere; but my secret wish cannot be fulfilled, which is to have high command with British soldiers. Rather let me command Esquimaux than be a subaltern of Rifles forty years old."

Before he was twenty-eight Napier had commanded a regiment for one campaign, was foremost in fight with it, and desperately wounded. In 1802 he was sent on a recruiting mission to Ireland, and soon afterwards rejoined his regiment at Shorncliffe. In the following June (the year that Wellington won the battle of Assaye, which made us masters of India) he went to Dublin as *aide-de-camp* to a relation, General Fox, who was made commander-in-chief in Ireland. He writes to his mother:–

"My uniform is expensive: the dress-coat twenty guineas, exclusive of epaulettes. Nothing of mine except linen will do for an A.D.C. My pantaloons are green, and I have only one pair; my jacket twice turned! a green waistcoat is useless; one pair of boots without soles or heels; a green feather and a helmet not worth sixpence. This is the state of my Rifling kit!"

Napier did not remain long in Ireland. Disputes arose between General Fox and the Irish Government, and he was recalled. He was, however, appointed to the London district: his staff accompanied him. While on the staff Charles Napier met the most important men of the day, and was frequently thrown into the society of Charles Fox. "And the young soldier used to describe with good-humour the manifestations of the orator's earnest and natural disposition. How at cricket he would strike the ball and recklessly run for a score, bat on shoulder, his Sancho Panza figure fully displayed and his head thrown back, laughing in childish delight amidst reproachful cries, while his opponents struck down the wickets behind him." Charles Fox took a deep interest in Sir John Moore, then the most honoured military character of the day. "One evening, hearing some person relate an advantageous anecdote—as what other could ever be justly told of Moore—he threw down his cards and called out,

'Tell that again! I know a great deal of General Moore and
everything good; tell me that again.' " About the middle of
1805 Napier's quarters were removed to Hythe, and he was
then placed under Sir John Moore, who had at Shorncliffe
created a real camp of instruction. His improvements in
drill, discipline, dress, arms, formations, and movements
entitle him, as William Napier states, to a high place on the
roll of military reformers.

"His materials were the 43rd and 52nd and Rifle
Regiments, and he so fashioned them that afterwards,
as the Light Division under Wellington, they were found
to be soldiers unsurpassable, perhaps never equalled.
The separate successful careers of the officers strikingly
attest the merit of the school: so long a list of notable men
could not be presented by three regiments of any service
in the world." Though drill was an important part of the
instruction, it was not, as one of his pupils tells us, by that
alone the soldier was there formed. "It was the internal and
moral system, the constant superintendence of the officers,
the real government and responsibility of the captains,
which carried the discipline to such perfection."

In that great school Napier's natural gifts for high
command were trained, and the time was fast approaching
when they would be perfected in the greater school of war.
In 1806 Charles Fox, now in power, gave him a majority,
but in a Cape colonial corps. He was going to embark for the
Cape when a remarkable incident gave a new turn to his
fortunes. "Contrary winds had detained him at Portsmouth,
and being there thrown into the society of the 50th
Regiment, he so won on the officers that they proposed to

him to exchange at a small cost. He refused to pay money, as contrary to the regulations; but they would not be so baffled, and contrived to have him gazetted without payment,–how, he never knew, but it was a signal proof of regard." Two years later he was suddenly called to join the first battalion of the 50th at Lisbon. His colonel obtained leave of absence, the regiment fell to Napier, and Sir John Moore incorporated it in the army going to Spain.

The retreat from Astorga to Corunna is an old story, but it is one of those scenes of history on which one loves to dwell. The heroic, the awful, and the picturesque are blended in the account given in that immortal book, the 'History of the Peninsular War.' The three brothers were in that dark retreat in Spain of a small British army before the French host, and they were together when the great explosion took place, which William has described in a sentence which will last as long as our English. "Stillness, slightly interrupted by the lashing of the waves on the shore, succeeded as the business of the war went on." Charles Napier himself has described how the men of the 50th met the greatest assailing column on the fatal field of Corunna:–

The imperial troops, on higher ground, hung over us like threatening clouds, and about one o'clock the storm burst. Our line was under arms, silent, motionless, yet all were anxious for the appearance of Sir John Moore. There was a feeling that under him we could not he beaten, and this was so strong at all times as to be a great cause of discontent during the retreat wherever he was not. "Where is the general?" was now heard along that part of the line where I was, for only of what my eyes saw and my ears heard I speak. This agitation augmented as the cries of men stricken by cannon-shot arose. I stood in front of my left wing, on a knoll, from whence the greatest part of the field could be seen, and my pickets were fifty yards below, disputing the ground with the French skirmishers; but a heavy French column, which had descended the mountain at a run, was coming on behind with great rapidity, and shouting, *"En avant, tuc, tile! en avant, tue!"* their cannon at the same time, plunging from above, ploughed the ground and tore our ranks. Suddenly I heard the gallop of horses and saw Moore. He came at speed and pulled up so sharp and close he seemed to have alighted from the air; man and horse looking at the approaching foe with an intenseness that seemed to concentrate all feeling in their eyes. The sudden stop of the animal, a cream-coloured one with black tail and mane, had cast the latter streaming forward, its ears were pushed out like horns, while its eyes flashed fire, and it snorted loudly with expanded nostrils, expressing terror, astonishment, and muscular exertion. My first thought was, It will be away like the wind! but then I looked at the rider, and horse was forgotten. Thrown on its haunches, the animal came sliding and dashing the dirt up with its foreeet, thus bending the general forward almost to its neck; but his head was thrown back and his look more keenly piercing than I ever before saw it. He glanced to the right and left, and then fixed his eyes intently on the enemy's advancing column, at the same time grasping the reins with both hands and pressing the horse firmly with his knees; his body thus seemed to deal with the animal while his mind was intent on the enemy, and his aspect was one of searching intenseness beyond the power of words to describe; for a while he looked, and then galloped to the left without uttering a word.

The fire from the village of Elvira had grown very sharp, and our pickets were being driven in by the attacking column, when Moore returned, and Napier asked leave to throw his grenadiers, who were losing men fast, into the enclosures in front. " 'No,' he said, 'they will fire on our own pickets in the villages.' 'Sir, our pickets, and those of the 4th Regiment also, were driven from thence when you went to the left.' 'Were they?

then you are right, send out your grenadiers;' and again he galloped away." Turning round, Napier saw Captain Clunes of the 50th, and said to him, "Clunes, take your grenadiers and open the ball." He stalked forward alone, like Goliath before the Philistines, for six feet five he was in height and of proportionate bulk and strength, his grenadiers followed, and thus the battle began on our side. Charles Napier's regiment was driving back the French column with fire and shell beneath the eyes of the general, who with exultant applause gave instant orders to support the impetuous counter-stroke; but just then "the heroic Moore fell, and error followed when the presiding spirit was gone." The 50th was not supported, and, fighting among lanes, houses, and vineyards, was scattered in small bands, when fresh enemies came down and overwhelmed them. Napier was stooping down to assist a wounded soldier when a musket-ball broke the small bones of his leg some inches above the ankle. In great pain, hardly able to walk, he made his way to a spot where two lanes met near a church. Here he found three privates of the 50th and one of the 42nd, an Irishman. They said they were cut off, and Frenchmen were rushing up the lanes. The nearest were now thirty yards distant. Napier, forgetting his leg, said to the four soldiers, " 'Follow me, and we'll cut through them'; then with a shout I rushed forward."

The Frenchmen had halted, but now ran on to us, and just as my spring was made the wounded leg failed, and I felt a stab in the back; it gave me no pain, but felt cold, and threw me on my face. Turning to rise, I saw the man who had stabbed me making a second thrust. Whereupon, letting go my sabre, I caught his bayonet by the socket turned the thrust, and raising myself by the exertion, grasped his firelock with both hands, thus in mortal struggle regaining my feet. His companions had now come up, and I heard the dying cries of the four men with me, who were all instantly bayoneted. We had been attacked from behind by men not before seen, as we stood with our backs to a doorway, out of which must have rushed several men, for we were all stabbed in an instant, before the two parties coming up the road reached us. They did so, however, just as my struggle with the man who had wounded me was begun. That was a contest for life, and being the strongest, I forced him between myself and his comrades, who appeared to be the men whose lives I had saved when they pretended to be dead on our advance through the village. They struck me with their muskets, clubbed and bruised me much, whereupon seeing no help near, and being overpowered by numbers and in great pain from my wounded leg, I called out *"Je me rend,"* remembering the expression correctly from an old story of a fat officer, whose name being James, called out "Jemmy round." Finding they had no disposition to spare me, I kept hold of the little Italian who had first wounded me; but I soon grew faint, or rather tired. At that moment a tall dark man came up, seized the end of the musket with his left hand, whirled his brass-hilted sabre round, and struck me a powerful blow on the head, which was bare, for my cocked hat had fallen off. Expecting the blow would finish me, I had stooped my head in hopes it might fall on my back, or at least on the thickest part of the head, and not on the left temple. So far I succeeded, for it fell exactly on the top, cutting me to the bone but not through it. Fire sparkled from my eyes. I fell on my knees, blinded, but not quite losing my senses, and holding still on to the musket. Recovering in a moment, I saw a florid, handsome young French drummer holding the arm of the dark Italian, who was in the act of repeating the blow. Quarter was then given; but they tore my pantaloons in tearing my watch and purse from my pocket and a little locket of hair which hung round my neck. But while this went on two of them were wounded, and the drummer, Guibert, ordered the dark man who had sabred me to take me to the rear. When we began to move, I resting on him because hardly able to walk, I saw him look back over his shoulder to see if Guibert was gone; and so did I, for his rascally face made me suspect him. Guibert's back was towards us; he was walking off, and the Italian again drew his sword, which he had before sheathed. I called out to the drummer, "This rascal is going to kill me; brave Frenchmen don't kill prisoners." Guibert ran back, swore furiously at the Italian, shoved him away, almost down, and putting his arms round my waist supported me himself. Thus this generous Frenchman saved me twice, for the Italian was bent on slaying.

Thus was Napier taken prisoner. Sixty years after, when floating down the Indus, he wrote:–

January 16.–On this day the glorious Moore fell at Corunna. It was my first battle. I felt great anxiety, no fear: curiosity also. It was unpleasant until the fire, and then only one idea possessed me–that of keeping the soldiers steady and animated. Personal danger did not enter my thoughts until I was cut off and had to fight, man to man, or rather with many men. When overpowered and struggling, thinking my life gone, fear made me desperate. Had I not lost my sabre I think I could have cut my way through; but while striving for the man's musket nothing else was thought of: there was but one weapon for both, and death for the man who lost it.

Charles Napier's family mourned him as dead, but nevertheless induced the Government after three months to send to ascertain his fate. Clouet received the flag and hastened to inform Ney, who replied, "Let him see his friends, and tell them he is well and well treated." Clouet looked earnestly but moved not, and Ney, smiling, asked, "Why he waited." "He has an old mother, a widow, and blind." "Has he? Let him go, then, and tell her himself that he is alive." Charles Napier rejoined his regiment and renewed his letters to his mother and his fighting. His two years in the Peninsula produced six wounds. At Busaco he received a severe one in the jaw. As he was borne away the Duke asked who he was; but he could not answer, but took off his hat and waved it, muttering, "I could not die at a better moment."

Thirty-nine years afterwards, when he was Commander-in-Chief in India, he wrote in his journal on the 27th of September:–

Well, Busaco was the great test, and a very beautiful fight it was. The French were in the valley, shrouded in mist, when the morning broke and the running fire of the outposts began; soon an irregular but very sharp musketry rang through the gradually dispersing mist, which, mingled with smoke, came up the mountain, and from it many wounded men broke out. The pickets then appeared, being driven back, but firing so hard that our line loudly cheered them from the crest above; following last came the enemy's columns, and eighty pieces of cannon opened with a roar from the summit of the mountain, sending shrapnels, shells, and round-shot down on them. The battle was thus begun, and soon they reached us. The firing rolled loud and heavy, the shouts of our men were grand, and their charges in different parts of the line went fiercely home. I was hit, woe the while for me! Now, thirty-nine years after, the horrid suffocation of that wound is scarcely endurable. Oh! it shakes my very soul, the horror of this feeling does! I was carried into a small chapel of the convent of Busaco. It had a large arch in the wall, officers high of rank, in the next room, eating and drinking, though the battle was not yet over! Some talked of my father and mother, praising them and their extraordina﹃ beauty. I was so delighted at this as hardly to feel pain; but finally disgust at these men for being out of the battle so excited me that I got up from the pallet on which I had been laid, walked clean out, and got to the convent door, looking for my horse. I was, however, seized by

Edward Packenham, and led back with this expression, "Damn it, Napier, are you mad, to think you can go back in this state to the action? Be quiet, for God's sake." I could not speak plain, as my jaw was broke, and blood flowed freely from my mouth, so my looks were worse than the reality.

Napier made his way to Lisbon, where he rested some months in great suffering from his wound. "It is said that my sight may be lost; but it is not dim, and if it goes, why, Hannibal having one eye, I have a mind to pluck it out." When the Light Division began to pursue Massena, and combat followed combat, Charles Napier could no longer bear to remain inactive, and with his wound still bandaged, he rode above ninety miles on one horse and in one course to reach the army. Having found his corps, he pushed it forward to support the Light Division. Hearing the sounds of the fighting in front, he had hourly to ask if his brothers were living. Thus advancing, he met a litter of branches borne by soldiers and covered with a blanket, "What wounded officer is that? "Captain Napier, of the 52nd; a broken limb." Another litter followed. "Who is that?" "Captain Napier, 43rd, mortally wounded; "it was thought so then. Charles Napier looked at them and passed on to the fight in front.

Just as the army of the Peninsula was entering on a course of victory Charles Napier had to quit it. He was appointed to the command of the 102nd; raised as the New South Wales Fencibles, this regiment had gone out there by the Cape of Good Hope and returned by Cape Horn, and was probably the only regiment that ever circumnavigated the globe. The state of discipline in the corps required that their new conmmander should join it without loss of time. Early in 1812 Napier took the command, and after spending a few months at Guernsey, proceeded with the regiment to Bermuda. He was not pleased with his new station. "This island, beautiful to look at, but food and all things but rogues so scarce as to make a miserable quarter." When the 102nd landed in Bermuda, writes a comrade, "even casual observers perceived it was commanded by no common man. He made soldiers of all under him, and had the rare quality of rendering the most familiar intercourse compatible with absolute authority." He made good soldiers, because he knew his profession. "His was no adjutant's regiment; he was himself drill-master, and master also of every detail: with the exception of beating the drums, there was no part of a soldier's duty from the sentinel to the sergeant-major which he could not teach and do as smartly as the smartest non-commissioned officer. Nor was his knowledge restricted to his own arm: he was conversant with engineer's duties, and with those of artillery, whose practice he generally attended." The regiment contained a large number of Irishmen, and in February he writes to his mother: "All hope of reclaiming my men is not extinct. Severity of punishment, and disgracing all when one sins, has had an effect, for Pat fears odium for getting his comrades into trouble more than punishment. He does some bloody mischief in his cups, but it is horrible to flog him when you know he is as sorry as possible himself." He adds: "The letter is filled with Paddy's tricks, which I hope to get out of him with as little flogging as possible. Poor fellows, with all their sins, they are fine soldiers, and their blood should be kept for better than being drawn with a cat-o'-nine-tails. I allow them to box, it is the best issue for the rum, and such a parade of black eyes was never before beheld. Oh, Pat! thou art a very odd fish, very odd." His efforts to reform Pat were, however, successful, and when he left the regiment it presented him with a sword of honour. Napier had not been long in Bermuda when he was employed on active service. Wellington had just begun to succeed in the Peninsula when we went to war with America, and plunged into a contest as purposeless, as foolish, as unnecessary as it was ill-managed, useless, and merely as war discreditable to us. Napier landed with Admiral Cochrane's forces first in North Carolina and then on the York Town peninsula, and was present at the disgraceful burning of Hampton. The spirit of the high-minded soldier revolted from the work he had to perform. It is quite shocking," he writes, " to have men who speak our own language brought in wounded: one feels as if they were peasants, and that we are killing our own people." He was heartily glad when he was able to exchange back into his old regiment, and he sailed for England in September 1813. When Napier reached England the war with France was over, and being reduced to half-pay, his prospects were not cheering. But he resolved to prepare himself for whatever duties fortune might. bestow on him. He joined the Military College at Farnham.

Napier had, however, hardly begun his studies when Napoleon escaped from Elba, and Europe once more rushed to arms. Charles Napier went as a volunteer to Ghent, but Waterloo was fought and won before he could join the army. He accompanied the victorious army into Paris, where he stayed for a few days, and then returned to Farnham, where

he spent some industrious years. Many of his reflections
which he jotted down in his notes are worth recalling to
memory. Eighty years ago Charles Napier wrote regarding
cavalry:–

In the British army we have not considered this arm much in
a scientific point of view; that is to say, its use in the field and
its equipment as suited to its duties and dependent on them. .
. . In the British army we know little of the uses of cavalry, and
our cavalry officers are perhaps the least informed on the subject:
we have not war enough to teach them. The forming of officers is
perhaps the most difficult part. A general wants neither farriers
nor jockeys for officers; both are natural consequences of being
a good cavalry officer: but a good officer is not a consequence of
being a farrier or jockey. To form English cavalry officers they
should be encouraged to serve abroad when we are at peace. War
alone can form them. No service requires experience so much,
and new officers are suddenly thrown into very critical situations
before they have an idea of war: this draws on them unmerited
discredit. Our cavalry have thus been ruined, and some old
German regiments, full of experienced officers, have gained more
credit, though in all qualities but experience inferior to our native
regiments: with equal practice our cavalry would send all the
French and German cavalry to the devil.

In India, long afterwards, Napier helped John Jacob to
organise and teach the Sind horsemen on the principle he
laid down, and no better cavalry ever took the field. He was
not satisfied with the beaten path of professional study, but
made an excursion into general literature. He also took an
interest in agriculture and political economy, because the
lives and sufferings of the poor deeply affected his generous
mind. Endowed with a sensitive nature and a strong sense
of justice, he was a Liberal in the best sense of the word.
Regarding Ireland he wrote: "I am of no party, but

when people are starving in the midst of abundance, my blood first runs cold with horror and then boils with indignation."

Two years after gaining a first-class certificate at the Staff College, Napier was appointed inspecting field officer in the Ionian Islands, and afterwards made military resident of Cephalonia. Here it was first discovered that he was as great an administrator as he was a soldier. He checked feudal oppression, established courts of justice, and developed the material prosperity of the island by building roads and bridges. The moral welfare of the inhabitants was not neglected. Napier writes: "I have built eight bridges since my return, and made a road from the quay to the town of Luxine, three miles. My long quay, a mile Long, is completed, and looks magnificent. Meanwhile, to bless us, we have got a bishop appointed. An excellent, pious man, who formerly lived by sheep-stealing, which he now calls his pastoral life."

Early in 1830 Charles Napier, owing to his wife's health, left Cephalonia never to return. Ten years of inactive life followed, during which he had to struggle against the deep melancholy caused by want of work and want of means. This decade was also one of exceptional misery and suffering to his countrymen. Steam-engines and powerlooms had worked a revolution in trade, and brought the misery which attends on every economical revolution. In the manufacturing districts of the north starvation produced frequent riots, and the services of the military were in constant request. At this crisis the command of the Northern District became vacant, and it was offered to Napier. No better choice could have been made: his commiseration for the people, his tact and firmness, prevented bloodshed. He had held this post at home a couple of years when, unexpectedly, the command of the Poona division was offered to him. The appointment was accepted, and on the 28th of December 1841 he assumed command at the capital of the Deccan. Charles Napier was now sixty years old, and had been forty-eight years in the army, but he was a young man in mind and body. Neither age nor wounds nor hardships could wither his energy. He never was too old to learn. From Poona he writes: "My wish is to be left quiet a little while in each clay, to obtain an insight of Indian wars, history, and country; for knowledge and thought only can enable us to act wisely in such positions. This the world will not believe, and idle talk is thought more important than reason and reflection. If my morning hours only were secure from worry it would content me; but only by snatches can needful knowledge be obtained." His energy in command provoked hostile criticism. He writes: "All the stuff in the 'United Service Gazette' about myself and my drill is pure nonsense; they are very few, and more to get my own hand in than anything else, for it requires habit to move large bodies. There are two awkward things to think of in a field—viz., what to do and how to do. These three arms have never been worked together, and the infantry only in the same dull formal round on the smooth piece of ground which tired them to death. Now they go out all together, and over the hills, which they like; my belief is no one before did this, so it makes a talk. The sepoys are capital soldiers." After he had resided for a year in the Deccan, Napier was ordered to take the command in Sind. In the story of John Jacob's career we have told how Sind was subdued and subjected to

British rule. Napier had now another opportunity of showing his ability as an administrator. A newly conquered country he felt for a time must be under military rule, and as a military ruler his administration must be judged. But, like Mountstuart Elphinstone in the Deccan, he availed himself as much as possible of the framework of government that existed under the *Ameers*. "Make no avoidable change in the ancient laws and customs," he said to his subordinates; "the conquest of a country is sufficient convulsion for the people without abrupt innovations in their habits and social life." One custom, however, he did insist on abolishing. He suppressed the practice of *suttee*. When he made known his intention of suppressing it, the priests came to him to protest, on the ground that all nations had customs which should be respected, and *suttee* was a very sacred one. Napier, affecting to be struck by the argument, replied: "Be it so. This burning of widows is your custom, prepare the pile. But my nation has also a custom. When men burn women alive we hang them, and confiscate all their property. My carpenters shall therefore erect gibbets on which to hang all concerned when the widow is consumed. Let us all act according to national customs." As in Cephalonia, he devoted his energies to develop the resources of the land. He saw that Sind only required water to become a fertile land, and he planned and started an irrigation department. He also drew up a plan for supplying Kurrachee with fresh water from a neighbouring stream, but the scheme did not receive the sanction of the Supreme Government. He had a great belief in the future prosperity of the capital of Sind. He wrote to the governor of Bombay: "You know Kurrachee was my hobby long before I came to Sind, and now that I know the place I am more sanguine than ever. Suez, Bombay, and Kurrachee will hit Calcutta hard before twenty years pass; but Bombay will beat Kurrachee and be the Liverpool, if not the London, of India." After four years of great responsibility and labour, unbroken by any rest or relaxation, Napier bade farewell to Sind. During that time the victorious commander constructed the entire machinery, of civil government. He held strongly enough that our rule in India depended on our might as conquerors, but he never considered that view as conflicting with the duty or necessity of developing the native capacity for self-government. "It is not by moderation but by victory that we must hold India; and we must mix with the people, give them justice, give them riches, give them honours, give them a share of all things, until we blend with them and become one nation." Sir Bartle Frere used to endorse Sir William Napier's fine summary of his brother's rule: "He left a united, regenerated people, rejoicing in a rising civilisation, the work of his beneficent genius."

In October 1847 Napier embarked for Europe and proceeded to Nice, where he stayed some time to recruit his strength. At Paris he had an interview with Marshal Soult. "He paid me the highest compliments, as he had studied all my operations in China and entirely approved of them. This was flattering. Depend upon it that when a French soul is damned, it puts on a greatcoat and compliments the devil on his fine climate, though *un peu froid*." In London, however, he received a splendid genuine compliment from Sir Robert Peel. "Sir Charles Napier," he said, "were I to begin life again and be a soldier, I would enlist under you in preference to

any other general." Peel always had the highest opinion of
Napier's ability, and was inclined to rank him above his
brother as a writer of English prose. He declared he had
"no hesitation in placing Napier's despatches in comparison
with those of Wellington, or with the best things of the
kind which have ever been written." When the details of
the battles, called victories, fought at the opening of the
second Sikh war, reached England, all men's minds were
filled with misgiving and dread. Napier's period of rest at
home was of short duration. The want of confidence in Lord
Gough had become so general that there was a loud call in
England for a change of command. The directors asked the
Duke of Wellington to recommend them a general for the
crisis, and he named Sir Charles Napier. But Napier felt
great hesitation in accepting the post. "When the Duke of
Wellington first told me of my appointment, I objected, that
my many enemies in India would mar all usefulness; "he
laughed, pressed the matter home, and concluded thus: "If
you don't go, I must." Napier went.

On 6th of May 1849, Napier landed at Calcutta. At daylight on the same day he reviewed the 96th Regiment,
which had lately arrived. He reached the parade before a
single officer of the regiment had made his appearance,
and walked into the barracks. He soon returned, and after
a minute inspection addressed the men in a characteristic
speech. After alluding to his former connection with the
regiment, he said:—

I am very glad to meet the 96th again. We have both been
a good deal about the world since we were last together, and
I am very glad to hear such a good account of the regiment.

Your colonel tells me that you are not only in good health, but that you are good in conduct–that you have few men in hospital. Now this is all right. I hope you will continue to bear a good character. But let me give you a bit of advice –that is, don't drink. I know young men don't think much about advice from old men. They put their tongues in their cheek and think they know a good deal better than the old cove that's giving them advice. But let me tell you that you've come to a country where, if you drink, you're dead men. If you be sober and steady, you'll get on well. But if you drink, you're done for–you will either be invalided or die. I, know two regiments in this country–one drank, the other didn't drink. The one that didn't drink is one of the finest regiments, and has got on as well as any regiment in existence. The one that did drink has been all but destroyed. For any regiment for which I have a respect I should always try to persuade them to keep from drinking. I know there are some men who will drink in spite of the devil and their officers; but such men will soon be in hospital, and very few that go in in this country ever come out again. I wish the 96th Regiment every success, and am very glad to see it in the state it is.

At a dinner given to him at the Military Club at Calcutta, he said:–

It is with no ordinary feeling of pleasure that I now return to India, proud of the position which I hold among you. I owe much to the army of India, both Queen's and Company's, and now that I am at its head I will endeavour to pay back that debt of obligation. I will endeavour to acquit myself without partiality, favour, or affection. I will endeavour to do justice to all, and I will maintain that discipline in the army of India which, aided by the gallantry of the soldiers, will ever lead us on from victory to victory, and point out to the whole world that we are the paramount Power in India, and that those glorious sepoys who have so often fought side by side with their European officers, striving with them even unto their death, are invincible. I feel proud whenever I see the native soldier bearing the same medals on his breast which I wear, though his are perhaps better deserved, and I feel double pleasure in the knowledge that such decorations excite the emulation and raise the confidence of the sepoy.

On the 22nd of May Sir Charles Napier left Calcutta, but he did not reach Simla till the end of June. The hope of again leading an Indian army to victory was gone, but he determined to make that army as efficient as possible. His whole career as commander-in-chief was a severe battle to introduce necessary military reforms. On reaching Simla he at once bent himself to the stiff and thankless task. In his journal he tells us that his three great objects were—" (1) To make the army know that, good or bad, I am commander myself. (2) To restore discipline in various ways. (3) To give a better tone to the officers."

"I go thoroughly into courts-martial, and endeavour by my remarks on sentences to amend the general notion, which is to think that the offence of every culprit–that is officers, not soldiers–is to be passed over, as he is a 'good fellow,' a 'poor fellow,' and so forth. Thus every *bad* fellow that the articles of war force a court-martial to cashier has a recommendation tacked to his sentence, and half the courts acquit a blackguard if they can. But the army is full of fine fellows, and I am sure of support against this maudlin mercy, which in every instance I have rejected."

The state of society in India at the time is illustrated by the fact that in the short period–not much exceeding a year and a half–during which Sir Charles Napier commanded the Indian army, fourteen officers of her Majesty's regiments in India and thirty-six officers of the Bengal military service were tried by general court-martial. Only one of the former and two of the latter were acquitted. Of those convicted six Queen's officers and fifteen Company's officers were cashiered or dismissed. Two of the former and one of the latter were pardoned by the commander-in-chief. In the case of one Bengal officer Sir Charles refused to reprimand. Lieutenant Robert Renny, 47th Native Infantry, was tried "for great disrespect to his Excellency the Commander-in-Chief, in having at Cawnpore between the 6th, and 22nd of June 1849 repeated to several persons at the station certain observations on the proceedings of a court-martial which had been recently held at Cawnpore, which he stated to have been made to him by the commander-in-chief in person, and having represented these observations as a good joke, or in disrespectful terms to that effect." Lieutenant Renny was found guilty with the exception of the words, "great disrespect to his Excellency the Commander-in-Chief." He was sentenced to be reprimanded in such manner as his Excellency the Commander-in-Chief may be pleased to direct. The sentence was approved and confirmed with the following remark: "Except that I cannot agree with the court in thinking that this gallant officer has done anything to demand a reprimand, and therefore I must decline giving him the slightest reprimand. On the contrary, his trial has given me a very high opinion of him as an officer." The majority of officers owed their downfall to drink, duelling, gambling, and debt. Shortly after Sir Charles Napier assumed command an officer was tried for drunkenness, and was sentenced to be dismissed the service. The court recommended the prisoner to the merciful consideration of his Excellency the Commander-in-Chief. He remarked:–

There are few things that are more painful than to refuse mercy, but it is my duty to support discipline in the vast army of India, and discipline cannot be upheld if officers, who are by law the judges that try private soldiers for drunkenness, set an example of the crime. This Lieutenant —— has done; and though it is by far the worst part of the delinquent's conduct, it is not all. The being intoxicated after dinner, however unbecoming and disgraceful it is to the character of a well-bred gentleman, may still have the pretext of conviviality for a thoughtless but culpable excess in a young man. This, however, is not the crime of the prisoner. His has been deliberate drunkenness, a glaring disregard of decency in the broad face of day, an act destructive to all society, all discipline, all moral feelings, and calculated to make the uniform of a British officer a byword and shame! The court has recommended Lieutenant —— to mercy, but it has offered no reason for this recommendation. The above are mine for refusing a recommendation which has no apparent foundation; and therefore, while it adds much to the pain of performing a distressing duty, cannot divert me from the paramount object of a commander-in-chief —namely, that of supporting the integrity of military discipline and the high character of British officers. I will not pardon Lieutenant —— Headquarters, 30th August 1849.

After the sentence of the court-martial was published the mother of the young officer made earnest intercession for her son's restoration. She said he was not a habitual drunkard, and if inquiry were made it would be found that he had never before been intoxicated. He had been a good son, and had regularly remitted to her a considerable portion of his meagre allowances to assist in supporting herself and his younger brothers and sisters. The Commander-in-Chief in reply expressed his regret that these details had not been furnished at a previous date, as a knowledge of them might have mitigated the severity of his sentence, which,

however, was not too great for the proved offence, and could
not be reversed. After some further correspondence Sir
Charles Napier, in the kindness of his nature, sent her from
his own purse the price of an ensign's commission.

Duelling Napier put down with a strong hand. On the
26th of August 1850, Ensign T. W. White, 48th Native
Infantry, and Lieutenant G. T. Smith of the same regiment,
were tried for having assisted as seconds at a duel between
Lieutenant E. B. Letchford and Ensign G. C. Huxham of
the same regiment. Both were found guilty, sentenced to be
cashiered, and recommended to the merciful consideration
of the commander-in-chief. Sir Charles Napier remarked: "I
cannot attend to the recommendation of the court on account
of youth and inexperience. The prisoner is above twenty-one
years of age; he had the command of veteran soldiers; he
has, I conclude, received the education of a gentleman; yet
he has taken part in the active promotion of a duel for which
there was not the slightest pretext or any possible excuse
whatever, except on the part of Ensign Huxham. In contrast
to the conduct of Ensign White and Lieutenant Smith, I am
bound to express my approbation of the admirable conduct of
Ensign Ogilvie, who through this proceeding has acted with
the greatest good sense and honour both as an officer and a
gentleman." The stern example had its effect, and this was
the last case of duelling tried by a court-martial in India.

The danger of running into debt was the subject of
Napier's farewell address to the officers of the army.
He reminds them that it is not the case of a rich man
speaking to those who are poor. "I have known poverty,
and have lived for years on less than half what every

ensign in this army receives, and so lived, too, in a more expensive country than India. I take no merit to myself for this: I only state it as a fact, that I may not be taunted, on the threshold of my argument, by being told I know nothing of the difficulties of poverty. I do know them perfectly." He further reminds them that "the families of many officers" have made great sacrifices to gain them their commissions, "and these last have no right whatever to live as if they were gentlemen of landed property, nor as men do who have served long and earned a higher rank and greater income than themselves. It is the desire to imitate those above us, and not to regard our own means, that is mischievous to all, and most to young men.

"I do not say that a subaltern officer can give dinners; I do not say he can indulge in many *luxuries;* I do not say he can *cast off all self-denial,* nor do I see why he *should do any of these things.*"

Napier considered that the extravagance of messes was one of the main causes of debt; his remarks on the subject should be studied by every commanding officer, for extravagance in messes is still one of the great difficulties that beset the path of the military reformer. It was the commanding officer he held entirely responsible for this grave evil.

Many regiments (both Queen's and Company's) have economical messes, especially in the Queen's regiments, because the number of officers in the latter is so large. But many regiments are extravagant; and in all cases where a mess is extravagant the fault lies with the commanding officer. I have heard it said by some that "the commanding officer ought not to interfere with the mess, which should be considered as the private table of the officers." Now, people who talk thus forget that there is a wide difference between a mess and a private gentleman's table. The last is regulated by his income, and there is but one master to be consulted as to expense. But in a mess there are many masters, and the expenses must be regulated by the income of the poorest. The majority have no right to crush the poor and provident officers, with the extent of whose liabilities they are utterly ignorant; nor must an officer, because he belongs to a mess, explain all his distresses, his misfortunes, his generosities, his follies, to the members of a mess in order to prove his incompetency to meet its extravagances! Common-sense forbids this.

On the 22nd of October Sir Charles Napier left Simla, "where I have dwelt among the clouds for four months and six days, doing much hard work." At Jerrog he reviewed the little Gurkha battalion, and recognised the worth of "the brave little men," whom the Bengal officers, accustomed to the stalwart Brahmin sepoy, decried. "We should make much of them," he states in his journal; "take 15,000 or 20,000 of them into pay. . . . They should be in number equal to the British forces here, and then the Sepoys could not turn out." The following day he inspected the barracks, and the examination "leaves no wonder at the sickly state of the men. In rooms badly ventilated, and only 12 feet high, they put 152 men. The principle of the Military Board is that of the Black Hole of Calcutta: only 94 men should have been in these barracks at the most. How is it possible men should not be sickly and die." All during his command his effort to improve the condition of the Indian barrack was unceasing. "Such barracks," he wrote, "are expensive, no doubt; so are sick soldiers, so are dead soldiers. But the difference of these expenses is that the first is over and done with; the second goes on increasing like compound interest and quickly

outstrips the capital." Commissions and committees were
appointed to inquire into the matter, but for fifteen years
costly British soldiers continued to die in ordinary years at
the rate of sixty per thousand, till another strong man, John
Lawrence, took the matter in hand, and the new barracks,
large and airy, which are now to be found in every station
in India where the British soldier is quartered, began to be
built.

On the 31st of October Napier reached Delhi, "the queen
of cities," and visited the citadel palace where the great
Moghul was allowed to hold his mock court. What courts are
here! What seats of marble from which to issue edicts to an
empire! On this palace, once worthy of India, now the marble
even cannot be seen from filth. Would that I were King of
India! I would make Moscow and Pekin shake. Before this
no palace ever met my eye that excited a wish to become
its master." After inspecting the troops and presenting
colours to the 41st Native Infantry, Sir Charles departed for
Agra, where he was received "by the Lieutenant-Governor
Thomason with a kindness of manner which distinguishes
this very distinguished member of the Civil Service. Of him I
have heard and seen enough to convince me that he is one of
the few I have met who take really great views for this noble
empire." The day after his arrival he inspected the brigade,
and having called the commanding officers to the front, he
said, "I know that preconcerted manoeuvres always go off
swimmingly, and I therefore purposely gave you one which
you could not be prepared for, and I am highly satisfied with
the result." He then told them to take their regiments to
their quarters. He rode with the 2nd European Regiment

to their barracks to inspect the latter, as also the hospital. He tasted the bread served to the soldiers, and abused the commissariat contractors. He said he would like to hang every contractor in India. The welfare of the British soldier was ever uppermost in his thoughts.

Returning from Agra to Delhi, Sir Charles discovered that the 41st N.I. showed a disposition to mutiny against going to Multan. Resenting the loss of extra allowance, caused by the conversion of a foreign country into a British province, the sepoys in the Punjab, and those who had been ordered there, had quietly agreed to strike for higher pay. In July 1849 the 22nd N.I., stationed at Rawal Pindi in the Punjab, refused the reduced pay, and the 13th Regiment soon followed their example. Some of the ringleaders at Rawal Pindi were tried and sentenced to be dismissed the service—a punishment wholly inadequate for the crime of mutiny, and not sufficient to deter others from following their example. The sepoys of the 41st at Delhi were somewhat foolishly conciliated by a liberal grant of furlough which had before been withheld, and the regiment marched to its destination. When Napier reached Wuzzeerabad Brigadier Hearsey informed him that "the sepoys, and especially the younger ones, said, 'When other regiments come up we will do as they do; the reduction of pay is tyranny, but what can we do alone?' He further said that an unusual degree of correspondence is going on between regiments–which he considered very bad, and wished that the Government could prevent it or appoint a person to read all the sepoys' letters. I told him that was quite impossible: that neither could Government abridge correspondence nor open private letters except on some occasion which would bear out such an act." Sir Henry Lawrence afterwards stated that a large number of these letters were seized and examined, and they were found to contain nothing on the subject of the allowance. But documents have come to light since the Mutiny which prove that at the time native regiments had begun to communicate with each other by emissaries on the subject of their real or supposed grievances, and had established by an understood general consent an armed trade-union. The sepoy resented that the victories which he had helped to gain should result in a pecuniary loss to himself. And a petty economy increased his annoyance and shook his belief in the good faith of the Government. There had always been an understanding that when the price of certain things, part of his rations, exceeded certain limits there should be a small addition to the sepoy's pay. In 1844 an elaborate financial regulation was issued by which there was a small petty reserving of public moneys to the loss of the sepoy in respect of the allowance. Thus was created that state of disaffection which, by another act of incredible stupidity, the use of the greased cartridge, burst out into open mutiny seven years later.

Brigadier Hearsey, who commanded at Wuzzeerabad, was a gallant soldier of thirty years' service, who knew perfectly the language, the habits, and temper of the sepoy. The man who best knows the Oriental likes him best, and Hearsey respected the courage and patience of the sepoy. He had also a sympathy for his prejudices. When the 32nd Native Infantry. at Wuzzeerabad refused its pay, he had them drawn up on parade, and addressed them in their own vulgar tongue. The majority expressed their sorrow

at what they had done; but some still refused to receive
their pay. The first four were tried at once and sentenced to
imprisonment with hard labour. Five ringleaders, who had gone
from company to company instigating and fomenting rebellion,
were tried by court-martial and sentenced to imprisonment
with hard labour for fourteen years. The commander-in-chief
remarked: "The prisoners, like infamous agitators as they
are, have been convicted by the court of having gone from
company to company exciting their comrades to making and
administering unlawful oaths, and I revise the sentence passed
upon them as inadequate to the magnitude of their crime. I beg
of the court to reconsider its sense of the consequences which
may result from the crime of these heinous offenders. Let it
sentence a punishment commensurate with their damnable
projects." The revised sentence was "death by hanging." Sir
Charles Napier remarked: "These five men have been guilty,
sentenced to die, but I commute their sentence into that
of transportation for life. In eternal exile they will expiate
their crimes. For ever separated from their country and their
relations, in a strange land beyond the seas, they will linger
out their miserable lives! It is a change, but I do not consider
this to be an amelioration of their punishment: they will remain
living examples of the terrible fate which awaits traitors to
their colours."

Napier was on his way to Peshawar when he confirmed
the sentence on the mutineers of the 32nd. On reaching that
cantonment he found he had "very bad work on hand." "The
Afreedis, a hill tribe, have massacred a detachment of our
men on the road between this place and Kohat, and they are
said to have fortified the pass, and I will open it. The ground

is very strong, and these chaps are bold men; but we shall try them the 10th and 11th of this month, for then I will go through the pass or know the reason why." He adds: "Letters from the south this day tell me that the determination of the sepoys to have higher pay is breaking out everywhere! This is not unexpected news for me, but how it is to be dealt with I know not. All in my power has been done, and if they persevere we must come to blows: altogether it endangers India; our rule is in greater jeopardy than it has ever been. . . . I am in doubt whether to go to Kohat about the Afreedis or to Lahore about the mutineers. Kohat I must see before deciding on important military matters, while Lahore is the point of danger as to the mutiny."

Fifty miles from Lahore, outside the holy Sikh city of Umritsar, is the fort of Govindgarh. The 66th Regiment had lately arrived there from Lucknow, the heart of the recruiting-ground of the old Brahmin sepoy. On the and of February they broke into mutiny and attempted to seize the fort, but they were prevented by the gallantry of Captain Macdonald and the fidelity of the 1st Bengal Cavalry. A hundred and seventy ringleaders, picked out by their native officers, were awaiting the award of the court-martial which the General had promptly ordered to assemble at Govindgarh. On the 8th of February the trial began, and the following day Sir Charles Napier, accompanied by a force under Brigadier Sir Colin Campbell, started to punish the mutineers.

On the 10th the column entered the pass, and Sir Charles was met by some Afreedis, who endeavoured to excuse themselves. Sir Charles answered that their people must give themselves and their arms up to him, "that they had received money from the British Government for protecting the road, and that instead of affording that protection they had murdered a detachment of our soldiers. I gave them an hour to consider what answer they would give to my summons to surrender themselves." At the end of the hour they returned and said their companions would not listen to them. Napier ordered Sir Colin Campbell to cover the heights round the village, but not to fire unless fired on. The moment our troops advanced the Afreedis' matchlock-men opened their fire, which was instantly returned, our troops driving the enemy before them in every direction. "Then commenced the work of destruction. Every village we came to was attacked and destroyed under a desultory fire from the surrounding hills, some of which were covered by our troops, whose advance was covered by artillery." When the burning of the villages became known in England, a clamour was commenced about Sir Charles Napier's ferocity. The burning of them, however, was the act of the civil authorities, and both Sir Charles Napier and Sir Colin opposed that system of warfare. The latter wrote, "Punish those of the leading men who have shown enmity or have done injury to those we are bound to protect, but leave the cultivators of the soil of the land unmolested." Sir Charles reluctantly acquiesced in the burning of the villages, because they had been entirely abandoned except by the fighting men, and "the blame of the long frontier war thus sure to be created was as sure to be attributed to my preventing the arson."

The next day the column continued its march through the defile and encamped immediately under the Pass of Kohat, which was in possession of some of our irregular troops. On the 12th Sir Charles, accompanied by his staff, rode to Kohat and examined its defences and position. On returning to camp he was informed of one of those unfortunate accidents inseparable from warfare in a mountainous country. Two companies of the 31st, under Lieutenants Dunmore and Sitwell, were ordered to ascend a height in rear of our camp, and to hold it during the night. They reached the summit without opposition, held it till the following morning without being disturbed, and were then ordered to withdraw. Dunmore, who commanded the party, then carefully surveyed the hill, which was very steep, high, and rugged, and finding none of the enemy in sight, proceeded to descend leisurely, but at the same time took the precaution to do so by alternate companies, the one covering the other in its descent. When Dunmore's company had nearly reached the foot of the hill, with Sitwell's some distance above him covering his retirement, he met a party of twenty men of the 31st Regiment, under a native officer, on their way up to replace him and hold the hill during the daytime. After having cautioned the native officer to be careful and vigilant, he continued his descent, and had nearly accomplished it, when he heard some firing above which induced him to halt and ascertain the cause. Owing to the precipitous nature of the hill it was some time before he could see what was going on, when he perceived that the enemy had opened fire and were throwing down stones. He immediately commenced reascending, and met a party of Sitwell's company, from whom he learnt that the party which had been sent to hold the hill during the day had been attacked before it quite reached the summit, and Sitwell on hearing the news had gone back. "He fell rushing against the enemy, and calling on his men to follow, and they obeyed him. When he fell, he tried in vain to make them leave him to an unsparing foe, and save their lives; they obeyed not then but died with him! Heroic was the young spirit who inspired such deeds! "A native officer and two sepoys attempted to carry off their wounded leader. The native officer was killed and the two sepoys desperately wounded. They were afterwards rescued by their comrades.

A native non-commissioned officer went four times up the hill in the face of the enemy, accompanied by a sepoy, and brought away a wounded man each time. But these were not the only deeds of valour and devotion done during that brief campaign. Napier writes:–

In our Afreedi fight three young men distinguished themselves much: chance gave me three vacant posts in that week; one went to each of those three officers. This seemed a fair thing, I never having seen one of them until in fight; yet three times three dozen, in the whole army, have greater claims, but not the luck to fight gallantly and notably under the eye of the commander-in-chief. This, therefore, was not strictly just; but two of them went three times up a precipitous hill, leaping from crag to crag, under a heavy matchlock fire and rolling down of stones, and brought off four wounded men from under the noses of the Afreedis. These wounded men had been lying under the rocks above, seen by us from below but the enemy, though just above them, saw them not. Up went Lieutenant Norman[1] and Lieutenant Murray in full red uniform with a parcel of sepoys as gallant as themselves, and in three trips brought the poor wounded fellows down. The third officer was Hilliard, who, when gallantly carrying a cliff, was shot down while cheering on his men.

---

[1] Now General Sir Henry Norman, G.C.B., G.C.M.G., later Governor of Queensland.

On the morning of the 13th the force was put in motion to return to Peshawar, the baggage being in the centre, so that its head and tail were free to act in repelling the enemy. As soon as the columns entered the long and winding defile flanked by formidable precipices, the foe opened fire from above and vigorously attacked the front and rear. Skirmishing in front, flank, and rear, our troops slowly made their way. Then a body of Afreedis were seen gathered on a sugar-loaf top, terminating a spur from the precipitous hills on our flank. Being close to the road, it barred progress, and the column halted.

On the summit a warrior stood like Fuseli's picture of Satan, with legs wide apart and arms high in the air: waving a sword and shaking a shield, he shouted and defied us! A young artillery officer–Maister or Delane–laid his gun with a shell the flying death whizzing through the air, burst at the moment it struck the brave Afreedi. His head, his legs, his arms, flew like radii from a centre into the air, and a shout of exultation burst from the troops! The amusements of a field of battle are grim. Condemn not that shout. Life was played for in the rough game, and they who won naturally rejoiced. It is, however, a painful remembrance.

When he fell the others flew. The troops again advanced, but on our rear-guard reaching a narrow gorge the overturning of a carriage caused another halt, and the enemy pressed on skirmishing. "While Sir Colin was placing some sepoys to cover the men about the gun the Afreedis closed gallantly, whereupon he rode forward calling for a charge; but to reach mountaineers is easier said than done. Terrified by the sepoys' rush, they fled without firing for a great distance. Campbell saved lives by this ebullition of military spirit, which he had previously more grandly displayed at Chillianwallah, when at a terrible moment he charged the Sikh guns with the 61st Regiment and decided the crisis of that bloody field!" After this event the road opened on a small plain surrounded by rocks, where the enemy was ensconced, and from a projecting spur smote the column. "One of the young artillery officers threw some round-shot against them, and every bullet struck where the smoke of a jezail appeared, but the brave barbarians did not move." Shells were then thrown, and another gun opened in vain, and Captain Douglas of the Rifles was moving to attack, but the column then resumed its march and he was recalled. A neighbouring hill was seen covered with the enemy. Among the irregular troops commanded by Colonel George Lawrence there was a small band of Khaibaris, of the Malekom khel clan, commanded by Futteh Khan. "He was six feet four inches high, and always accompanied by his standard-bearer, a tall spare man not less daring, yet slight to look at near his gigantic master. This Futteh Khan and his followers attacked the hill, he with his flag-man conspicuously leading. The Afreedis held their ground, firing fast; but on the summit were charged sword in hand by Futteh, who slew their chief with a single stroke. 'With one blow I split him down,–no man wants a second from me,' was his speech, and it was no empty boast. All had fallen who came within the sweep of his sword. He was certainly one of the finest men ever seen." Storming heights and skirmishing, the troops steadily made their way through thirteen miles of pass without a single beast of burden or article of baggage falling into the hands of the Afghans, " renowned for being the most daring and dexterous plunderers in the world." On the 14th of February the column marched into Peshawar, and in honour of his bravery Napier made Futteh Khan ride in front of it on an elephant, "with his standard-bearer behind the *howdah* waving the flag over his head."

Such was the Kohat expedition, the last of Charles Napier's exploits in war. "I am glad," he writes – "at least I pray to feel glad–at having no more battles: I never sought one, thank God! His hand directed me in all things. I glory in Meeanee and Hyderabad when I think of them, which, however, I rarely do; I glory in my hill campaign when I think of it, which I rarely do: but I ask for no more battles." A little later he writes in his journal: "I shall now go to Oaklands" (his home in Hampshire) "and look at my father's sword, and think of the day he gave it into my young hands, and of the motto on a Spanish blade he had, 'Draw me not without cause, put me not up without honour.' I have not drawn his sword without cause, nor put it up without honour."

Soon after reaching Peshawar the proceedings of the court-martial at Govindgarh were sent to the commander-in-chief. Of the 170 ringleaders 13 were acquitted and 85 dismissed the service, while the remainder were sentenced to imprisonment with hard labour for terms ranging from six months to fourteen years. On the 26th of February the whole proceedings reached the commander-in-chief: he considered the sentences too lenient for the crime of mutiny, but they could not be altered, as they had been approved and carried into effect by the major-general cominanding on the spot. He considered a prompt and strong blow was necessary, and he struck it. The next day the following appeared in the orders issued from the headquarter's camp: "The native officers, non-commissioned officers, and private sepoys of the 66th Regiment are to be marched from Umballa, and there struck off from the service of the Honourable East India Company, and his Excellency directs that the colours of the 66th are to be delivered over to the loyal and brave men of the Nurseree Gurkha battalion, and that the 66th Regiment shall in future be denominated the 66th Gurkha Regiment. The 66th have brought down ruin and disgrace upon the regiment! When a mutinous corps had endeavoured to seize a fortress which a confiding Government believed it had entrusted to faithful soldiers, it is time that vengeance should fall upon the whole."

When the 66th mutinied Lord Dalhousie was at sea, but on his return, though the disbandment of the 66th and the consequent measures were beyond the competency of the commander-in-chief, "feeling that under such circumstances the commander-in-chief should receive a support without any qualification, gave publicly to them all a full, cordial, and unqualified approbation."

Twelve days before the 66th mutinied, when the crisis was evidently approaching, Brigadier Hearsey, writing officially from Wuzzeerabad after the sepoys there had declared they would await the arrival of more regiments to enforce their demand for higher pay, ended an analysis of the different allowance regulations of a partial nature with these words: "It *appears* to me to be altogether a new regulation, and ought to be carefully explained to the sepoys on parade if it is to be the rule for the future and to be enforced, and not thus introduced for the first time in a new *addition of pay and audit regulations.*" Countersigned by Sir Walter Gilbert in approval, this letter reached Napier when going to Peshawar about a fortnight after quitting Wuzzeerabad, and Lieut.-Colonel Grain, the adjutant-general, in laying the matter before the commander-in-chief, expressed his entire agreement with

Hearsey and Gilbert. He said: *"The regulation in question has been concocted by subordinates in office merely to save trouble, and he did not believe the Governor-General or the Commander-in-Chief of the time were hard on the sepoys.* He added that from its nature it only came into operation locally, and could be known but to a few regiments: *to enforce it at Wuzzeerabad would be dangerous."* The representations of two of the most capable judges in India from their position, their abilities, and their long experience in the Indian army, guided the conduct of Napier. He issued an order that the compensation should be adjusted in accordance with the old regulations, *"pending the result of a reference which will be made to the Supreme Government on the subject."* The day the order was issued the reference was made. Sir Charles Napier, after expressing his belief that the alteration had been introduced without the circumstances of the case being fully and clearly explained to the Supreme Government, wrote:

The Commander-in-Chief considers the change that has been made, to the injury of the soldier, to be both impolitic and unjust, and he feels assured that it only requires to be brought before the notice of the Government to ensure its immediate rectification.

In the mean time, confident of the support of the Government, the Commander-in-Chief has directed that compensation shall be issued to the native troops serving in the Punjab, in accordance with the rules laid down in the old regulations, as in the present state of transition from Scinde pay and allowances to the regular pay of the troops, a transition which has produced a most unprovoked state of insubordination in some regiments, the Commander-in-Chief thinks that no cause of dissatisfaction should be given to the troops.

This letter reached Calcutta on the 13th of February; the answer came back on the 26th. One month and seven days, therefore, were required for the commander-in-chief to communicate with the Supreme Council. "Yet Lord Dalhousie," writes Napier, "condemned me for exercising my discretion at a moment so full of danger and on a point so purely military. He would have had me wait for an answer, which might have come as waste-paper in the midst of terrible disasters caused by the delay. Is this the way to govern? Let it be recollected that I was of the Supreme Council as well as Commander-in-Chief, not that my rights as such were adverted to at the time; there was no reason, none imagined the proceedings could be thought an encroachment on the civil powers of Lord Dalhousie. He was far away on the Pacific Ocean, and had left me full assurance of support." The self-willed old warrior did not see that it was an encroachment on the financial and general control of the army vested in the Governor-General by Parliament. The President in Council in their reply elaborately explained by dates that Brigadier Hearsey "has wholly misled his Excellency in stating the rule to be altogether a new regulation, that it was adopted as being perfectly just by the late Governor-General (Lord Hardinge) in Council and by the late Commander-in-Chief (Lord Gough)." A regulation which was regarded as new by an officer who had thirty years' experience of every detail of the Bengal army must have been regarded as new by the sepoy. When Lord Hardinge sanctioned the regulation he had just arrived in India, he had to deal with great events, and he had no knowledge of the country or its army. And as to Lord Gough, his son-in-law, his chief staff officer, his amanuensis, Colonel Grant, officially assured Sir Charles Napier that Lord Gough had adopted the regulation under an entire misconception of its import and bearing. Sir Henry Lawrence wrote at the time: "At present there are not three officers in the Bengal army who could with certainty tell what they and the people under them are entitled to in every position in which they are liable to be placed. The audit officer seldom affords help. He is considered an enemy ready to take advantage of difficulties, not an umpire between man and man." The memorandum defending a regulation whose import and bearing the commander-in-chief and the sepoy could not understand ended by informing Sir Charles Napier that the President in Council could not but regret that his Excellency should have acted without previous communication with Government.

Napier returned to Simla just six months after his departure from it–six months spent in marching and under canvas or fighting. On the 30th of March he wrote to Dalhousie: " I am on my way to Noorpore and Kangra, just to see that frontier and report upon it to your lordship. I expect a grilling, but for that there is no help. I have taken 'Bentinck Castle' for the season, where I hope soon to have the honour of again meeting your lordship, the only satisfaction I have drawn from the mutiny, for had it not been for that I should have been far on my way to England." A month after this letter, and six months after the events, Sir Charles received an official letter from the military secretary informing him "that the Governor-General and Council viewed with regret and dissatisfaction his Excellency's act," which, it was stated, "called for no haste, while it interfered materially with

the measures which the Government was pursuing." Sir
Charles Napier was further informed, "for his future guidance,
that the Governor-General in Council will not again permit the
commander-in-chief under any circumstances to issue orders
which shall change the pay and allowance of the troops serving
in India, and thus practically to exercise an authority which
has been reserved, and must properly be reserved, for the
Supreme Government alone." Lord Dalhousie in his minute
dated 25th January 1851 states: "The order of the commander-
in-chief was confirmed. Whatever it gave was continued, and
his Excellency's authority was upheld before the army." Every
soldier and sepoy in the army, however, learnt that the head of
the army, a great and illustrious soldier, had been reprimanded
by the Governor-General as if he were a young subaltern. It was
right that Lord Dalhousie should have maintained the powers
of the Governor-General in Council, but there can hardly be a
question that the rebuke should not have been public. There is
an air of simple candour in the Governor-General's avowal of
motive. "The official papers addressed by Sir Charles Napier
have for some time past been habitually rude and discourteous
in expression." But that does not justify a statesman for
unhappily addressing to the general commanding our Indian
army a reprimand for taking an unauthorised step to avoid
a great danger. Napier wrote: "But I do not consider that the
real question is whether I acted with judgment or without
judgment. I consider the real question to be this, whether the
commander-in-chief in India, removed to a great distance from
all higher authority (the highest being at sea), in a moment
of great danger, surrounded by a hostile population, and
with an army of upwards of 40,000 men infected with a

mutinous spirit, was justified or not justified in using his
discretion and promptly dealing with danger in the manner
which he thought most effectual for the safety of India. This
is the real question."

The object of Lord Dalhousie's minutes, composed with
elaborate art, which is the more striking the more frequently
we peruse them, is to combat this practice of Napier's. By
subtle argument, by clever quotations of seeming contradictory
statements gathered from the old warrior's impulsive speeches,
he even draws the conclusion that a formidable mutiny did
not exist, that the army of 40,000 men was not tainted with
mutiny to such an extent as to justify the assertion that the
feeling was general. But no State Papers were ever composed
which are less convincing in proportion to their ability.
They display the powers rather of a subtle logician than of a
statesman who commands your confidence. It is impossible
to explain the results, but you are not convinced. The facts
remain, that a dangerous mutinous spirit was evinced openly
by five regiments; that circumstances went to show eight
regiments combined for an outbreak when time should serve;
that officers competent to judge believed their regiments
infected with the same spirit. Of the five regiments who openly
evinced a dangerous mutinous spirit, one attempted to
seize a strong fortress; and when Sir Charles Napier by
a prompt and daring measure contrived to extinguish
the flame ere it had spread over the empire, he was told
it did not exist. "I have confronted," wrote Dalhousie,
"the assertions of the commander-in-chief on this head
with undisputed facts and with the authority of recorded
documents. Fortified by these facts and documents, and

my convictions strengthened by the information which the Government commands, I desire to record my entire dissent from the statement that the army has been in mutiny and the empire in danger." The information which Government commands is, as a rule, the popular official view of a matter. A year after the foregoing was written Lord Dalhousie requested the 38th Regiment to proceed to Burma. They refused on account of caste prejudice. As with the pay regulations, and the issue of greased cartridges, no one had considered the question before the order was issued from the sepoys' point of view. Lord Dalhousie and the mild old gentleman of refined tastes who succeeded Charles Napier as commander-in-chief succumbed. The 38th Native Infantry was not disbanded. Five years later the regiment mutinied at Delhi and shot its officers. Napier's prophecy of a mutiny had been fulfilled. "He [the Sepoy] is devoted to us as yet, but we take no pains to preserve his attachment. It is no concern of mine, I shall be dead before what I foresee will take place, but it will take place."

On the 22nd of May Sir Charles Napier wrote to the Home Military Secretary a letter of resignation, which ended as follows:—

I have been treated as if I had assumed the powers of government, which I had not done: I merely acted with decision in a dangerous crisis—so dangerous that in a few days after the mutinous troops attempted to seize the strongest fortress in the Punjab. On that occasion also, although the Governor-General publicly approved of what I did, he in a private letter regretted that I had not consulted the Supreme Council at Calcutta! Such dangerous moments do not admit of slow and undecided councils; yet I am reprimanded.

Therefore I request, most humbly, that his Grace will obtain for me her Majesty's most gracious permission to resign the chief command in India. And the more so, as being now nearly seventy years of age, during the last ten years of which I have gone through considerable fatigue of body and mind, during the last year, my health requires that relief from climate and labour which public service in India does not admit of. I hope that his Grace will allow of my being relieved in October next, or as soon as may be convenient."

Lord Dalhousie, who was somewhat prone to write imperious reprimands to the rulers of provinces, expressed great surprise that a soldier who had won victories, subdued a great kingdom by arms and legislation, "should have permitted himself thus hastily to resign his high command on grounds so insufficient and untenable." But when a soldier of high repute finds he cannot with credit to himself or advantage to the State exercise the functions of his high command owing to friction with the civil power, he is bound in honour to himself, to the army, and the Crown, to resign that command.

Charles Napier felt regret at parting with the Indian army, but he did not feel the slightest repentance of having sent in his resignation. On the 25th of September he wrote in his journal: "I have just got the Court of Directors' answer to the Laird of Cockpen—Dalhousie. . . . They merely approve of his conduct, and say that, as I have resigned, the less said the soonest mended." Fourteen days later the old soldier lets off his spleen, as he always did, with a jest: "The laird having returned, I wrote to the *aide-de-camp* in waiting to know if the Governor-General had any orders for the Commander-in-Chief? The Governor-General had no commands for the Commander-in-Chief, but he would be happy to receive his

Excellency on whatever day he might wish to see him! Now
the commander-in-chief never wishes to see the G.-G. again."
On November the 15th he wrote, "To-morrow I leave Simla,
after seventeen months of hard work, no thanks, and a great
deal of abuse." In December 1850 he formally took leave of
the army, which he had so well and zealously laboured to
improve: "I have not in twenty months done what could be
done if I remained; but having no real power, I could only
give a vigorous tone to the army, which it had in a great
degree lost. Next to tone I ought to have drawn the cords
of drill and discipline tight, but could not without time and
camps of instruction, neither of which I could obtain." He
travelled down the Indus and stopped at Meeanee to take a
last look at the scenes of his great victories. Belooch sirdars
came from hundreds of miles distant to meet him and to
shake hands with him, "Before you leave us for ever." On
the 9th of January 1851 he left Hyderabad.

"All the sirdars accompanied me to the river. How different
from the day I first entered Hyderabad! These sirdars were
then sent out to meet and escort me to the *Ameers!* The
same numbers, the same men, the same show and state
were present now, but all were my friends! Between these
two occasions I entered it as a conqueror hot from the field
of battle; but then no sirdars were there: British troops,
British colours, British cannon accompanied me. How full
of events my life has been!

"The sirdars resolved to present him with a sword of
honour worth 300 guineas, as a mark of their gratitude
for saving them from the miseries of conquest, and for
honouring their courage and fidelity to the *Ameers*. No
man has a better or finer eye for a great man than the

Oriental. Napier was greatly moved by the reception he received at Kurachce from the men of the 64th and 84th.

If we had troubles in England [He writes] I should be a dangerous man, for half the troops would follow me: it is wonderful what a little success and kind feeling towards them does. I owe much to my soldiers, and it is my pride and pleasure to acknowledge it: they know this and are attached to me. A commander who would make the most of an army, especially a large army, must be popular, but he must earn his popularity by stern justice and by kindness to all who need it—that is, every one under him, and most to those lowest in rank; the private soldier requires it most, because he is least at ease and has the greatest physical suffering. To be kind to him is no more than justice, it is the first duty of a commander,—a duty which the private and officers equally appreciate and repay on the battlefield. A commander should always share fatigue: I did so with the 50th Regiment in Spain, and with the 102nd in America; no man went through so much as I did, but then I was thirty, and in India seventy.

In Sind he states the body would not keep pace with his thoughts. "Still, in 1845 I rode a camel seventy-two miles without a halt in one night, which is said to be equal in fatigue to riding 140 on horseback, and I was not tired. On the hill campaign I indeed wore myself out much; though even then I was on horse-back for twenty-two hours without being knocked up."

On the 28th of January Napier landed at Bombay. On proceeding from the pier he observed along the Esplanade a horse artilleryman in the crowd. His eye rested on the man for a moment. Then he stepped out and grasped him by the hand and exclaimed, "Delaney, I am delighted to see you. How have you been since we last met? How is your wife and dear little boy? To what troop do you belong? "The man having answered these questions as quickly as possible, stating that he had some years since volunteered from the Queen's service into the Company's, said, "Sir, I thought my heart would have leaped to my mouth as I saw you land." Sir Charles, addressing those nearest him, said, "Gentlemen, this fine fellow belonged to H.M.'s 22nd, and was my bugler at Meeanee; and when I had roared myself hoarse, and almost speechless, wound many a cheering blast, such as a sound-hearted soldier in the hour of danger knows how to send forth to his comrades in arms."

At Bombay all classes joined in a public banquet to his honour, and he was much affected by the respect shown him. "This very day," he said, "fifty-seven years ago, I received my commission as an ensign, and girded on this sword, my father's sword, which has for these long years hung at my side. I received that commission rejoicing as a boy; your kindness has made me finish my career rejoicing as a man."

In March 1851 he was back in England. On the 3rd of February he writes to his brother: "I never was so kindly and graciously received as just now by the Duke. I thought he would have embraced me. 'Will your Grace let me put your name on my card for the levee on Wednesday? 'Oh, yes! yes; and I will go there, and take care to tell the Queen that you are there; she will be glad to see you back, and so am I, and so is everybody.' " The next few years were devoted to serving his country with his pen. His last service to her was the letter he published on the defence of England by a corps of Volunteers and Militia. It was written with spirit and vigour, and did much to prepare the way for the Volunteer movement. He was a pallbearer for his great commander, and soon after struggles and controversies were over, and Charles Napier sank to rest. He was, with all his infirmities of temper, undoubtedly a great man. He had those qualities which make a hero. He was loving, gentle, and brave, and one of the most honest of men.

SIR HERBERT B. EDWARDES.

HERBERT EDWARDES, a member of the illustrious brotherhood of the Punjab which surrounded Henry Lawrence, and wielded power, not from mere love of ruling, but to curb the wild and lawless and to protect the weak, to redress all grievances and to answer the plaints of the poor, was born at Trodesley, about seven miles from Shrewsbury, in 1819. He was left an orphan at an early age and was adopted by a near relative. After passing some years at a school at Richmond in Surrey he attended classes at King's College, London. At twenty he received a direct appointment to India, and landed at Calcutta in the beginning of 1841. On arriving in India Edwardes was posted to the 1st Regiment Bengal Fusiliers, and was ordered to join his regiment at Kurnaul. He spent three profitable years at that station studying Hindustani and Persian. From Kurnaul his regiment was moved to Subathoo, where Edwardes wrote the 'Brahminee Bull's Letters' in India to his Cousin John Bull in England.' The ability and freedom of speech displayed attracted great attention to them. And it was reading these letters which first interested Captain

SIR HERBERT B. EDWARDES.

Henry Lawrence in their author. In 1845 Edwardes was appointed *aide-de-camp* to Sir Hugh Gough, and in the following month the Sikhs crossed the Sutlej and invaded our territories. He was wounded at the doubtful victory of Moodkee, and was in hospital when Ferozesha was fought, but he was sufficiently recovered to take part in the crowning victory of Sobraon, which closed the Sikh campaign. Then followed the chivalrous attempt of Henry Lawrence to teach the Sikh Government to learn to govern the empire which Runjeet Singh had founded. But vice and corruption made the task impossible, and England had to govern the province. Colonel Lawrence became president of a board and Herbert Edwardes was his private secretary.

Soon after Henry Lawrence became president his attention was drawn to the "outstanding revenue of Bunnu Tak," a district on the far-off borders of the Sikh kingdom of Runjeet Singh. The Sikhs professed to have won it by the sword, and kept up their claim by biennial devastation of the valley country they could not hold. They just took what they could and came away. In 1846 the Sikh Chancellor informed Henry Lawrence that "there are two and a half years' revenue due at this moment, so it is high time to send an army." Henry Lawrence said it was his duty to maintain the boundaries of the Sikh kingdom as he found them, and if the tribes of Bunnu refused to pay a reasonable revenue the Sikh durbar might send a force to compel them; but a British officer chosen from the Resident's staff of assistants must accompany that force to see that it resorted to arms only in extremity, and committed no excesses. Edwardes was chosen to accompany the force, which left in the middle of February 1847. "We

entered Bunnu on the 15th of March, and were burnt out
of it by the sun on the 1st of May." Only a small portion
of the revenue was collected, and the Bunnuchees refused
to enter into any peaceable settlement with regard to
the payment of the revenue in future. For the first time,
however, a Sikh army, under the influence of a single
officer, had passed through that country unmolesting and
unmolested. Edwardes had also reconnoitred the whole
valley, ascertained the strength of the tribes, and saw
how both might be subdued. On his return to Lahore he
submitted a full report on Bunnu, proposing that the old
Sikh system should now be abandoned and the permanent
subjugation and occupation of the valley undertaken, and
concluding with a detailed military plan for effecting it, the
main points of which were to level all the forts of Bunnu
to the ground and build one large one for the Crown. This
plan was approved by Henry Lawrence, and the Governor-
General, Lord Hardinge, directed it should be carried out the
next cold season. It was also decided that the troops for the
purpose should move in two columns, the one from Lahore
and the other from Peshawar, and form a junction on the
border of Bunnu at a place called Kurrak. The Peshawar
column was conducted by Lieutenant George Reynell Taylor
of the 11th Regiment of Bengal Light Cavalry, who had at
Punnear and Moodkee won a name as a chivalrous leader,
and was destined to complete the great work which Edwardes
began at Bunnu. The other column, which Edwardes
accompanied, was commanded by General Van Cortlandt
of the Sikh service, who "was indebted for a very rare
combination of qualities to his descent, inheriting at once

the best characteristics of the East and West." Carefully educated in England, he returned to seek his fortune in his native land, and had been eighteen years in the Sikh army when he commanded a brigade in the first expedition. On the 8th of December 1847 the Peshawar column, after a most fatiguing march across the desert, effected its junction with General Cortlandt's division at a solitary place in the desert called *Joor*, which means in the Pushtoo language 'The Wells.' "Not a house, or hut, or field was to be seen in this wild spot; and save for an occasional thin column of smoke, seen for a moment in the sandy distance and then lost in the blue sky, we might have deemed ourselves out of the reach of man." The next morning the whole force, consisting of five infantry regiments, one regiment of regular cavalry, about 2000 irregular horse, three troops of horse artillery, and eighty *zumbooruhs* or camel-swivels, crossed the border of Bunnu. All who have read one of the most fascinating books in our English, as Milton proudly calls it, 'A Year on the Punjab Frontier,' by Herbert Edwardes, are familiar with the fair and fertile valley of Bunnu, watered even as the garden of the Lord.

In spring [he writes] it is a vegetable emerald, and in winter its many-coloured harvests look as if Ceres had stumbled against the great Salt Range, and spilt half her cornucopia in this favoured vale. As if to make the landscape perfect, a graceful variety of the sheeshum-tree, whose boughs droop like the willow, is found here and there alone; while along streams, and round villages, the thick mulberry, festooned with the wild vine, throws a fragrant shade, beneath which well-fed *Syuds* look exquisitely happy, sleeping midway through their

beads. Roses, too, without which Englishmen have learnt from
the East to think no scenery complete, abound in the upper
parts, at the close of spring. Most of the fruits of Kabul are
found wild, and culture would bring them to perfection. As it
is, the limes, mulberries, and melons are delicious. Altogether,
nature has so smiled on Bunnu that the stranger thinks it
paradise; and when he turns to the people, wonders how such
spirits of evil ever found admittance.

The spirits of evil are the Bunnuchees, or, as they generally
style themselves, Bunnurwals, a mongrel Afghan tribe, who
"have all the vices of Pathans rankly luxuriant, the virtues
stunted." Armed to the teeth, they fought among themselves
for the fat meads of this country. Every village threw a
wall around its limits, chose its own *mullick* (master), and
went to war with its neighbours. A native who made a tour
through parts of the Punjab and Afghanistan in the year
1837 reported that there were full 400 if not 500 forts and
villages in the district. Ten years later Edwardes sent a
spy before him into Bunnu to draw a rough map of it. He
returned with a sheet of paper completely covered over with
little squares and lozenges and a name written on each,
with no space between.

" 'Why, Nizamooddeen,' I said, 'what is this?'

'That,' he replied triumphantly; 'why, that's Bunnu.' "

" 'And what are all these squares? '

'Oh! these are the forts.' "

Subsequently, in making a revenue assessment, 278
forts were actually registered in Bunnu alone, without
counting those in the uitland or those on the borders. The
Bunnuchees were not the only race inhabiting Bunnu.

There were the *Ooluma* or religious characters, the Hindus, and the Wuzeeree interlopers.

Far and near, from the barren and ungrateful hills around, the *Moollah* and the *Kazee*, the *Peer* and the *Syud*, descended to the smiling vale, armed in a panoply of spectacles and owl-like beaks, miraculous rosaries, infallible amulets, and tables of descent from Muhommud. Each new-comer, like St Peter, held the keys of heaven; and the whole, like Irish beggars, were equally prepared to bless or curse to all eternity who gave or who withheld. These were "air-drawn daggers" against which the Bunnuchee peasant had no defence. For him the whistle of the far-thrown bullet or the nearer sheen of his enemy's *Shumsheer* had no terrors; blood was simply a red fluid; and to remove a neighbour's head at the shoulder as easy as cutting cucumbers. But to be cursed in Arabic, or anything that sounded like it; to be told that the blessed Prophet had put a black mark against his soul for not giving his best field to one of the Prophet's own posterity; to have the saliva of a disappointed saint left in anger on his doorpost; or behold a *Hajee*, who had gone three times to Mecca, deliberately sit down and enchant his camels with the itch and his sheep with the rot,–these were things which made the dagger drop out of the hand of the awestricken savage, his knees to knock together, his liver to turn to water, and his parched tongue to be scarce able to articulate a full and complete concession of the blasphemous demand.

It is no wonder, therefore, that when Edwardes came to register the land he found one-sixth of Bunnu in grasp of the *Ooluma* as owners, while fully two-thirds of that prolific valley had passed into their hands as mortgagees. These impudent impostors throve alike on the abundance and the want of the superstitious Bunnuchees. The position of the despised and infidel Hindu was very different to that of the privileged Mohammedan priest in Bunnu. The educated Hindu, who chafes at our rule, is apt to forget the nature

of the Mussulman yoke from which we relieved him. The
Hindus were entirely dependent on the individual *mullicks*,
who harboured them in their forts. They could not, indeed,
venture outside the walls or visit their brethren in other forts
without a safeguard from their own chief, who conducted
and brought them back, and was paid for his protection. No
Hindu in Bunnu was permitted to wear a turban, that being
too sacred a symbol of Mohammedanism; and a small cotton
skull-cap was all that they had to protect their brains from
the keen Bunnu sun. The fourth division of the inhabitants
of the province was the Wuzeerees, who occupy the wild
undulating waste called the *theell* or desert which lies
between the cultivated lands of Bunnu and the hills of the
Kuttucks. It is not exactly a desert, but a wilderness dotted
over with scrubby vegetation and the prickly bushes of the
camel-thorn. However–

Even this is a paradise to the Viziri tribes, who, expelled from
their own stony and pine-clad mountains by the snow, yearly
set before them their flocks of broad-tailed sheep and goats, and
strings of woolly camels, and curved-eared horses, and migrate
to the sheltered plains of Bunnu. Here they stretch their black
blankets or reed mats on the bare earth, over two sticks set up like
the letter T, the four sides straggling on the ground, or fastened
with a stone if the wind gets high. Under this miserable shelter
huddle men, women, and children, afraid neither of the rain's
cold nor the sun's hot beams, in happy ignorance of better things.
From the corner of the tent the shaggy muzzle of a hill sheep-dog
peeps out, and watches over the tethered donkey and sick goat
left at home with the women, while the flocks are out at graze.
Tall and stately as a pine the daughter of the mountains stands at
the tent door in her indigo-dyed petticoat and hood, smiling on the
gambols of her naked brats, or else sits down and rubs out corn
for her lord, who is afield. The men, stout, fierce, and fearless of

man or beast, and clad in shaggy cloaks of brown camel's hair, drive out the herds to feed, and, with long *jazail* in hand and burning match, lie full-length along the ground, and listen for strange footsteps on the horizon. Should an enemy approach, the discharge of a single matchlock would be heard over the whole plain, and summon thousands of the tribe to the point where danger threatened or plunder allured.

Such were the inhabitants whom Edwardes was sent to subdue, to raise, and to civilise. Murder was considered but a small affair, and the chiefs were anxious to ascertain Edwardes' views regarding past incidents of so trivial a nature.

In the course of some other business, Ursula Khan, a fine young lad, sixteen years old, son of one of the Surauni *mullicks*, came in to impart to me his own and his father's uneasiness about past murders. "What," he asked, "is to be the law?" I asked him, jokingly, "What does it signify to a lad like you?" He replied modestly, "Oh! I've only killed four, but father has killed eighty!" One gets accustomed to this state of society; but in England what monsters of cruelty would this father and son be considered! Indeed, few people would like to be in the same room with them. Yet, *cateris paribus*, in Bunnu they are rather respectable men.

Edwardes at once set to work to measure the land, but this proceeding did not meet with the approval of the Wuzeerees. Swahn Khan, a leading chief of the clan, said that "the measurement was doubtless a very nice idea, but that if it was done with any intention of taking revenue, it might as well be dispensed with, as such a thing was altogether visionary, and could certainly never come to pass." Edwardes, however, told him at once that it must come to pass, and that no Wuzeeree should stay in Bunnu who did not pay the same as his neighbours. Then Swahn Khan began to inquire what revenue

would be required, and, after a hard fight about the terms, this
old chief at last consented on his part, but said seriously that he
could not answer for the rest, whose chiefs he must collect and
hold a *jeeniza* or council. On the 16th it was held in Edwardes'
camp. Under a large awning outside his tent door they seated
themselves in a circle on a carpet. Clothed in their cumbrous
posteens and storm-stained *choguhs* of camel's hair; with long
elfin locks of rusty black or grey, dyed red with henna, hanging
about their shoulders, and weather-beaten countenances, each
grasped his brass-bound *jazail*, or felt that his knife was near
him, in case the *Feringhee* chief should have drawn them into
an ambush under pretence of a council. Edwardes seated
himself among them and read out a paper in Persian, which
a chief from a neighbouring Afghan valley friendly with the
Wuzcerees interpreted. Edwardes boldly told them–

If you do not like laws and paying revenue, you are quite at
liberty to give up your lands to the Bunnuchees, from whom
you took them, and return to those happy hills where there is
no revenue to give and no corn to eat. Of one thing be assured,
that I will either make you pay revenue like the Bunnuchees
or expel you from Bunnu. I have troops enough here to destroy
your whole tribe. I do not believe, however, that you will be
fools enough to forsake in a day the lands which you have been
thirty years in conquering, or forego the whole of your rich
harvests rather than pay a part.

After the terms Edwardes offered had been read, the
chiefs proceeded to discuss them, and the debate grew so
warm that they adjourned to their own camp. They accused
Mullick Swahn Khan of having sold himself and his tribe
to Edwardes, but as they had no faith in a Bunnuchee
alliance the council returned to make an unconditional

surrender. "I caused each chief to sign the 'terms,' or rather to make a scratch where he was told; and as none of them had ever had a pen in their hands before, much laughter was occasioned by this approach to the slavery of civilisation; and the assembly broke up in good-humour, to which I further contributed by a feast in honour of the alliance."

The next day at noon the foundation of the new fort was commenced on a well-chosen site at Bureyree, within a few yards of the principal canal which irrigated the valley. "To please the Sikhs the usual native ceremonies were performed: the soil turned up and oil poured in, sweetmeats distributed, a royal salute of twenty-one guns fired, and the infant fort named the 'Dhuleepgarh,' in honour of the little Maharajah, whose sovereignty it is intended to establish." In 'A Year on the Punjab Frontier' there is a sketch of the fort drawn by Reynell Taylor, with the Kafir Kote range in the background. It represents a large fortress with castellated walls and circular bastions at each corner of the outer as well as the inner lines. The structure was swiftly raised by the hands of the Sikh army. By the 4th of January the walls of the inner fort had risen to such a height as to form a complete and almost impregnable intrenched position. During the night Edwardes prepared the following proclamation and issued it next morning:–

Where just laws are in force, every *fakeer's* hut is a castle, because no one dare enter it to injure him.

You are hereby ordered, therefore, to throw down to the ground the walls of every fort and enclosed village within the boundaries of Bunnu; and I hold the *mullicks* responsible for the carrying out of this order within fifteen days.

By the end of the month, in spite of being preached against in the mosques, in spite of two open attempts at assassination, and a third plot to murder him in a gateway, Herbert Edwardes had carried that measure out, and left but two Bunnuchee forts standing in the valley, and these two by permission. An entry in Reynell Taylor's diary shows how much Edwardes had done in two months. On the 11th of February he returned to Bunnu from Peshawar, and writes: "It really is wonderful what Edwardes has accomplished in my absence. The whole of the fortified villages, amounting to 400, have been knocked down by the people themselves, and in their places the walls of the new fort of Dhuleepgarh, surrounded by a cantonment wall, have arisen. The triumph of making the people knock down their own walls is worth anything. A military road has been marked out between this and Sukkee in Murrine, and about two *coss* (miles) of it have been made."

Bunnu was the most northern of the ten provinces into which the district of Derah Ishmael Khan (the camp of Ishmael) was divided. As political officer Edwardes was charged with the revenue settlement of the whole district. After three months, having peacefully annexed to the Punjab the valley of Bunnu, which had defied the Sikh arms five-and-twenty years, and having subjugated without a shot being fired the Wuzeerees and the Bunnuchees, he made over charge of the civil administration to Reynell Taylor, and proceeded south to the sister country of Murrine, whose sandy soil and dry air were different to the well-irrigated humid Bunnu, and whose inhabitants are almost the immediate reverse of their neighbours. Fine, tall, muscular Pathans, they have a profound contempt for the Bunnuchces. On the 1st of March he reached Sukkee, the capital of Murrine, and found it a thriving and well-peopled town. Two days later he passed the Pezzod Pass and encamped in the province of Tak. He wrote to the governor of Tak to meet him that he might hear how he and his country got on. The governor was no stranger to the English officer. In 1846, when Edwardes was travelling in the hills of Jummu, upwards of 300 miles from Tak, his native assistant introduced two Pathans who, he said, were in distress. "They were dressed in the commonest white clothing, and had an air of misery mingled with being ashamed to beg. They talked of places I had never heard of across the Indus, and of rivers of which I was ignorant; but I gathered that they had seen better days, and without attending much to the story, gave them ten rupees between them." They took the money gratefully and started. However, when Edwardes started on his first expedition to Bunnu they appeared again and asked permission to accompany him, as their native country was across the Indus. Their wives and families had taken refuge in Bunnu, and they might be of service to Edwardes. He consented, and the two Pathans started with him from Lahore. On the march Edwardes used during the heat of the day to collect a knot of natives under the shade of a tree and gather information regarding the countries he was about to visit. One afternoon the talk turned on Tak, and Edwardes, with his finger on the map, asked who knew anything about that country. "One of the two Pathans modestly lifted up his head and said, 'My father was once king of it'!" It was Shah Niwaz Khan, the son of the cruel voluptuary from whom the Sikhs had taken Tak, and grandson of Surwur Khan, the chief who had brought streams from the mountains to fertilise it, and turned its desert plain into a richly-cultivated land. Edwardes on inquiry found that Shah Niwaz had had no food for two days, after selling his arms and a few remaining ornaments, so he ordered him 500 rupees out of the treasury and sent him on rejoicing to see his exiled family. On the return of the first expedition Edwardes persuaded Colonel Henry Lawrence to give the charge of Tak to Shah Niwaz. On the 4th of March Edwardes enters in his diary—

Shah Niwaz Khan of Tak arrived in camp, and gives a modest but satisfactory account of his country. His best report, however, is in the mouths of the common people of the districts round, who already compare him to his wise grandfather, Surwur Khan. He shows as much moderation in his prosperity as he did fortitude in his troubles. I cannot say what a happiness it is to me to have had it in my power at once to restore him to his home, and to recover a whole people from ruin. It is, perhaps, the best thing I have done on this frontier; yet it was only a happy hit—a thought that it would do—a recommendation to Lawrence—his order—and it was done! Talk of conjuring trees with singing birds out of a mere cherry-stone—why, here is a populous country conjured up, in a waste, by the scratch of a pen. Happy Asia, where such things may alone be done! Sad Asia, whose princes so seldom do them!

From Tukwarah Edwardes continued his southern march to Kolachee. "There is hardly a vestige of cultivation to be seen in the land. The rain fell too late. Waste, waste—waste on every side. On arriving at the city (6th March) the whole population moved out in a body, and raising their hands in the air, cried out with one voice, 'Furyad, Sahib log! Furyad!' (A complaint, O Englishman! A complaint!) I felt it to be a powerful appeal, and by the help of God will, before I leave, lighten the burdens of the poor." Whilst working all the day and half the night at settling the assessment of the country, news reached Edwardes that a recusant chief, Shahzad Khan, the head of the Nassur tribe, was lying hid sixteen miles away under the Sheraunee hills. He was a thorough Afghan in his hatred of all Hindus and all forms of taxation. "He boasted that he had defied Dost Mahommed, the *Ameer* of Kabul, and the Nawab of Dera; and was it to be supposed he would knuckle down to the dogs of Sikhs? "Edwardes wrote to him from Bunnu and asked him to come and talk the delicate subject of taxation over with him, but he refused. "I then ordered him to come, or else to be off the limits of the Sikh kingdom, whose laws he did not like. He refused to do either. It was disagreeable to put these things in one's pockets, but I was obliged to do so from Christmas to the present time. Now, however, I was quite determined to clear the account; for the man who hopes to rule a barbarous country must first make his orders law, else the barbarians will very soon rule him." Edwardes, resolute and quick in all his movements, started at once with a force of 300 men to seize Shahzad Khan in the midst of his people, and carry him off prisoner. Pushing on through a very ugly night, Edwardes came in sight of the watch-fires of the Nassur's camps about daybreak. "The guides pointed out Shahzad's, far away in the rear of all, under the outer ridges, which lie like pebble-stones beneath the mountain called Solomon's Throne; and I called a halt under the shelter of a ravine to look at it, breathe the horses, and let the stragglers close up." When morning broke, great was Edwardes' surprise to find that his band of nearly 300 men had dwindled down to about eighty. "The heroes had taken advantage of the night to lose their way." It was hardly to be expected that eighty men could defeat the stout rebel who had fought Dost Mahommed. But Edwardes felt that if he hoped for influence in that wild country it would be more honourable and wise to be defeated in a bold attempt than not to make it. So, getting his men together, "with a heart not over-high," he led them on at a gentle trot to the rebel camp.

"The grey dawn was just removing the friendly veil that had hitherto concealed us, the watchfires of the mountaineers were dying out, and we could see the savage Kabul dogs of the merchants spring up from beside the ashes, before their accursed howl of alarm and warning reached our ears." The Nassurs at the baying of the dogs turned out like a nest of hornets. To ensure that his small band did not retreat Edwardes led them round to the rear of the rebels' camp, and drew them up between it and the hills. Then beckoning with his hand to the Nassurs he told one of his Afghan troopers to shout to them to surrender. The Nassurs replied with a volley of bullets and abuse. "Come on," they cried; "come on, you *Feringhee* dog! and don't stand talking about surrender." As their fire grew warmer Edwardes drew his sword, stuck his spurs into his big chestnut Arab, and calling on his men to follow, plunged into the camp. But not fifteen of his men charged, and scarcely a dozen reached the middle of the encampment.

The dozen was composed of Muhommud Alim Khan (I think I see him now with his blue-and-gold shawl turban all knocked about his ears!), Kaloo Khan, and Lumsden's *Duffadar* of Guidcs; each backed by a few faithful henchmen.

The only officer *non-inventus* was the Sikh *Russaldar*. The *mêlée*, therefore, was much thicker in our neighbourhood than was at all pleasant, and how we ever got out of it is unaccountable; but we did, after cutting our way from one end to the other of the Nassur camp. Somewhere about the middle of it a tall ruffian, whom I was told afterwards was Shahzad's brother, walked deliberately at me with his *jazail*, and sticking it into my stomach, so that the muzzle almost pushed me out of my saddle, fired! The priming flashed in the pan, and as he drew back the *jazail* I cut him full over the head; but I might as well have hit a cannon-ball—the sword turned in my hand; and the Nassur, without even resettling his turban, commenced repriming his *jazail*, an operation which I did not stay to see completed. Between 1845 and 1849 there was no lack of peril in the Punjab frontier, and I, like all the rest, had my share; but I have always looked back to the moment when that *jazail* missed fire as the one of all my life when I looked death closest in the face.

Shahzad Khan struck his camp immediately after the fight, and marched away out of the Derajat into the Sheraunee hills, with his flocks and herds and people, and did not again descend from his mountain hiding-place. "Nor was I ever again told by any other Kabul merchant in the province under my charge that he would not come when he was called, or would not obey the laws of the Sikh territory in which he lived and bought and sold." Soon after this affray an event occurred which launched Edwardes on a career of exploits equalled by few and surpassed by none in the annals of Indian warfare.

On the evening of April 22, 1848, at Derah Futteh Khan, on the Indus, Edwardes was sitting in a tent full of Beluchees conducting a trial, when the *purdah* was lifted and a messenger stripped to the waist and steaming with heat entered and presented a letter-bag. "It was from the sahib in Multan," he said, "to the sahib in Bunnu." It was addressed to General Cortlandt. There was something in the *kossid's* manner which compelled Edwardes to open it. He found the copy of a letter to the Resident at Lahore, written by Mr P. Vans Agnew, one of his assistants at Multan, informing Sir Frederick Currie that he and Lieutenant Anderson, who commanded the Sikh escort, had been treacherously wounded. "During the perusal of this letter I felt that all eyes were upon me, for no one spoke, not a pen moved, and there was that kind of hush which comes over an assembly under some indefinite feeling of alarm. I never remember in my life being more moved, or feeling more painfully the necessity of betraying no emotion. After lingering over the last few sentences as long as I could, I looked up at the *kossid* and said, 'Very good, sit down in that corner of the tent, and I'll attend to you as soon as I have done this trial.' Then turning to the gaping *moonshees* I bade them 'go on with the evidence,' and the disappointed crowd once more bent their attention on the witnesses. But from that moment I heard no more. My eyes, indeed, were fixed mechanically on the speakers, but my thoughts were at Multan with my wounded countrymen, resolving how I ought to act to assist them." His resolution was quickly made. The trial concluded, he wrote to Agnew: "I need scarcely say that I have made arrangements for marching to your assistance at once. I have one infantry regiment and four extra companies, two horse-artillery guns, twenty *zumbooruhs* (camel-mounted guns), and between three and four hundred horse. This is a small force, but such as it is, you are welcome to it, and *me*." Edwardes also persuaded the mountain tribes he had so lately subdued to follow him to punish the rebel chieftain. The wild force was kept together by the firm will and the kindness of their commander. "The officers," he writes, "I learnt to know well–their characters, their circumstances, and their wants; and, by living the same life they do, wearing the same dress, talking the same language, and sharing with them all dangers and fatigues, they became attached to me and I to them. I believe that, when the war was over and we had seen our mutual enemy subdued, to part was a mutual sorrow. Wild, barbarous, indifferent to human life, they were yet free, simple as children, brave, faithful to their masters, sincere towards their God. During the whole war I never lost by desertion one man of all whom I had enlisted."

The crowded city has its virtues, but so have the desert and the mountain, and he who walks the world aright will find something good wherever he finds man, and nothing barren, from Dan to Beersheba. Edwardes' life teaches us that confidence begets confidence. The rudest and wildest tribes admired the guileless honesty of the man and nobly rewarded the faith he put in them. On the 24th April Edwardes crossed the Indus with his force to relieve the wounded officers, but the sad news reached him that they had been massacred. He, however, saw that if rebellion was not to spread over the Punjab, Mulraj, the traitor and murderer, must be driven into the fort of Multan. Edwardes implored the Resident to reinforce him with regular troops, but Lord Gough, then commander- in - chief, refused because it was the hottest season of the year.

On the 17th of June the troops of Mulraj and the army of

Bhawul Khan, the Nawab of Bhawulpoor, who had thrown
in his lot with us, were on the left bank of the river Chenab
on the point of coming into collision. Edwardes' force,
consisting of two divisions (one of about 1500 men and ten
guns under General Cortlandt, and another of about 5000
irregular horse and five-and-thirty falconettes under his
own personal command), were on the right bank of the river,
hastening to the scene of action. During the night 3000
Pathan irregulars, with about fifty mounted chiefs, crossed
the river and joined Bhawul Khan's army at sunrise. As the
day began to break Edwardes with a few horsemen in two
small ferry-boats commenced to cross the stream. Cortlandt
was to follow with the guns and the rest of his force as rapidly
as he could. As Edwardes was nearing the left bank he was
roused from a "brown-study" by a burst of artillery within a
mile or two from the shore. "A second cannonade replied, was
answered, and replied again, and two tall opposite columns
of white smoke rose out of the jungle, higher and higher at
every discharge, as if each strove to get above its adversary,
then broke and pursued each other in thick clouds over the
fair and peaceful sky. The horsemen knit their brows and
devoutly cried 'Allah! Allah!' They quite felt there was a
fight going on. For my own part, I felt so too; and as I stepped
on shore, and buckled the strap of my cap under my chin, I
remember thinking that no Englishman could be beaten on
the 18th of June." Accompanied by three or four troopers
and half a dozen guides of Lieutenant Lumsden's corps,
he set out for the field of battle. On reaching it Edwardes
found the Daudputra [1] army disorganised, and their general

[1.] *Daudputra* means descendants of David, and is the family name of
the Bhawulpoor chief and his tribe.

seated under a peepul-tree surrounded by a crowd. "A little old man, in dirty clothes and with nothing but a skullcap on his head, sitting under the tree with a rosary in his hands, the beads of which he was rapidly telling, and muttering in a peevish helpless manner, *'Ulhum doolillah! Ulhum doolillah!'* (God be praised! God be praised!) apparently quite abstracted from the scene around him." Excitement had completed the imbecility of his years. Edwardes, after learning from the Nuwab's officers the general nature of the position, told them that he would write to General Cortlandt to send over the guns, and until they came not a move was to be made. They must keep their men under cover as much as possible while their artillery played on the enemy's guns. "Above all, stand fast and be patient." Then amidst the loud greetings of the soldiers the one solitary British officer rode down the line to the left, where his own 3000 men had stuck their standards upright in the turf and were lying down between them. Dismounting from his horse Edwardes asked if any one had got pen and paper.

"Sahib!" replied a well-known voice behind me, and turning, I beheld Sudda Sookh, the *moonshee* of my office, pulling out a Cashmere pen-box and paper from his girdle just as quietly as if he had been in *cutcherry*. He had no sword or other implements of war, but merely the writing materials with which it was his duty to be furnished; and though he looked serious and grave, he was perfectly calm amid the roar of hostile cannon, and men's heads occasionally going off before his eyes.

"What are you doing here, Sudda Sookh?" I asked in astonishment. He put up his hands respectfully and answered, "My place is with my master! I live by his service; and when he dies, I die!" A more striking instance of the quiet endurance of the Hindu character I never saw.

Seating himself under a bush, Edwardes wrote two short notes to Cortlandt informing him of his critical position. If the guns did not arrive by 3 P.M. the battle must be lost. At 8 A.M. the messenger was despatched. Hour after hour passed and the artillery duel continued. The wild Pathans did not understand civilised warfare. Continually springing up, they demanded to be led on against the enemy. "Look here!" they cried, "and there, and there!" pointing to men as they were hit. "Are we all to be killed without a blow? What sort of war do you call this? there is iron on one side and only flesh and blood on the other, Lead us on and let us strike a blow for our lives." The officers crowded round Edwardes, "and every one thought he was a general, and if I would only listen to *him* (pulling me by the sleeve to interrupt my rebuke to some one else) the battle would be mine." Edwardes strove hour after hour to calm the rash and excited throng, and assured them that when the right moment came he himself would lead them on. Seven hours passed—no signs of the guns. The cannonade became heavier and the foe no longer could be kept back. Their guns, covered by a swarm of cavalry, advanced. A supreme moment. Edwardes implored the infantry to be still a little longer, and ordered Foujdar Khan (the adjutant-general of the Pathan levies) and all the chiefs and officers who had horses to mount, and form themselves into a compact body. Then he gave the word about 3 P.M., "Charge the rebel cavalry and hurl them back on the foot!" "Put off the fight," I whispered to Foujdar Khan, "or not a man of us will leave the field." On Edwardes' order, "spreading their hands to heaven, the noble band solemnly repeated the creed of their religion, as though it were their last act on earth, then passed their hands over their beards with the haughtiness of martyrs, and drawing their swords, dashed out of the jungle into the ranks of the enemy's horse, who, taken wholly by surprise, turned round and fled, pursued by Foujdar and his companions to within a few hundred yards of the rebel line, which halted to receive its panic-stricken friends."

Many fell, and few of that brave band who returned came back without a wound. But they saved the day. At that moment was heard the bright note of the artillery bugle in the rear. Every ear was strained to catch that friendly sound again. "Again it sounds, again, and there is no mistake. The guns have come at last, thank God!" Straightway Edwardes spake to the chiefs gathered around him in a circle: "With all speed hasten to your tribes and bid the footmen arise and form line. Let every chief keep his own standard in a line with the standard right and left of him. Break the line, and you will be beaten; keep it, and you are sure of victory." Then the captains in haste went to their respective clans, urging them to fight, and with a loud shout like to a wave on a steep shore they stood up. "Standards were shaken in the wind, ranks closed, swords grasped, and matches blown, and the long line waved backwards and forwards with agitation as it stood between the coming friend and the coming foe." Louder and louder grew the murmurs of the advancing host, more distinct and clear the bugles of the friendly guns. Then the rattling of wheels was heard: the crowds fell back, a road was cleared, and the foremost gun amidst the cracks of whips and shouts of welcome galloped to the front. Five more swiftly followed. Behind them came panting two regiments of regular infantry–Soobhan Khan's

corps of Mussulmans and General Cortlandt's Sikhs. And
first Edwardes arrayed the artillery, and close behind them
the two regiments, and he charged the horsemen under
Foujdar Khan to advance steadily in line in the rear. So he
led the guns through the trees on to a cultivated plain, and
saw on its opposite edge the serried battalions of infantry
of the enemy, and a long line of horse bristling with shields
and swords. Then one of Edwardes' guns rang out; soon a
second and third rent the air. A loud roar came from across
the plain, and the whole line of the enemy, completely taken
by surprise, as they hadn't heard of the arrival of the Sikh
guns, sank down among the long stalks of the sugar-cane.
To and fro their astonished officers rode, uncertain what to
do, and while the guns maintained the battle, a messenger
was sent in hot haste to the rebel general, who, seated on an
elephant, looked safely down upon the fight from the hills
around. Edwardes' gunners grew warm. " 'Grape! grape!' at
length shouted the commandant; 'it's close enough for grape!'
And the enemy thought so too, for the next round rushed
over our heads like a flight of eagles." Two of their guns
were silenced, and as the fire of the others began to slacken,
Edwardes gave the order to Soobhan Khan's regiment to
attack, "and away they went, Soobhan Khan himself, a stout
heavy soldier, leading them on and leaping over bushes like
a boy. While they are stealing rapidly on the battery, half
a dozen troopers darted out from the trees, dashed past
the advancing corps, and swept down on the guns. Their
leader received the ball full in his face and fell over the
'cannon's mouth.' " It was Shah Niwaz Khan of Esaukheyl,
whose family I had recalled from exile to rule over his

own country. The Sikhs came rushing up and captured the other gun at the point of the bayonet. "Confusion fell among their artillery; ours advanced, and cruelly harassed them with grape; the infantry followed up; a momentary struggle ensued for the mastery, and the next minute the rebels were in full flight. Bravely, I must allow, did they labour to carry off their guns, but one by one they all fell to either the sword or the bayonet. In the morning they commenced the action with ten guns, and in the afternoon advanced with six across a *nullah* which was between them and us, leaving four guns behind. All six are now in our possession, but they managed to carry off the more distant four, though we followed them up for four miles after they broke." The enemy's camp and all their ammunition fell into our hands, and they left 500 dead on the field. On Edwardes' side upwards of 300 men were killed or wounded. And so ended the battle of Kineyree, won by irregular levies commanded by a single British officer, a subaltern aged twenty-nine.

After his victory Edwardes continued his advance against Multan. He once more encountered the rebel army at Suddoosam, routed them, and drove them within the walls of the fortress. But to capture that stronghold he found no easy task. It was not till nine months had lapsed that the prophecy of the dying Agnew was fulfilled. "They can kill us too if they like, but we are not the last of the English. *Thousands of Englishmen will come down here when we are gone, and annihilate Mulraj and his soldiers and his fort.*" It was three companies of the very same regiment to which Anderson, Agnew's companion, belonged (the 1st Bombay Fusiliers) who assaulted the Bloody Bastion and captured Multan. The bodies of the two murdered officers were carefully removed from the grave where they lay side by side, and were borne by the soldiers of the Bombay Fusiliers through the broad and sloping breach which had been made by the British guns to a resting-place in the summit of Mulraj's citadel.

After the capture of Multan, congratulations and honours were showered on Edwardes for the leading part he had played and the victories he had gained. The Queen was graciously pleased to ordain a special statute of the Order of the Bath to appoint him an extra Companion of that order, and the Court of Directors bestowed upon him a gold medal in acknowledgment of his services. The anxieties and hardships of the campaign had left their mark upon him, and shortly after leaving Multan he was compelled to take furlough to England. John Lawrence and his wife urged him to take charge of their two little girls, aged six and seven. He consented, and never had any children more loving and careful protection. The young loved him, as they do all true natures. At the close of 1849 Edwardes left Lahore, and, accompanied by his friend John Nicholson, dropped down the Indus. They stopped every night to let the boatmen rest and to give the girls a run on the land to hunt for tigers' footprints on the sandy shore. The friendship between him and Nicholson, which ripened during the voyage, only perished when the heroic Nicholson died on the ridge at Delhi. On the 27th January 1850 Edwardes landed in England, and found himself an object of general interest and admiration. He received the thanks of the House, and, what pleased him more, the marked approval of the great Duke.

When the rewards for the campaign were being discussed in the House of Lords, it was remarked that "these would be unprecedented honours won for so young a man." The Duke replied, "Gentlemen, Lieutenant Edwardes' *services* have been *unprecedented*, and his rewards must be unprecedented too." Oxford bestowed upon him the honorary degree of D.C.L., his own college, King's, an honorary fellowship, and Liverpool feted him. He told the citizens of that city that few changes struck him more after a ten years' absence from England than the change of feeling on the subject of England's colonies. It had become a moot point whether colonies are of any use at all. "Citizens of Liverpool, I would answer that question thus. The use of colonies is *not to abuse them.* A colony well treated and liberally governed is certain to repay the mother country with interest and honour, with commerce in peace and sympathy in war." But a reward far greater than titles and decorations came in England. On the 9th July 1850 he was married to her whom he had loved from boyhood, who became the helpmeet of his life, and whose hand has traced the outline story of his life. During the year after his marriage–his "first happy year," as he called it–he wrote 'A Year on the Punjab Frontier,' a work which always repays reading.

On March 20, 1851, Edwardes and his wife returned to India. He proceeded to Jullundur, and remained there fifteen months administering his district. Then came the sudden uprooting so common in Indian life. House and furniture had to be sold at once, for Edwardes was ordered to move to Hazara as quickly as possible,–Lord Dalhousie "hoped within ten days." The devoted wife writes, It was my first lesson on the uncertainty of an Indian life. But it was a happy lesson to learn (as I learned it) that the happiest of homes consists in the companionship and fellowship of the being who is the most dearly beloved on earth; and home and the very best of society can be comprised within the four canvas walls of a tent in the jungle, and far from the sight of another white face, even with the thermometer at 100⁰ Fahr." The stay at Hazara was of short duration. On the murder of Colonel Mackison, Commissioner of Peshawar, Edwardes was ordered by the Governor-General to succeed him. Lord Dalhousie wrote to him: "In the whole range of Indian charges I know none which at the present time is more arduous than the commissionership of Peshawar. Holding it, you hold the outpost of the Indian empire. Your past career and your personal qualities and abilities give me assurance that, in selecting you, I have chosen well for its command. . . .You have a fine career before you. God speed you in it both for your own sake and for the sake of this empire." Edwardes more than justified the confidence which the Governor-General placed in him. As Chief Commissioner he displayed the same power of ruling and conciliating wild races which he did at Bunnu, but he also found himself to be a successful diplomat. Edwardes had not been long at Peshawar before he saw the value of cultivating friendly relations with Kabul, and he proposed to make a treaty with Dost Mahommed. John Lawrence, who was then Chief Commissioner of the Punjab, wrote: "I have two reasons against it: (1) That you will never be able to get the Afghans to make a treaty; and (2) if they make it, they will not keep it." In February 1854 Edwardes wrote to Lord Dalhousie, "I should be very glad to see a new account opened on the basis of an open treaty of friendship and alliance."

The Chief Commissioner, in forwarding the letter, noted on the margin that he "doubted whether a treaty would be good policy with the Dost, who would only be bound by it as long as he liked." The Governor-General's opinion, however, fortunately coincided with that of Edwardes in favour of a treaty being made. The negotiations for an alliance proceeded in spite of John Lawrence's adverse criticism. Writing to Edwardes, he says: "I daresay you are right; still I cannot divest myself of the idea that it is a mistake, and will end in mixing us up in Afghan politics and affairs more than is desirable. The strength which a treaty can give us seems to be a delusion. It will be like the reed on which, if a man lean, it will break and pierce his hand." Again he wrote, "Nothing that we could do would make him a real ally and friend." Lord Dalhousie remarked on this: "I do not agree with him. I think his views founded on a fallacy. It proceeds on the assumption that the Afghans are fools, whereas I think they are, in general, quite as clever fellows as we are." The Chief Commissioner's opposition, however, did not abate. He wrote to Edwardes: "A treaty with the Afghans might be a dead letter so far as Russia and Persia are concerned. But while of no real value to us, it would at home be thought of some value, and might lead them into a mistaken line of policy. . . . I so far agree with the Governor-General that I think all the merit of the affair, whatever it may be, is good." After long negotiations and exercise of considerable tact and skill, a treaty of friendship was drafted, and Dost Mahommed determined to send his son and heir to sign it. The Supreme Government gave Edwardes orders to meet the *Ameer's* representative in full *durbar* and sign the treaty on their part. But Edwardes, with rare self-abnegation, suggested that it might enhance the importance of the treaty in the eyes of the Afghans if the Chief Commissioner of the Punjab were ordered to Peshawar to meet the son of Dost Mahommed. The suggestion was acted upon, and John Lawrence was ordered to Peshawar to sign the treaty in conjunction with Major Edwardes. Lord Dalhousie wrote to Edwardes: "I am exceedingly vexed that you should not have had, *as I intended you should,* the crowning credit of bringing to a close the negotiations you have conducted so well and so successfully to their present port." The signature of the treaty was all that John Lawrence had to do regarding it. It was negotiated and completed in spite of his opposition, but to him in England was given the credit of making it, and for it he received the honour of knighthood.

The misapprehension at home was in a great measure due to the Governor-General. In 1855 Lord Dalhousie informed John Lawrence that the Governor - General intended to seek an honour for him from the Queen, "well earned before for other times and other causes," but that he considered the completion of the treaty a fitting cause to bring his name forward, " because the great importance of the entire change in the relations between England and Afghanistan would be well understood by her Majesty's advisers at home." John Lawrence wrote to Edwardes, "I may say with perfect truth that I consider you deserve at least as much, if not more, for the late treaty than I do." But years passed away, and John Lawrence never publicly put forward the facts in their true light. The treaty of 1855 bound "the Afghans to be friends of our friends and enemies of our enemies." Edwardes followed this up at the close of 1856 by recommending that active aid should be given to the *Ameer*. On the 26th of January 1857 was signed "an agreement confrming the treaty of 1855." The agrccmcnt not only confirmed the treaty, but it arranged the payment subsidy by the British Government to the *Ameer* to enable him to strengthen his frontier. We were at the time at war with Persia, and the majority of the articles of agreement have reference to the exigencies of that war. Lord Canning, with the generous and hearty recognition of good service which was habitual to him, wrote to Edwardes on January 19, 1857, as follows: "I must ask you to accept my best thanks for the part you have taken in the recent negotiations and for their satisfactory issue. I feel the more bound to do this because the first suggestion of a meeting came from you." Not only was the first suggestion made by Edwardes, but the interview was equally opposed by John Lawrence. Ten years later (1868), when our Afghan policy was being keenly discussed in the *'Times,'* an old friend of John Lawrence, who evidently was at the time a member of the Secretary of State Council, sent the correspondence to Edwardes and asked his opinion concerning it. In acknowledging the receipt of Edwardes' letter written in reply, the old friend of John Lawrence remarked:–

It has left me with the feeling that you have not had justice done you, and with a desire to help to see right done. . . . A better mode would be that you should yourself take the subject in hand, and tell the whole truth about it, which nobody is so well qualified to do as you are. . . . Unless I hear from you to the contrary I shall show it to Kaye, our Indian historiographer. From its bearing on the truth of history, it is valuable.

The letter called forth a reply, in which the diffidence and generosity of Herbert Edwardes were strikingly illustrated:—

I have not the least wish to make a stir about it. These sparks are simply struck out of me by our discussion, and Sir John's reputation is as dear to me as my own, though I certainly lament that he has never felt the impulse to give the credit where it was due.

I feel it more that on the occasion of each treaty (in 1855 and in 1857) I successively forewent the legitimate opportunity that was offered me of being the representative of the British Government in the formal act of signing the treaties, and urged Government to honour the Ameer (and so promote the policy) by deputing John Lawrence alone to make the first treaty, and associated with me to make the second. Very much ashamed of myself should I be if I had acted otherwise: but it grieves poor human nature not to be treated in the same spirit.

The foregoing was a private letter not intended for publication. Edwardes always declined to make public the credit due to him in originating and negotiating the two treaties with Afghanistan. When a similar request was made to him two years after the treaty was signed, he wrote—

Not a finger will I move in the matter. We all think it a defect in John Lawrence that he praises no one. But I acquit him of all mean and selfish motives in it. It is not that he *wishes* to keep the credit to himself, though practically it has that effect. It is a *principle* of his *not* to praise public servants, for fear of its "putting wind into their heads," as he expresses it! This is, I think, a mistaken argument; for there is a higher necessity—in justice, to praise the good men do, as well as blame their evil. John Lawrence's blame is an ever-impending thunderbolt, but he is a Jupiter Tonans who never smiles upon his world. I am as indignant as any one about it, when it touches a friend like John Nicholson, and I have had a hot correspondence with J. L. on this subject. But it does not do any good. He is emphatically a hard man in public matters, and so all one has to do is to love him in private, and respect him in public.

The treaty which Edwardes negotiated and John Lawrence signed, proved of great service to us in the dark days of the Mutiny; for Dost Mahommed, in spite of the fanatical taunts of the priests and the ambitious councils of his followers, remained true to it, and abstained from raising the green flag of Islam and marching on the fertile valley of Peshawar, which once formed the boundary of the Afghan kingdom. As Commissioner of the most important district on the frontier, Edwardes naturally devoted much time and thought to the study of the frontier question and our policy with regard to Afghanistan. In 1858 he wrote:–

Afghanistan must be admitted to be a great physical difficulty. It is difficult to conquer, difficult to hold, difficult to sustain an army, and most difficult of all to leave. The very native Government of the country lives from hand to mouth, and is savage with its own embarrassments. Finding such a country between us and Russia, why should we divide the difficulty? Every mile that we advance beyond the present British border is a relief to the enemy, and is taking on our own shoulders a share of the burden which the invader ought to bear. After all, every conquest is a question of resources. Experience has shown us that military operations in Afghanistan can, from the nature of the country, only be carried on at an enormous sacrifice of money. To take on that expenditure on ourselves would surely be a blunder; and to throw it on the enemy, the most obvious dictate of strategy.

In 1865, after he had left India, he wrote to John Lawrence: "Somehow or other, I do not think you fully care enough for keeping Afghanistan as *netural ground between us and Russia,* which can only be done by keeping her *friendly and independent.*" Edwardes' days at Peshawar were occupied not only in watching the frontier and curbing wild tribes, but in founding a Christian mission in the heart of the fanatical city. The experiment was a dangerous one, but it proved a success. A beautiful church, around which a congregation of Christian Afghans has been gathered, now adorns Peshawar. The founder did not lose his power over his people by his zeal for his creed. The Mussulman is a fanatic, he hates the infidel, but he despises the man who is so tolerant as to have no creed. The Oriental is essentially a religious man, and he admires those who have a religion and lead religious lives. The life of Edwardes was the life of a Christian. To men of all races and creeds he extended the melting hand of charity. All cases of real distress won a ready sympathy from his chivalrous heart. The widow of a clerk, who was very ill, said to her doctor: "Now I shall die, I am sure; I shall make over my two girls to Colonel Edwardes." When told of it, he remarked, "I heartily wish the good lady a long life." His own happy home was broken up by the sickness of his wife, and he had to take her down to Calcutta, for it was absolutely necessary that she should go to England. At the capital he had the opportunity of discussing State affairs with the new Governor-General, Lord Canning. John Nicholson at that time, owing to friction with John Lawrence, was anxious to leave the Punjab, and Edwards brought to the notice of Lord Canning the great qualities of Nicholson and the great loss the province would sustain by his departure. "If your lordship ever has a thing of real difficulty to be done,

I could answer for it John Nicholson is the man to it." Lord Canning replied with a smile, "I will remember what you say, and I will take you for Major Nicholson's godfather." Edwardes had not been back at Peshawar a month when from an apparently clear sky burst the great storm which almost wrecked our empire in the East. The day after he heard the news of the Mutiny he wrote to John Lawrence: "I write to tell you that Nicholson and I are of opinion that a strong movable column of reliable troops (European and irregulars) should take the field in the Punjab at once, and move on the first station that stirs next, and bring the matter without further delay *to the bayonet.* This disaffection will never be talked down now. It must be put down." At Peshawar there were three strong men—Nicholson, Edwardes, and Cotton—capable of grappling with a great danger. Cotton had fortunately succeeded Hewitt as brigadier, who had been removed because he was physically unfit for the duties on the frontier. "During the time he commanded the Peshawar Division it is believed he never once visited the outposts, and he used to inspect his troops in a buggy. Yet he was appointed to another large division at Meerut, no doubt a quieter place. But wherever it is necessary to keep troops, it is surely necessary to keep a commander who can head them in the field. It is not a question of age, but of efficiency." Edwardes' remarks are mere platitudes, but the world is apt to underrate the value of platitudes. A competent man at Meerut would probably have crushed the Mutiny at the outset, and saved England and India the greatest calamity of the century. But the habit of appointing incompetent men will continue as long as people will not learn that the welfare of the individual is nothing in comparison to the public weal. At a council of war held at Peshawar Nicholson's idea of having a movable column of trustworthy troops to suppress mutiny, wherever it might appear in the Punjab, met with approval. Edwardes, in forwarding the proceedings of the council of war, also asked leave to raise levies among the Mooltanees of the Derajat, whom he had led in his youth; but Lawrence replied, "I would not raise Mooltanee Horse without the orders from Government, *nor do I think they are necessary,* at any rate at present." A few days afterwards John Lawrence summoned Edwardes to Rawul Pindi, and after consulting with him gave his consent to raise the levies.

The night that Edwardes returned from Rawul Pindi he heard that some companies of the regiment at Nowshera had mutinied. He knew from intercepted letters that disloyalty existed among the native troops at Peshawar, and he felt certain that they would follow the example of their neighbours the moment they heard the news. There was only one way of grappling with the danger. The native troops at Peshawar must be disarmed. Nicholson and Edwardes went at once to Cotton, roused him from his sleep, and told him what they had heard. The next day the native troops were disarmed in spite of the vigorous protests of their officers, who had a blind belief in their loyalty. "It was a painful and affecting thing," writes Edwardes, "to see them putting their own firelocks into the artillery waggons–weapons which they had used honourably for years. The officers of a cavalry regiment, a very fine set of fellows, threw in their own swords with those of their men, and even tore off their spurs. It was impossible not to feel for and with them; but duty must be done, and I know that we shall never regret the counsel we gave."

The result was instantaneous. To take the place of the mutinous sepoys offers of service came from the tribes. By disarming the troops, and by prompt and severe punishment dealt to the evil-doers, Edwardes had impressed them with the fact that the English were the masters. One day a man came into his study saying, "O, sahib! a number of armed hill-men are coming into the cantonment and calling out for your house. What are we to do?" And so it truly was. Nearly 300 Afreedees, armed in every imaginable manner, came down from the hills and asked him to enlist them. They were men who, on account of their crimes, had taken to the hills to escape from justice. They saw the time had come to get the score removed by service. "I went among them," Edwardes writes, "and picked out their youths, and enrolled them as recruits; then brought the older ones, weather-beaten, scarred, and scored with frays, into our willow-walk in the garden, set them down in the shade, and, after talking to them, dismissed them to their hills again with a rupee each, quite satisfied that they had been honourably treated. I was not sorry, however, to get them out of the cantonment." Levies were raised and troops sent to Delhi, but the imperial city did not fall. However long the siege might be, John Lawrence determined that he should not fail in sending reinforcements. To accomplish this he was ready to make a great sacrifice. On the 9th June he wrote to Edwardes that "in the event of disaster at Delhi he was prepared to reinstate Dost Mahommed, to take possession of Peshawar, and send the European troops to Delhi." He

told him to consult Cotton and Nicholson. Edwardes replied:
"We are unanimously of opinion that, with God's help, we
can and will hold Peshawar, let the worst come to the worst;
and that it would be a fatal policy to abandon it and retire
beyond the Indus. It is the anchor of the Punjab, and if you
take it up, the whole ship will drift to sea." John Lawrence
was not convinced by the arguments of his lieutenants, and
reminded them that "there was no one thing which tended
so much to the ruin of Napoleon in 1814 as the tenacity with
which, after the disasters at Leipsic, he clung to the Rhine."
Edwardes sent another warm letter of remonstrance against
the course John Lawrence seemed bent on following. "It is
absurd to engulf everything in the Delhi whirlpool," he wrote.
"Let us hold the frontier province, at all events, in strength,
and that will facilitate the reconquest of Central India by
the troops from England. But if we let go the frontier, all
India and the Punjab will have to be reconquered, and
perhaps a war with Afghanistan be added to it.   . . . My
belief is that on the reinforcements now being sent reaching
General Reid, Delhi will be stormed successfully; if not,
another thousand will not turn the scale, while their removal
will endanger the Punjab. It is not selfish. It is the good of the
empire. Don't get engulfed in Delhi." John Lawrence had in the
mean time written to Lord Canning and asked that an answer
might be sent in one of two forms–"Hold on Peshawar to the
last," or "You may act as may appear expedient regarding
Peshawar." He informed the Governor-General that Cotton,
Edwardes, and Nicholson were against the plan, but he
did not forward their letters of remonstrance. Edwardes on
learning this requested they should be sent. In August came

the telegram from Lord Canning, "Hold on Peshawar to the last." The controversy regarding the evacuation of Peshawar has been discussed with more passion than judgment. John Lawrence thought that the safety of the empire depended on Delhi being taken even if Peshawar had to be abandoned; Edwardes thought that the safety of the empire depended on retaining Peshawar even if the siege of Delhi had to be raised. Edwardes was right. In India we can never afford to retreat. The abandonment of Peshawar would most probably have led to the loss of the Punjab, and then the siege of Delhi must have been abandoned.

It was a choice between two great evils, but happily such a choice never became necessary. On September 14 came the telegram, "Delhi assaulted, and fighting still going on. The attack successful." Then came the sad tidings that Nicholson, the dearest friend of his life, was severely wounded, and after days of keen suspense that the hero was dead. On his deathbed the stern warrior sent a message of tender humility to Edwardes: "Tell him I should have been a better man if I had continued to live with him, and our heavy public duties had not prevented my seeing more of him privately. I was always the better for a residence, however short, with him and his wife. Give my love to them both." "The fall of Delhi has pacified wonderfully," wrote Edwardes to his wife. "At Peshawar nearly all interest in the struggle seems to have dropped among the people. Their whole energies are now thrown into illuminating their own city in honour of the English victory." The crisis over, Edwardes, who sadly needed rest, wished to join his wife at home, but public duties kept him at his post, and he did not reach England till June 1859.

Before leaving Peshawar he gave his house to the mission as a "parting offering of my own and my dear wife's goodwill and earnest wish for its increasing prosperity and usefulness. The house is in good order and should rent, I think, for Rs. 110 or Rs. 120 a-month, which would replace our failing help, and provide also for the annual repairs. I have no conditions to impose whatever. Do with it whatever is best for the interests of the mission, as that is our object."

Edwardes came home to rest, but to a nature like his complete rest was an impossibility. He was asked by the family of Sir Henry Lawrence to write the biography of the old friend, of whom he wrote, "If I have been able to serve Government to any purpose, I owe it to your teaching and example," [1] and he consented. It was a labour of love, but it was severe labour. Fragmentary letters, scraps of writing, important and unimportant, had to be carefully arranged and examined; and the handwriting was difficult to decipher. The writing of the Life fully occupied his time till the summer came, when he had to take his wife to Kissingen for the benefit of the waters. Before he left England the offer came to him of the appointment of the Commissioner of Umballa and Governor-General's agent for the Cis-Sutlej states. He had hoped for another year at home to finish the Life, but the appointment could not be kept open, and in 1862 Edwardes and his wife returned to India. During his stay in England he received a K.C.B., and the honorary degree from the University of Cambridge. After a short stay at Calcutta Edwardes joined his new appointment. He did good work for the State, but it grieved him to find that individual

---

[1.] Dedication of *'A Year on the Punjab Frontier.'*

administration in the Punjab had been supplanted by office forms and regulations. He wrote: "Very soon we shall have all the estrangement and class-feeling and ignorance of the old North-West Provinces. It passes my comprehension to find how things have gone exactly the wrong way. How palpably every one felt during the Mutiny that India ought to be unregulationised, yet it has ended by a greater flood of regulations, and yet all, I believe, with the best possible intentions." In a letter written to his old friend, Sir Donald Macleod, he says: "Perhaps one of the things which chafed me so of late years, and made the last three years that I was at Umballa the most burdensome and unhappy of my public life, was the state of machinery to which we had all been reduced, and the daily sense that I had less power than I had eighteen years before, when dear Sir Henry Lawrence sent us forth to do our best for chiefs and people, and supported us in doing it." Only one appointment in India would have caused Sir Herbert Edwardes to have stayed in India after his pension had been earned—the lieutenant - governorship of the Punjab, but when the high office became vacant he wrote to John Lawrence: "I would repeat now, with all my heart, what I have said often to you at home and in letters, that if my voice could get the Punjab for Donald Macleod he should have it. But truly do I consider that not only his claim is *first*, but that he is the *best* man for the Punjab." Not all his deeds in the field reflect greater honour on Herbert Edwardes than this act of self-sacrifice, for his claims to the office were undoubtedly great, and in many respects superior to those of his friend. Five years afterwards, when there seemed a prospect of the lieutenant-governorship again falling vacant, the Governor-General telegraphed to England to ask Sir Herbert to take it. But he was too ill to accept the offer. The day of toil and labour was flitting away and the hour of rest was fast drawing nigh. It came on the 23rd December 1868. Love for all that is good and true, reverence for all that is great and noble, a spirit of humility, had their roots in the depths of his soul. Such a man makes us prouder of our race, and the memory of men like Darcy Tod, Havelock, Henry Lawrence, Herbert Edwardes, is a precious inheritance of all Englishmen.

SIR THOMAS MUNRO.

SIR THOMAS MUNRO.

Sir Thomas Munro was born at Glasgow on the 27th May 1761; his father was engaged in trade; and at the age of sixteen young Munro entered the counting-house of some West India merchants. He remained in this employment for two years, when, his father's affairs becoming involved, he accepted a commission and landed at Madras on the 15th January 1780. In July of the same year the hosts of Hyder Ali came pouring through those wild passes which, torn by mountain torrents and dark with jungle, lead down from the table-land of Mysore to the plains of the Carnatic. Hyder was everywhere triumphant. The English inhabitants of Madras could see by night from the top of Mount Thomas the eastern sky reddened by a vast semicircle of blazing villages. Munro's first active service was with the army under the command of his namesake, Lieutenant-General Munro, which had been sent to meet the invading force. He was present at the General's disastrous retreat–which might be called a flight–and he took part in the great victory of Porto Novo, by which Coote retrieved the honour of English arms. Munro spent the three years of peace which followed the death of Hyder Ali in garrison duties at different stations. He was for a short time employed in the Intelligence Department, being selected on account of his proficiency in Hindustani and Persian. When war broke out afresh with Tippoo, he rejoined his regiment and was again engaged in active service. During the years 1791 and 1792 he was present at most of the operations under Lord Cornwallis, and took part in the siege of Bangalore. He was at Seringapatam when Lord Cornwallis on the 24th of February 1792 issued the following order: "Lord Cornwallis has great pleasure in announcing to the army that preliminaries of peace have been settled between the confederate Powers and Tippoo Sultan." Lord Cornwallis was apprehensive that he should have been driven to the necessity of taking Seringapatam, and frequently exclaimed, "Great God! what shall I do with this place?" "I could have said," writes Munro to his father, "'Keep it, as the best barrier you have to your own countries; and be confident that, with it and such a frontier as the Cavery, skirted by vast ranges of rugged mountains, no Indian Power will ever venture to attack you.'" Munro, in the masterly narrative of events sent to his father, describes Tippoo as incomparably the most powerful and dangerous enemy of the English at the time, and points at the mockery of making a peace with an inveterate foe which deprived him of half his revenue, "though he has by no means lost half his power." The folly of making peace with Tippoo was the burden of all his arguments, and the justness of his views was proved by the decisive policy adopted by the Marquess of Wellesley. In March 1792 Munro accompanied the detachment in charge of the two sons of Tippoo, who were sent as hostages to Madras; and in the following month

he was appointed one of the three military assistants
deputed to conduct the civil administration of the
Baramahal.

The greater part of the present district of Salem was then
designated the Baramahal, and was ceded to us under the
treaty of Seringapatam. Lord Cornwallis determined that the
newly acquired territory should be administered by military
officers. The chief place was given to Captain Alexander Read
and Munro, and two other young officers were appointed his
assistants. Munro's life in his new charge was a life of incessant
labour. He described the system of revenue management as
one of "plain hard labour." He acquired experience in dealing
with men and a thorough acquaintance with all the details
connected with the tenure of land by going from village to
village settling the rent of the inhabitants. The *ryotwar* system,
which prevails in the greater part of the Madras Presidency
and in the Bombay Presidency, was originated by Read in
the Baramahal, and extended by the powerful advocacy of
his subordinates. Munro was a staunch advocate of moderate
assessments, and he was ever in favour of fixity in the rate of
assessment, so far as this could be conceded with a due regard
to the necessities of the State. "The great point in making a
settlement," wrote Munro, "is the rate of assessment—all other
regulations connected with it are of very inferior importance."
He strongly objected to the taxation of improvements effected
by the *ryots* themselves, as, for instance, the imposition of a
higher assessment upon land watered from a well constructed
by a *ryot* at his own expense. He clearly saw that India
not only wants gigantic works of irrigation—enduring
monuments of our engineering skill—but also small works,

which will irrigate those districts and villages most likely to
be visited by the calamity of famine. Munro wrote—

Nothing could more tend to secure a country from famine than
numerous wells. They are so little affected by the seasons that
their crops seldom fail; they require no expensive repairs; they
do not fill up, nor are they liable to be swept away by floods, or
to be destroyed by an enemy, like tanks; but they enable the
cultivator to resume his labour, without even waiting for rain,
the moment the danger is over.

Had it ever been the practice under Indian Governments,
instead of building tanks themselves, to have let the *ryots*
do it, without raising their rents, there would now have been
infinitely more wet-lands than there are: an equal or greater
revenue from them, and without any expense to the public.
If the old system of imposing an additional rent on every
improvement be persevered in, the people will remain for ever
poor, and revenue uncertain.

Though the work was hard Munro found life extremely
enjoyable in Baramahal. India was not to him "a dull and
beastly land," because he surveyed everything with the
vigilance and delight of a cultivated and active intellect. No
man has ever painted with so much fidelity the rural life
of India, and he carries us into the very heart of the scenes
he describes. Having all the sympathies of an English
gentleman and the training of an administrator, he was not
only an exact observer but also a liberal judge of the natives.
He could appreciate the charity, the kindness to old and
young, the patience and good-humour of the most thrifty
and law-abiding peasantry in the world. His ability, his
accessibility, his firmness, his sense of justice, his profound
knowledge of the native language and character, of the
husbandry and domestic habits of the cultivator, gained for

him from the natives whom he governed the title of their "father." He gives us some charming pictures of his familiar intercourse with them as he travelled from village to village settling their rent. The following places us at once by the side of the district officer and the scenes which he passes through:—

At this moment, while I am writing, there are a dozen of people talking around me: it is now twelve o'clock, and they have been coming and going in parties ever since seven in the morning, when I began this letter. They have frequently interrupted me for an hour at a time. One man has a long story of a debt of thirty years' standing, contracted by his father. Another tells me that his brother made away with his property when he was absent during the war; and a third tells me that he cannot afford to pay his usual rent, because his wife is dead, who used to do more work than his best bullock. I am obliged to listen to all these relations; and as every man has a knack at description, like Sancho, I think myself fortunate when I get through any one of them in half an hour. It is in vain that I sometimes recommend to them to begin at the end of the story. They persist in their own way of making me full master of all the particulars; and I must, after making my objections and hearing their replies, dictate answers in the same copious style to them all.

The following throws more light upon the character of the rustic population than many a learned essay by the modern traveller:—

At this season of the year I take so much pleasure in these rambles, that I find it difficult to confine myself to my tent. They are not so solitary as I could wish; for I often fall in with story-tellers, who keep me company all the way. The farmers of this country are, I believe, the most talkative race on the face of the earth. A party of them met me this evening with a complaint against some unknown conjurer, who had set fire to their village twice in the course of the year. I told them I had a great antipathy to all conjurers, and would give them satisfaction on their producing him. They said they had concerted a plan for discovering him, but that it could not be executed without my assistance. I was to take my station at a little distance from the village, with a spying-glass in my hand all the inhabitants were to pass in review before me; when I could not fail, by means of the virtues of the glass, to discover the felon who had done so much mischief. I answered that it was an excellent thought, but that the trial must be deferred till I should get a new glass, as my old one was broken; and as we should then certainly catch the conjurer, I asked what punishment it would be proper to inflict upon him. They said, no other than drawing two of his teeth, with which he would lose all his magic powers. I replied that this could not be done till he was taken; but that, in the mean time, there was another remedy, equally simple, at hand–to defend themselves from him in future: any person who had any suspicion of his having evil designs upon himself, had only to get two of his own teeth drawn, which would secure both himself and his property against all the art of the enemy. I said I had some years ago parted with two of my own teeth; and offered, if they would accompany me back, to get them all made magic-proof at the same cheap rate. They asked leave to go home and consult about my proposal, and promised to give me their answer in the morning; but I suspect that I shall hear no more of the matter.

Munro's administration in Baramahal is a vivid exemplification of the personal rule which created our Indian Empire. Munro, Metcalfe, Elphinstone, Jonathan Duncan, Thomason, knew the people, and by their sympathy and frankness gained their confidence. The rule by a centralised bureaucracy will go far to destroy it. The modern collector, on whose administration the happiness and prosperity of the people and the stability of the empire mainly depends, is no longer, like Munro, the "father" of the people. He is fast becoming a mere instrument for carrying the orders of centralised bureaucracy, and all originality and independence are fast perishing. Men no longer administer large areas, but boys carry out orders. The gulf between the rulers and the ruled grows wider day by day. The effects of government by bureaucratic resolutions, by reports and statistics, are to be read in letter of blood in the history of the *ancien régime*. Munro left the scene of his benevolent exertions in 1799, when war with Tippoo having again broken out, his chief, Colonel Read, was appointed to command a force, and Munro accompanied him as his secretary. The war was of short duration, and ended in the gallant capture of Seringapatam and the death of Tippoo. Munro, on the conclusion of the campaign, was appointed to the charge of Canara, one of the territories which now became British. He found it in a state of anarchy and poverty, and met with the greatest difficulty in even commencing a settlement of the revenue. The *ryots* refused to attend for the purpose save under certain conditions. Patience and firmness, however, won the day, and by a careful examination into the circumstances of the district, and a scrutiny into its ancient records, he was able to make a settlement which has formed the basis of all subsequent arrangements with reference to the land revenue of Canara, now one of the most flourishing provinces of India.

After having been sixteen months in Canara, Munro was transferred to the charge of the districts which had just been ceded to the Company by the *Nizam*. The area of the territory which he was now called upon to administer was little short of 27,000 square miles. The seven years which he spent in governing it formed probably the most important period in his official life. He won the confidence and attachment of all classes of the population. The memory of his good work still survives. The appellation by which Munro was most commonly known to the people of the ceded districts was that of the Colonel "Dora," with reference to the military rank which he held during the greater part of his service as Principal Collector; and to this day it is considered a sufficient answer to inquiries regarding the reason for any revenue rule that it was laid down by Colonel Dora.

After Munro had been a couple of years in the ceded districts the second war with the Mahrattas took place. On the 2nd of December 1802 the Peshwa, a fugitive from Poona, made with the British a "treaty of defensive alliance and reciprocal protection." The treaty of Bassein gave great offence to the other Mahratta chiefs, who were shrewd enough to see that the system of subsidiary alliances with the British was fatal to the independence of native states. The treaty, though it was not the immediate, was the real *casus belli*. The first great blow delivered in the war was the capture of Ahmednagar, Scindia's great arsenal, August 12, 1803. This was followed on the 23rd of September by the decisive victory of Assaye. On the 14th of October Munro wrote to his friend:—

I have seen several accounts of your late glorious victory over the combined armies of Scindia and the Berar man, but none of them so full as to give me anything like a correct idea of it. I can, however, see dimly through the smoke of the Mahratta guns (for yours, it is said, were silenced) that a gallanter action has not been fought for many years in any part of the world. When not only the disparity of numbers, but also of real military force, is considered, it is beyond all comparison a more brilliant and arduous exploit than that of Aboukir. The detaching of Stevenson was so dangerous a measure that I am almost tempted to think that you did it with a view of sharing the glory with the smallest possible numbers. The object of this movement was probably to turn the enemy's flank, or to cut them off from the Ajunta Pass; but these ends would have been attained with as much certainty and more security by keeping him with you. As a reserve he would have supported your attack, secured it against any disaster, and when it succeeded, he would have been at hand to have followed the enemy vigorously. A native army once routed, if followed by a good body of cavalry, never affords any effectual opposition. Had Stevenson been with you, it is likely that you would have destroyed the greatest part of the enemy's infantry: as to their cavalry, when cavalry are determined to run, it is not easy to do them much harm unless you are strong enough to disperse your own in pursuit of them. Whether the detaching of Stevenson was right or wrong, the noble manner in which the battle was conducted makes up for everything.

On the 1st of November General Wellesley replied:–

CAMP AT Cherikain, *November 1st*, 1803.

MY DEAR MUNRO,—As you are a judge of a military operation, and as I am desirous of having your opinion on my side, I am about to give you an account of the battle at Assye[1] in answer to your letter of the 19th October; in which I think I shall solve all the doubts which must naturally occur to any man who looks at that transaction without a sufficient knowledge of the facts. Before you will receive this, you will most probably have seen my public letter to the Governor-General regarding the action, a copy of which was sent to General Campbell. That letter will give you a general outline of the facts. Your principal objection to the action is,

---

[1] The Duke of Wellington always spelt it Assye. The most correct way of spelling the name of the village is Asai.

that I detached Colonel Stevenson. The fact is, I did not detach
Colonel Stevenson. His was a separate corps equally strong,
if not stronger than mine. We were desirous to engage the
enemy at the same time, and settled a plan accordingly for
an attack on the morning of the 24th. We separated on the
22nd—he to march by the western, I by the eastern road, round
the hills between Budnapore and Jalna; and I have to observe
that this separation was necessary,—first, because both corps
could not pass through the same defiles in one day; secondly,
because it was to be apprehended that if we left open one of the
roads through those hills, the enemy might have passed to the
southward while we were going to the northward, and then the
action would have been delayed, or probably avoided altogether.
Colonel Stevenson and I were never more than twelve miles
distant from each other; and when I moved forward to the
action of the 23rd, we were not much more than eight miles. As
usual, we depended for our intelligence of the enemy's position
on the common *hircarrahs* of the country. Their horse were so
numerous, that without an army their position could not be
reconnoitred by an European officer; and even the *hircarrahs*
in our own service, who were accustomed to examine and report
on positions, cannot be employed here, as, being natives of the
Carnatic, they are as well known as an European.

The *hircarrahs* reported the enemy to be at Bokerdun. Their
right was at Bokerdun, which was the principal place in their
position, and gave the name to the district in which they were
encamped; but their left, in which was their infantry, which I
was to attack, was at Assye, which was six or eight miles from
Bokerdun.

I directed my march so as to be within twelve or fourteen
miles of their army at Bokerdun, as I thought, on the 23rd.
But when I arrived at the ground of encampment, I found
that I was not more than five or six miles from it. I was then
informed that the cavalry had marched, and the infantry was
about to follow, but was still on the ground: at all events, it was
necessary to ascertain these points, and I could not venture
to reconnoitre without my whole force. But I believed the
report to be true, and I determined to attack the infantry if it

remained still upon the ground. I apprised Colonel Stevenson of this determination, and desired him to move forward. Upon marching on I found not only their infantry but their cavalry encamped in a most formidable position which, by the by, it could have been impossible for me to attack, if, when the infantry changed their front, they had taken care to occupy the only passage there was across the Kaitna.

When I found their whole army, and contemplated their position, of course I considered whether I should attack immediately, or should delay till the following morning. I determined upon the immediate attack, because I saw clearly that if I attempted to return to my camp at Naulniah, I should have been followed thither by the whole of the enemy's cavalry, and I might have suffered some loss: instead of attacking, I might have been attacked there in the morning; and, at all events, I should have found it very difficult to secure my baggage, as I did, in any place so near the enemy's camp, in which they should know it was. I therefore determined upon the attack immediately.

It was certainly a most desperate one; but our guns were not silenced. Our bullocks, and the people who were employed to draw them, were shot, and they could not all be drawn on, but some were; and all continued to fire as long as the fire could be of any use.

Desperate as the action was, our loss would not have exceeded one-half of its present amount, if it had not been for a mistake in the officer who led the picquets which were on the right of the first line.

When the enemy changed their position, they threw their left to Assye, in which village they had some infantry; and it was surrounded by cannon. As soon as I saw that, I directed the officer commanding the picquets to keep out of shot from that village. Instead of that, he led directly upon it; the 79th, which were on the right of the first line, followed the picquets, and the great loss we sustained was in these two bodies. Another evil which resulted from this mistake was the necessity of introducing the cavalry into the cannonade and the action, long before it was time, by which that corps lost many men, and its unity and efficiency, which I intended to bring forward in a close pursuit at the heel of the day. But it was necessary to bring forward the cavalry to save the remains of the 79th and the picquets, which would otherwise have been entirely destroyed. Another evil resulting from it was, that we had then no reserve left, and a parcel of straggling horse cut up our wounded; and straggling infantry who had pretended to be dead, turned their guns upon our backs.

After all, notwithstanding this attack upon Assye by our right and the cavalry, no impression was made upon the corps collected there, till I made a movement upon it with some troops taken from our left, after the enemy's right had been defeated; and it would have been as well to have left it alone entirely till that movement was made. However, I do not wish to cast any reflection upon the officer who led the picquets. I lament the consequences of his mistake; but I must acknowledge that it was not possible for a man to lead a body into a hotter fire than he did the picquets on that day against Assye.

After the action there was no pursuit, because our cavalry was not then in a state to pursue. It was near dark when the action was over; and we passed the night on the field of battle.

Colonel Stevenson marched with part of his corps as soon as he heard that I was about to move forward, and he also moved upon Bokerdun. He did not receive my letter till evening. He got entangled in a *nullah* in the night, and arrived at Bokerdun, about eight miles from me to the westward, at eight in the morning of the 24th.

The enemy passed the night of the 23rd at about twelve miles from the field of battle, twelve from the Adjuntee [Ajunta] Ghaut, and eight from Bokerdun. As soon as they heard that Colonel Stevenson was advancing to the latter place, they set off, and never stopped till they had got down the Ghaut, where they arrived in the course of the night of the 24th. After his difficulties of the night of the 23rd, Colonel Stevenson was in no state to follow them, and did not do so till the 26th. The reason for which he was detained till that day was, that I might have the benefit of the assistance of his surgeons to dress my wounded soldiers, many of whom, after all, were not dressed for nearly a week, for want of the necessary number of medical men.

Munro, who by the light of the rules of war had criticised the mode of attack, admitted that "though it might not have been the safest it was undoubtedly the most decided and heroic; it will have the effect of striking greater terror into the hostile armies than could have been done by any victory gained with the assistance of Colonel Stevenson's division, and of raising the national military character, already high in India, still higher."

After having administered the ceded districts for seven years, Munro resigned his appointment and took furlough to England. He had not been home for twenty-eight years. After a passage of rather more than five months he landed at Deal on the 5th of April 1808. Time had wrought its usual effects. His mother, whom he had so fondly loved, his two brothers, and many of his acquaintances were dead; his father was fast approaching his end. There was now little in common between him and the old friends who had survived. Nature, however, remained the same, and with him the love of nature was a strong passion. The mysteries of mountains, woods, and rivers appealed to his imagination. He writes to his sister:—

A solitary walk is almost the only thing in which I have any enjoyment. I have been twice at Northside, and though it rained without ceasing on both days, it did not prevent me from rambling up and down the river from Claysloup to the aqueduct bridge. I stood above an hour at Jackson's dam, looking at the water rushing over, while the rain and withered leaves were descending thick about me, and while I recalled the days that are past. The wind whistling through the trees, and the water tumbling over the dam, had still the same sound as before; but the darkness of the day, and the little smart box perched upon the opposite bank, destroyed much of the illusion, and made me feel that former times were gone. I don't know how it is, but, when I look back to early years, I always associate sunshine with them; when I think of Northwood-side, I always think of a fine day, with the sunbeams down upon Kelvin and its woody banks. I do not enter completelyinto early scenes of life in gloomy, drizzling weather.

But Munro had mixed in the great game. The poison was in his veins. He repaired to London, where a searching inquiry regarding Indian affairs was at that time being instituted by the House of Commons, and Munro's evidence regarding the organisation of the army and the great departments of the civil administration was of the highest value to the Parliamentary Committee. He strongly advocated that every officer on first going out to India should be employed one or two years with a European regiment until he had learnt his duty, and that "he ought not to be transferred to a *sepoy* corps until, by previously serving with a European one, he had made himself master of all his duties, and likewise, by being in some degree acquainted with the character of the natives, qualified to command and to act with *sepoys*." The judicial and police arrangements in the Madras Presidency were regarded by Munro as involving too great a departure from native institutions to work with success. He strongly advocated the revival of the *panchayet* or village council. In the summer of 1814 Munro, having been married barely seven weeks, sailed for Madras to be the head of a Special Commission formed to carry out his recommendations. The Commission was viewed with disfavour by the Madras authorities, who did all they could to obstruct it. However,

Munro, backed up by the home authorities, overcame all difficulties, and in two years a series of enactments framed by him was passed. These measures have been extended in principle, if not in form, throughout India. Within the last few years the various administrations have been invited to consider the expediency of extending the Madras system of village tribunals to their respective provinces. The labours of the judicial Commissioner had hardly been concluded when circumstances occurred which led to Munro's re-employment in a military capacity. The aggressions of the *Pindarees* had forced the Governor-General—the Marquess of Hastings—to take up the gauntlet against them. A few weeks before the *Pindaree* war began the Peshwa, on account of his intrigues, had been compelled by the English to cede certain districts, and Munro had to proceed to Dharwar to take charge of the newly acquired territory, the military as well as civil command of which was placed under him. Shortly after he took charge the war broke out, and Munro was at once invested with the rank of Brigadier-General and the command of the reserve division formed to reduce the southern Mahratta country. The Peshwa had been defeated at Kirkee and was moving southwards. At this crisis Munro displayed both spirit and fertility of resource. With a very slender force he entered the enemy's country, took several of his strongest forts, followed up a large body of the Peshwa's infantry with thirteen guns to Sholapore, where he defeated them, and the capture of the strong fort of Sholapore followed. With the reduction of Sholapore the subjugation of the southern Mahratta country was complete. The war being over, Munro relinquished his command and prepared to go to England. His services elicited his praise from the Governor-General; and Canning spoke of him in the House of Commons as a gentleman "than whom Europe never produced a more accomplished statesman, nor India, fertile in heroes, a more skilful soldier."

Munro's stay at home was very short. A few weeks after his arrival he received intimation that he had been nominated Governor of Madras. When the chairman of the East India Directors mentioned the name of Munro to Canning, the last of a dynasty of statesmen said, "Nay, if you have such a card as that, it must be played." It was not without reluctance that Munro decided on accepting it. He was already fifty-eight years of age, and had spent upwards of thirty-two years in India. In the last days of 1819 Munro embarked for India, and he assumed office on the 8th June 1820. A bureaucratic world improves but slowly. Munro, like all Indian governors after him, found not only that his time was occupied by the necessary business of office, but that much of it was taken up in reading masses of papers and useless altercations between different departments." He wrote to Mr Canning: "By not coming to India you have escaped the irksome task of toiling daily through heaps of heavy long-drawn papers. I never had a very high opinion of our records, but it was not until my last return that I knew that they contained such a mass of trash." There are no exciting events, no exceptional circumstances, for the biographer to record in Munro's administration. He was a good ruler, because he studied those whom he governed, and gained a place in their hearts by his justice and sympathy. He made frequent tours through the country which he governed, and was always accessible to the people. He writes to Lady Munro, "I like to recognise among them a great number of my old acquaintances, who, I hope, are as glad to see me as I to see them." But though Munro enjoyed his tours, and took deep interest in his responsible and laborious office, he had returned to Madras with the fixed determination of leaving India for ever 1823 he after a residence of three or four years. In addressed to the Directors a memorial to be relieved, but before he received an answer the first Burmese war broke out. The calm verdict of history is that it was one of defence and violated territory, but there were not wanting multitudes at the moment to condemn both the cause and the conduct. "The case is," Munro wrote to his old friend, now his Grace the Duke of Wellington, "a clear one of self-defence and violated territory, and I have little doubt but that fortune will on this occasion take the right side." Eager as he was to return home, Munro at once volunteered, in the event of no successor being appointed, to continue at the head of the Madras Government. The offer was readily embraced by the Court of Directors. "We are happy," they wrote, "to signify to you our unanimous desire to avail ourselves of an extension of Sir Thomas Munro's services in that high station, at a period when his distinguished talents and peculiar qualifications cannot fail of being eminently beneficial to the country under your government as well as to our interests." His distinguished talents are shown in the minutes and letters he wrote to the Governor-General regarding the prosecution of the war, and his peculiar qualifications as an administrator by the zeal and energy he displayed in sending troops, ships, boats, transport bullocks, and supplies to the seat of war. It was through the prompt and indefatigable exertions of Munro that the army of invasion was saved from perishing from lack of food. As it was in the beginning, now, and ever shall be, we had begun the campaign with an inadequate force. Munro writes:—

It is always dangerous, and often fatal to success, to have a force only sufficient to maintain themselves in a hostile country, and none to spare for detachments or distant offensive operations which it may occasionally be found advisable to undertake. It was a great advantage to begin a campaign with commanding force, particularly in a country recently conquered. It discourages the enemy, and encourages the people of the country to join and aid us, in the hope of regaining their independence. The occupation of Rangoon ought not to make us relax in the smallest degree our preparations, or to believe that it will bring us any nearer to a peace. Our safest and our speediest way of arriving at an honourable peace is to consider the first success as only the beginning of a general war with the Burman empire, and to engage in it with our whole disposable force.

Munro adds:—

I do know of only one thing likely to induce the king to hold out–the idea that we would not keep the country, but would get tired of the war and withdraw our forces. Whatever may be intended in this respect, it will be advisable to indicate by our whole conduct a fixed desire of keeping our conquests.

For two years after the occupation of Rangoon a war was carried on, and then concluded by a peace far too moderate. The arrogance of the Burmese suffered no abatement, and a second war was necessary to ensure what should have been ensured by the first war–the peace and prosperity of Further India.

For his distinguished exertions in the conduct of the Burmese war Munro was raised to the dignity of baronet. The honour was won by a costly sacrifice, for it entailed upon him separation from his wife and child. Owing to the indisposition of Lady Munro and the severe illness of their second son, who was born to them at Madras, they left in March 1826 for England. Munro describes, in a few simple words, perhaps the most common and the most melancholy scene in an Indian career,—the farewell on deck, the walk down the ladder, the watching of the ship till the masts sink beneath the horizon, the drive home, the empty house, and the toy lying on the floor. Soon after his wife's departure he wrote to her from Government House at Guinde:—

We came here for the first time since you went away. We alighted at the old place near the well. It was nearly dark, and we passed through the garden without finding you. . . . The cause which occasioned the desertion of this house gives everything about it a melancholy appearance. I dislike to enter Kamen's room (his son's nursery name). How delightful it was to see him walking or running, or stopping to endeavour to explain something with his hands to explain his language! How easy and artless and beautiful are all the motions of a child—everything that he does is graceful! All his little ways are endearing, and they are the arms which nature has given him for his protection—because they make everybody feel an attachment for him. . . . Your rooms look very desolate; they are empty all day, and in the evening have one solitary lamp. I now go along the passage without seeing a human being, and often think of him running out to pull my coat. I cannot tell you how much I long to see him playing again.

He never saw him playing again. On the very day that the news of the definite treaty with Ava reached

Madras, Sir Thomas despatched several copies of a letter to
the Directors expressing his earnest wish to be relieved at
once. Pending the arrival of his successor he determined on
making a tour of inspection in the ceded districts. Towards
the end of March 1827 he set out, attended by a small escort,
and experienced "the great pleasure of passing through
countries enjoying profound peace and full of industrious
inhabitants which he had formerly seen desolate and laid
waste by a destructive enemy." To do this work is the
destiny of the English race. On the morning of the 16th of
July, whilst transacting business in the audience-tent, he
was suddenly seized with cholera.

He spoke with perfect calmness and collectedness, assured
his friends that he had frequently been as ill before, regretted
the trouble he occasioned to those about him, and entreated
them to quit the tent. "This is not fair," said he, "to keep you
in an infected chamber;" and when told that no apprehensions
were entertained, because there was no risk of infection, he
repeated his usual observation, "That point has not been
determined; you had better be on the safe side and leave me."
It was now one o'clock in the day, and his pulse being full and
good, sanguine hopes were encouraged that all might yet be
well; but from that time he failed rapidly, and the fears of his
friends and attendants became seriously excited. About three,
however, he rallied, and feeling better, exclaimed, with a tone
of peculiar sweetness, "that it was almost worth while to be
ill in order to be so kindly nursed." Between three and four
no event of importance occurred, except that he repeatedly
alluded to the trouble which he gave, and constantly urged
the gentlemen around him to withdraw; but soon after he
himself remarked that his voice was getting weaker and his
sense of hearing more acute. These were the last articulate
sounds which he uttered, for the disease increased rapidly
upon him; and though faint hopes were more than once

entertained, owing to the appearance of certain favourable symptoms, for the apprehensions that accompanied them there was too much ground. Sir Thomas Munro lingered till half-past nine in the evening, and then fell asleep.

About an hour after his death they took the corpse to Gooty, and hundreds of natives who had flocked there to see the man whom they remembered by the name of Father wept as they lowered it into the grave. "The situation of the churchyard," writes one who was present, "the melancholy sound of the minute-guns reverberating among the hills, the grand and frowning appearance of the fortress towering above Gooty—all tended to make the awful ceremony more impressive." Not far from where his dust rests there is a *choultry* or rest-house for travellers built by the natives of the district, and it is shaded by a grove which they reverentially planted. The *choultry* at Gooty, in Southern India, the monument to Cleveland, who won the confidence of the hill tribes on the Bengal frontier, Jacob's tomb on the Sind frontier, bear witness how by justice and conciliation the loyalty of vanquished races has been won. Every Indian statesman who is engaged in the task of ruling the people and winning over their minds should study Munro's weighty utterances on the great perennial questions of Indian politics. His views on the progress of education and the duty of admitting the natives of India to their fair share in the government of their country were much in advance of his own day. He attached little value to schemes for improving the education of natives, unless, *pari passu*, steps were taken for extending to them a greater share in the honours and

emoluments of office. The following are some of the truest
words ever written by an Indian statesman:—

There can be no hope of any great zeal for improvement when
the highest acquirements can lead to nothing beyond some
petty office, and can confer neither wealth nor honour. While
the prospects of the natives are so bounded, every project for
bettering their characters must fail, and no such projects can
have the smallest chance of success unless some of these objects
are placed within their reach for the sake of which men are
urged to exertion in other countries. This work of improvement,
in whatever way it may be accepted, must be very slow, but
it will be in proportion to the degree of confidence which we
repose in them, and to the share which we give them in the
administration of public affairs.

SIR DAVID BAIRD.

SIR DAVID BAIRD AND A FORGOTTEN INDIAN EXPEDITION TO EGYPT.

DAVID BAIRD was born in the year that Clive laid the foundation-stone of the fabric of our Indian Empire at Plassey. At the early age of fifteen he entered the army as an ensign in the 2nd Regiment of Foot, and joined the corps at Gibraltar in the year 1773. Four years afterwards he was appointed captain in the famous 73rd, and sailed with them to India in the spring of 1779. At the Cape, which then belonged to the Dutch, the fleet remained three months, and it was not till January 1780 that the gallant Highlanders landed at Madras. Six months after their arrival Hyder found his way through the Ghauts and burst like a mountain torrent into the Carnatic. Ruthlessly he laid waste the whole country, and in a few days he was only fifty miles from Fort St George. It was proposed to place Lord Macleod, who commanded the Highlanders, at the head of a small force of 6000 men to be despatched at once to meet the host of Hyder. Lord Macleod, however, was an able and cautious soldier. He agreed to assume the command of the army, but only when it should be properly formed and equipped for service.

In his remonstrance to the Government of Madras he used the following rough expression, which deserves to be borne in mind. "I," said his lordship, "have been a great many years in the service, and I have always observed that when you despise the enemy he generally gives you a d—d rap over the knuckles." In consequence of Lord Macleod's refusal, Sir Hector Munro, the commander-in-chief, proceeded with a small force to meet Hyder, and Lord Macleod's words came true. Orders were sent to Colonel Baillie, who was in the Northern Circars, to meet the commander-in-chief at Conjeveram, about forty miles from Madras, on the road to Arcot. Sir Henry Munro reached Conjeveram, but Hyder, by a skilful manoeuvre, placed the main body of his army between the two English corps, and on the 10th of September surrounded the small detachment of Baillie's. His brave force fought with desperate valour against overwhelming odds, and were on the eve of achieving victory when the explosion of their tumbrils deprived them of their ammunition and the services of their artillery. Baillie formed his men into a square, and without ammunition received and repulsed thirteen attacks of the enemy's squadrons. After the contest had lasted one hour and a quarter, and the force had been reduced to 400 men, Baillie resolved to surrender. Hyder promised to spare their lives, and Colonel Baillie directed Captain Baird to order his men to ground their arms. The instant the order was obeyed, the enemy's cavalry rushed upon them and attacked the defenceless and the wounded. The greater part of Captain Baird's company of Highlanders were cut to pieces, and he himself, having received two sabre-wounds on his head, a ball in his thigh, and a pike-wound in his arm, fell senseless to the ground.

One of Hyder's horsemen found Baird on the field and gave him water to drink. Baird attempted to walk to camp aided by his generous foe, but he fainted thrice on the road, and the patience of the soldier being exhausted, he was left to die. Baird was discovered by a sergeant and a private of his own company, and they, though themselves severely wounded, helped their captain to reach the French camp. Here he was made prisoner and eventually sent by Hyder to Seringapatam, where he spent three years in one of its most noisome prisons. The journal which recounts the tortures the captives suffered, the hunger and scanty fare they had to endure, is one of the most ghastly tales of suffering ever recorded. The darkness of the picture is, however, lighted by noble acts of heroism and generosity. The boy Lang deserves to be remembered by Englishmen. Hyder ordered him to write to his father, who commanded Vellore, and offer him a splendid establishment if he surrendered the place, or the death of his son if he refused. Bravely did the lad reply. "If you consider *me*," said he, "base enough to write such a letter, on what ground can you think so meanly *of my father*? It is in your power to present me before the ramparts of Vellore and cut me into a thousand pieces in my father's presence, but it is out of your power to make him a traitor." All threats were found ineffectual, and the lad was remanded to the quarters of the other prisoners.

After the treaty of Mangalore in 1784, Baird, with the few who had survived the wasting effects of wounds and sickness, was released. Three years afterwards he received his majority and proceeded to England, and returned in 1791 to Madras to command his old regiment. Lord Cornwallis was now at war with Tippoo, and Colonel Baird was appointed to the command of a brigade of sepoys. He served with distinction in all the operations of the third Mysore war, and was present at Seringapatam when peace was concluded (1792). Next year he was present at Pondicherry, where all preparations had been made for a siege when the garrison surrendered. The British troops while before the place received accounts of the execution of Louis XVI., and newspapers and prints descriptive of the execution were thrown into the place in dead shells by the commanding officer of the artillery. After the surrender of Pondicherry the 71st was ordered to Tanjore, of which place Baird was appointed commandant. He displayed his honesty and generosity by taking the part of the Rajah against the Political Resident, who wished to annex the territory of Tanjore. The independent conduct of Baird did not please the Madras Government, and the regiment was removed to Walajabad. Here Colonel Baird remained till 1797, when, without any warning, he received an order immediately to break up his regiment and draft the men fit for service into the 73rd and 74th. To read the order to his men, with whom he had so often fought and bled, was too severe a task for the hero of Seringapatam, and he gave the paper to the adjutant, who read it. The effect produced was great. It seemed as if sudden dismay had seized the whole corps. Baird addressed to his old comrades a few words: "My poor fellows–not a word–the order must be obeyed," and then he ordered the band to strike up the popular Scottish air–

> "The King commands, and we'll obey,
> Over the hills and far away."

Colonel Baird, with the colours, officers, band, and invalids of his own regiment, arrived at the Cape of Good Hope in December 1797. He was not destined to reach England with the skeleton of his old corps, for Lord Macartney, the governor of the Cape, appointed him Brigadier-General, and gave him the command of a brigade. He only held his new command a year when he returned to India as Major-General. At Madras he found the Governor-General, the Marquess of Wellesley, who had come there for the purpose of collecting and forming the army which he had determined should take the field against Tippoo, who sent nothing but evasive or misleading answers to all his warnings, remonstrances, demands, and proposals. In February 1799 the Governor-General's forbearance could hold out no longer, and the English army was ordered to advance. General Baird was appointed to the command of the first European brigade and the Scottish brigade. The advance of the army was slow, for the troops were encumbered with materials for a siege, and delays were occasioned by the failure of the carriage-bullocks, which died in great numbers during the march. It was the 5th April before the army took up its position for the siege of Tippoo's island capital. On the 3rd May the breach was reported to be practicable, and preparations were made for the assault on the following day. The storming-party was placed under the command of Baird. On the forenoon of the 4th the silence which reigned in the trenches was broken by the voice of Baird. "Come, my brave fellows," he exclaimed, "follow me and show yourselves worthy of the name of British soldiers!" The effect was like magic. The men rushed forward, and after a short and severe struggle the breach was carried and the British colours were proudly floating on the summit of it.

"The moment," writes an eyewitness, "was one of agony; and we continued with aching eyes to watch the result, until after a short and appalling interval we saw the acclivity of the breach covered with a cloud of crimson; and in a very few minutes afterwards, observing the files passing rapidly to the right and left at the summit of the breach, I could not help exclaiming, 'Thank God, the business is done.'" [1]

Tippoo was dining when news was brought to him of the assault. He instantly washed his hands and called for his sword and fusils. Whilst buckling on his sword a messenger came running to tell him that Syed Goffar, his best officer, was killed. "Syed Goffar was never afraid of death," he said. "Let Mahommed Cawn take charge of Syed Goffar's division." The Sultan then ascended the north rampart, followed by four men who carried his fusils, by a fifth who carried a blunderbuss, and by two or three eunuchs. Standing behind one of the traverses on the ramparts he fired seven or eight times at the advancing assailants, and he brought down three or four of them. But on they pressed. The Mysoreans, fighting stubbornly, reluctantly abandoned every traverse. In vain did Tippoo mix with his struggling troops to sustain the fight,—he was carried by the retreating mass along the north rampart. Coming up with one of his horses, he mounted, complaining of fatigue and of the aching of a leg in which he had been slightly wounded. The

---

[1] *Memoirs of a Field Officer on the Retired List of the Indian Army,* p. 427.

water-gate was near, and he might have escaped through it; but he rode slowly towards a covered gateway which led through the inner rampart into the city.[1] He crossed the bridge which passed over the inner ditch, and as he was entering the sally-port he was again struck by a musket-shot. He pressed onwards, but he could not make his way through the crowd of fugitives. The assailants poured a murderous fire into each side of the arch. Tippoo was again struck, and his horse fell wounded. His attendants placed him in his palanquin, but it was impossible to carry him through the solid mass of dead and dying. On entering the gateway a British soldier, attracted by the glittering of the golden buckle, snatched at the sword-belt of Tippoo, who had crawled out of the litter. "The Sultan instantly stretched out his right hand (the lower part of his body being entangled amongst dead bodies), and snatching a drawn sword which happened to lie within his reach, made a stroke at the soldier. The blow falling upon his musket, he makes another stroke at another soldier with more effect, and immediately afterwards was killed by a musket -ball which penetrated his temple." [2] How the body was

---

[1] "Rajah Cauwn the only person now living who accompanied him during the whole forenoon of the 4th of May, declares that he could not discover where the Sultaun intended to go if he had succeeded in making his way into the town through the gate. He imagines, however, that his greatest anxiety was on account of his family; and that from some expressions which had fallen from him, he had conceived the design of putting them to death, under an apprehension that they would be exposed to indignities in the tumult and fury of the assault."—*A View of the Origin and Conduct of the War with Tippoo Sultaun,* by Lieut.-Colonel Alexander Beatson, p. 165.
[2] Ibid.

found hidden beneath a heap of slain is told in the following narrative [1]:–

On the 4th May 1799, after the complete possession of the fort of Seringapatam, a man by name Meer Nudeen, *killedar* of the fort and *depogah* of the *tosha khanee* or treasury, said that the *Badshaw* [for so Tippoo was then called by all his subjects] had been wounded and was then in the water-gate [called by the Hindus the *Huli Bagh*], upon which General Baird gave orders for a body of troops to move with all expedition to that gate, and the 33rd being on the spot were ordered there. General Baird accompanied us—the regiment marched left in front, and I was then in command of the light infantry company, which being in front caused General Baird to put the two natives before mentioned in my charge. They now became our guards, and were threatened with death if they deceived us. They led us to the gate, which we found filled with dead and dying heaped one over the other. General Baird ordered the regiment to pile their arms and look for Tippoo, who, it was now imagined, must have died of his wounds or made his escape, no wounded person like him being there. The light infantry of the 33rd were then ordered into the gate by Lieut.-Colonel Shee, who commanded the regiment, and a search was immediately commenced. The bodies were taken out one by one—they were at the time all on fire, as the cartouch-boxes had caught fire by accident and communicated from one to another. A palanquin was at one side of the gate and a dead horse at the other. After a tedious search, during which it appeared as if there were very little hope of finding Tippoo, which circumstance was then of the utmost consequence, the people came to a body, at which our guides looked very attentively and said it must be disengaged from the dead bodies which lay over it. After great difficulty this was effected, and on examination it was found to be Tippoo himself, although two Frenchmen who were sent for said it was a *jeminidar* who was remarkably like Tippoo, but on the body

---

[1] It has never before been printed, and has been kindly lent to me by the Misses Holland of Brenchley.

being brought out of the gate and laid upon the ground the *killedar* and the other native again examined it, as did also Rajah Khan, a favourite of Tippoo's, and by certain marks which they recognised they unanimously declared it was the *Badshaw*. At first Lieut.-Colonel Wallace and others suggested that life might still remain, and the former cleared the way to let the air to him; but upon his being examined by Mr Fraser of the 33rd and a surgeon who had accompanied General Baird, it was found he was quite cold and that not the least particle of life remained. General Baird cut off a small pouch he wore, which was made of crimson velvet, and gave it to a soldier of the light infantry, 33rd; but the man mislaid it, and General Baird never recovered it. The General said, "I never plunder, but I will keep this as a memorial of him." I expressed a wish at this time to Lieut.-Colonel Wallace, who stood near me, to get a bit of his crimson sash and jacket, but was diffident from the General's presence. Colonel Wallace immediately pulled out his penknife and cut off the two pieces contained in this box, and some time after I myself cut off a small piece of his payjamas or trousers, and before he was carried off a piece of his mustaches or whiskers, all of which is contained in this box.[1] There being now no doubt as to the identity of his person, the palanquin was taken out of the gate, the body put into it, and the light infantry of the 33rd acted the palanquin-boys, and with many hearty curses hoisted him upon their shoulders; but they had not advanced two paces when the bottom fell out of the palanquin, and all were again at a stand how to proceed; but some person having suggested putting the firelocks across, six or eight firelocks were immediately put across the frame, on which the body was again laid, and with the additional weight, and consequently some additional imprecations from the soldiers, he was again lifted on their shoulders, and they staggered on with him to his own palace, not a little vexed at being made palanquin-boys. He was laid down in the palace, and then recognised by some of his children. A guard of the 12th regiment was placed over the body, and in this situation

---

[1.] The box and hair are now at Brenchley.

it was viewed the next day by every officer in the British
army who could crawl from camp for that purpose. It began to
smell the next morning, but it was necessary that it should be
recognised by his children and others to place it beyond a doubt,
and buried with as much decency as possible, which took place
on the evening of the 5th May. The funeral party consisted of
the flank companies of the 12th and 33rd regiments under the
command of Lieutenant Goodlad, 33rd, who happened to be the
oldest officer present. Much has been said of the finding the
body, and I could enlarge here a good deal on it, and if I entered
into particulars, make the account very voluminous, but as this
paper is merely to show how the contents of the box came into
my possession, what I have here said is sufficient. In searching
for the body, that of a most beautiful girl was found lying
over Tippoo's: she had no mark of violence, being, I suppose,
smothered, but was quite dead. Lieut.-Colonel Shee and myself
had her taken out by the man, and she was examined by us,
but life had left her. She was very fair, about sixteen years
old, and the most beautiful girl I ever beheld even in death.
Colonel Shee got a handsome ornament she had on her neck,
and I got one that was on her neck also, and one on her hand. It
gave rise to many conjectures of Tippoo having his women with
him; but this was ridiculous, and from what we know of the
Mohammedan customs, could not have been the case. She must
have been a Brahmin girl who was going for water (for that is
the gate through which the Brahmins go, and indeed during
the siege all the inhabitants went there). I am confirmed in this
opinion since, by knowing that the ornaments are those worn
by Brahmins and not by tMohammedans.

The officers I perceived during the finding of Tippoo's body were
General Baird and Lieut.-Colonels Wallace and Shee, Captain
Keith Young, Lieutenant Lambton, a surgeon who accompanied
General Baird, and most of the officers of the 33rd.[1]

JOHN KING.

---

[1] Major Allan's (afterwards Sir Alexander Allan) account of the
finding of the body of Tippoo is annexed to Beatson's 'View of the War
with Tippoo Sultaun.' He writes: "When Tippoo was brought from
under the gate-way his eyes were open, and the body was so warm

After the capture of Seringapatam, Colonel Wellesley was appointed to the command of the city. General Baird deeply felt a junior being placed over him, and remonstrated against what he considered an act of favouritism. But the remonstrance had no effect.[1] However, his services did not remain unacknowledged. The sword of Tippoo was presented to him in the name of the army as a testimonial of their high admiration of his courage and conduct in the assault, and the thanks of both Houses of Parliament were voted on the 4th of October 1799 to General Baird and the other officers who commanded at Seringapatam.

General Baird afterwards proceeded to Madras,

---

that for a few moments Colonel Wellesley and myself were doubtful whether he was not alive. On feeling his pulse and heart that doubt was removed. He had four wounds, three in the body and one in the temple, the ball having entered a little above the right ear and lodged in the cheek. His dress consisted of a jacket of fine white linen, loose drawers of flowered silk, with a crimson cloth of silk and cotton round his waist; a handsome pouch, with a red and green silk belt hung across his shoulder; his head was uncovered, his turban being lost in the confusion of his fall; he had an amulet on his arm, but no ornament whatever. Tippoo was of low stature, corpulent, with huge shoulders, and a short thick neck, but his feet and hands were remarkably small; his complexion was rather dark, his eyes large and prominent, with small arched eyebrows, and his nose aquiline; he had an appearance of dignity, or perhaps of sternness in his countenance, which distinguished him above the common order of people."

Major Price in 'Memoirs of a Field Officer' writes: "The individual—an officer of great merit–has long since gone to his account, otherwise I might have forborne to mention what I am about to state, This officer, one of the bystanders, asked me if I could lend him a penknife, which I accordingly did. Before I could recollect myself he had cut off one of the Sultaun's mustachios, which he said he had promised to his friend Dr Cruso, of our establishment. For the moment I consoled myself with the reflection that there were few, if any, of the Sultaun's followers witnesses of the circumstance; but there were reasons to apprehend that the act was neither unobserved nor forgotten."

---

[1] See *Wellington*, p. 35.

where he found the Governor-General, who gave him a most cordial reception. Lord Wellesley persuaded Baird to accompany him to Calcutta, and gave him the command at Dinapore. He had only held the command for a short time when rumours reached him of an expedition being fitted out at Madras, the object of which it was generally believed was the capture of Batavia and the Isle of France. Baird hastened to Calcutta, and had an interview with the Marquess of Wellesley, and in the course of a stormy conversation urged the injustice that would be committed if the command of the proposed expedition was given to a junior colonel. His lordship told him that if he meant to ask him any questions as to the destination of the expedition he would not give him any answer. Baird replied that he had no desire to know where the expedition was going, all he wished to know was who was to command. The interview was brought to a close by Baird saying, "I suppose then, my lord, I am to consider your lordship's answer final, and that I am not to command (or to be employed) in this expedition." Next morning he received a letter informing him that his Excellency had finally arranged matters so that he (General Baird) should command the expedition. The object of the expedition, as it was surmised, was to seize Batavia and the Mauritius, and the troops to carry it out assembled at Trincomalee. On the 5th February 1801 General Baird received orders to proceed to that place to assume chief command, the Hon. Colonel Wellesley being the second in command. Shortly before the expedition was to start the Marquess of Wellesley received a letter from Downing Street, which induced him to turn the whole power of his resources to another plan which he had projected a year before. The plan was to apply the resources of India to the ejectment of the French from Egypt. The necessary instructions for effecting the change were immediately forwarded to General Baird. The General, when he reached Trincomalee, found that Colonel Wellesley had sailed for that place, and he quickly followed him to Bombay, which place he reached on the 31st March.

General Baird found that, owing to the activity of Governor Duncan and Colonel Wellesley, several of the transports were nearly ready, and before three days elapsed six of them sailed under Colonel Beresford with sealed orders. On the morning of the 6th April General Baird left Bombay: he was much disappointed that, owing to an attack of fever, Colonel Wellesley could not accompany him. Mocha was reached on the nineteenth day after leaving Bombay, and Jeddah on the 18th of May. On his arrival at that port he heard that the Bombay detachment and Colonel Beresford's division had proceeded up the Gulf of Suez, and he was told of the victory of Aboukir and the death of the gallant Abercrombie. Just as General Baird was about to leave Jeddah, Sir Hume Popham with the Cape detachment reached it. On the 26th May the contingent sailed for Kosseir, and on the 8th June that miserable cluster of wretched hovels built with shells and mud was reached. A letter from General Hutchinson, who commanded the forces in Egypt, saying that he intended to besiege the citadel of Cairo, hastened General Baird's anxiety for despatch, and accordingly the troops were ordered to advance by divisions. The first corps which started was commanded by Colonel Beresford. General Baird accompanied the division to its first halting-place, nearly twelve miles from Kosseir, and it was then discovered

that a very great number of the leather water-bags had
entirely emptied themselves through the leakage. This
discovery seriously retarded the movement of the troops, for
General Baird was compelled to forward the camels laden with
water, which were ready and intended for the second division,
to Colonel Beresford. One hundred camels were immediately
forwarded, fifty of which were laden with water. When the
second division, to which was attached the first company of
sepoys, began their march, it was discovered that their water-
bags were in as bad a condition as those of the first corps.
General Baird now began to doubt the possibility of carrying
into execution his march through a country in which there were
neither trees, shrubs, nor herbs, in which there was no water
on the surface, sweet or brackish, and no trace of any living
creatures. However, his resolution remained unshaken, and he
returned to Kosseir to make further arrangements. No sooner
had General Baird in some degree overcome the main difficulty
regarding water when a fresh misfortune assailed him.
The troops that had advanced were attacked with a dreadful
dysenteric complaint brought on by bad water. Another source
of uneasiness to the General was the delay in the arrival of
the detachments from Bombay, and they only arrived on the
day fixed for his departure from Kosseir. On the 30th of June
General Baird quitted Kosseir, and on the 1st July took up his
headquarters at Moilah, determined to move the army with
all possible expedition. On the 3rd he removed from Moilah
Wells, and on the 6th he arrived at Genneh. The difficulties
and trials of the march are well described by Count de Noe in
'Memoires relatifs a l'Expedition anglaise de l'Inde en Egypte.'
The Count was an officer in the 10th H.M., and accompanied

his corps in the expedition. The Count says, "General Baird came to pay us a visit, and told us that Colonel Beresford was in want of provisions and water. We immediately despatched as much of both as we could possibly spare, and sent them forward, notwithstanding that our own stock was by no means abundant. The springs were nearly dry, and we were obliged frequently to wait till nature replenished them. In the midst of the suffocating heat only two bottles and a half of water per man per diem could be spared. But our comrades at Moilah were in absolute want, and we did not pause for a moment to calculate the probability of any distress which might arise to ourselves, but gave them all we could spare." He declares tea to be the best beverage that can be used in crossing the desert, and attributes his escape from ophthalmia, which was very prevalent, to his having used a veil.

General Baird grew very uneasy at not having heard from General Hutchinson for a long period of time. When in this state of suspense as to the position of affairs the welcome news reached him that the Governor of Cairo had entered into a treaty with Hutchinson, and soon afterwards he got a despatch from the general himself. The despatch brought him the intelligence that the general was about to besiege Alexandria and that the Indian troops were to garrison that town. The general expressed a wish that Baird should join him as soon as possible. The prospect of active service delighted Baird, and he issued orders that the army should march at once to Genneh. He had made arrangements that they should receive provisions from the depots he had established in the desert, and had concentrated a supply of camels for the carriage of water, and had dug more wells in various places along the route. He thus saved his army much of the toil and fatigue he himself had undergone, and it marched across the burning sands of the desert with the loss of *only three men* between Kosseir and Genneh. But fresh difficulties of another kind now threatened him in his forward advance.

The new impediment that General Baird had to contend against was the Nile, which had begun to overflow its banks. The ancient stream, swelled by the rains in the uplands of Abyssinia, begins to rise in Egypt about the month of May, and its vast volume of water rapidly grows greater. Towards the end of June, when the river has risen five or six cubits, the fact is proclaimed in the streets of Cairo by the public crier, and when it rises to sixteen cubits the public rejoicing is great, and the people exclaim *"Waffah Allah"* (God has given us abundance). The rising of the Nile compelled Baird to abandon the idea of marching his whole force by its banks, but he was determined to convey some of his troops by water to Cairo. About this period the General was reinforced by the arrival at Kosseir of four companies of the 61st and two companies of the 80th, the Horse Artillery from Bengal, and the Artillery and Pioneers from Madras. The pleasure of receiving reinforcements was much diminished by the loss of the ships bringing stores for his army. *The Susannah,* the ship in which the future Duke of Wellington was to have sailed, was lost on the passage, and another storeship was wrecked near Jeddah and had to remain behind.

Having made all arrangements for the march of his forces, General Baird embarked for Lower Egypt on the 31st July. Colonel Murray was placed in command of the whole army of Upper Egypt until the rear had come up from

Genneh, whence it was to be sent forward with all possible speed to Gizeh. To the 9th Bombay N.I. and two companies of the 1st Bombay N.I. was intrusted the task of keeping the route open between Genneh and Kosseir. It was not in those days the settled policy of the Government of India to snub the Bombay army on every possible occasion. The General reached Gizeh on the 8th August, and, having laid in a store of supplies, he removed to the little island of Rhonda, situated on the Nile between Gizeh and Cairo. By the 27th August the whole of his army was collected on the island, and on the same night the right wing began to advance forward. An eyewitness has supplied us with an enthusiastic account of the Indian force on the island. "At this hour," he writes, "we often resorted to the island of Rhonda to view the magnificent parade: an immense grove of the most enormous sycamore fig-trees, larger than any of our forest trees, secured almost the whole army from the rays of the sun. Troops in such a state of military perfection, or better suited for active service, were never seen, not even in the famous parades of the chosen 10,000 belonging to Buonaparte's legion, which he was so vain of displaying before the present war in front of the Tuileries at Paris: not an unhealthy soldier was to be seen." Three days after leaving Rhonda General Baird reached Rosetta, and being so near Alexandria he was most anxious to push on without any loss of time. His enthusiasm was checked by hearing from General Hutchinson that the French had sent a flag of truce to treat for the surrender of the place. Next day the General proceeded to the chief's headquarters and found that the capitulation was actually signed.

Sir John Hutchinson, having accomplished his task, left
Egypt and handed over the command of the whole army to
Lord Cavan. In April news reached the army of the Peace of
Amiens, which had been concluded in the previous month on
terms of mutual restitution. France promised to retire from
Southern Italy and England to give up her newly conquered
colonies. "It is a peace which everybody is glad of, and
nobody is proud of," said a witty critic. On the 7th of May
Baird quitted Alexandria to return to India, and reached
Gizeh after a march of four days through a fertile country.
Immediately after his arrival at Gizeh he put the army in
motion, and began the march to Suez. "The troops crossed
the desert in successive divisions in five easy marches each,
without experiencing much inconvenience and with the loss
of only three Europeans." This brief account of the march
is written by Baird himself. In those days English generals
had not learnt the art of writing flowery despatches. But it
must be borne in mind that Baird's march was through a
desert, twenty-three leagues, in which not a drop of water
could be procured without digging a well. On the 5th June
the army sailed for India, and reached Calcutta on the last
day of July. The flag was hoisted at Fort William, and a royal
salute was fired in honour of the return of the army from
Egypt. The Indian troops, though they had no opportunity of
reaping the honour of victories, won for themselves the name
of being thoroughly good soldiers. The Earl of Cavan writes:
" Their excellent discipline and obedience, and their patience
under great fatigue and hardship, have been equalled by
their highly exemplary conduct in the correct and regular
discharge of every duty of soldiers; and though they may

lament that circumstances rendered it impossible for them to have taken part in the brilliant actions of this country during the last campaign, it must be a satisfaction for them to know that their services in Egypt have been as important and as essential to their country as those of their brother soldiers that gained such distinguished victories."

Shortly after his arrival at Calcutta, Baird quitted the capital of Bengal for Madras, where he was again called into active service. By the treaty of Bassein (31st December 1800) the Peshwa had virtually surrendered his independence to the English, but he had no sooner signed it than he had ignored it by sending private letters to India and the Rajah of Berar, urging them to march on Poona. It was now necessary to carry out the provisions of the treaty and place the Peshwa in authority at Poona. To accomplish this General Wellesley moved up from Mysore, and when he crossed the Toombudra he took with him a very large portion of the Madras army. General Baird was annoyed at the serious reduction made in his force, and asked for leave of absence, which was granted. It is impossible to justify his conduct. No soldier has a right to relinquish a command at the opening of a campaign. General Baird hastened to Fort St George, and with as little delay as possible embarked for England, accompanied by several officers of his staff. In crossing the Bay of Biscay they were captured by a French privateer. General Baird and his officers were allowed to remain in their ship on the expressed condition that they should consider themselves prisoners of war and not impede the voyage of the prize to Bordeaux. On the way to that port the ship was recaptured by the English, and at length

the General reached Falmouth in safety. It was decided
by the military authorities that he could not serve again
until exchanged with a French officer of equal rank. This
exchange was effected, and General Baird was appointed to
the staff of the Eastern District.

He had not been long in his new command when he received
a communication informing him that he was to command
an expedition to retake the Cape of Good Hope, which had
been given up by the Addington Administration. On the 4th
January 1806 General Baird reached the coast of Africa, a short
distance to the northward of Cape Town, and by the morning
of the 8th the whole of the troops were landed and the General
commenced his march to Cape Town. After a slight engagement
the town surrendered, and a few days afterwards the whole
of the colony of the Cape of Good Hope and its dependencies,
and all the rights and privileges held and exercised by the
Batavian Government, were surrendered to his Britannic
Majesty. General Baird quickly restored order in the colony
and governed it wisely; but he, unfortunately, committed one
grave error, which led to his recall. Admiral Popham, having no
further work at the Cape, determined, without any authority
from home, to attack the Spanish colonies in South America,
and he induced Baird to let him have a portion of his force.
The expedition at first proved successful, and while Fox was
breathing his last the Tower guns were firing for the capture
of Buenos Ayres. Before he was laid in his grave our force
was able only to secure itself at a post on the shore. At first
the Cabinet acquiesced in the enterprise, but when it proved
unsuccessful Popham was superseded and Baird recalled from
the Cape for having lent him aid.

When General Baird arrived in England the Grenville Administration had resigned, and the Duke of Portland was First Lord of the Treasury and Canning occupied the post of Foreign Secretary. Canning was Pitt's pupil. He entered heart and soul into his master's contest with France. Like Pitt, he did not believe in crying Peace, peace, when there was no peace. He had bitterly condemned the Peace of Amiens. "I would never have signed," he wrote. "I would have cut off my right hand rather." When Canning became Foreign Secretary it was a critical time for England. Napoleon was at the climax of his power. "Poll up that map," Pitt had said, pointing to a map of Europe which hung upon the wall; "it will not be wanted these ten years!" England alone opposed the ambitious schemes of Napoleon. Alexander had written to George III. that "there was no salvation to himself or to Europe but by eternal resistance to Buonaparte," and yet within four weeks the Czar and Napoleon had formed a plan of the complete spoliation of Europe, and had agreed that the fleets of the neutral Powers should be seized to enable them to carry out their designs. The intrigue was, however, disclosed to Canning, who acted promptly. The Danish fleet was the object of the confederates, and a minister was sent to the Danish Government to require that the Danish navy should be delivered over to England to be taken care of in British ports and restored at the end of the war. He went escorted by twenty ships of the line, forty frigates and other assistant vessels, and a fleet of transports conveying 27,000 land troops. It was to this force, commanded by Lord Cathcart, that Sir David Baird was attached. The affair was soon decided. On the 16th of August the English troops landed on Danish soil, and on the 8th of September all was over: the Danish navy and arsenal were surrendered. One-fourth of the buildings of Copenhagen were by that time destroyed, and in one street 500 persons were killed by the bombardment. Canning endured great blame for a long time on account of the peremptory way in which he acted, and for the bombardment of the city, but he could not justify himself because the Government were pledged to secrecy. However, since the facts were revealed, there has been a universal agreement that he was right. The Danish fleet was the property of the Danish Government, with whom we were at peace; but it was practically in the possession of the Allies, with whom we were at war. If it was not used by *us*, it would certainly have been used *against us*. " England was in great and imminent peril; to the supreme moral fearlessness of Mr Canning we owe in no small measure her deliverance."[1] At the siege of Copenhagen Baird was twice wounded. One finger of his left hand was broken by a musket-shot, and he was also hit on the collar-bone. The Danish fleet having been given up, the object of the expedition was accomplished, and the troops returned to England. Shortly after his arrival Baird was appointed to the command of the camp of instruction at the Curragh.

The capture of the Danish fleet checked France at sea, but Napoleon was master of Western Europe. Mad with success, he committed a gross act of treachery, and made a fatal blunder. The French army entered Madrid and proclaimed Joseph

---

[1.] "But our negotiations failed, and finally we seized, as belonging to a Power which was certain to become our enemy, the ships with which she refused to aid us as an ally."–*Historical Characters,* by Sir Henry Lytton Bulwer, p. 393.

Buonaparte King of Spain. "It was the unhappy war in the peninsula that ruined me," Napoleon said years afterwards to Las Cases. "The unfortunate war in Spain proved a real wound–the first cause of the misfortunes of France." Canning sent supplies, money, and troops under the command of Sir John Moore and Sir Arthur Wellesley to the aid of the Spanish insurgents. The latter won the victories of Roliga and Vimiero; but the fruits of victory were destroyed by that Convention of Cintra which called forth from England's great poet one of the most eloquent invectives in our language. Three months after the Convention Sir John Moore set out from Lisbon to relieve Spain from the collar of France. He thought an enthusiastic nation of cavaliers would aid him, but he found no enthusiasm and little civility on his route. On the 13th of October Sir David Baird landed at Corunna with a detachment of 11,000 men, with which he was to join Sir John Moore at Salamanca. He was thwarted and delayed in every possible way by the Spaniards. Before the two armies could join the defeat of the Spaniards in every quarter rendered the success of the expedition hopeless. Sir John Moore ordered Baird to retreat to Corunna and embark his detachment, but the order was countermanded. He next began to hope that the two forces joined with the troops of the Spanish General Romana might be able to strike a decisive blow at the French under Soult. On the 19th of December 1808 the long-anticipated junction of the armies of Moore and Baird was effected, and just as they were on the point of advancing, news reached Sir John Moore that Napoleon had left Madrid with 50,000 men and was hurrying on to annihilate him. No course but the better one of retreat was open to the English general. Napoleon conducted the pursuit himself as far as Astorga, where he gave up the command to Soult. "Through the mountains of Galicia the three armies passed like a tempest, yet Moore, with unflinching resolution, amidst winter rains and appalling difficulties, and without one gleam of good fortune to nourish energy, reached Corunna with a gain of two marches on his pursuers. His retreat was one of suffering, of privation and fatigue, but he met with no disaster in arms, and in many combats taught the enemy to beware of his sword."

As to Sir David Baird's division, its sufferings and privations were no less than those of the main body with Sir John Moore. At Corunna the English general found that the ships had not arrived, and he was compelled to accept battle with inferior numbers and in a bad position. The battle proved that neither suffering nor danger had quelled the courage of the gallant troops. The weight of the conflict at its commencement fell chiefly on Sir David Baird's division. As the French advanced to attack the division he asked Sir John if he would give the word to move forward. He replied, "No, Baird; do you." As Baird gave the word, and was animating his men, he received a grave shot on his left arm which compelled him to withdraw from the field. Notwithstanding the pain he suffered from a wound which had literally shattered the bone to pieces, his countenance and manner were so calm and unchanged that several officers whom he passed as he was *walking* into Corunna were perfectly unconscious that he was even wounded. When he arrived on board the *Ville de Paris,* the surgeon of that ship and of the *Barfleur* declared that an operation was absolutely necessary for the preservation of his life. The wound was so near the shoulder that the ordinary mode of amputation could not be adopted, and it was therefore determined to remove the arm out of the socket. The preparations for the operation were immediately made; and during its progress David Baird exhibited the same firmness of nerve which so eminently distinguished him on every occasion in life." He sat leaning his right arm on a table without uttering one syllable of complaint, except at the moment when the joint was finally separated, when one single exclamation of pain escaped his lips." News reached Baird at the close of the day of the glorious victory won, but won at the cost of the life of the hero who commanded the victors. A letter from Captain Hardinge, the young soldier with the eye of a general and the soul of a hero, who turned the tide in the battle of Albuera, and the Governor-General who turned it in Ferozeshah and Sobraon, gives a vivid picture of the last moments of Sir John Moore. William Napier's famous account, how Moore was borne from the fight in a manner so becoming to a soldier, was taken from Hardinge's, and we prefer the simple relation of the latter without any literary skill or pathos. It is a story which Englishmen cannot read too often:–

I had been ordered [says Captain Hardinge] by the commander-in-chief to desire a battalion of the Guards to advance, which battalion was at one time intended to dislodge a corps of the enemy from a large house and garden on the opposite side of the valley. I was pointing out to the General the situation of the battalion, and our horses were touching at the very moment that a cannon-shot from the enemy's battery carried away his left shoulder and part of the collar-bone, leaving his arm hanging by the flesh.

The violence of the stroke threw him off his horse on his back: not a muscle of his face altered, nor did a sign betray the least sensation of pain.

I dismounted, and taking his hand, he pressed mine forcibly, casting his eyes very anxiously towards the 42nd Regiment, which was hotly engaged; and his countenance expressed satisfaction when I informed him that the regiment was advancing.

Assisted by a soldier of the 42nd, he was removed a few yards behind the shelter of a wall. Colonel Graham and Captain Woodford about this time came up, and perceiving the state of Sir John's wound, rode off for a surgeon.

The blood flowed fast, but the attempt to stop it with my sash was useless from the size of the wound. Sir John assented to being removed in a blanket to the rear. In raising him for that purpose, his sword, hanging on the wounded side, touched his arm, and became entangled between his legs. I perceived the inconvenience, and was in the act of unbuckling it from his waist, when he said in a very distinct manner, "It is well as it is. I had rather it should go out of the field with me."

Here I feel it would be improper for my pen to venture to express the admiration with which I am penetrated in thus faithfully recording this instance of the invincible fortitude and military delicacy of this great man.

He was borne by six soldiers of the 42nd and Guards, with my sash supporting him.

Observing the resolution and composure of his features, I caught at the hope that I might be mistaken in my fears of the wound being mortal, and remarked that I hinted, when the surgeon dressed the wound, that he would be spared to us and recover. He then turned his head round, and looking steadfastly at the wound for a few seconds, said, "No, Hardinge, I feel that to be impossible."

I wished to accompany him to the rear, when he said, "You need not go with me–report to General Hope that I am wounded and carried to the rear."

A sergeant of the 42nd and two spare files, in case of accident, were ordered to conduct their brave General to Corunna, and I hastened to report to General Hope.

Two days after leaving the Peninsula Baird landed in England. On the 25th of January he and his officers and troops received the thanks of Parliament for their gallant conduct in repulsing a superior French force before Corunna. On the 13th of April 1809 he was created a baronet: next year he married Miss Preston, and the union in every way proved a happy one. His last active service was as Commander of the Forces in Ireland, which post he resigned in 1822. Seven years after he had put off harness passed away one of the most thorough soldiers that ever devoted their lives to the service of their country.

GENERAL JOHN JACOB.

WE are so accustomed to rely on the courage, the confidence, and the administrative capacity of our countrymen, that we do not always pay sufficient honour to those who, by the exercise of these qualities, have built our empire. The biography of John Jacob,[1] one of the last of the great servants of the East India Company, does, therefore, good service in arousing us to the perception of what we owe to the men whose intellect and strength enable them to confront and grapple with the duties and perils of imperial sovereignty. The story of his life has been too long left untold, and all who take a pride in England's worthies will be grateful to Mr Shand for making John Jacob known to them, and for having done it with a judicious and reticent hand. It is difficult to sketch in plain speech his character, for the imagination is fascinated by the strong nature and the darting and vigorous intellect of the man. He was the daring leader of cavalry, with a dash of ancient chivalry, and he organised a military system. He subdued the proud and warlike mountaineers of the Afghan and Beluchee

---

[1] *General John Jacob.* By Alexander Innes Shand. London: Seeley & Co. 1900.

GENERAL JOHN JACOB.

frontier, and over them he acquired a remarkable influence. He liked them, and treated them kindly or sternly as the case required, but always with justice and honesty. By constructing roads, digging canals, and the encouragement of agriculture and commerce, he converted what was a desert waste into a thriving agricultural community. He wrote as well as he fought and governed. His judgments may be often hasty and his economics open to question; but in his letters and despatches, as in his conduct of war and government, there is a masculine sense and vigour united to imaginative power. His views regarding some of the most delicate and intricate problems of administration cannot be too closely studied by the statesman, and his opinions regarding our military system may be serviceable in this time. Many of his suggestions regarding army reform, which he had so long pressed in vain on the Government, were adopted after a mutiny he had long foretold had shaken to its foundation our Indian empire.

On the 11th of January 1812, three years before the battle of Waterloo, John Jacob was born at Woolavington, in Somersetshire. He was the fifth son of Stephen Long Jacob, vicar of the parish, who came of an old country stock whose healthy minds had been developed by culture and study. The Jacob lads were reared in simple living and the restraints of an honourable poverty, a training which enables high or low, civilians or soldiers, to play their part in life with advantage. The vicar, owing to a slender income, had to teach his own boys, and John Jacob on receiving his cadetship went straight from his father's vicarage to Addiscombe, the Military College of the East India Company, which did such a splendid work in its day, and sent to the Indian army such soldiers as Eldred Pottinger, Henry Lawrence, James Brind, Napier of Magdala, and Roberts of Candahar. In January 1828, John Jacob, having been appointed to the Bombay Artillery, set sail for India, where thirty years of strenuous labour awaited him, and where he made his sepulchre. Immediately after his arrival at Bombay he began to work diligently at his profession, and for seven years he had the best training a young soldier can have–regimental duty. He was then intrusted with a small detached command, and he held an administrative post in Gujerat when the first Afghan war broke the long peace in which India had reposed.

The base of our operations for the first invasion of Afghanistan lay in Sind, and in 1838 John Jacob sailed with his battery for Kurrachee, then a small fishing village, now one of the great seaports of our Indian empire. He accompanied as far as Sukkur the Bombay column of the army of the Indus under the command of Sir John Keane. Here he and Lieutenant Corry of her Majesty's 17th Regiment were left behind in charge of 150 Europeans, chosen from every regiment of the army, Royal and Company, and from every troop of horse and company of foot artillery. But Jacob soon had an opportunity of showing his skill and daring in war. No sooner had Keane and his army passed the Bolan than the predatory tribes inhabiting the mountains which run along the entire frontier of Sind from the Bolan to the sea attacked his line of communication. They cut off his envoys and murdered his messengers. By negotiations and offers of money vain efforts were made to obtain a safe passage through their lowland territory. The chiefs were deaf to all persuasion and scorned every offer. Then it was determined to try force. In June 1839 a detachment was ordered to proceed from Sukkur and Shikarpoor against Beja khan, a stout old bandit, the head of the Doombkees, one of the principal clans, and Jacob was now directed to choose men from the Europeans to form a company of artillery to proceed with the force to Kutchee, the great arid plain between the mountains and Sind, the country of the "blasts of death." Having selected twenty artillerymen and twenty men belonging to the infantry, Jacob with Lieutenant Corry marched from Sukkur on the 3rd of June. "The season," writes Jacob, "was one of intense heat, which has never since been equalled: the thermometer in the hospital-shed at Shikarpoor stood commonly at 130°, and on several days reached the astonishing height of 140°. One day it even stood at 143°. The wind appeared like a blast from a furnace, and this even at midnight." On the first day's march of ten miles seven of the soldiers were struck dead by the heat, and Lieutenant Corry was brought in dying. " The poor fellow rallied a little at night, but as the heat returned next day he also relapsed and died." Before reaching Shikarpoor, out of a detachment of two officers and forty men, one officer and fifteen men had been struck dead. The military authorities somewhat tardily realised that it was impossible at such a season to prosecute the proposed expedition, and the attempt was abandoned till the following October. Early in that month Major Billamore with about 500 native infantry, a single bullock battery of two 24-pounder howitzers and one 6-pounder gun, set forth to chastise the wild tribes of Eastern Beluchistan. As it was thought unadvisable to have any Europeans with the force, Lieutenant Jacob was ordered to form a native company

of artillery. He selected some men from the Bombay 5th
Regiment of Native Infantry, whose men were, Jacob
states, perfect specimens of the Bombay sepoys as described
by Sir John Malcolm,–"The true descendants of Seevagi's
(Shivaji) mountain rats, whom not all the pride and power
of the armies of Hindustan could prevent from marching to
the gates of Delhi." Jacob himself describes them as "small
and not at all good-looking, but of an amazing energy and
activity, and full of zeal and courage, and with sinews that
no labour could tire, and hearts that no danger could taint."
It is well to bear in mind that the Sikhs, Afghans, and
Gurkhas are not the only warlike races from whom we can
recruit our Indian army.

The little force crossed the desert and proceeded without
opposition to Chuttur and Pooligee, two townships belonging
to Beja Khan, who with his people fled to the neighbouring
mountains. Major Billamore represented at headquarters that
without cavalry he could not act effectively against tribes of
horsemen, and a detachment of 180 irregular horse under
command of Lieutenant Clarke was ordered to join the force.
This detachment had just before been transferred from the
Poona Irregular Horse in order to form the nucleus of the new
corps at that time to be raised in Sind. Its official title was
the Sind Irregulars, but men always spoke and wrote of it
as Jacob's Horse. The day that Clarke with his detachment
reached Chuttur he got information of a strong band of
horsemen having left the hills to plunder. With half his men
he went out about midnight, and just before daybreak found
them, about 300 in number, dismounted in a corn-field. They
had barely time to spring on their mares when Clarke charged,

and after a sharp tussle the marauders fled up the dry bed of a river, vigorously pursued by the Sind Horse. About fifty of them were killed and eleven were taken prisoners.

The country round Shahpoor now began to be nightly raided by numerous bands of tribesmen, who had assembled at Ooch, about twelve miles distant. Major Billamore, with thirty infantry and sixty of the Sind Irregulars, accompanied by Captain Brown, Lieutenants Clarke and Jacob, set forth for it. To understand the operations, the nature of the country must be kept in mind. A sea of gleaming sand spreads westward to a range of bare and barren sandstone hills, at whose entrance there is a little valley some 500 or 600 yards wide, through which runs a mountain torrent of fresh water out of hills of salt. Along the northern end of the torrent-bed the water exudes from the banks and creates a green and moist spot called Ooch. "This place Major Billamore and party had to discover for themselves; no one could be found to guide them; the general direction alone was pointed out and the distance given." After advancing some miles, seeing single horsemen hastening in a certain direction, the officers and troopers galloped after them, and soon found themselves in the middle of the Beluch encampment. Their horsemen, about 100 in number, sprang on their mares, which were always kept saddled, and escaped unhurt. An equal number of men who had no horses, accompanied by some women and children, climbed to the top of the hills, and having placed the women and children in caves, opened a smart matchlock-fire. The troopers were dismounted, and Billamore and his officers led them to the assault. The Beluchees fought hard, and twenty were killed and several wounded before the remainder surrendered. Billamore heard from the prisoners that the party he had surprised were led by two of the most enterprising and most famous of the Beluch warriors, Janee and Rahmut. He determined to remain the night at Ooch, in the hope that they would attack him. But they did not appear, and the next morning he went into the hills with his troopers in quest of them. No trace of them, however, could be found in the unknown and pathless waste. The pursuit was abandoned, and the party returned to Ooch. No sooner had they reached the watering-place and the horses had begun to drink, when as if by magic there suddenly appeared not half a mile off, opposite to an opening in the hills, Janee, Rahmut, and 100 Beluchees, mounted and drawn up in a regular line. In a second the men of the Sind Horse were in their saddles, the next instant they were formed and riding at the enemy:–

Janee and his men drew their swords and advanced with a shout, and valiant deeds appeared about to take place: the ground looked firm and level for a fair passage of arms, when suddenly every horse of the British detachment sank into the earth, some plunged over girth and saddle-flap, many rolled over and over, and all in hopeless confusion. The cunning Beluch had drawn them into an extensive quicksand. One European officer of the whole party, being admirably mounted, alone struggled on through it; but Janee, carelessly or generously, took no notice of him as he still rode towards him, but with shouts of laughter the Beluch riders went off at speed, and disappeared from, almost as suddenly as they appeared on, the scene.

Billamore, baffled by his active foe, returned to Sherpoor. The following November his force proceeded in two detachments to enter the Murree and Boogtee hills, wherein the two great tribes, the Doombkees and Jekranees, had found refuge. After defeating the fierce warriors at their fastness called Tructnee, he determined to advance with a portion of his scanty force to Kahun in the heart of the mountains. He considered it important that his artillery should accompany him, in order to show the tribes that their most difficult, high, and rugged hills were not inaccessible to our guns. The nature of the road was, however, stated to be absolutely unfit for the transport of artillery. But Jacob was confident, and Billamorc allowed him to take a detachment and examine it for himself. He found the road bad in many places, but soon by means of his pioneers made it passable for his guns. Over the hills the artillery carriage was transported with great labour, and Billamore's detachment with their guns reached Kahun in safety. The mountain tribes, finding they were not safe in their rocky fastnesses, came in and surrendered. The object of the expedition having been accomplished, it was determined to return to the plain country as soon as possible. Jacob thought they might make their way back by a nearer route. A herdsman told him there did exist a path over the mountains bounding the south side of the valley of Kahun, which he was willing to point out. Under his guidancc Jacob proceeded to the top of the mountain: "The path was only a sheep-walk, and seemed tremendously difficult even for a single horseman; the part over and through the mountain was alone four miles in length. Thus was the pass of Nuffoosk, a place whose name has since become so familiar, then first beheld by European eyes." Jacob and his pioneers set to work at the road over the pass, and in three days it was thought practicable for the artillery. On the fourth the 24-pounder howitzer and the other carriages were dragged over the mountain, and before evening the detachment had crossed Nuffoosk. Next day they descended the great mountain of Surtoff, and reached without adventure Pooligee on the 11th February 1840, about three and a half months after they had left it to enter the hills, then an unknown land. As Jacob writes: "Every object had been fully accomplished without serious loss and without a shadow of a disaster. The mountaineers had been thoroughly beaten whenever encountered: the robbers, who had fled for shelter among them, compelled to surrender. The mountains had been penetrated in every direction, and roads made in the very heart of them." The commander of the expedition had not the pen of a ready writer, and contented himself with making a verbal report to his superiors, and the gallant adventure would long since have been forgotten had not Sir William Napier's 'History of the Conquest of Sind' provoked "Major Billamore's surviving subaltern" to give an account of it, and to correct the inaccuracies of the historian.

When the field force was disbanded, Jacob returned to regimental duty at Hyderabad. Here he met Outram, who was then Political Agent for Sind, and between the two men, who had much in common, there was laid the foundation of a lifelong friendship. The exertions of Jacob on the frontier became known through field and general orders, and led Outram to appoint him to make a reconnaissance of the route from Hyderabad to Naggur Parkur on the Sind frontier. The Government, not caring

to be entirely dependent on the sea-communication
between Bombay and Kurrachee, were anxious to discover a
land-route from the centre of Sind to the province of Gujerat.
Accompanied by only three tribesmen in the service of one
of the *Ameers*, Jacob did the journey in the hottest season
of the year at considerable risk. He carefully measured and
mapped the road, and made minute notes of the villages, the
water-supply, and the agricultural and pastoral resources of
the country. In forwarding his report to the Government,
Outram wrote: "I have the honour to transmit a report on
the route from Hyderabad to Naggur Parkur by Lieutenant
Jacob of the Bombay Artillery, a scientific and enterprising
officer, whose zeal and intrepidity in undertaking the
journey during the hottest period that has been known in
Sind during the memory of man, in preference to continuing
the far easier voyage down the river or by sea, on which
that officer was engaged when requested by me to survey
this road, will, I hope, be appreciated by his lordship and
considered worthy of notice."

For the important services he had rendered during the
hill campaign and his daring reconnaissance, Jacob was
appointed in March 1842 to command the Sind Irregular
Horse, when that body was augmented and placed in charge
of all the Kutchee frontier. On assuming the command he at
once took active measures to put down the forays made by the
Beluch chiefs across the border. He not only beat them off,
but when they planned a bloody inroad he frustrated them
by making a raid into their fastnesses. These retaliations
laid the foundation of that knowledge of our power which
enabled his subsequent conciliatory measures to have their

full effect. When Outram was about to leave Scinde he wrote, on the 9th of November 1842: "For the first time within the memory of man Kutchee and Upper Sind have been for a whole year entirely free from the irruptions of the hill-tribes, by which villages were annually destroyed, lives and property sacrificed, and the whole country kept in a state of fever." On the 27th of November Jacob was ordered to Sukkur to join the forces that were gathering there under Sir Charles Napier. Two days after he reached it, and on the 3rd of December the regiment was reviewed by Napier, who expressed himself highly pleased with it, and the old veteran was not easy to please.

The story of the annexation of Sind cannot be both shortly and adequately told; and as the conquest was the result of a policy for which Jacob was in no degree responsible, it would have been wiser if his biographer had not touched so thorny a subject. It is a difficult task to elicit the historic truth from a mass of blue-books, original documents, and miserable personalities. Mr Shand is, however, to be commended for avoiding as much as possible the raking up of the ashes of long-forgotten animosities. The pity of it, that a bitter controversy should have arisen between two noble and generous souls! Napier and Outram regarded the position from totally opposed points of view. Napier considered that as Governor and Commander of the forces he was bound to enforce the acceptance of the treaty which the Governor-General dictated, and this could be done only by an appeal to the God of battles. Outram, as Political Resident, considered it could be done by negotiation. The *Ameers* were indignant at the terms of the treaty, but in dread of further consequences they signed it. The signing was a mere mockery. War was certain: Napier maintained, and it is not easy to deny it, that not only the *Ameers* but also their friends and others were gathering a vast force to extirpate the English. Delay might be fatal. He determined, therefore, to attack before they could all assemble and crush him by mere weight of numbers. With a force numbering 2200 men, of whom 700 were cavalry and only 800 were Europeans, he attacked at Meeanee an army of more than 20,000 men, and won one of those splendid victories which illustrate the annals of the British in India. For three hours the stubborn contest on the bank of the river Fullailee continued, and still the Beluchees, undismayed at their losses, pressed onwards with furious force. "The bayonet and the sword clashed in full and frequent conflict." At last the Beluch swordsmen began to waver, and the 22nd leaping forward with shouts of victory pushed them backwards into the deep ravine. The superb 9th Cavalry of Bengal broke the line of the enemy on the left, and Jacob's Sind Horse charged into the *Ameer's* camp, sabring to right and left. "Captain Jacob, though slight of person, meeting a horseman at full gallop, passed his sword with such force through shield and body that the hilt struck strongly against the former." Napier, in his despatch after the battle, said that Jacob had rendered "the most active services long previous to and during the combat. He broke the enemy's camp, from which he drove a body of 3000 or 4000 cavalry."

After the battle of Meeanee Napier entered Hyderabad as a conqueror, and there prepared to meet the new army which was advancing to crush him. Having called up succours, he moved out of Hyderabad, and ten miles from the city he found himself in a plain in front of the

Beluch army. Far and wide it stretched. There were more
than 36,000 fighting men before him with sword and shield
and matchlock, and they had fifteen guns, eleven being in
battery. He had 5000 men all told. The front of the enemy's
infantry was covered by a *nullah* extending a mile, twenty
feet wide, eight deep, and scarped so as to form a parapet.
His right rested on the river Fullailee, a deep channel which
quits the main stream of the Indus. It is a flowing river only
when the Indus is in flood: at that time the Indus was low
and the Fullailee was dry, but deep in mud. Beyond was
a thick *shekargah* or jungle, which prevented the position
being turned except by a wide movement. Near the river was
the village of Dubba, with loopholed houses filled with armed
men. Between Dubba and the front ran another deep *nullah*,
which was planted with the second line of Belooch infantry.
Here, too, his guns were placed. His left extended to a wood,
and was protected by a *nullah* in front and a ravine which
divided it from the right. All the cavalry were behind in one
great mass. The British column formed line–the cavalry being
drawn up on the wings, the artillery in the intervals between
the regiments. At nine o'clock the battle commenced. Napier,
seeing many Beluchees hurrying from their left towards the
village, thought they had neglected their right and were
hurrying to repair their error. He at once put his troops into
movement. Leslie's Horse Artillery advanced, and the rest
followed in succession by batteries. Rapidly gaining ground to
the extreme right, they obtained raking positions, "crossing
their fire with the Horse Artillery so that the bullets tore the
thick masses of the enemy's infantry in a terrible manner."
Previous to this "Lieutenant Smith, thinking of his duty and

not of his life, with desperate valour rode foremost and alone to the bank of the first *nullah* and ascended it. He sought for a place where his guns could pass, and found death! The *nullah* was filled with Beluchees, and *there the hero fell.*" Meanwhile the 22nd Regiment, followed by a sepoy regiment, had advanced against Dubba. Their march was marked by the dead: "Half the light company were driven by fire from the first *nullah*, and beyond it the second and greater one was seen more strongly lined with men, while the village suddenly became alive with warriors whose matchlocks could also reach the advancing line." Napier discovered he had made a mistake, and that the rush of men towards the village was to strengthen that flank. "He had neither time nor means to countercheck them, and, as generally happens even with the greatest captains, had to remedy his error by courage." Placing himself at the head of the 22nd, he was meaning to head the charge, when suddenly came a horseman from the right to tell him all the cavalry of that wing was charging. He went there at full speed, and found the report was correct. Jacob, seeing the enemy moving to the left, thought they were returning, and charged them.

The whole body of cavalry was at full speed, clearing the *nullahs* without a check, the riders' spurs deep in their horses' sides, their different war-cries pealing high and clear, their swords whirling above their heads in gleaming circles: there was the fiery Jacob and the terrible Fitzgerald careering alike in the same path of error, while the splendid troopers of the 32nd Cavalry and the red turbans of the wild horsemen of Sind, speeding through smoke and dust, streamed like meteors behind them.

For a moment the General gazed at first with anger and then with admiration, and, putting spur to his horse, he went back with such speed as to reach the 22nd at the moment it was rushing to storm the first *nullah*.

Riding to the front rank, he raised that clear high-pitched cry of war which had, at Meeanee, sent the same fiery soldiers to the charge. It was responded to with even greater ardour; for here no check occurred, though the danger and difficulty was greater. Lieutenant Coote first gained the summit of the bank, and tearing a Beluch standard from its bearer, waved it in triumph, while he reeled along the narrow edge fainting from a deep wound in his side. Then, with a deafening shout, the soldiers leaped into the midst of the swordsmen; and they were no sluggards to deal with, for there the black hero Hoche and all the Scindes fought and there they fell.

Strongly and fiercely the enemy fought, but they were driven from Dubba and joined the retreating masses, who were vigorously followed. "The fiery Jacob, with his usual impetuosity, had pushed so far ahead that he caught sight of the elephant which was bearing Shere Ahmed (the Lion *Ameer*) away. He might have caught the *Ameer* and ended the war had not Colonel Pattle, the second in command, deemed it prudent to stop the pursuit." The *Ameer* fled to his capital; but abandoning it, he sought safety in his desert fortress at Omercote. Jacob was present at its surrender, and continued the pursuit of the *Ameer*, who, however, made good his escape across the Indus into the hills. For his services Napier recommended Jacob for the brevet rank of major and the companionship of the Bath. The General Orders by the Governor-General announced that "the conduct of Brevet Captain Jacob is considered to have entitled him to honorary distinction, which cannot be at present conferred on account of his want of rank." The announcement was a severe disappointment to Jacob, and he wrote to his father that he wished he had died at Meeanee.

The victories of Meeanee and Hyderabad were decisive. The *Ameers* came and submitted and were deposed. The victorious general issued a wise proclamation, announcing that the rights of the landowners would be scrupulously observed, and no man should suffer any injury in person or property. Two months after the battle of Meeanee Sind was conquered and annexed, amidst the joyful acclamations of the people, who had been the victims of a cruel, grinding, alien tyranny. Napier set at once to work to consolidate his conquest by a firm and beneficent administration. He took strenuous means to prevent the disbanded armies of the Beloochees from becoming hordes of banditti, and many a bold robber he converted into a soldier or a policeman. He made the tribes on the border understand that if they raided our frontier or killed our people he could penetrate their most inaccessible strongholds and capture them, and deal out punishment with a heavy hand. The hill-tribes of Kutchee, under the leadership of Beja Khan, had again begun their raids and ravages, and as the winter of 1844-45 drew on, Napier made his preparations for another expedition against them. On the 12th of January 1845 he left Sukkur for Khanghur, the future Jacobabad. The day he reached it Jacob pushed forward to Roza, nine miles to the west. Having refreshed his men, he rode thirty-five miles farther, and when within two miles of Sherpoor he learnt that a son of the chief was holding the village in force.

I pushed on at a trot, and completely surrounded the village before the alarm was given or any one could escape. Knowing the place well, I at once galloped into an enclosure on one side

of the village. The enemy now opened a heavy fire upon us
from a high tower and from the houses. I immediately picketed
a troop, and took the men into the village on foot, when all
opposition ceased, and the robbers were anxious only to hide
their arms.

In these few modest words Jacob narrates a prompt and
daring feat of arms, which Napier made the subject of a
separate order. He writes:–

This is a very rare and very glorious instance of perfect
discipline, as well as courage, on the part of the Sind Horse;
and though to men less acquainted with war it may appear
trifling, yet in the mind of the Major-General and Governor it
stamps both the Sind Horse and its commandant as first-rate
soldiers—prompt, resolute, obedient, and humane, even in the
momentary excitement of action against the most furious of
enemies.

Another gallant exploit also drew forth the warm approval
of the old chief, and it is best told in his own words:–

Twenty-five brave robbers on foot, well armed with swords
and shields and matchlocks, met twenty of the Sind Horse
patrolling in the desert. The robbers gave a volley and charged.
The Sind Horse met them; a combat with sabres ensued. The
Sind Horse had one man killed and two wounded; four horses
killed and two wounded. Of the enemy every man fell sword in
hand. Quarter was repeatedly offered to those stern gladiators,
but they refused, and every robber bit the dust. Honour be to
their courage–more honour to their conquerors. Another laurel-
leaf has been added to the rich wreath of Jacob's Horse.

After the campaign had been brought to a successful
close by the able plan, skilful execution, and personal
activity and intrepidity of Napier, Jacob's Horse returned
to Hyderabad. Their commander had recommended that
the corps should be increased by a second regiment. The

Governor-General and Sir Charles Napier were willing to accede to his proposal, but military precedent was against his claim to command both regiments. Jacob wrote to Napier: "What I want is to be the real commander, on whom everything centres, or else to have nothing to do with the matter. I do not write hastily, but have considered the matter well. Let us be a regiment of English squadrons—you can always detach as many of these squadrons as you please, but whatever distance may separate the corps, let us be one as regards command, with one chain of authority throughout." After much correspondence, lengthy and involved, as too often is the nature of official correspondence, the order was received for raising the new regiment, and the Governor-General "deemed it expedient that for the present it shall be under the command of Captain Jacob, that he might superintend the formation and drill." From precedents, the Governor-General observed, "he had been induced in this single instance to depart out of regard to Captain Jacob's reputation and success." The time had, however, come for the great leader of light horse to show his ability as a diplomat and administrator. In January 1847 there is a notice in the regimental records that, "under instructions from Colonel Forbes, commanding at Shekarpoor, and General Hunter, C.B., commanding in Upper Sind, Captain Jacob assumed command of the frontier." He was to establish his headquarters at Khanghur, and the whole of the lower land from the Punjab to Shahpoor in Kutchee was to be under his sway. It was a dreary waste of sand, swept for eight months in the year by burning and noxious winds, and was almost wholly deserted. At Khanghur there was a mud fort and five miserable families, amounting to about twenty souls. The old mud fort has long since disappeared, and near its site there is the large and flourishing town, which Dalhousie commanded should be called after its founder, Jacobabad, or the city of Jacob. Jacob, determined to impress on the people that our occupation was going to be permanent, built for himself and his staff a massive and handsome residence. He planted a garden and embarrassed the Khan of Khelat by sending a present of vegetables. The chief tried the cabbages unsuccessfully as salads, and served the turnips among the rare fruits at dessert. Along the frontier were dotted similar mud forts in which the troops were stationed, and the officers and men were necessarily totally ignorant of the country and of the people. Jacob had the forts dismantled, and abandoned all idea of defensive operations. Every detachment was posted in the open plain, and patrols sent in every direction. Whenever a party of the Sind Horse came on any of the raiders, they attacked them at once, charging any number, however superior, without the slightest hesitation. Jacob's first year on the border was one of enormous bodily labour. "We had, literally, to lie down to rest with boots and sword on for many months together." Having by the use of force made himself respected, Jacob was able to apply better means and to appeal to higher motives than fear.

It is moral more than physical force [he writes] which is required to control predatory tribes: both are doubtless necessary, but the latter is so chiefly to enable us to apply the other. Justice, honesty, high principles, unswerving firmness, and force without violence succeed best with these men, as with others. If we imitate their crimes in pretence of retaliation we only perpetuate the evil. The power of the border marauder does not wholly consist in the damage he is able to cause, or in the terror he is able to inspire, but in the fact that his name and deeds are associated, even in the minds of those he injures, with chivalric daring and attributes not altogether bad. But if the trade of the marauder be proved to be unsuccessful and disreputable, it soon receives the ridicule and contempt of all.

Jacob proved the trade of the marauder to be unsuccessful and disreputable, and under his rule the most active and the most violent of the old robber tribes became cheerful and thriving agriculturists. "And," Jacob adds in memorable words, "believe me, the principles which have guided proceedings in this instance are of universal application. If we arc just and true we shall be trusted even by the Afghans, whatever measures we may find it necessary to undertake." John Jacob was no believer in the strictly close system which discouraged English officers from having intercourse with the barbarians on their confines; he had no faith in the policy of punitive expeditions followed by a precipitate and complete withdrawal, a policy which the late Lord Lytton very aptly described as one of alternate vengeance and inaction. Unhappily for the repose and finances of our Indian empire, the system recommended by the wisdom of John Jacob, and followed by Herbert Edwardes and Nicholson, has not been adopted in later days in our northern marches.

The suppression of crime on the border was accompanied by a settlement of the land revenue. Jacob saw that in a country like India the good government of the country and the security and contentment of the people mainly depend on the revenue administration. "We cannot," he writes, "too earnestly bear in mind that a revenue, survey, and settlement is merely a short name for proceedings involving the rights, good order, and advancement of the true interests of the Government we serve and of the people confided to our charge." He realised that it is of the highest importance to a people that the taxes should be of a moderate amount, and they should be so assessed and levied as not to interfere injuriously with industry. Jacob also recognised, what is too often forgotten at the present time, that to leave the people alone and let things grow is the essence of a good administration: "Above all, avoid over-governing and unnecessarily interfering. Depend on it, the people understand their own interests better than you. See that all men know and feel secure in their rights. Remove all obstructions to free inter-communication; and then stand by and keep the peace."

The eight years of Jacob's strong rule on the frontier passed away, and in 1856, when Sir Bartle Frere, who had worthily continued the great work which Napier began, had to go home on sick-leave, John Jacob was appointed to succeed him as acting Commissioner of Sind. He addressed himself to his new work with characteristic energy and activity, and was soon deep in plans for the material development of the province. He wished to construct a great canal along the boundary-line between Sind and Khelat territory into the heart of the desert, and to build a railway which should some day run from Kurrachee through the Bolan. Jacob was looking forward to a quiet administration, the only duty of which would be by improved institutions and public works to promote the happiness and prosperity of a contented population, when the sky suddenly became overcast. In October 1856 Bartle Frere wrote to him: "You will see that things look stormy in Europe. I fear they will not leave you long at the ploughshare, and ere long the din of the battle will be putting thoughts of sabres into your head again." In his next letter he informed him that the Persian campaign had been decided on. Jacob strongly disapproved of the war as a needless extension of our responsibilities. He and Bartle Frere agreed it was but a momentary expedient to obtain redress for evils brought on by the weakness and vacillation of statesmen at home. The best security for India, he considered, from threat, insult, or real attack, was to obtain a strong frontier. He proposed the permanent establishment of an outpost at Quetta, commanding on the north and west all the direct routes from Kandahar to the Punjab and on the south the passes leading into Sind. Lord Canning objected, on the ground that "the red line of the map would be again pushed forward westward, and without finding so good a resting-place as now." Twenty years after Jacob's death the red line had again to be pushed westward: Quetta became an outpost of our empire, and by following the principle laid down by Jacob the province of Beluchistan has been reduced from anarchy to order.

When war with Persia was declared Jacob was appointed, at the request of Outram, to command the cavalry. Sudden disturbances in Khelat, however, delayed the Sind Horse and their commandant, and he found Outram at Bushire the very day he was about to embark on his expedition against Mohamerah, a strongly fortified town on the Euphrates. Three thousand men were left at Bushire, and Jacob was

placed in command of the garrison. He was mortified at not
going forward at the head of his Horse, but Outram softened
the unwelcome order by appealing to his soldierly spirit and
reminding him of the importance of securing the base. On
the 26th of March the forts at Mohamerah were occupied;
but all further operations were stopped by news reaching
Outram (5th April) that peace with Persia had been signed
at Paris. A month later Lord Canning telegraphed to Lord
Elphinstone: "Write to Sir James Outram that I wish him
to return to India immediately, and the same to General
Jacob. We want all our best men here." The mutiny that
Jacob had foretold had burst. In June Outram left for India,
but Jacob was detained, at the desire of the British Minister,
in Persia. Four months later he arrived at Bombay. A
sore disappointment awaited him. Outram had written to
him that he had urged the Governor-General to give him
command of the army of Central India then assembling,
"and he appears most highly to approve of the idea, satisfied
as he is that you, of all men, are best fitted for the great
military and political responsibilities which must rest on
that commander." On his arrival at Bombay Jacob received
a letter from Lord Elphinstone informing him that, as he
was unable to wait for him, the command had been given
to Sir Hugh Rose, and John Jacob returned to his old duties
at Jacobabad. He found the work much increased, and for
the first time in his life he found his strength unequal to the
task. He was no more than forty-six, but the keen, untiring
spirit had fretted the body to decay. He worked on, however,
from early morning to midnight. He wrote: "The business I
strive to get through daily would be sufficient to overwhelm

fifty brains instead of one. I seldom get above three hours'
sleep in the twenty-four, and the work will kill me, but I do
not regret; for I have proved and established principles and
built foundations on which others will be able to work." A
friend found him in the desert suffering from sleeplessness
and weakness from loss of blood. He consented to return
to headquarters, but refused to be carried. He insisted on
riding to Jacobabad—a distance of twenty miles—though
often bent double in the saddle. His officers entreated him
to have medical assistance, but he refused, declaring that
all he needed was rest. At midnight on the 6th of December,
as his strength was fast ebbing away, they brought to his
bedside the troopers whom he had often led to the charge
and the Beluch chiefs whom he had tamed. Their eyes were
dimmed with tears. The next day they carried him to his
rest. The officers of the garrison, the troops of the Sind
Horse, and the Beluch warriors followed his bier, and many
of the peasants joined the procession as it moved to the
churchyard. They lowered the body into the grave, and the
Beluchees believe that as it lies in their earth his spirit still
watches over them. He being dead yet speaketh, how man
may be won by courage, love, and justice.

SIR DONALD STEWART AND SIR WILLIAM LOCKHART.

DEATH has recently taken two men of the old type, lofty in valour and honour, who founded our Indian Empire. The individual must pass away, but let us hope the type will never be lost, for such men as Donald Stewart and William Lockhart are the true builders of our nation's greatness. They both belonged to the Bengal Army, and, like Munro, Malcolm, Herbert Edwardes, and Henry Lawrence, were of the great line of statesmen-soldiers who have so materially aided in the establishment and administration of our splendid dependency. Their tact and ability as civilians were only equalled by their ardour and bravery in the field. The story of their lives deserves to be known, for it reminds us by what virtues, and by what toils, a fame so clear and great as theirs is won, and by what thoughts and actions an empire is made and held together.

Donald Stewart and William Lockhart both belonged to the race which has scored so deep a mark in our Imperial history, and were proud of their old Scottish blood. On both sides of his house Donald Stewart was a Highlander,

SIR DONALD STEWART.

and his strong Norse features and well-knit frame were evidence of his descent. By birth he was a Morayshire man, for in 1824 he came into the world at Mount Pleasant, near Forres. When he was a year old his father, Richard Stewart, moved to Sea Park, also near Forres. And from there Donald was sent, in the first instance, to the village school at Findhorn, a small fishing hamlet near his home, where he picked up the elements of knowledge. Donald Stewart was a product of the old education which formed the character of the English and Scottish nations. At the parish school of Dufftown the dominie not only imparted to him whatever knowledge of Greek and Latin he was able to provide, but he also moulded his character and imbued him with a love of the fine art of salmon-fishing. At the age of fourteen, in order to improve his scholarship before he entered the University of Aberdeen, Donald was sent to the Elgin Academy, then considered the best school in the north of Scotland. The result was satisfactory. He had been there but a year when he gained a small bursary by open competition, and proceeded to the university which has sent to India some of her bravest soldiers and ablest administrators. Before the close of the year, by dint of hard work, he gained a brilliant victory over many competitors. "My object," he says, "was to get a fair place at the examination, to please my parents, and I did my best. The result far exceeded my expectation, and no one was more astonished than myself when I heard my name called as the winner of the first prize in Greek and first in the order of merit in Latin. Every one in the class thought it must be a mistake, and my name had to be called more than once before I moved from my seat."

He adds, "I was proud of my success, but I had a feeling
that it was hardly deserved, as I knew there were many of
my term who were infinitely better scholars than myself."
Donald Stewart always did his best, and this was the chief
secret of his success; and all through his life the essentially
chivalrous nobleness of his disposition was in no respect
more conspicuously manifested than in the modest estimate
it induced him to form of his own work, and the enthusiasm
with which he acknowledged the soldierly qualities and
triumphs of his military comrades.

Not letters but arms were destined to be Donald Stewart's
vocation. His college career came to an end by a nomination
to the military service of the East India Company, and in
1840, twelve years before Lord Roberts landed in India, he
was appointed an ensign in the 9th Bengal Native Infantry.
It was the pattern regiment of that great army whose history
abounds with many examples of courage shown in brilliant
attack; of courage shown in coolness under danger; of patient
stoicism under pain, and self-denying devotion to duty. That
the evil that men do lives after them, while the good is often
interred with their bones, was amply illustrated in the case
of the old Bengal army. But history will record that it was
by the aid of the Bengal sepoy the masters of Fort William
became the masters of Bengal, and the masters of Bengal
became the masters of India. A triumphant mercenary army,
however, grew ungovernable; there were not sufficient officers
to maintain discipline; and an act of signal imprudence–the
issue of greased cartridges–caused a sudden conflagration
and explosion. The Indian Mutiny shone with "the sudden
making of noble names." Among these names must be enrolled

that of Donald Stewart. He was stationed at Alyghur, an important station about eighty miles from Meerut and sixty from Agra, when his regiment mutinied. The sepoys plundered the treasury, broke open the jail doors, and released the prisoners; but they did not lay hands on their officers. After his men had marched away in a body to Delhi, Stewart remained at Alyghur and took command of a body of volunteers sent by the Lieutenant-Governor of the North-Western Provinces to aid the civil authorities in maintaining order in the district. But he was too keen a soldier to care for the work, and after a short time he went to Agra and placed his services at the disposal of the Lieutenant-Governor. Despatches had arrived from the Governor-General for the Commander-in-Chief. But all communication between Agra and Delhi was closed. Donald Stewart was told he might be the bearer of the despatches if he chose to undertake so perilous a journey. But no journey was too perilous for Stewart when a duty had to be performed. On the 18th June, as the sun was setting over the broad waters of the Jumna, he set forth on his ride. Darkness swiftly fell. All night he rode, and the sun had risen before he reached the sacred city of Muttra, thirty-five miles distant, without mishap. Armed men thronged its narrow and tortuous streets; but England's prestige had not fallen, and they did not attempt to molest the solitary British officer. A Brahmin official received him with courtesy, and offered him two native troopers belonging to a neighbouring chief, to accompany him thirty miles on his road, to the town of Hodul. They were ill-looking swashbucklers, and Stewart would fain have declined their company, but he dared not show any

distrust. At daybreak he resumed his ride, accompanied by
his escort. But he had not gone sixteen miles when his horse
fell down, utterly worn out. The two troopers laughed and rode
away, while Stewart, taking his saddle and bridle, tramped
to the nearest village. But no horse could be got for love or
money. The future field-marshal siezed a donkey grazing in a
field, and at sunset arrived at Hodul, having done thirty-seven
miles in the day. The native magistrate courteously received
him, and gave him some bread and milk; but he would not
hear of his staying one night, as the arrival of a European
had created considerable commotion in the town. Stewart was
worn by the adventures of the day and wanted rest, but the
magistrate was firm, and he at last consented to start if he
were provided with a horse. The native promptly lent him
his own pony, and Stewart was again under way. Day had
long flooded the wide plains when he reached the camp of
the prime minister of Jaipur, where he found the political
resident and several English refugees. He persuaded one of
them, Mr Ford, a district magistrate, to accompany him in
his ride. Late on the 27th of June they started forth, and
during their journey they passed through towns and villages
filled with rebel sepoys breathing death, and once or twice
narrowly escaped being attacked by gangs of bandits. The
next morning they halted at a village to escape the heat
of the day, and they received, as many Englishmen and
Englishwomen did in these evil days, much kindness from
the villagers. A notorious cattle-lifter guided them all the
following night. At dawn they saw "the tall red minarets
of Delhi rise out of the morning mist, when an occasional
shell might be seen bursting near the city." The cattle-lifter

refused to proceed any farther. He would take no reward, but he hoped his services would be remembered when quieter times came. Stewart found a villager who conducted them to one of our pickets. A splendid feat of gallantry was done, but Stewart's modesty has covered the greatness of the deed. Lord Roberts writes: "I was waiting outside Sir Henry Barnard's tent, anxious to hear what decision had been come to, when two men rode up, both looking greatly fatigued and half starved, one of them being Stewart. He told me they had had a most adventurous ride; but before waiting to hear his story I asked Norman to suggest Stewart for the new appointment—a case of one word for Stewart and two for myself, I am afraid, for I had set my heart on returning to the quartermaster-general's department, and so it became settled to our mutual satisfaction, Stewart becoming the D.A.A.G.[1] of the Delhi Field Force, and I the D.A.Q.M.G.[2] with the artillery." As deputy-assistant adjutant-general he took part in that great siege, and conducted the duties of that important department to the satisfaction of the general commanding the field forces, who mentions him in his despatch, and writes of him as " the gallant and energetic Captain Stewart." He served in the same capacity throughout the siege and capture of Lucknow by Sir Colin Campbell, and the Rohilkund campaign. On the 30th of December 1857 he was transferred as assistant adjutant-general to army headquarters. For his services in the Mutiny Donald Stewart was rewarded with a brevet majority, and in July 1858 he reached the rank of lieutenant-colonel.

---

[1] Deputy Assistant Adjutant–General.
[2] Deputy Assistant Quartermaster-General.

When the old Bengal army disappeared a new Bengal army had to be created, and as assistant adjutant-general from 1857 to 1862 and deputy adjutant-general from 1862 to 1867, Donald Stewart did much towards its formation. His homely sense and careful forethought were of the highest value in adjusting the new system to the varying circumstances to be dealt with. The ability he had shown as a military administrator, and the reputation he had won as a gallant officer in the Mutiny, led to Brigadier-General D. M. Stewart being nominated in 1867 to command the Bengal portion of the force for service in Abyssinia. Major Roberts, R.A., was appointed to be his assistant quartermaster-general. Lord Roberts writes: "I had often read and heard of the difficulties and delays experienced by troops landing in a foreign country, in consequence of their requirements not being all shipped in the same vessel with themselves,– men in one ship, camp-equipage in another, transport and field-hospital in a third, or perhaps the mules in one and their pack-saddles in another,–and I determined to try and prevent these mistakes upon this occasion. With Stewart's approval, I arranged that each detachment should embark complete in every detail, which resulted in the troops being landed and marched off without the least delay as each vessel reached its destination." This arrangement has been followed with conspicuous success in subsequent expeditions sent from India.

When the Bengal brigade reached Africa, Sir Robert Napier had already begun his march to Magdala. But before launching his army into an unknown and hostile country he had, like a wise commander, organised his base and provided for his communications. Senafe, 8000 feet above the level of the sea, and distant twenty-seven miles from the port of Zeila, was the secondary base of operations in the campaign, and the great store- house for supplies and provisions which, after being carried through the Kumayli Pass, were pushed on to the front. Soon after he landed Brigadier Stewart was ordered to take command of the post, and displayed all the qualities of an energetic and sound administrator. For his services in the expedition he received the Abyssinian medal and a Companionship of the Bath.

On his return to India Donald Stewart was appointed to the command of the Peshawar Brigade. He was no stranger to the great frontier station which guards the Khyber defiles, for his regiment had been stationed there, and he had won his first medal and clasp for distinguished service in two expeditions against the wild tribes on our northern frontier. He held the command of the Peshawar brigade only a short time, as he had to vacate it in December 1868 on promotion to the rank of major-general. Tempting offers of permanent civil employment had been made to him at different times, but he clung to his profession. However, in 1871, an offer was made him of an appointment which required both military and civil capacity.

In the spring of that year it came to the notice of Lord Mayo that a cruel and mysterious murder had been committed in the penal settlement of the Andaman Islands. He ordered a strict inquiry to be made, which disclosed a laxity of discipline productive of scandalous results. He therefore determined to create a new government for the settlement, which, while enforcing stricter discipline, should allow of a career to the industrious and well-behaved. A code of regulations was drafted under his immediate orders, and supervised by his own pen. Then, "true to his maxim that for any piece of hard administrative work 'a man is required,' he sought out the best officer he could find for the practical reorganisation of the settlement." He chose Donald Stewart. "The charge which Major-General Stewart is about to assume," wrote Lord Mayo, "is one of great responsibility. In fact, I scarcely know of any charge under the Government of India which will afford greater scope for ability and energy, or where a greater public service can be performed."

In the summer Donald Stewart became Chief Commissioner of the Andamans and Nicobars, and at once set to work to carry out Lord Mayo's scheme, which was a great and most humane conception. The whole force and earnestness of his character were directed upon the general peace and upon the most subordinate detail. But he had a difficult and delicate work to perform, and he desired that Lord Mayo should "personally realise the magnitude and difficulty of the task." The Viceroy resolved to visit the Andamans when returning from his first visit to Burma.

On the 8th of February 1872 Lord Mayo cast anchor off Hopetown in the Andamans. The day was spent in visiting the different convict settlements, and every possible provision was taken for the Viceroy's protection. In the evening Lord Mayo insisted on visiting Mount Harriet, a lofty hill about a mile and a half inland from the jetty. He lingered some time on the top watching the sun set in the ocean. "It is the loveliest thing I think I ever saw," he said. Darkness had fallen when he reached the foot. Preceded by two torch-bearers, he walked down the pier between his private secretary and Donald Stewart, closely followed by a strong body of police. On reaching the stairs, Lord Mayo stepped aside from his companions. In a moment a convict, who had been stalking him all day, rushed out and stabbed him to death. Men of all classes and creeds mourned the death of a Viceroy much beloved, and there was also universal sympathy for the gallant soldier in whose territory the tragedy occurred. But, as the subsequent investigations showed, Donald Stewart had done all that prudence and foresight could suggest to guard Lord Mayo, who, being a strong man full of pluck, had during the day let it be seen that he regarded the precautions taken for his safety as not only irksome but somewhat superfluous. The shock to Donald Stewart was naturally a severe one, and he soon after was compelled to take leave to England to recover his health.

In 1875 General Stewart returned to India, and the following year he was again brought on to the military establishment by being appointed to the command of the Meean Meer Division. In 1878 he was promoted to the rank of lieutenant-general. Early that year the startling intelligence reached India that a Russian mission had visited Kabul, and had been favourably received by the Ameer. A counter-mission was sent, which was not allowed to enter Afghan territory, and war was thereupon declared against Shere Ali, the Ameer. On the commencement of hostilities Donald Stewart was appointed to command the Southern Field Force, destined for the reinforcement of our Quetta garrison and the capture of Kandahar. They had to be pushed forward from Sukkur *via* Dadur through the

Bolan Pass over the Khojak, and at that time there were in
those regions no roads worthy of the name. The transport
difficulties, aggravated by the death of the camels, were
enormous. The loss of life among the unfortunate camp-
followers was great, and the sufferings of the troops were
unusually severe; but all difficulties were overcome, and
on the 8th January 1879 Kandahar was reached without
serious resistance having been attempted. Donald Stewart
made Southern Afghanistan a tranquil province, and the
methods of his administration must always be instructive.
He pursued the same policy that Mountstuart Elphinstone
did after the conquest of the Deccan. He did not subvert
the existing authority, but he made use of every Afghan
official who was willing to render him true and loyal service.
A foreign occupation must gall; but he made the yoke fall
as light as possible on the shoulders of the people. From
Kelai-i-Ghazai to the Helmund British authority began to
be respected. Donald Stewart was a successful Governor,
not only because he was a shrewd sensible man, but because
he was a modest honest man. "The inhabitants of the city,
of the neighbouring villages, and of the country generally,"
writes an eye-witness, "learnt to know and trust the man who
treated them with justice, and always spoke the truth."

After the treaty of Gundamuk Kandahar was in process of
being evacuated; but when the outbreak at Kabul, resulting
in the murder of our envoy, occurred, General Stewart
was told to reoccupy it. A month after the murder of Major
Cavagnari Lord Roberts took possession of Kabul. Then
followed the investment of our intrenchments at Sherpur,
and the desperate attempt of the enemy to take it, which

was foiled by the steady fire of the defenders. Kabul was once again in our hands, and during the winter months General Roberts strengthened his position. In order to overawe more completely the warlike tribes of the north, General Stewart was ordered to march with the Bengal troops by way of Ghazni to Kabul.

On the 31st of March 1880 General Stewart, leaving Southern Afghanistan to be protected by the Bombay troops, set out to reduce Ghazni and join General Roberts at Kabul. Two long marches from the famous fortress he found, on the 19th of April, the enemy drawn up on a low range of hills through which passes the road to Ghazni. Donald Stewart determined to force his way. He knew that if he stopped to disperse every body of Afghans that gathered on the hills that lined his route, Kabul would never be reached in any reasonable time. He therefore continued his march till the head of the column was within three miles of the enemy; then he began to make his arrangements for the impending battle. Before he completed them the whole upper range, for a distance of two miles, was seen to be swarming with the enemy, and a large body of horsemen threatened our left. Our guns had scarcely opened fire when a torrent of men poured forth from the slopes, and, breaking against our line, spread out right and left and enveloped it. The wave struck the lancers, and forced them back on the infantry. Mules and riderless horses went dashing through the ranks. The fanatics were engaged in a hand-to-hand contest with our infantry. They broke through it on the left, and some penetrated to within twenty yards of the spot where the general and his staff were watching the action. All drew their swords for self-defence. At that critical moment the cool promptitude of Colonel Lyster, V.C., commanding the 3rd Gurkhas, saved us from a terrible disaster. He formed his men into company squares, and poured volley after volley into the fanatics as they surged onwards. The attack had now spread along the line. The general's escort and the 59th had to fall back. An order issued to this regiment to throw back their right to stem the rush was understood to imply the retirement of the whole regiment, and the movement was carried out. The Ghazis were upon them, and there was a tendency to huddle for common protection. General Hughes, observing this, galloped down, and with a fiery exhortation calmed the men; then by a steady fire they kept the Ghazis at bay, and covered the plain with dead. The fanatics charged with the same desperate valour as the followers of the man of Mecca did when they broke the ranks of the Roman Legion. Beaten back by our force, they returned again and again to the attack. After an hour's desperate fighting our reinforcements and the heavy artillery came up, and the enemy, finding all assaults hopeless, spread broadcast over the country. Thus ended the battle of Ahmed Keyl, the most hard-fought contest of the Afghan war. Ghazni surrendered without a struggle, and the road to the capital of Afghanistan lay open. General Roberts had sent from Kabul a detachment to co-operate with the Kandahar force, and on April 28th these two forces joined. On the 2nd of May Sir Donald Stewart arrived at Kabul, and, as senior officer, assumed from Sir Frederick Roberts the chief command as well as political control. Sufficient credit has hardly ever been given to Sir Donald Stewart for his daring march from Kandahar to Kabul. But it was undoubtedly a fine feat of arms.

For some time negotiations had been going on between the Indian Government and Abdul Rahman as to his succession to the throne of Kabul, one chief point of difference being that the Government would not recognise his claim to have Kandahar handed over to him. At length all was arranged, and on July 22nd Sirdar Abdul Rahman was formally recognised by the British Government as Ameer of Kabul. A few days after the proclamation of the new Ameer news reached Kabul of the disaster at Maiwand and the investment of Kandahar by Ayub Khan's army. With the consent of Sir Donald Stewart, Roberts telegraphed at once to headquarters at Simla a proposal that he should lead a relieving force straight from Kabul to Kandahar, and the Viceroy agreed. As Lord Roberts tells us in his *Forty-one Years in India,'* Donald Stewart gave him every possible encouragement and assistance in the organisation of his column. By lending to him his tried troops, he crowned his career in the field by a noble and generous act. After Lord Roberts had left for Kandahar, General Stewart, with masterly skill, marched his troops out of Afghanistan without firing a shot.

For his great military and political services in the war, Donald Stewart received the thanks of Parliament. His sovereign, ever ready to reward the services of her soldiers, bestowed on him the Grand Cross of the Bath, and created him a baronet. In October 1880 he was appointed military member of the Governor-General's Council, and six months after he became Commander-in-Chief in India. The long campaign in Afghanistan had laid bare the deficiencies in our military system; and during his tenure of office were laid by Sir George Chesney–a brave soldier, a great

administrator, and a man of genius–the foundations of
those military reforms which marked the administrations
of Lord Dufferin, and were completed by his successor, Lord
Lansdowne. A simple, modest man, Donald Stewart looked
at military problems apart from any personal bearing, and
the power of taking an unselfish view prevented him from
clashing with his colleagues. To make the Bengal army
worthy of its old traditions he laboured hard, and when he
resigned his command he had done much to make it what it
is now, one of the best fighting machines in the world. When
he left the land in which he had spent the best years of his
life, his connection with India did not cease, for on arriving
in England he was appointed one of the official advisers
of the Secretary of State. And in the consideration of the
numerous political and military problems which from time
to time arose his opinion carried great weight, because it was
founded on calm judgment and long experience. He worked
on till his death, modestly, intelligently, and without fear.
The old veteran has gone, but he has left us an example of a
noble and blameless career.

It would be difficult to imagine two men more different in
their intellect and their character than Donald Stewart and
William Lockhart. Stewart was a brave soldier, endowed
with a vigorous intellect, Scottish common-sense, and
Scottish caution. Lockhart was a dashing captain, full of life
and humour, with a strong love of adventure. He possessed
in no small degree the brilliant literary instincts of his uncle,
John Gibson Lockhart, and his brother, Lawrence Lockhart,
gallant soldier and novelist. He had almost every quality
fitted to make him a favourite in society. His presence

SIR WILLIAM LOCKHART.

was commanding, his features mobile and handsome, and in every movement there was an air of high breeding and aristocratic culture which bore witness to his old Scottish descent from the "Lockharts of the Lee."

A year after Donald Stewart went to India, William Lockhart was born at Milton Lockhart, where his father was the laird-parson. At the age of seventeen (4th of October he joined the Bengal army as ensign 1858), nominally in the 44th Bengal Native Infantry, but he was attached to the 5th Fusiliers, and shared in the pursuit of the rebels. In 1859 Lockhart joined the cavalry, and the 14th Bengal Lancers, Murray's Jat Horse, was his regiment for several years. He had been six years in the service when the chance of being employed on active service first came to him. On the 4th December 1863 a mission left Darjeeling for Bhutan, and returned on the 12th of April 1864, having been not only received without honour but even subjected to insult and outrage. War was the inevitable consequence. In the military operations against the Bhutanese, Lockhart, as adjutant of his regiment, first proved himself to be a brave and daring soldier. He had inherited from his Scottish ancestors a keen instinct for scouting and an eye for mountain topography. The services he rendered by his reconnaissance to Checrung were acknowledged by the Government of India, and he obtained a medal and clasp. The dash and daring he had displayed led to his being appointed *aide-de-camp* to Brigadier-General Merewether in the Abyssinian expedition. Four future commanders-in-chief of India were employed in that wonderful campaign—Napier, the able commander; Donald Stewart, the brigadier; Roberts, transport officer;

and Lockhart, the *aide-de-camp*,–a group of soldiers of whom any army in the world might well be proud. John Merewether had been one of John Jacob's most trusted lieutenants, and he managed the various chiefs of Zeila with the same conspicuous success that he had managed the chiefs on the borders of Upper Sind. Merewether reported "very favourably of the services of his *aide-de-camp*, Lieutenant Lockhart of the Bengal cavalry." Lockhart was present when the Abyssinians were driven down the slopes of Arogic, and at the subsequent capture of Magdala.

On his return to India, Lockhart was for the first time engaged in one of those punitive expeditions, the need for which will always exist till the other side of the line is held by a civilised government. In July 1868 the Pathans of the Black Mountains attacked a police post, the establishment of which they deeply resented. For four months they raided and destroyed British villages. Then a force of 12,000 men was sent to punish the aggressors. It penetrated without serious opposition to the crest of the Black Mountain, explored the enemy's country, occupied their strong-holds, and reduced them to submission. The work of exploration suited Lockhart. The 2nd Brigade bivouacked for the night at a small village preparatory to the ascent of the Black Mountain the next day by the way of the Sumbulboot spur. Brigadier-General T.L. Vaughan, C.B., who commanded the brigade, determined to reconnoitre that evening the road between the village and spur. "This duty," he writes in his despatch, "was most ably and resolutely performed by Lieutenant Lockhart, deputy-assistant quartermaster-general attached to the brigade, who at much personal risk reconnoitred for some distance beyond the village of Belean up the spur, and brought me most important information."

The next few years were spent in carrying on his ordinary regimental duties. But garrison life did not suit his ardent spirit. Not for honour, nor for expectation of advancement, but from sheer love of adventure and a feeling of genuine chivalry, he went forth to pursue and to conquer. It was the unrest in him which led him in 1876 to visit Acheen, where the Dutch were waging a vigorous war against the tribesmen who resented their intrusion into Sumatra. He took part in the assault on Lambada, displayed his wonted gallantry, and received from the Dutch their war-medal and clasp. In the malarious Dutch settlement he was smitten with the cruel blasting fever, and would have been left to die in a shed on the wharf if he had not insisted on being carried on board the Singapore steamer. The sea-breeze restored his health. At the outbreak of the Afghan war he was attached to the Quartermaster-General's department, and, to his sore disappointment, was left in India. In the second phase of the campaign, after the murder of Cavagnari, he was posted as assistant quartermaster-general with Lord Roberts, and took part in the three days' hard fighting around Kabul, before we had to concentrate our forces at the cantonment of Sherpur. During the investment Lockhart was the life and soul of the party, who had many a merry evening together in the headquarters of the gateway at Sherpur. For his services during the Afghan campaign he received the insignia of a Companion of the Bath, with another medal and clasp.

After the war Lockhart went to Simla as deputy quartermaster-general in charge of the newly formed

Intelligence branch. But neither the life of the Himalayan capital nor the routine of office-work suited him, and on the expiration of his term of office he assumed command of the 24th Punjab Infantry, and returned to the rugged borderland where he was to win his best laurels. Among the illustrious men, Cleveland, Outram, John Jacob, Herbert Edwardes, Reynell Taylor, and John Nicholson, who, from Burma in the far south to Kashmir in the far north, have raised and civilised the warlike tribes on our border, Lockhart has a right to a not undistinguished niche. The mode in which they accomplished their object was in all cases fundamentally the same. It was effected by the power of individual character. They explored the countries beyond the border, and there was no expedition so hazardous that they were not found ready to undertake it. They trusted themselves to the people, and by their courage and frankness they gained their confidence. Lockhart's great influence among the tribes was due to his good-humoured, confident, fearless way of dealing with them. They felt that they had his sympathy, but they also knew that he was not in the least afraid of them, and that he would not allow them to take the slightest liberty. Like Nicholson, his name was a power on the frontier.

When Lord Dufferin determined in 1885 to send a mission to Chitral, then an almost unknown land, he chose Lockhart to be his envoy. On the 25th of June the mission started from Kashmir, and on the 13th of the following month the Kamri Pass, about 13,100 feet above the sea, was passed. For many miles the road ran through snow. On the 29th of July the mission reached Gilgit. Here it was found advisable to halt for some time, in order that the streams on the Chitral route, swollen by the melting snow, might subside. During their stay the officers of the mission acquired a good deal of useful knowledge regarding the surrounding countries. Surgeon Giles, who accompanied the party, was beset by patients. Among the operations he performed none excited so much interest as the reconstruction of noses (by a flap from the forehead),–for the deprivation of that organ was a common form of punishment in those regions. On the 8th of August the officers rode out of Gilgit, and the party made their way over roads often passing round the face of a precipice, with the foaming torrent far below. Mules fell over, and the party had to halt to recover the lost loads. Clefts in the face of the rock often broke the continuity of the path, and had to be crossed by a few unfixed logs thrown across, which moved and turned under the foot of the traveller. Over these places animals could not go, and they had to take some higher path which zigzagged over the mountains. Rivers had to be crossed by bridges, primitive and shaky. On the 23rd of August the Shandar Pass, 12,100 feet above the sea, was crossed, and three days later Masting was reached. Here a halt of ten days was made, to await the return of a detached party who had started to explore some of the neighbouring passes. Not till the 11th of September was Chitral reached. The *mehtar* (chief), with the *Nizam-ul-Mulk,* his heir, and a large following, met the party some four miles from the city and brought them in.

At two miles from the fort [writes Lockhart], the opposite bank of the river was lined by some hundreds of horse and foot, who fired a succession of *feux-de-joie* on our approach, and made a great noise, shouting, fifing, and drumming, the

horsemen manoeuvring parallel to our course, circling and
firing. The men were clad in many colours, and the effect
was good. Weather threatening, sky overcast, drops of rain
occasionally, and distant thunder, all pronounced to be good
omens. The *mehtar* is about 5 feet 9, and enormously' broad,
with a fist like a prize-fighter's. Age perhaps seventy, large
head, aquiline features, complexion (the little of it seen above a
red-dyed beard) pretty fair, hands very much so. A fine bearing
and a determined cast of countenance. We rode hand-in-hand,
according to a very disagreeable habit of the country, and,
on passing his fort, were greeted by an artillery salute, most
irregularly fired.

They found their camp pitched in a mulberry grove half a
mile north of the fort:–

The weather was warm, and a shady camp was most grateful
to all. From it the *mehtar's* mud fort just showed through a
mass of *chinar* and fruit-trees. Away to the east rose the huge
snowy Torach-Mir (25,000 feet), like a mass of frosted silver in
sunshine; at dawn receiving the sun's rays whilst the valley
was in profound darkness, thus presenting the phenomenon of
"a pillar of fire," a mass of burnished copper, and passing as the
sun rose through gold to the silver aspect it wore throughout
day. There can be few more beautiful and striking sights than
this in the world; and it is not surprising that the Torach-Mir
should be the subject of fairy legend throughout the land.

On the 19th of September the officers of the mission with
a small escort started to pay a visit to Kafiristan. After
visiting the Durah Pass (14,800 feet), they crossed by the
Zedek Pass (14,850 feet) into Kafiristan, and marched
through the Bashgal country as far as Lut-Dih. For the
first time Bashgal women and men were seen in their own
country by a European. At two miles from Shui a deputation
of Kaffirs–some fifty men and boys–met the party, with a

very small pony, which Colonel Lockhart had to mount. The path ran through woods of birch and *deodar* on springy turf, and down the centre rushed a sparkling stream over granite boulders, widening and pursuing a more tranquil course over sand and pebbles as Shui was approached. The English officers marched in the midst of their strange hosts, "who satisfied their curiosities as to the colour of their guests' skin under their garments, the texture of their clothes, and the make of their boots, without any false modesty. The men and boys nearly all carried the national dagger, the hilt of carved steel and brass, and a short axe. In front of the procession went three musicians, playing on reed-pipes. A single reed was used by blowing across one end–as in pan-pipes–and the sound was modulated by several holes. The airs played were soft and melodious, different from anything before heard by the officers. There was nothing at all harsh or unpleasant in the music, the character of which was plaintive and melancholy." The camp was pitched in the village, and in the evening the men came down to it and danced by a great log-fire: "It was a mixture of country-dance and Highland schottische. Advancing and retiring in lines, intermingling in couples, they kept excellent time to the music of reed-pipes and two small drums, and marked points in the dance by ear-piercing whistles on their fingers, and the brandishing of axes. The red firelight, the savage figures, and their fierce but perfectly timed gestures, presented a weird spectacle, which it would be difficult for an onlooker ever to forget."

From Shui the party proceeded to Lut-Dih (6660 feet), which means "The Great Village" in the Chitral tongue. It contains 5000 inhabitants, and vines, apricot, mulberry,

and walnut trees are abundant. After staying there a short
time they returned to Chitral, from whence they proceeded
back to Gilgit. Here they had to pass the winter, as all
issues from the valley were closed by the snows. In April
the mission again went forth to explore, and on the 9th of
May they crossed the Wakhugrins Pass, whose crest they
found to be 16,200 feet. On arriving at the plateau at the
top, two miles broad, they discovered the ponies stuck—the
snow was too soft. Some of their carriers, hardy mountain
men, broke down and refused to go on, although their loads
were taken from them. Two were stricken to death.

"Every effort was made by the Sikh havildar and four men,"
writes Lockhart, "who endeavoured to crawl with the dying
men on their backs; but both legs and arms disappeared in
the soft upper snow, and the exertion at 16,200 feet above
sea was more than could be endured. The two creatures
fainted continually, and, although I am pretty strong, I
found that I was quite exhausted by mid-day from lifting an
insensible man from the snow, reviving him, getting him on
a few yards, and then having to lift him again." Lockhart,
the brave and generous soldier, carrying through the snow
the dying coolie, makes a fine picture.

On the 26th day of August the mission returned to Kashmir,
the officers having accomplished a most adventurous and
interesting journey. They had succeeded in penetrating into
Kafiristan farther than any European had ever gone, and had
laid the foundation of our political influence beyond Gilgit.

"The results of your mission," wrote the Foreign Secretary
to Lockhart, "are of high value to the Government of India,
and the Viceroy desires me first to inform you, as the

responsible head of the undertaking, that he has noticed with much satisfaction the firmness, temper, and discretion which you have shown in circumstances of unusual difficulty and hardship."

On his return from Chitral Lockhart was sent to command the Eastern Division in Upper Burma, and took a very prominent part in reducing the country to order. After the occupation of Mandalay and the nominal termination of the war, British authority hardly extended beyond the limits of our camps, and it was unsafe for an Englishman to move without a strong escort. Guerilla bands held the peaceable portion of the peasantry in terror. Here and there chiefs arose with sufficient influence to collect a force which amounted to a small army. These scattered bands had little communication with each other. But they moved quickly, and the character of the country, thickly covered with dense scrub jungle, and the sympathy and co-operation of the people, enabled them to elude pursuit. All who saw Sir William Lockhart's work in 1886-87 bear witness to the able manner in which he conducted the campaign, and the untiring energy with which he followed the enemy. The thorough way in which Lockhart did the military work was a great help to the Chief Commissioner in establishing the civil administration. If there had been more Lockharts in command of brigades, the final pacification and settlement of the country would have taken less time to complete. For his services in Burma Lockhart received the degree of Knight Commander of the Bath. Then he enjoyed a brief period of rest as assistant military secretary for Indian affairs at army headquarters. But London as little suited the active

soldier as Simla, and at the end of 1890 he gladly accepted
the command of the Punjab Frontier Force. During his
period of command he conducted four frontier expeditions.
He was no believer in "the policy of the bayonet and the
firebrand," but his aim was, by personal intercourse and
neighbourly good offices, to "make mild a rugged people, and
thro' soft degrees subdue them to the useful and the good."
He, however, held that if an aggression had to be punished
it should be done thoroughly. He harried Waziristan for
months till he made the chiefs thoroughly understand the
power of the British arm. He had a profound knowledge of
the Pathan character, appreciated its good points, and had
much sympathy for the Afghans, with their love of their
Highlands, and admired their courage. When Sir Robert
Sandeman died, Lockhart would probably have succeeded
him as chief commissioner of Baluchistan if his services had
been available. If a chief commissionership for the Trans-
Indus territory had been created, Lockhart would, there is
little doubt, have been appointed to the office. No man in
India was so well suited to be the Warden of the Marches,
and if he had been Warden no Tirah campaign would in all
probability have been necessary.

Lockhart was on sick leave in England when the Afreedis
sacked our forts and closed the Khyber. The frontier was in a
flame, and he was hastily summoned to command the "Tirah
expeditionary force," which had been gathered to punish the
aggressors. The Afreedis are a large tribe, inhabiting the
lower and easternmost spurs of the great Safed Koh or White
Range, to the west and south of the Peshawar district. The
area of the country inhabited by them is about 900 miles.

The principal streams that drain these hills are the northern branch of the Bara river or Bara proper, the Bazar or Chuya river, and the Khyber stream, all flowing into the Peshawar valley. The valleys lying near the sources of the Bara river are included in the general name of Tirah, which comprises an area of 600 or 700 miles. By the camp-fires the Afreedi soldier loved to boast of the beauties and fertility of Tirah, and he used to state with swelling pride that it was a virgin land which had never been desecrated by the footsteps of a foreigner. Lockhart lifted the veil from Tirah, and its valleys were traversed by the British soldier. Lockhart had under him an army of 40,000 men, and he showed his military capacity by the way he handled them in a mountainous and almost impracticable country. It was the hardest bit of fighting we had done since the Crimea and the Mutiny. The storming of the heights of Dargai and the gallantry of the Gurkhas and Gordon Highlanders will be remembered as long as Englishmen reverence deeds of valour. The war did not strike the imagination of the British nation like the Soudan campaign. The skill and bravery displayed were not sufficiently appreciated, owing to newspaper correspondents sending home sensational accounts of insignificant untoward incidents which must occur in a war against a brave foe, armed with modern weapons, fighting in a difficult country of which he knows every inch. Sir William Lockhart told the present writer that the Tirah campaign had revealed to him that modern weapons had revolutionised the art of war. The methods practised on the parade would not answer against an enemy accustomed from childhood to carry arms, full of resources and wiles, fighting in their own land. "But what

gave me the greatest satisfaction," he added, "is the proof
it afforded that the British soldier can fight as well as the
British soldier fought in the Crimea or the Peninsula."

After the war Lockhart was made a G.C.B. and appointed
Commander-in-Chief in India. But the hand of death was on
him. He struggled hard to perform the multifarious duties
which the high and responsible office entailed, but illness
again and again laid him low. Then came "one fight more,
the best and the last," and he fought it, as he fought all his
fights, full of hope and courage.

On Sunday, the 20th of March 1900, William Lockhart
died. He was a fine example of those virtues which a soldier
should possess. He was brave, unselfish, and true, and the
wild men of the frontier recognised the essentially chivalrous
nobleness of his disposition.

FIELD–MARSHAL LORD ROBERTS.

FIELD-MARSHAL LORD ROBERTS.

On the 18th of April 1852 Frederick Roberts, having been appointed to the Bengal Artillery, arrived at Calcutta and joined the headquarters of his illustrious corps at Dumdum, a military station about five and a half miles from the capital. He began to work diligently at his profession, but he longed impatiently for the period when the irksome routine of garrison duty should be exchanged for the substantial delights of war. The Court of Ava having refused to make amends for the injuries and insults which British subjects had suffered at the hands of its servants, Lord Dalhousie resolved to exact reparation by force of arms. Two months 10th February 1852) before Roberts landed war had been declared, and he wrote to his father, General Abraham Roberts, a gallant officer who had commanded a brigade in the first Afghan war, begging him to use his influence to get him sent to Burma. The father replied that he expected soon to get the command of the Peshawar Division, and that he would like his son to join him. Four months after young Roberts got his marching orders, and his sorrow at not being sent on active service was mitigated by the thought

that he was going to the great school of Indian soldiers–the
northern marches of our empire.

Early in August Roberts left Dumdum for Peshawar,
the great frontier station which guards the Khyber defiles,
commanding the best known and most famous road from
India to Kabul. The material change wrought in India during
the reign of her late Imperial Majesty is brought home to us
when we find that the journey to Peshawar, which now can
be done in three days by rail, then occupied Roberts three
months. As far as the sacred city of Benares he travelled up
the noble Ganges in a barge towed by a steamer, and spent
nearly a month on the river. From Benares to the important
military station of Meerut, situated thirty-six miles from the
imperial city of Delhi, the journey was done in a *dak-garry*
(post-chaise), a vehicle now as extinct as the dodo. At Meerut
Roberts came across for the first time the far-famed Bengal
Horse Artillery, which had gained renown in many Indian
fields of honour. Sir Charles Napier said of it, "Second to
none in the world." The best recruits were picked for it, and
if interest had a hand in the selection of the officers, so also
had a good record on service. The uniform was picturesque
and effective: a handsome helmet with red horsehair plume,
a richly laced jacket, pouch and pouch-box with silver
mountings, sabretasche and shabrasque, with the sphinx,
Egypt, Ava, and Bhurtpore devices, a hussar sash, buckskin
breeches, and huge boots. It was "the red men " whom the
Afghans most dreaded, and so felt the Sikhs.

At Meerut the metalled and bridged imperial high-
way which the East India Company constructed from
Calcutta to Peshawar then ended, and the remainder of the

journey was done in a palanquin. It was not till November that Roberts reached Peshawar. Born at Cawnpore, and leaving India as an infant, he had enjoyed but little intercourse with his father, and they met almost as strangers. "We did not, however, long remain so: his affectionate greetings put an end to any feeling of shyness on my part, and the genial and kindly spirit which enabled him to enter into and sympathise with the feelings and aspirations of men younger than himself rendered the year I spent with him at Peshawar one of the brightest and happiest of my early life." [1] The son bears testimony that from his father he learned much about Afghanistan and the best mode of dealing with its people, thus gaining information which proved invaluable to him when, twenty years later, he found himself in command of an army on the field in that country.

From his arrival at Peshawar until the autumn of 1853 Lieutenant Roberts acted as aide-de-camp to his father, whilst at the same time he did duty with the artillery. In November he got the much-coveted jacket, but his joy was somewhat lessened by the fact of the troop to which he was posted being stationed at Umballa. Life on the frontier has a charm for young men of the right stuff, and Roberts did not wish to quit Peshawar. A vacancy opportunely occurred in one of the troops of Horse Artillery at the station, and it was given to him. The troop to which he was posted "was composed of a magnificent body of men, nearly all Irishmen, most of whom could have lifted me up with one hand. They were fine riders, and needed to be so, for the stud-horses used

---

[1] *Forty-one Years in India,* by Field-Marshal Lord Roberts, V.C., G.C.B., Vol. i. p. 18.

for artillery purposes at that time were not the quiet, well-broken animals of the present day. I used to try my hand at riding them all in turn, and thus learnt to understand the amount of nerve, patience, and skill necessary to the making of a good Horse Artillery driver, with the additional advantage that I was brought into constant contact with the men. It also qualified me to ride in the officers' team for the regimental brake. The brake, it must be understood, was drawn by six horses, each ridden postilion-fashion by an officer."

When Lieutenant Roberts arrived at Peshawar Colonel Mackeson was the commissioner or chief civil officer. "He was," wrote Lord Dalhousie, "the *beau ideal* of a soldier—cool to conceive, brave to dare, and strong to do. The Indian army was proud of his noble presence in its ranks—not without cause. On the dark pages of the Afghan war the name of Mackeson shone brightly, but the frontier was his post, and the future his field. The defiles of the Khyber and the peaks of the Black Mountains alike witness his exploits." On the evening of the 10th of September 1853 Colonel Mackeson was seated in his verandah listening to appeals from his subordinate officers when a man came up to him and presented a paper. He had spread his carpet, the Mohammedan's chapel, within sight of the house, and the attendants had noticed him all day earnestly engaged in prayer. Mackeson raised his arm to take the paper from his hand, when the assassin plunged a dagger into his breast. A brave native official threw himself upon the man, and was wounded in the struggle to secure him. "Secure the man, but don't kill him," cried Mackeson as his strength swiftly ebbed away, and he was carried into the house. He died of the wound in a few days, and Herbert Edwardes, the great soldier-statesman, was ordered by the Governor-General to succeed him. Lord Dalhousie wrote to him: "In the whole range of Indian charges I know none which at the present time is more arduous than the commissionership of Peshawar. Holding it, you hold the outpost of the Indian Empire. Your past career and your personal qualities and abilities give me assurance that in selecting you I have chosen well for its command. . . . You have a fine career before you. God speed you in it, both for your own sake and for the sake of this empire." Edwardes had not been long at Peshawar before he concurred in the opinion expressed by General Abraham Roberts, that the time had come for cultivating friendly relations with Kabul. He therefore proposed to make a treaty with Dost Mahommed, but John Lawrence, who was then Chief Commissioner of the Punjab, opposed it on the grounds (1) "that you will never be able to get the Afghans to make a treaty, and (2) if they make it, they will not keep it. Lord Dalhousie's opinion, however, fortunately coincided with that of Edwardes in favour of a treaty, and after long negotiations and the exercise of considerable tact and skill a treaty of friendship was drafted and signed on the 3rd of March 1855. In the autumn of the following year, when India was startled by the news of the fall of Herat into Persian hands, Edwardes put forward proposals for rendering effective aid to the Afghan *Ameer*. John Lawrence opposed the proposals, but they were accepted by the Governor of India, and the *Ameer* was invited to a conference at Peshawar. On the 1st of January 1857 took place the meeting between the Afghan *Ameer* and the Chief Commissioner of the Punjab. The English camp was pitched on the plain near Jumrud, and as his troop of Horse Artillery formed part of the escort, Roberts "was in the midst of it all."

Soon after the Peshawar conference the general commanding the division started on his tour of inspection, taking Roberts with him as his staff officer. He had already acted for some time as a deputy-assistant quartermaster-general, and with characteristic earnestness had thrown himself into the work and won the confidence of his chief. During the tour of inspection he met John Lawrence in camp at Rawal Pindi, and that shrewd judge of character, after he had been present at the general's inspection, offered him an appointment in the Public Works department. Happily he refused the offer, for it meant forsaking soldiering, and towards the end of April 1857 Roberts was ordered to report on the capabilities of Cherat, a hill not far from Peshawar, as a sanatorium for European soldiers. Here he first met Nicholson, who was engaged in introducing peace and order in the Peshawar valley.

"Nicholson impressed me more profoundly than any man I have ever met before, or have ever met since. I have never seen any one like him. He was the *beau ideal* of a soldier and a gentleman. His appearance was distinguished and commanding, with a sense of power about him which to my mind was the result of his having passed so much of his life amongst the wild and lawless tribesmen, with whom his authority was supreme. Intercourse with this man amongst men made me more eager than ever to remain on the frontier, and I was seized with ambition to follow in his footsteps."

But the young soldier was not destined to remain on the

frontier. On the night of the 11th of May 1857 Herbert Edwardes wrote to his wife: "The telegraph officer has just sent me a sad piece of news from Delhi, that the sepoys from Meerut had come over and burnt the bungalows there and killed several Europeans! This is serious, and we must expect the Mutiny to spread to every station, if not put down with the bayonet at some one cantonment." The following day he wrote: "The plot is thickening. This morning we got the following telegraphic message from the deputy adjutant - general at Meerut, dated twelve at night of May 10: 'Native troops in open mutiny. Cantonments south of Mall burnt. Several European officers killed. European troops under arms defending barracks. Electric telegraph wires cut.' " On the forenoon of the 13th Brigadier Cotton, Brigadier Chamberlain, Colonel Nicholson, and Herbert Edwardes met in a council of war, convened by its president, General Reid, to decide what steps should be taken to ensure the safety of the Punjab. Lieutenant Roberts was present, having been summoned to record its decisions, and he was "greatly impressed by the calm view of the situation taken by Edwardes and Nicholson." The decisions, according to the memorandum agreed upon, were: "First, General Reid, as senior officer in the Punjab, assumes the chief military command; and it is hereby resolved to organise a movable force instantly of thoroughly reliable troops to take the field, and get between the stations that have mutinied and those that have not, and move on any point in the Punjab where mutiny has to be put down by force of arms." The formation of the movable column was approved by Sir John Lawrence and carried into execution without delay. Brigadier Neville

Chamberlain was appointed to command it, and he chose the future Field-Marshal for his staff officer. When Neville Chamberlain relinquished the command on proceeding to Delhi as adjutant-general, Nicholson succeeded him, and as his staff officer Captain Roberts had opportunities of observing closely his splendid soldierly qualities and the workings of his grand but simple mind. "Nicholson was a born commander," he writes, "and this was felt by every officer and man with the column before he had been amongst them many days." Captain Roberts was at the fort of Philour when a message came from Sir Henry Barnard, who commanded at Delhi, begging that all artillery officers not doing regimental duty might be sent to Delhi, where their services were urgently required. Roberts at once felt that the message applied to him. Nicholson was loth to part with him, but he agreed that his first duty was to his regiment. At dawn next morning he left by mail-cart for Delhi. He proceeded to Umballa as fast as horses could carry him, but here a difficulty arose. He had to change mail-carts, but the seats in the fresh vehicle had been engaged some days in advance. But Roberts determined to get on "by hook or by crook"–to use a classic expression from the 'Faerie Queen.' He called on Douglas Forsyth, the Deputy Commissioner, who said that he might have a seat in an extra cart that was leaving that night laden with small-arm ammunition. The offer was gladly accepted, and the journey resumed. On the evening of the 29th of June Roberts, after a narrow escape of falling into the enemy's hands, reached our pickets at Delhi.

"The relief to us when we found ourselves safe beside our own pickets may be imagined. My father's old staff officer, Henry Norman, who was then assistant adjutant-general at headquarters, kindly asked me to share his tent until I could make other arrangements. He had no bed to offer me, but I required none, as I was thoroughly tired out, and all I wanted was a spot in which to throw myself down. A good night's rest quite set me up. I awoke early, scarcely able to believe in my good fortune. I was actually in Delhi, and the city was still in the possession of the mutineers." And it remained for many a long day in their possession.

On joining the camp at Delhi Roberts was appointed deputy-assistant quartermaster-general with the artillery. Two days after he first found himself under fire, and in the hard-fought encounter on the 14th of July he was wounded. On the afternoon of that day a column was formed to drive the enemy out of the suburbs. It consisted of six Horse Artillery guns under Major Turner and Captain Money, the 1st Fusiliers under Major Jacob, and Major Coke's corps of Punjab Rifles, with a few of the Guides cavalry and Hodson's Horse and the Kohat *Risala*. Brigadier-General Chamberlain accompanied the column, and on passing the front of Hindu Rao's ridge it was joined by Major Reid with all the available men from his position. Under a shower of grape the troops moved on till they came to a wall lined with the enemy, and they stopped short instead of pushing up to it. "Then Chamberlain, seeing that the men hesitated to advance, leaped his horse clean over the wall into the midst of the enemy, and dared the men to follow, which they did, but he got a ball in his shoulder."

While the Fusiliers and Coke's men were driving the mass of the enemy through the gardens to the right,

Hodson went with the Guides, Gurkhas, and part of the Fusiliers along the Grand Trunk Road leading right into the gates of Delhi. "We were exposed to a heavy fire of grape from the walls, and musketry from behind trees and rocks; but pushing on, we drove them right up to the very walls, and then were ordered to retire. This was done too quickly by the artillery, and some confusion ensued, the troops hurrying back too fast. The consequence was the enemy rallied, bringing up infantry, then a large body of cavalry, and behind them again two guns to bear on us." Hodson managed to get eight of his horsemen in front, and to rally some of the Guides infantry; Greville and Major Jacob coming up at that moment, brought forward a few scattered Fusiliers. A body of the enemy's horse now advanced to the charge. But at Hodson's command his scanty band opened fire and the rebel cavalry stopped, reeled, turned, and fled in confusion. Their guns were left deserted, and Hodson attempted to steady his men for a charge to capture them.

We were within thirty paces; twenty-five resolute men would have been enough; but the soldiers were blown, and could not push on in the face of such odds, unsupported as we were, for the whole of the rest of the troops had retired. My eight horsemen stood their ground, and the little knot of officers used every exertion to aid us, when suddenly two rascals rushed forward with lighted portfires in their hands and fired the guns loaded with grape in our faces; and when the smoke cleared away we found, to our infinite disgust and chagrin, that they had limbered up the guns and were off at a gallop. We had then to effect our retreat to rejoin the column under a heavy fire of grape and musketry, and many men and officers were hit in doing it. I managed to get the Guides to retire quietly, fighting as they went, and fairly checking the enemy, on which I galloped back and brought up two guns, when we soon stopped all opposition, and drove the last Pandy into Delhi.

Our loss was 15 men killed, 16 officers and 177 men wounded. Among the wounded were "Chamberlain shot through the arm, and little Roberts." Little Roberts, while helping the artillery-driver to keep the horses quiet under an incessant fire, suddenly felt "a tremendous blow on my back, which made me faint and sick, and I was afraid I should not be able to remain on my horse. The powerless feeling, however, passed off, and I managed to stick on until I got back to camp. I had been hit close to the spine by a bullet, and the wound would probably have been fatal but for the fact that a leather pouch for caps, which I usually wore in front near my pistol, had somehow slipped round to the back: the bullet passed through this before entering my body, and was thus prevented from penetrating very deep."

The wound, though comparatively slight, kept Roberts on the sick-list for a fortnight, and for more than a month he could not mount a horse or put on a sword. He, however, recovered in time to serve in No. 2 Battery, which was constructed immediately in front of Ludlow Castle, 500 yards from the Cashmere Bastion. Here he had a narrow escape, being knocked down by a round-shot which came through an embrasure. On the morning of the assault, being no longer required with the breaching battery, he was ordered to return to staff duty, and accordingly joined the general at Ludlow Castle. Discouraging reports were received as to the progress of the assaulting columns, and Roberts was sent to find out how far they were true.

Just after starting on my errand, while riding through the Cashmere gate, I observed by the side of the road a *doolie* (palanquin), without bearers, and with evidently a wounded man inside. I dismounted to see if I could be of any use to the occupant, when I found, to my grief and consternation, that it was John Nicholson, with death written on his face. He told me that the bearers had put the *doolie* down and gone off to plunder; that he was in great pain, and wished to be taken to the hospital. He was lying on his back, no wound was visible, and but for the pallor of his face, always colourless, there was no sign of the agony he must have been enduring. On my expressing a hope that he was not seriously wounded, he said, "I am dying: there is no chance for me." The sight of that great man lying helpless and on the point of death was almost more than I could bear. Other men had daily died around me, friends and comrades had been killed beside me, but I never felt as I felt then,—to lose Nicholson seemed to me at that moment to lose everything.

On the morning of the 24th of September, whilst Nicholson's funeral was taking place, Roberts marched out of Delhi with the column that was despatched to Cawnpore. "It was a matter of regret to me that I was unable to pay a last tribute of respect to my loved and honoured friend and commander by following his body to the grave, but I could not leave the column."

Six-and-thirty years after, the present writer drove with Lord Roberts to the old cemetery near the Cashmere gate. It stands by the road and is surrounded by lofty trees. The inside is bright with budding flowers. Near the entrance is the grave of John Nicholson. A few roses were placed on the tomb by his old comrade, and he stood for many minutes gazing at the resting-place of his loved and honoured friend. He then joined us at the gate, and as we drove away, beyond the cemetery walls we had, through the trees, a glimpse of the breach through which Nicholson led his victorious soldiers. "I never saw any one like him," was the only remark that broke the silence.

Before dawn, September 29, the advanced-guard of the column arrived at four cross-roads about a mile and a half from Bulandshahr. It is a civil station forty-two miles from Meerut and about five from the fort of Malagarh. One of the roads led to Malagarh and one straight ahead to the town and civil station. At sight of our approach a picket of the enemy fell back, and the scouts brought the news that they intended to give battle at the station. The rebels' position was undoubtedly strong. Their guns in battery commanded the entrance, the gardens and offices were occupied by their infantry, around which bodies of horse hovered. At the junction of the four roads a reserve was immediately formed under Major Turner to protect the baggage. It was at once attacked in flank by cavalry and guns, but they were quickly driven off with loss. The remainder of the infantry and the artillery were drawn up on the left of the road. The advanced-guard was strengthened by two of Captain Remington's Horse Artillery guns, and soon were in action, as the enemy opened at once down the road. Remington's guns swiftly returned the fire, and he was reinforced by the remainder of his troops. Bourchier with his battery took up his position more to the right, supported by a squadron of Punjab cavalry and a portion of her Majesty's 75th. The enemy's guns awaken on them, while from the high crops and surrounding gardens the rebels send a stream of

musketry. But the cross-fire was fatal to their battery, and
it was silenced. A few salvos of grape cleared the front, and
the artillery was ordered to advance. "Lieutenant Roberts of
the artillery, who seemed ubiquitous, brought the order at
a gallop. The guns charged and took the battery, the enemy
scampering before us as we came up to it. Lieutenant Roberts
was first at the guns. A second burst, after clearing our front
with grape, brought us to the goal, the enemy flying before
us like sheep."

Meanwhile a second column, consisting of the greater
portion of the cavalry with two guns under Lieutenant
Cracklow, had advanced into the town, and were for a time
exposed to a most severe fire in the street. "Four men out
of one gun crew were wounded, and the gun was worked
with difficulty. The cavalry charged and routed several
large bodies of the enemy. In pursuing them they became
entangled in the narrow streets, and at a gateway leading
out of the town a hard fight ensued." "Sarel was wounded in
the act of running a sepoy through the body, the forefinger
of his right hand being taken off by a bullet, which then
passed through his left arm; Anson was surrounded by
mutineers and performed prodigies of valour, for which he
was rewarded with the Victoria Cross." Lieutenant Roberts
had a narrow escape. In the midst of the melee he observed
a sepoy taking deliberate aim at him and tried to get at him.
"He fired; my frightened animal reared and received in his
head the bullet which was intended for me."

Early on the morning of the 10th of October 1857 the column
reached Agra. As the local authorities said that the enemy
were nowhere in the neighbourhood, the brigadier gave

orders for the camp to be pitched as soon as the tents should arrive, and he considered (wrongly, as Lord Roberts frankly admits) there was no necessity for posting pickets until the evening. Roberts and Norman (now General Sir Henry Norman),[1] with a few others, got permission to breakfast in the fort. They had scarcely sat down when they were startled by the report of a gun, then another and another. Hurrying down the stairs, they jumped on their horses and galloped out of the fort and along the road in the direction of the firing. On reaching the scene of action a strange sight broke upon them. "Independent fights were going on all over the parade-ground. Here, a couple of cavalry soldiers were charging each other. There, the game of bayonet versus sword was being carried on in real earnest." Roberts and Norman rode off in different directions to search for the brigadier. While thus employed the former was stopped by a dismounted *sowar*, who danced about in front of me, waving his *pagri* (turban) before the eyes of my horse with one hand and brandishing his sword with the other. I could not get the frightened animal near enough to use my sword, and my pistol (a Deane & Adams revolver), with which I tried to shoot my opponent, refused to go off, so I felt myself pretty well at his mercy, when, to my relief, I saw him fall, having been run through the body by a man of the 9th Lancers who had come to my rescue."

Gradually the enemy were beaten off, hotly pursued, and their camp captured. After a halt of three days the column continued its march, and reached Cawnpore on the 26th of October, and for the first time Lord Roberts heard the details of that great tragedy, and saw the sights which had driven

---

[1.] See Napier, *ante*, p. 162.

our soldiers mad. But the day after the arrival of the Delhi column orders reached Hope Grant from Sir Colin Campbell to get into communication with the Alumbagh, a garden-house surrounded by a lofty wall, where Havelock and Outram had left their sick and wounded and spare stores. On the 31st of October Hope Grant left Cawnpore and crossed the Ganges, but the next day the brigadier was bidden to halt until the commander-in-chief should arrive. On the 9th of November Sir Colin joined the column, accompanied by his chief of the staff, Brigadier-General Mansfield. The following morning arrived Kavanagh, the brave Irishman, who, disguised as a native, had passed through the enemy's lines. He brought a letter from Outram stating his views with regard to the route that should be followed by Sir Colin Campbell, in which the line proposed was clearly marked. Sir Colin readily accepted Outram's plan of advance, and strictly adhered to it. On the morning of the 12th the column began its march to the Alumbagh, and after halting there for two days to perfect the smallest detail, Sir Colin Campbell set forth for the relief of the Residency. By noon on the 14th he had occupied the Dilkusha and Martiniere, where he fixed his headquarters. The next day was devoted to making preparations for a further advance. In the evening Roberts was told that the commander-in-chief desired his presence at the Martiniere. On reporting himself to his Excellency, Sir Colin Campbell informed him that he was not satisfied that a sufficient reserve of small-arm ammunition had been brought with the force, and that the only chance of getting more in time was to send back to the Alumbagh for it that night. Sir Colin asked Roberts if he thought he could find his way back in the dark. "I answered, 'I am sure I can.'" The commander-in-chief impressed upon him strongly the necessity for caution, told him that he might take what escort he thought necessary, but that whatever happened he must be back by daybreak, as he had signalled to Outram that the force would advance on the morrow. The old Scotsman grimly desired that the ordnance officer whose fault it was that sufficient ammunition had not been brought should go back with Roberts and be left at the Alumbagh. Accompanied by the unfortunate ordnance officer, Younghusband, Gough, two squadrons of cavalry, and 150 camels, Roberts started at 9 P.M. for the Alumbagh. After an adventurous ride in the dark the Alumbagh was reached, and at dawn he returned with the ammunition, and as he rode up to the Martiniere he could see old Sir Colin, only partially dressed, standing on the steps in evident anxiety at his not having arrived. He congratulated him on the success of the expedition, and told him to get something to eat as quickly as possible, for they were to start immediately the men had breakfasted. "I went off to the artillery camp, and refreshed the inner man with a steak cut off a gun-bullock which had been killed by a round-shot on the 14th."

As soon as the men had breakfasted on the 16th the force advanced. Roberts was ordered to accompany the advance-guard, behind which rode Sir Colin, who had Kavanagh with him, and his general knowledge of the locality proved of great service. As the force was feeling its way along a narrow and tortuous lane it reached a corner which turns sharply to the left, and, winding round it, the British were suddenly deluged by a storm of bullets from the Sikandarbagh. The bank was so steep that it seemed

impossible for artillery to ascend it, But men and horses
did manage to clamber up it, the guns opened fire, and in
an hour a breach was made. The bugle sounded for the
assault.

It was a magnificent sight–a sight never to be forgotten–
that glorious struggle to be the first to enter the deadly
breach, the prize to the winner of the race being certain
death! Highlanders and Sikhs, Punjabi Mohammedans,
Dogras, and Pathans, all vied with each other in the
generous competition. A Highlander was the first to reach
the goal, and was shot dead as he jumped into the enclosure;
a man of the 4th Punjab Infantry came next, and met the
same fate. Then followed Lieutenant Cooper of the 93rd,
and immediately behind him his colonel [Ewart], Captain
Lumsden of the 30th Bengal Infantry, and a number of Sikhs
and Highlanders as fast as they could scramble through the
opening. A drummer-boy of the 93rd must have been one of
the first to pass that grim boundary between life and death,
for when I got in I found him just inside the breach, lying on
his back quite dead—a pretty, innocent-looking, fair-haired
lad, not more than fourteen years of age.

A party made a rush for the gateway, the doors of which
were on the point of being closed, when a Mohammedan
(Mukarrab Khan by name) "pushed his left arm, on which
he carried a shield, between them, thus preventing their
being shut: on his hand being badly wounded by a sword-
cut, he drew it out, instantly thrusting in the other arm,
when the right hand was all but severed from the wrist. But
he gained his object–the doors could not be closed, and were
soon forced open altogether, upon which the 4th Punjab
Infantry, the 53rd, 93rd, and some of the detachments,
swarmed in."

Roberts entered immediately behind the storming party, and the scene that ensued, he states, "requires the pen of a Zola to depict." The pen of Tolstoi would do it more justice.

The rebels, never dreaming that we should stop to attack such a formidable position, had collected in the Sikandarbagh to the number of upwards of 2000, with the intention of falling upon our right flank as soon as we should become entangled amongst the streets and houses of the Hazratganj. They were now completely caught in a trap, the only outlets being by the gateway and the breach, through which our troops continued to pour. There could therefore be no thought of escape, and they fought with the desperation of men without hope of mercy, and determined to sell their lives as dearly as they could. Inch by inch they were forced back to the pavilion, and into the space between it and the north wall, where they were all shot or bayoneted. There they lay in a heap as high as my head, a heaving, surging mass of dead and dying inextricably entangled. It was a sickening sight, one of those which, even in the excitement of battle and the flush of victory, make one feel strongly what a horrible side there is to war. The wretched wounded men could not get clear of their dead comrades, however great their struggles, and those near the top of this ghastly pile of writhing humanity vented their rage and disappointment on every British officer who approached by showering upon him abuse of the grossest description.

After the capture of the Sikandarbagh the troops, fighting for every inch of the ground, proceeded to the Shah Najif mausoleum, enclosed by high masonry, loopholed walls, and reached it as the afternoon was waning. Sir Colin Campbell desired to carry it before nightfall, and Barnston was instructed to bring up his battalion of detachments under cover of the guns. As the troops advanced in skirmishing order their leader fell, and it was seen that the men were wavering.

"Norman [General Sir Henry Norman] was the first to grasp the situation. Putting spurs to his horse, he galloped into their midst, and called on them to pull themselves together: the men rallied at once, and advanced into the cover from which they had for the moment retreated. I had many opportunities for noting Norman's coolness and presence of mind under fire. On this particular occasion these qualities were most marked, and his action was most timely."

More infantry were brought up without avail. The afternoon was passing away, and it seemed essential to carry the Shah Najif. The old chief placed himself at the head of the 93rd, and under a heavy fire led them to some cover in close proximity to the walls. The naval guns were dragged by the seamen and the Madras Fusiliers close to the walls, and commenced to breach. The enemy at length lost heart and fled out the other side, so that an entrance was effected without difficulty.

Night came on, and the troops lay down in lines with their arms. Next morning the contest was renewed. Fire was opened on the mess-house, and in the afternoon it was captured. As from thence the advancing troops could see the British flag flying on the positions captured by Sir J. Outram the previous day, Lord Roberts states Sir Colin Campbell ordered him to procure a regimental colour and place it on one of the turrets of the building.

I rode off accordingly to the and Punjab Infantry standing close by, and requested the commandant, Captain Green, to let me have one of his colours. He at once complied, and I galloped with it to the mess-house. As I entered I was met by Sir David Baird (one of Sir Colin's aides-de-camp) and Captain Hopkins of the 53rd Foot, by both of whom I was assisted in getting the flag with its long staff up the inconveniently narrow staircase, and in planting it on the turret nearest the Kaiserbagh, which was about 850 yards off. No sooner did the enemy perceive what we were about than shot after shot was aimed at the colour, and in a very few minutes it was knocked over, falling into the ditch below. I ran down, picked it up, and again placed it in position, only for it to be once more shot down and hurled into the ditch just as Norman and Lennox (who had been sent by Sir Colin to report what was going on in the interior of the Kaiserbagh) appeared on the roof. Once more I picked up the colour, and found that this time the staff had been broken in two. Notwithstanding, I managed to prop it up a third time on the turret, and it was not again hit, though the enemy continued to fire at it for some time.

After the capture of the mess-house the troops pressed forward with great vigour and lined the wall separating us from the Moti Mahal. Here the enemy made their last stand. Captain Wolseley[1] sent for some sappers, who coming up made openings in the wall through which the troops poured and attacked the network of buildings within. The rebels fought stubbornly, but they were driven at the bayonet from room to room, and after the lapse of some time thrust forth from the vast enclosure. The relieving force and the garrison were now separated only by a space not more than 450 yards across, but it was exposed to a hot fire of musketry and a heavy cannonade. Outram and Havelock and their respective staffs, however, safely made the dangerous passage across. The party then proceeded to meet Sir Colin at the mess-house. While threading the passages and courts of the Moti Mahal they nearly lost their lives. A shell fell near Havelock, and bounding against a

---

[1] Field-Marshal Viscount Wolseley, K. P., &c.

wall, burst at his feet. He was prostrated by the concussion but sustained no other injury. The distance from the Moti Mahal to the mess-house was only twenty-five yards, but an iron tempest swept across the road. Colonel Napier (Lord Napier of Magdala) and Lieutenant Sitwell were wounded in running the gauntlet of fire, but Outram and Havelock crossed over unhurt to the outside wall of the mess-house enclosure. An opening was quickly made by the sappers, through which they entered. On the sward sloping down from the mess-house stood Colin Campbell, and a blaze of shot and musketry from the Kaiserbagh rose upon them as the three veterans met.

Norman and Roberts obtained permission to accompany Havelock to the Residency, and as they entered it they saw a strange sight. Not only the old garrison but also the men belonging to the first relieving force bore manifest tokens of what they had gone through–bad food, foul air, and noisome exhalations had left their mark.

In the ragged summer clothing in which they had entered, these men looked worn and hungry, and in one corner was seen the curious spectacle–I suppose common enough in the garrison–of a British soldier making *chuppaties* (unleavened cakes) for himself out of his scanty allowance of flour. Entering a battery which was trying to silence some of the enemy's guns across the river, these officers saw a few men grimed with smoke and without coat or waistcoat, all so alike in costume and appearance that it was only by asking which was the officer that they ascertained they were standing close to one they well knew–one of the bravest officers of the Bengal Artillery.

When they came to the Bailey Guard and looked at the battered wall and gateway, not an inch without a mark from a round shot or bullet, "we marvelled," writes Lord Roberts, "that Aitken and Loughman could have managed to defend it for nearly five months. There were plenty of evidences on all the surrounding buildings of the dangerous nature of the service which they and their gallant native comrades had so admirably performed. Although we were pressed for time, we could not resist stopping to speak to some of the native officers and sepoys, whose magnificent loyalty throughout the siege was one of the most gratifying features of the Mutiny."

On the 23rd of November Sir Colin Campbell accomplished the removal of the garrison from the Residency, a skilful movement which merits every praise. The sound judgment of the commander was manifested in the foresight with which he examined and provided for every contingency. On the afternoon of the next day he moved to the Alumbagh. Leaving Outram with a strong column to guard it, Sir Colin on the morning of the 27th of November, with the women and children rescued from Lucknow, the wounded of his own and Outram's force, together with treasure and artillery and engineers' packs, started from the Alumbagh. The convoy extended along at least ten miles of road. To guard it Sir Colin had only 3000 men, amongst whom were the remnant of the gallant 32nd who had so stoutly defended the Residency, the sepoys whose fidelity and courage can never be too highly appraised, and the few native pensioners who had loyally responded to the call of Sir Henry Lawrence to come to our aid in the darkest hour. Slowly did the long train wend its way, and it was sunset before Sir Colin passed Bunnee bridge and encamped two miles beyond. During the

day had been heard heavy firing the low tremulous sound
which denotes at a distance, and on reaching Bunnee the
officer commanding that outpost reported that he had not
only heard a cannonade during the day, but it had been
audible during the greater part of the previous day. No news
had reached Sir Colin from Cawnpore for some time, and
now the cause of the silence became evident: the Gwalior
Contingent were attacking Windham. The contingency of
which he had never lost sight, and which had influenced him
in limiting his operations at Lucknow to the withdrawal of
the garrison, had arisen. Sir Colin also knew how slender
was the force at Windham's disposal, how strong the enemy
were, and the grave consequences of Windham's not being
able to hold his own. With Cawnpore and the bridge of boats
in the hands of the enemy, the situation of his force in Oudh
would indeed be grave. To abandon the charge of the convoy
was impossible. All must be pressed forward without delay.
Orders were issued for a march on Cawnpore the following
morning, and Cawnpore was thirty miles away.

At 9 A.M. on the 28th of November the column, preceded
by the cavalry and artillery, resumed its march. At every
step the sound of heavy but distant cannonade became
more distinct, but mile after mile was passed over and
no news could be obtained. The anxiety and impatience
of all became evident. "Louder and louder grew the roar;
faster and faster became the march; long and weary was
the way; tired and foot-sore grew the infantry; death fell
on the exhausted wounded with a terrible rapidity; the
travel-worn bearers could hardly stagger along under
their loads; the sick men groaned and died,—but still On!

on! was the cry." They had tramped on till noon without
news, when a native suddenly jumped out of cover in a field
and handed a letter in Greek characters to the staff at the
head of the advance-guard. It was addressed, "Most urgent,
to General Sir Colin Campbell, or any officer commanding
troops on the Lucknow road." "The letter was dated two days
previously, and said that unless affairs took a favourable
turn the troops would have to retire into the intrenchment;
that the fighting had been hard and most severe; and that the
enemy was very powerful, especially in artillery. It concluded
by expressing a hope that the commander-in-chief would
therefore see the necessity of pushing to their assistance
with the utmost speed." Soon he received two other notes in
succession, announcing that "Windham was hard pressed;
that he had been obliged to fall back from outside the city to
his intrenchment." Three salvos were fired from the battery
of the advanced-guard to intimate the approach of coming
aid, but it is doubtful whether they were ever heard, or, if
heard, understood. Desirous of learning the exact state of the
case, Sir Colin ordered Roberts to ride on as far as he could to
the river Ganges, and if he found the bridge broken to return
at once; but if it were still in existence, to cross over, try to
see the general, and bring back all the information he could
obtain. Roberts started, took two *sowars*, found the bridge
intact, pushed across, and got into the intrenchments. He
was about to return to headquarters when loud cheers broke
from the men, caused by the appearance of the commander-
in-chief. Sir Colin Campbell had grown impatient, and
leaving the infantry and artillery to follow, had pushed
forward with the cavalry. On reaching Mungalwar, a strong

and elevated position, he left these behind, with orders to
Sir Hope Grant to pitch his camp there, and galloped on,
escorted only by some of his staff. Six miles lay between him
and the river-bank. On they sped till they saw rising above
the flat plain the city of Cawnpore, and the forks of flames
which flashed across the sky told it was in the hands of the
enemy; the roar of guns proclaimed that a battle was raging.
The Ganges, gilded with the rays of the setting sun, lay
before them, and across its wide expanse they could trace a
dark thread. The bridge of boats was safe. Harder they went
till they reached the bank of the river, where they found a
guard of British soldiers under a subaltern. He expressed his
joy at seeing them, and stammered out, "We are at our last
gasp." Unfortunate man! Sir Colin flew at him as only Colin
Campbell could when roused, and asked him how he dared to
say of her Majesty's troops that they were "at their last gasp."
Then spurring his horse, Sir Colin, followed by his staff,
galloped over the bridge and down the road till they rode into
some infantry defending the outworks of the intrenchment.
As Sir Colin entered the gate of the fort the men of the Rifle
Brigade recognised the well-known face and wiry figure they
had so often seen in the Crimea, and sent forth cheer after
cheer. They knew that Cawnpore was saved.

The next morning Sir Colin ranged Peel's naval guns
along the north bank of the river, and having driven off
the enemy, took his whole force and a vast convoy across
the bridge. On the 3rd of December the women, children,
and wounded were despatched to Allahabad. On the 6th
Sir Colin attacked and defeated the trained soldiers of the
Gwalior Contingent. Roberts watched the advance as one of

the chief's staff, and took part in the chase after the flying enemy, which the old chief himself headed.

On the 23rd of December Sir Colin Campbell commenced his march towards Fatehgarh, and on the morning of the 2nd of January 1858 a strong force of the rebels were found posted at the village of Khudaganj. As our troops advanced the enemy hastily limbered up their guns and retired. A hot pursuit followed.

The chase continued for nearly five miles, until daylight began to fail and we appeared to have got to the end of the fugitives, when the order was given to wheel to the right and form up on the road. Before, however, this movement could be carried out, we overtook a batch of mutineers, who faced about and fired into the squadron at close quarters. I saw Younghusband fall, but I could not go to his assistance, as at that moment one of his *sowars* was in dire peril from a sepoy who was attacking him with his fixed bayonet, and had I not helped the man and disposed of his opponent he must have been killed. The next moment I descried in the distance two sepoys making off with a standard, which I determined must be captured, so I rode after the rebels and overtook them, and while wrenching the staff out of the hands of one of them, whom I cut down, the other put his musket close to my body and fired: fortunately for me it missed fire, and I carried off the standard.

A brief note states, "For these two acts I was awarded the Victoria Cross." A naval officer who was present with Peel's brigade wrote at this time:–

Lieutenant Roberts of the Bengal Artillery, General Grant's Assistant Quartermaster-General, also made himself conspicuous by his gallantry in the cavalry pursuit, and earned the much-coveted distinction of the Victoria Cross. He is one of those rare men who, to uncommon daring and bravery in the field, and unflinching, hard-working discharge of duty in the camp, adds the charm of cheery and unaffected kindness and hospitality in the tent, and his acquaintance and friendship are high prizes to those who obtain them.

When Lord Canning decided that the siege and capture of Lucknow were to be undertaken at once, Sir Colin Campbell issued a general order detailing the regiments, staff, and commanders who were to take part in it. Major-General Sir Hope Grant was appointed to the command of the cavalry division, and Roberts remained with him as deputy-assistant quartermaster-general. On the 8th of February Hope Grant reached Oano, a village on the road to Lucknow, from which Havelock's veterans had after a desperate hand-to-hand conflict driven forth the enemy. He had been there but a few days when he was despatched with a small compact force to make a detour to a small fortified place called Futtehpur Churassie, where the Nana was supposed to have taken refuge, about twenty-five miles north of the Cawnpore road and on the bank of the Ganges. On the morning of the 15th of February Hope Grant set out with his column, and making his way almost entirely across country, reached his destination in two days. But the Nana had flown. After having blown up the fort Hope Grant proceeded by short marches to Lucknow, clearing the country as he went of rebels. On the 23rd of February he reached Meeanjung, an old moderate-sized town surrounded with a high loop-holed wall, with circular bastions at the angles and at convenient distances along the sides. The gates were strongly fortified with bank, ditch, and palisade in front of them. After an hour's firing our guns had effected a practical breach. The 53rd were ordered up, and the general with a few words of encouragement sent them to the assault. When they got near the walls they raised a loud shout, and dashing through the water of the ditch entered the breach. A short fight ensued. The soldiers pushed forward with the bayonet, and the rebels fled through the gate. Dire destruction awaited them. The Lancers ran them through, the 7th Hussars and Irregulars cut them down. Five hundred were killed and 400 made prisoners; but as they were principally townspeople, Hope Grant directed, "to their inexpressible surprise and delight," that they should be set at liberty. With a vigorous hand he guarded the rights of life and property of the inhabitants, but a general can only mitigate the evils and horrors of war. At the capture of Meeanjung occurred many piteous events which illustrate the misery that attends the glory of arms. In a house was discovered a poor woman tending a wounded child who had been shot through the side, while a young man, her nephew, was lying dead by her side. Elsewhere in a small hut a workman was sitting at his loom dead with his hand in the act of arranging the thread. Another scene enacted itself that day more piteous than the poet's picture of Priam when he "braved what none other man on earth hath braved before, to stretch forth my hand toward the face of the slayer of my sons." The walls of the town and some of the streets had to be levelled in order to render the place incapable of defence. Roberts, the assistant quartermaster-general, was superintending the work of destruction when "an old infirm man, who was sitting at the door of a house, entreated him to spare it, saying that yesterday morning he was the happy father of five sons: three of them lie there, pointing to three corpses; where the other two are God only knows; that he was

old and a cripple, and that if his house was burned, he would
have nothing left but to lie down and die. Roberts, who is as
good as he is brave, gave directions for sparing the old man's
house; and I hope the two missing sons have escaped, and
have returned to comfort his few remaining days."

On the 25th of February Hope Grant's column marched to
Mohan, situated on the bank of the Sai Naddi, a picturesque
stream, and the next day, having crossed it by a beautiful
old bridge, encamped on a wide plain. On the 18th of March
Hope Grant received instructions from the commander-
in-chief to march to Bhuntera, the centre of his army. The
order, owing to some mistake of the messenger, had been
delayed. It was therefore late in the day before the force
started, and as the march was long, and a deep narrow river
had to be crossed, the moon had risen over the sandy-soiled
plain, covered for miles with white tents, before Hope Grant
and his column reached their encamping-ground.

Very early in the morning of the 2nd of March the first
bugle sounded. It was followed by the shrill pipe of the
boatswain's mate. Many a smouldering campfire cast its
fitful glance upon the regiments as they fell in. A few lances
glimmered in the firelight, and Sir Colin, accompanied by his
small cavalry escort, rode up and inspected the Highlanders.
As the grey dawn began to break they marched off with the
pipers playing "The Campbells are coming." The siege of
Lucknow had opened. The Dilkusha palace was reached,
and Hope Grant was placed in charge of the pickets which
were posted in and around it, a position for which he was
admirably adapted. "He rode well, without fatigue to himself
or his horse," writes Lord Roberts, " so that any duty entailing

long hours in the saddle was particularly congenial to him. I invariably accompanied him on his rounds, and in after-years I often felt that I owed Hope Grant a debt of gratitude for the practical lessons he gave me in outpost duty." Hope Grant accompanied Outram as second in command in the brilliant operations across the river which so greatly conduced to the capture of Lucknow. Roberts was by Outram's side when the Chukur Kothe (the race-stand of the former kings of Oude) was captured. After the Moosabagh had been captured and Lucknow was ours, Hope Grant was ordered on the 22nd of March to proceed to a town twenty-five miles away from the capital, reported to be occupied by the enemy. At midnight the column started, but it was delayed by the guns taking a wrong turn when leaving Lucknow, and the enemy had fled before they reached the town. Hope Grant pushed on with his horse, and came in sight of the enemy in full retreat. He had his own regiment (the 2nd Punjab Cavalry), a squadron of the 1st Punjab Cavalry under Captain Cosserat, and three Horse Artillery guns. Captain Browne (General Sir Samuel Browne, V.C., G.C.M.) was ordered to pursue. After a chase of two miles he came upon a body of mutineers formed up on an open plain. "The cavalry charged through them three times, each time thinning their ranks considerably; but they never wavered, and in the final charge avenged themselves by killing Macdonnel (the adjutant of the 2nd Punjab Cavalry) and mortally wounding Cosserat. I arrived on the ground with Hope Grant just in time to witness the last charge and the fall of these two officers, and, deplorable as we felt this was to be, it is impossible not to admire the gallantry and steadiness of the sepoys, every one of whom fought to the death."

On the 25th Hope Grant's division crossed the Goomtee and encamped near the Dilkusha. Roberts was feeling the ill-effects of exposure to the climate and hard work, and the doctors insisted on a trip to England. "On the 1st of April, the sixth anniversary of my arrival in India, I made over my office to Wolseley, who succeeded me as deputy-assistant quartermaster-general on Hope Grant's staff, and towards the middle of the month I left Lucknow."

The well-earned rest was enjoyed in the county of Waterford, where his father was at the time residing. On the 17th of May 1859 he was married to her "without whose loving help my 'Forty-one Years in India' could not be the happy retrospect it is." On the 30th of July 1859 Roberts and his wife returned to India. In 1863 he was again employed on active service in the Umbeyla expedition. Early that year Brigadier-General Sir Neville Chamberlain was appointed to command a force of 9000 men collected for the purpose of punishing the fanatic Mohammedans from India who had formed a colony amidst the fastnesses of the outlying spurs of the Hindu Kush, whence they had spread seditious exhortations to all true Mohammedans to aid with money, arms, and prayers in an unrelenting war against unbelievers. To their strong-holds of Sitana, Jadun, and Malka, in the Mataban or Mountains of the Great Forest, mutinous sepoys from India, Pathans, and Afreedis flocked in numbers, all eager to join in raiding the lowland villages with the hope of gaining plunder or Paradise. When Sir Neville Chamberlain reached the Umbeyla Pass he was met by 15,000 of these fanatics, his force was hemmed in, and for three weeks the camp could only hold its own, the

Punjab Government and the Government of India regarding the matter as so serious that they suggested a withdrawal of the whole force to the plains. Sir Hugh Rose, who was then commander-in-chief, very properly protested against any retirement, pointing out the danger of such a policy and the loss of prestige which would result. He promptly ordered larger forces to proceed to the frontier, and he sent the late Sir John Adye and Roberts, who knew the people and language, to Chamberlain in order to hear his views, take a personal survey of the country, and then return. On the 25th of November they reached Neville Chamberlain's camp. Having consulted the civil and military authorities on the spot, they informed the commander-in-chief that they were of opinion a withdrawal would be most unwise. On the 15th of December General Garvock, who on account of Sir Neville Chamberlain having been severely wounded had taken over the command, resumed the offensive by attacking the village of Laloo. A few hundred yards in front of it one of the great spurs running up from the Chumla valley terminated, and a lofty peak dominated the whole ridge. The heights were crowned by several groups of clansmen arrayed under their different standards, and they had fortified the steep ascent by numerous *sangars* or breastworks. The skirmishers having driven in the outlying mountaineers, halted about 600 yards in front of the conical peak, and, supported by the mountain guns, waited for the arrival of the main body. After the several regiments had come up, and all was ready, General Garvock sounded the "advance."

At that signal 5000 men rose from their cover, and with loud cheers and volleys of musketry rushed to the assault, the regiments of Pathans, Sikhs, and Gurkhas vying with the English soldiers as to who should first reach the enemy. From behind every rock and shrub at the foot of the peak small parties of mountaineers jumped up and fled as the advancing columns approached. It took but a few minutes to cross the open ground, and then the steep ascent began, our men having to climb from rock to rock, and their formation necessarily becoming much broken. Foremost among the many could be distinguished the scarlet uniforms of the 101st Fusiliers, who, led by Colonel Salusbury, steadily swarmed up the mountain and captured the defences in succession at the point of the bayonet, the enemy's standards dropping as their outworks fell; whilst here and there the prostrate figures of our men scattered along the rocks proved that the hillmen were striking hard to the last. Nothing, however, could withstand the impetuosity of the assault, and ere many minutes had elapsed the conical peak from foot to summit was in the possession of British soldiers.[1]

"It was a grand sight," writes Lord Roberts, "as Adye and I watched it from Hughes' battery." The next morning the force again pushed on past Umbeyla and approached the hill leading to Bonair. A body of Ghazis who had been lying concealed in the ravines and broken ground rushed out sword in hand and wildly attacked the 23rd Pioneers. In a few seconds five of the British officers were on the ground, one killed and four wounded. A number of the men were laid low. The rest, staggered by the suddenness of the onslaught, fell back on their reserve, "where they found the needed support, for the Fusiliers (7th Royal) stood firm as a rock." Roberts and Wright, the assistant adjutant-general, rushed

---

[1] *Recollections of a Military Life,* by General Sir John Adye, G.C.B., R.A.

in among the Pioneers, and having rallied them, led them
against the Ghazis, not a man of whom escaped.

The next morning the tribes who had come long distances
to join in the war disappeared from the
scene, and the Bonair chiefs came in to treat and make
peace. It was arranged that they should accompany a small
party of British officers to Mulkah, and that they themselves
should set fire to the stronghold of the Hindustani fanatics.
To Reynell Taylor, the political officer, of whom it was said
by his comrades that he feared nothing but God on earth,
the task was given of carrying out the operation. He was
accompanied by six British officers: they were Colonel Adye,
C.B., Colonel A. Taylor, R.E., Major Roberts, V.C., Major
Wright, Major Johnstone, and Lieutenant Carter. Twenty-
five cavalry and four companies of the Guides infantry
under four officers formed the escort. On the afternoon of the
19th of December the party set out. The distance was only
twenty-six miles, but owing to the severity of the weather
and the long and toilsome march up the mountain Mulkah
was not reached till the evening of the 22nd. It proved to be
a well-built village of wood, containing a rough gunpowder
factory and some few workshops. On the morning of the
22nd Mulkah was set on fire in the presence of a great
concourse of neighbouring tribesmen, and the smoke of the
burning village as it ascended high into the air proclaimed
to the wild mountaineers that British power could not be
abused and insulted with impunity. "The spectacle," writes
Reynell Taylor, "of a tribe like the Bonairs doing our bidding
and destroying the stronghold of their own allies in the war

at a distant spot, with British witnesses looking on, must have been a thoroughly convincing proof to the surrounding country of the nature of our success, and of the indubitable character of the prostration felt by the tribe which had been the foremost at Opposing us."

The Umbeyla compaign was over; the officers and their escort returned from Mulkah unopposed; the camp at the head of the pass was struck, and the force returned to British territory. On Christmas Day Roberts joined his wife at Peshawar. The commander-in-chief sent in his name for a brevet; "but the Viceroy refused to forward the recommendation, for the reason that I was 'too junior to be made a lieutenant-colonel.' I was then thirty-two."

Roberts returned to his duties in the quartermaster-general's department, but owing to ill-health he was obliged to proceed in February 1863 to England, and being given the command of a batch of 300 time-expired men, he sailed with them by the Cape route on board the *Renown*, one of Green's frigate-built ships, which was chartered for their conveyance. In the following March he returned to India, and was appointed assistant quartermaster-general, Allahabad Division, and he held this post till he was appointed to the same office with the Bengal Brigade that was to proceed to Abyssinia under the command of Colonel Donald Stewart. In nominating him the commander-in-chief, Sir William Mansfield, wrote on the 30th of September 1867 to the Government of India: "Sir William Mansfield would recommend Major F. S. Roberts, V.C., and assistant quartermaster-general, Allahabad Division, for the post. This officer is eminently qualified for the appointment by his activity and well-known military qualities, as well as by his experience in the quartermaster-general's department in peace and war for nearly ten years."

During the Abyssinian expedition Major Roberts served as senior staff at Zula, the landing-place for the force in Annesley Bay, and earned the thanks of the commander-in-chief for the efficient manner in which he performed his duties: "His Excellency has received with pleasure most favourable reports regarding the able and energetic manner in which Major Roberts has carried on the duties of the department at Zula, and it has been a source of regret to the commander-in-chief that he has been unable to avail himself of Major Roberts' services in front." After Magdala was taken Sir Robert Napier showed his appreciation of Major Roberts' services by making him the bearer of his despatches. On reaching London he took them to Sir Stafford Northcote, then Secretary of State for India, who, after reading them, asked him to take them without delay to the commander-in-chief.

"There was a dinner-party, however, that night at Gloucester House, and the servant told me it was quite impossible to disturb his Royal Highness; so, placing my card on the top of the despatches, I told the man to deliver them at once, and went back to my club. I had scarcely reached it when the Duke's aide-de-camp made his appearance and told me that he had been ordered to find me and take me back with him. The Commander-in-Chief received me very kindly, expressing regret that I had been sent away in the first instance; and their Royal Highnesses the Prince and Princess of Wales, who were present, were most gracious, and asked many questions about the Abyssinian expedition."

Towards the end of February 1868 Roberts, who had received the brevet rank of lieutenant-colonel for his services in the Abyssinian campaign, returned to Simla as first assistant quartermaster at army headquarters, and two years later he was appointed senior staff officer to the force who were going to punish the Lushais (one of the barbarous tribes that inhabit the large enclave of hilly country lying between Assam, Chittagong, and Burma) for raiding our territory and spreading havoc among the outlying tea-gardens of Cachar. In November two columns, formed mostly of native troops, led by Generals Bourchier and Brownlow, set out from Cachar and Chittagong. Colonel Roberts, to whom had been intrusted the organisation and equipment of the expedition, accompanied General Bourchier, who had made his mark at the siege of Delhi. Notwithstanding the extreme heat of the climate and the difficult nature of the country, which was one succession of rolling hills covered with dense jungle and crowned with stockaded villages, the two columns slowly but steadily pushed their way. They cut roads through the jungles, beat the enemy, and captured their villages. In an expedition against one of the villages Roberts first had the independent command of a small column, and he showed with what skill, daring, and precision he could carry out the operations of war. On Christmas Day 1871 Roberts and all the others assembled at headquarters mess and dined at "a table raised in a conspicuous position, with candles burning before them and Lushais firing from the jungle close by." By the end of February the expedition was brought to a successful close. To the great services rendered by his chief staff officer the general bore testimony in his final despatch: "Lieutenant-Colonel Roberts' untiring energy and sagacity are beyond all praise; working without guides, even without map and geography, thwarted by the Lochars, whose game was to delay our progress, he seemed never at a loss. But not only in his own department was it that he exerted himself. Whether piloting the advance-guard through the trackless forest or solving a commissariat or transport difficulty, his powerful aid was willingly given." For his services Colonel Roberts was awarded the Companionship of the Bath.

On the 31st of January 1875 Lord Napier nominated Colonel Roberts to the coveted post of Quartermaster-General. The next year he accompanied the commander-in-chief to Bombay on the eve of his departure, and while he was bidding Lord Napier farewell, the *Orontes* steamed into the harbour with Lord Lytton on board. "Little did I imagine when making Lord Lytton's acquaintance how much he would have to say to my future career. His Excellency received me very kindly, telling me that he felt I was not altogether a stranger, and he had been reading during the voyage a paper I had written for Lord Napier a year or two before, on our military position in India, and the arrangements that would be necessary in the event of Russia attempting to continue her advance south of the Oxus. Lord Napier had sent a copy of this memorandum to Lord Beaconsfield, by whom it had been given to Lord Lytton."

Lord Roberts maintains, as most men who have studied the subject maintain, that Lord Lytton's frontier policy, though at the time much misunderstood and criticised, was in essentials sound. But these are matters which must be left for final settlement in the calm court of history. When

the second Afghan war began General Roberts, on account
of the ability he had shown as quartermaster-general, was
appointed to command the Kuram field force, taking its name
from one of the passes through which our forces invaded
Afghanistan. To take a man from the desk to command an
army in the field is a hazardous experiment, but in this case it
was fully justified by the record of the officer. He had enjoyed
varied experiences in the field, and won three medals, the
Companionship of the Bath, and the Victoria Cross, and had
been mentioned twenty-three times in despatches.

On the 21st of November 1878 General Roberts made his first
advance into Afghanistan by entering the lower Kuram valley,
about sixty miles long and three to ten miles wide. "On every
side rose high and magnificently wooded mountains, those
on the north and east being the most lofty and precipitous,
while on the north-west projects the spur which runs from
Sika Ram, the highest peak of the Sufed Koh range, upwards
of 14,000 feet high. This spur forms the boundary between
Kuram and Afghanistan, and is crossed by the Peiwar Kotal."
Continuing his advance up the valley, General Roberts on
the 28th of November approached the *kotal* or pass over the
Peiwar ridge. A reconnaissance in force under the command of
Colonel John Gordon of the 29th Punjab Infantry showed that
the enemy's position, concealed by a high range of pine-clad
hills and precipitous cliffs, was almost impregnable in front
—a position strong by nature having been made more strong
by felled pine-trees and breastworks. Even if a frontal attack
proved successful, it would entail a heavy loss of life. General
Roberts therefore determined to turn the position by a flank
movement. By order of the General a thorough reconnaissance

of the different spurs which led from the Peiwar Kotal into the plain below was made, and those on the right and left of the camp carefully examined. Major Collett, assistant quartermaster-general to the division, and Captain Carr, deputy-assistant quartermaster-general of cavalry, having carefully reconnoitred the approaches to the Spingawan Pass, which crosses the ridge about one and a half miles north of the Peiwar, reported so favourably on the route that Roberts determined to make his chief attack on that point and so turn the enemy's left. At 10 P.M. on Sunday the 1st December, with a small force of only 1263 men, of whom only a few hundred were Europeans, he set forth to make his turning movement and surprise the enemy on the Peiwar ridge. Brigadier-General Cobbe, with a little more than 1000 men, was left for the feint and protection of the camp. Tents were left standing and camp-fires burning, and the preparations had been made with so much secrecy and carried out with so little noise that only a very few who were in the secret knew of the column's departure. Roberts led his men along a rough track which ran due north for two miles, and then turned sharp to the east, entered a wide gorge, and ran along the bed of a mountain stream covered by huge boulders over which the men had to pick their way. Moonlight had been followed by pitch-darkness, and a cutting wind swept down the gorge. On they toiled. Strict commands had been given that not a word should be spoken. Everything depended on silence and secrecy. About 2 A.M. the stillness was broken by the sound of two shots. They were fired by two men of the Pathan company of the 29th Punjab Native Infantry, but whether through accident or a warning to their countrymen

has not been indubitably proved. This untoward episode
caused a change in the order of the march. The 29th had been
leading, but now their place was taken by the 5th Gurkhas
and a company of the 72nd Highlanders. The force pushed
on in the darkness, and the Gurkhas reached the foot of the
Spingawai Pass unobserved by the enemy. Two shots fired by
the double sentries first announced our approach. Instantly
FitzHugh, who commanded the Gurkhas, gave the word to
charge, and the little mountaineers rushed up the steep side
of the mountain, and the flashes of their rifles were seen as
they made their way under the dark pine-trees. Led by their
gallant commander, they reached the first *sangar* and drove
the Afghans out. On they went, supported by a company of
the 72nd Highlanders, up the steep and wooded side of the
kotal. A second and third stockade were taken. The Afghans
fought stubbornly, and many bodies pierced by the bayonet
were stretched on the grass. After an hour's hard fighting
the Spingawai Kotal was won, the enemy retired along
the ridge towards the main road over the Peiwar. Roberts
reformed the troops who had led the assault on a *murg* or
open grassy plateau, and after a short halt he started again
in the direction of the Peiwar Kotal. The advance ran along
thickly wooded spurs covered with undergrowth, and was
necessarily slow. After two hours Roberts reached the ridge
of a deep hollow, and from the dense pine-woods beyond came
a smiting fire. He was alone with the 29th Punjab Native
Infantry. The Highlanders, Gurkhas, and the Mountain
Battery had not come up. A desperate position. Judging
at once that retreat was impossible without ruin, Roberts
"immediately sent his staff officers and others about him to

bring up reinforcements, and was for some time actually the only European officer in front, getting together little groups of men and trying to show fight with them till the others came up." The enemy were growing bolder and bolder when the lost force arrived. The mountain guns were brought into action, and the 23rd Pioneers under the command of Colonel Currie made a gallant attempt to dislodge the enemy, but in vain. "Their position could only be reached by a narrow causeway, which was swept by direct and cross-fire, and obstructed by trunks of trees and a series of barricades." Roberts determined to make another turning movement. At this juncture Lieutenant-Colonel Perkins, R.E., and Major M'Queen with the 5th Punjab Infantry arrived, and learning from them of a spur from which the *kotal* position could be fired upon, he planted his mountain guns there. Then with his column he set forth to take the enemy's centre in rear. A few rounds from the mountain guns and the knowledge that their rear was threatened, however, caused the Afghans to abandon their strong position on the crest of the *kotal*, leaving behind them their guns, stores, and a quantity of ammunition. General Hugh Gough was the first to reach the crest, and with his cavalry pursued the flying enemy. Night came on before Roberts could reach the Peiwar, and his troops bivouacked on the southern slope of the Sika Ram mountain. "It was hardly a pleasant experience lying on the ground without even cloaks at an elevation of 9000 feet, and with the thermometer marking twenty degrees of frost; but spite of cold and hunger, thoroughly content with the day's work and with my mind at rest, I slept as soundly as I had ever done in the most luxurious quarters, and I think the others did the same." Roberts had every reason to be thoroughly content with the day's work. At Peiwar Kotal he first gave a signal illustration of that intuitive perception which distinguishes the greatest generals. He saw that the *kotal* must be captured: a front attack might lead to disaster, it certainly must lead to heavy loss of life: he made the most thorough reconnaissance of the country, and by intuition he decided on the best course to follow. In following it he took the legitimate risk which every general must take who wishes to win a complete victory.

After his success General Roberts returned to Simla, and he was deep in the work of the Army Commission when news came of the massacre of our envoy at Kabul. Immediate steps were taken to retrieve the disaster. General Massy was ordered to seize again the Shutar Pass, and General Stewart was told to reoccupy Kandahar, which had been almost entirely evacuated. On the 29th of September General Roberts again took command of the Kuram force, and issued the following general order to the troops under his command:–

The Government of India having decided that the Kuram field force shall proceed with all possible despatch to Kabul, in response to his Highness the *Ameer's* appeal for aid, and with the object of avenging the dastardly murder of the British representative and his escort, Sir Frederick Roberts feels sure that the troops under his command will respond to the call with a determination to prove themselves worthy of the sacred duty intrusted to them, and of the high reputation they have maintained during the recent campaign. The Major-General need address no words of exhortation to soldiers whose courage and fortitude have been so well proved. The Afghan tribes are numerous, but without organisation, the regular army is undisciplined, and, whatever may be the disparity in numbers, such foes can never be formidable to British troops. The dictates of humanity require that a distinction should be made between the peaceable inhabitants of Afghanistan and the treacherous murderers, for whom a just retribution is in store, and Sir Frederick Roberts desires to impress on all ranks the necessity for treating the inoffensive population with justice, forbearance, and clemency. The future comfort and wellbeing of the force depend largely on the friendliness of our relations with the districts from which our supplies must be drawn; prompt payment is enjoined for all articles purchased by departments and individuals, and all disputes must be at once referred to a political officer for decision. The Major-General confidently looks forward to the successful accomplishment of the object of the expedition, and the re-establishment of order and settled government in Afghanistan.

The Kuram field force advanced as rapidly as possible, and on the evening of October 5 the village of Charasia was reached. Dawn discovered a large number of Afghan troops who had taken up a position happily formed by nature for withstanding the march of invaders. It consisted of a bay of hills running one above another, and with a front extending from two to three miles. In the centre of the crescent the enemy was posted on a strongly intrenched and almost inaccessible cliff some 2000 feet high: his right rested on a detached range which ended in a rugged summit 1800 feet above Charasia; his left was on a lofty plateau which rises 1000 feet above the defile through which the road and river run. Above the gorge on the other side of the river rise other heights which run down and bound the eastern part of the bay. The Afghans, as they saw the working party advance to the Sang-i-Nawishta defiles, considered that the main attack would be delivered on their left against the steep plateau that commanded the gorges. But General Roberts, considering that this position could only be captured by an immense sacrifice of life, determined to make the real attack by an outflanking movement to their right, while he distracted their attention by a feint attack on their left. He therefore ordered Major White, 72nd Highlanders, who commanded the party near the gorge, to threaten the pass, to prevent the enemy's advances towards the village of Charasia, to advance within artillery range of the enemy's position above the gorge, "and when the outflanking movement had been thoroughly developed and the enemy were in full retreat, but not before, to push the cavalry through the gorge and pursue." General Baker, with 702 British and 1293 native soldiers, he sent against the enemy's right. Baker's small force advanced in and from the extreme left of the village of Charasia, a company of the 72nd under Captain Hunt attacked the heights in front of the left peak, the extreme right of the enemy's position, while Lieut.-Colonel Clark with the remainder of the 72nd Highlanders, protected by the fires of two mountain guns, advanced in front against the Red Ridges, which connected the enemy's centre with the front of the left peak. The heights on the left were steep and rugged, and from behind their breastworks the Afghans plied them with a biting fire. The Highlanders, scrambling up from crag to crag, reached the first peak. Here they halted. Two companies of the 5th Gurkhas under Captain Cooke, V.C., were sent to support them. Then they again went forward, driving the Afghans from their coigns of vantage. The resistance to the front attack was a stubborn one, the advance equally slow, and two companies of the 5th Gurkhas under Major FitzHugh and

200 men of the 5th Punjab Infantry under Captain Hall were sent to reinforce it. Slowly they breasted the steep hillside. The Afghan commander, now perceiving the direction of the real attack, hurried reinforcements to his right: but it was too late. After two hours' hard fighting the Red Ridge was carried; the Afghans, exposed to a cross-fire, began to waver. "The general advance was now sounded, ands the first position gallantly carried by the 72nd Highlanders, 5th Gurkhas, and 5th Punjab Infantry. The enemy fought well to the last, and charged close up to the Gurkhas, who, however, commanded by Major FitzHugh, repulsed them with heavy loss. In this affair Lieutenant and Adjutant Martin was very forward." [1]

The enemy, driven over the crest, now took up a fresh position on a ridge some 600 yards farther back, but still well in advance of their main position at the centre of the crescent. Covered by the fire of the mountain battery, many a rush was made at it. For half an hour the Afghans held their own. Then a company of the 23rd Pioneers under Lieutenant Chesney, supported by the 72nd and the 5th Gurkhas and two companies of the 92nd (detached by Major White from the right attack), made one more rush, and the enemy again fell back on the main ridge. The British troops followed them at the double, and before they could make another stand the main ridge was carried. As the enemy's line of defence was now exposed to being taken in reverse, they soon began to retreat from their position on the Sang-i-Nawishta, advantage of which was speedily

[1.] From Major-General Sir F. S. Roberts, K.C.B., V.C., Commanding Kabul Field Forces, to the Chief of the Staff, Army Headquarters, Simla, Bala, Kabul, October 20, 1879.

taken by the troops under Major White, "who throughout
the day conducted the operations on the right in the most
satisfactory manner." A general advance was now made
(but no further resistance was offered), and General Baker
occupied the last peak overlooking the defile, through
which our cavalry, supported by a small body, had already
pushed. They were, however, held in check by the enemy's
rear-guard. The mountain guns opened on them from
the heights above, and the 23rd Pioneers and 5th Punjab
Infantry, rushing forward, dispersed them. Darkness
prevented the carrying on of the pursuit. The 23rd Pioneers
and 5th Gurkhas were pushed forward to the plain before
the defile, and the troops, after their hard-won victory,
bivouacked for the night. The Afghans fought stubbornly,
but the English General's dexterity in manoeuvring and the
valour of his soldiers gained the day.

At Charasia, as in every battle of the campaign, there
were some fine examples of individual heroism. Private
MacMahon of the 72nd Highlanders—who bore the brunt of
the fighting almost single-handed—scaled a hill, on the crest
of which was a *sangar* filled with men. Major White (the
gallant defender of Ladysmith), now General Sir George
White, of the same regiment, not caring to expose his men
on a particularly steep bit of ground which was enfiladed by
a few Afghans posted in rear of some rocks, took a rifle from
one of his men and stalked the enemy single-handed. Both
men received the Victoria Cross. During the day Lieutenant
Grant and Colour-Sergeant Hector MacDonald of the 72nd
also greatly distinguished themselves by dislodging with a

few men in a most daring manner a body of the enemy who from a height above were firing into the camp.[1]

After Charasia the enemy made no further stand, and General Roberts took possession of Kabul one month after the murder of Cavagnari, and for two months after the entry of the English into the Afghan capital no apprehension was entertained of any organised resistance to the occupation. Men are apt to forget that no one decisive battle ever subdued a brave and warlike nation. The work of the Normans only began after Senlac. In December tidings of general disaffection among the tribes began to reach the invaders, and to check the growing discontent a grand review of all the troops at Kabul was held on the 9th. The same afternoon a brigade was sent due west to Arghandeh to drive back the Afghan general, Mahomed Jan, who was reported to be attempting a junction with the Kohistanis from the north. On the next day General Baker's brigade marched south to Charasia. General Massy was told "that he was to advance cautiously and quietly by the road leading directly from the city of Kabul towards Arghandeh, feeling for the enemy; that he was to communicate with Macpherson and act in conformity with that officer's movements; and I impressed upon him that he was on no account to commit himself to an action until Macpherson had engaged the enemy." General Massy, Lord Roberts states, did not follow the route he was

---

[1] A few days before Colour-Sergeant Hector MacDonald and *Jemadar* There Mahomed, with a detachment of about sixty men of the 92nd Highlanders and 3rd Sikhs, had displayed great courage and skill in defeating a large body of the enemy in the Hazardarakoi defiles and opening the road to the advancing columns. For these two acts of skill and daring Hector MacDonald was awarded a commission. Now Brigadier-General Sir H. A. MacDonald, K.C.B., D.S.O.

told to take, and, marching straight across the country, he found himself face to face with the enemy before he could join Macpherson. General Roberts, warned by the firing that an engagement was taking place, galloped across the Chardeh valley, and on gaining the open ground beyond the village of Bhagwana he saw that an unbroken line, extending for about two miles, and formed of not less than between 9000 and 10,000 men, was moving rapidly towards me, all on foot save a small body of cavalry on their left flank—in fact, the greater part of Mahomed Jan's army. To meet this formidable array, instead of Macpherson's and Massy's forces, which I hoped I should have found combined, there were but four guns, 198 of the 9th Lancers under Lieut.-Colonel Cleland, 40 of the 14th Bengal Lancers under Captain Philip Neville, and at some little distance Gough's troops of the 9th Lancers, who were engaged in watching the enemy's cavalry."

Roberts, to save his guns, ordered the cavalry to charge. "But the ground, terraced for irrigation purposes and intercepted by dykes, so impeded our cavalry that the charge, heroic as it was, made little or no impression upon the overwhelming number of the enemy, now flushed with the triumph of having made our guns retire."

To assist the cavalry Roberts ordered two of the guns to halt and come into action while the other two continued to retire. They had not gone far when one of them fell into a deep narrow channel and had to be spiked and abandoned. The three remaining guns took up positions near the village of Bhagwana, and opened fire from behind a low wall which surrounded the houses. But the Afghans pressed on, and the ammunition being nearly expended, the gunners again fell back. The other side of the village they were stopped "by a ditch fully twelve feet deep, narrowing towards the bottom." The first gun was being taken across when a wheeler stumbled, and gun, men, and horses were in the ditch. A few hundred yards away were the Afghans, and the villagers began to fire from the roofs of the houses. Here was a critical moment. Roberts ordered the 9th Lancers to make another charge: it was gallantly done, but with exhausted troops and exhausted horses it could produce no results. The guns had to be spiked and abandoned. The cavalry retired slowly with great steadiness by alternate squadrons in the direction of the Deg-i-Mahan defiles through the hills immediately over-hanging Kabul city. He had sent for 200 men of the 72nd from Sherpur to hold the gorge, and it was of vital importance to keep the enemy back till they reached it. From Bhagwana to Deg-i-Mahan was three miles. The Afghans pressed forward to the fight, while the dismounted troopers of the 9th Lancers and the 12th Lancers and the gunners, standing up manfully, sent volleys into the approaching masses. Gradually their numbers began to diminish and the attack became less severe. Macpherson, on hearing the sound of the guns on his left, had pushed on to the Kabul road, and his advance-guard had engaged the rear portion of the Afghan army. Then a loud cheer arose from the Lancers as the Highlanders, led by Brownlow, were seen advancing at the double through the gorge. "It was literally touch and go who should reach the village first, but the Highlanders swept in, and swarming to the tops of the houses, the breechloaders soon checked the advancing tide." The Afghans, led by some Ghazis, streamed down upon the

village "like ants on a hill"; but, wrapped in the steady
fire poured upon them, they could not live. They broke
and fell back in confusion. Their entrance into Kabul had
been checked, but their standards floated on the hills
around. Sir Frederick Roberts waited at Deg-i-Mahan till
Macpherson arrived, and did not reach Sherpur till long
after dark.

Bad success in war, as William Napier has said, produces
much discussion. The conception of the operations around
Sherpur has been criticised, but on one point the verdict
has been unanimous. The comrades who rode by his side
bear marked testimony to the cool courage and judgment of
the commander in the handling of overmatched troops in a
perilous predicament. The General gives unqualified praise to
the steadiness and coolness of the squadron of the 14th Bengal
Cavalry under Captain Neville during the retirement, to the
gallantry of Lieutenants M'Innes and Tower, 9th Lancers, to
the devoted bravery shown by the Rev. J. W. Adams, which he
personally witnessed. In his despatch Sir Frederick Roberts
writes: "Mr Adams dismounted to assist a wounded man of
the 9th Lancers, and while so occupied lost his horse; when
making his way back on foot, and although the enemy were
but a few yards distant from him, Mr Adams, regardless of
his own safety, was mainly instrumental in saving the lives
of two men of the 9th Lancers who were caught under their
horses, which had fallen in a watercourse, and who but for
his aid must have been speedily killed by the advancing
enemy." For these two deeds of valour Adams was awarded
the Victoria Cross, being the first clergyman who won the
coveted decoration. The General himself nearly lost his life

in performing a similar act of bravery and mercy. "I was endeavouring to help some men out of the ditch when the headman of the village rushed at me with his knife, seeing which, a Mohammedan of the 18th Bengal Cavalry who was following me on foot, having just had his horse shot under him, sprang at my assailant, and seizing him round the waist, threw him to the bottom of the ditch, thereby saving my life."

The next day Sir Frederick Roberts resolved to dislodge the enemy from the heights above Kabul. Their most formidable position was on the crest of the Takht-i-Shah. The slopes leading up to it were covered with huge masses of jagged rock intersected by perpendicular cliffs, and their natural great strength was increased by breastworks and stockades thrown up on different points. After gallant attempts had been made during the greater part of the day to carry it, Roberts ordered the assault to be deferred till the following morning, when the arrival of Baker would enable him to assist the direct attack by a flanking movement. The next morning (December 13), under cover of artillery fire, the 92nd, supported by the Guides, rushed up the steep slopes. They were met by a furious onslaught, and a desperate conflict took place. The leading officer, Lieutenant Forbes, a lad of great promise, was killed, and Colour-Sergeant Drummond fell by his side. For a moment even the brave Highlanders were staggered by the numbers and fury of their antagonists, but only for a moment. Lieutenant Dick Cunyngham sprang forward to cheer them on, and confidence was restored. With a wild shriek the Highlanders threw themselves on the Afghans, and quickly succeeded in driving them down the farther side of the ridge."

The next day revealed that Lord Roberts was not fighting a gathering of hostile tribes but a well organised rebellion. He was therefore reluctantly compelled to evacuate all his isolated positions and to withdraw his force to his cantonments at Sherpur, where he was compelled with 5000 men to defend a position nearly five miles long, some two miles of which had no further protection than a slight shallow trench hastily constructed at a critical moment. If our troops had been systematically assailed they would have found it extremely difficult to have held their own inside the immense enclosure to which they had been committed. The enemy, however, did nothing but indulge in firing of a desultory kind until they heard that General Gough with reinforcements was approaching, and then they delivered their one real attack. On the morning of the 23rd December the signal-fire was lighted on the Asmai Heights. As it died out a brisk fire was opened upon the south-west angle of the camp. This, however, was only a feint. Led by their Ghazis, the main body of Afghans, waving swords and knives and shouting their war-cry, advanced on the north-east angle. As they came on the bullets fell thick on the besieged, but our soldiers patiently and silently waited the order to fire. When the enemy arrived within a few yards of the walls the order was given, and a crushing volley smote the head of the Afghan host. The dead and wounded filled the trench, the survivors took shelter behind walls and trees, from which they poured upon the defenders volleys which did but little damage. Once again did a few fanatics attempt to face the stream of fire from our ramparts, but even fanatical zeal could not nerve them to endure it. Then the news reached the Afghans that Gough's reinforcing column was crossing the river, and the besiegers became a mob.

Thus ended the investment of Sherpur. In a few days the enemy disappeared, and our troops were in Kabul. During the winter months General Roberts strengthened his position. In May 1880 Ayub Khan, the brother of Yakub, marched on Kandahar, and at the end of July news reached Kabul of the Maiwvand disaster. On the 6th of August the Kabul-Kandabar field force began its famous march. On August 31st, Sir Frederick Roberts reached Kandahar, and on September 1 he defeated Ayub outside the walls. In order to relieve the garrison General Roberts had given up all reliance on a base of operations, and with a force of 10,000 men marched through the heart of a hostile country 318 miles in twenty-three days. Such a feat will always be remembered. Its accomplishment was greatly facilitated by the previous daring march of Sir D. Stewart from Kandahar to Kabul, and the generous manner in which he handed over his tried troops to Sir Frederick Roberts. President Lincoln, on hearing a discussion as to the respective merits of Sherman and Grant, remarked, "I should have thought there was sufficient glory to cover both." There is quite sufficient glory to cover both Sir Donald Stewart and Lord Roberts.

At the close of the Afghan campaign Sir Frederick Roberts returned to England, and "was feted and feasted to almost an alarming extent." In 1881 he went to the Cape of Good Hope, having been nominated by Gladstone's Government Governor of Natal and Commander of the Forces in South Africa on the death of Sir George Colley and the receipt of the news of the disaster at Majuba Hill. "While I was on my way out to take up my command, peace was made with the Boers in the most marvellously rapid and unexpected manner. A peace, alas! 'without honour,' to which may be attributed the recent regrettable state of affairs in the Transvaal–a state of affairs which was foreseen and predicted by many at the time. My stay at Cape Town was limited to twenty-four hours, the Government being apparently as anxious to get me away from Africa as they had been to hurry me out there."

On the 27th of November 1881 Sir Frederick Roberts returned to India as Commander-in-Chief of the Madras army, having refused the appointment of Quartermaster-General at the Horse Guards. Two years after he succeeded Sir Donald Stewart as Commander-in-Chief in India.

Lord Roberts' speeches on Musketry Training and Artillery Practice bear witness to the minute trouble he took during the two years in which he commanded the Madras army and the eight years in which he held the high and responsible office of Commander-in-Chief in India, to make the forces under him as perfect a fighting-machine as possible, and they testify to the far sight of the soldier. The first speech was made fifteen years ago at a distribution of prizes at the Southern Indian Rifle Association meeting, held at the large and important military station of Bangalore. The Commander-in-Chief of the Madras army told the sepoys and soldiers who had gathered to compete for the prizes that it is not given to every one to possess all the qualities which combine to form the *beau ideal* of a soldier. Some are more intelligent than their neighbours; others are of finer physique; others, again, have greater endurance; while some are blessed with a constitution which is proof against all the vicissitudes of climate. "But every one," said his lordship, "with scarcely an exception, can become a good shot, and the more intelligent a man is, the easier it is for him to learn to shoot." The present war has demonstrated the truth of the proposition laid down by Lord Roberts, that "the smaller an army is, the greater necessity exists for its being able to shoot well:" "I have no hesitation in giving it as my opinion that, for ordinary fighting purposes, one good shot is nowadays equal to at least half-a-dozen bad ones. I may further add, and on this point I can speak with even more confidence, that if ever I have the honour of being employed again on field service, I shall endeavour to take with me those regiments which have gained the best reputation on the rifle-range."

The speeches are a fresh illustration of the truth that to achieve important results a commander must be assiduous in his care for details. It is often said that it is difficult to make our soldiers good marksmen on account of the scarcity of ranges available for the modern rifle. Lord Roberts' solution is simple. If you cannot get a long range, or if it is at an inconvenient distance from the barracks, it may be found possible to provide some kind of range nearer at hand: "I sincerely hope that this will be done, for I am persuaded that it is infinitely more important for the majority of our soldiers to shoot steadily and well at ranges varying from 50 to 300 yards, than for a few experts to be able to hit a solitary scout at 1000 or 1200 yards. Really good marksmen may with advantage be practised at long ranges, but we may be well satisfied if the greater number of men can hit a bull's-eye, or, better still, a moving object, pretty frequently at 300 yards."

Lord Roberts, without subscribing entirely to Napoleon's observation that " fire is everything, the rest is of no account," stated a decided opinion at the Simla Rifle meeting in 1888, that " in future wars superiority of fire will tell even more than it has in the past"; and at the Bengal Presidency Rifle Association meeting, held in the December of the same year, he said: "The more I study the question of modern fire tactics and the latest inventions in weapons of war, the more I become convinced that those troops who combine superior individual marksmanship with a sound and thoroughly well-mastered system of fire-control and discipline will in future be the victors whenever armies meet."

The Commander-in-Chief proceeded to inform his audience how this ideal was to be attained. Every officer must believe in musketry, and take a deep interest in it; every soldier must endeavour to have such a mastery over his rifle as to make him feel that he has, in the cool and steady use of it, the best form of defence against infantry. Throughout his tenure of office in India Lord Roberts never ceased to impress upon his officers that they should do all in their power to excel in musketry, and to train the soldier to combine straight shooting with the highest form of discipline which is demanded of those who in action aspire to fire steadily and by word of command.

Attempts have been made to separate these two qualifications of a good soldier, and exalt one at the expense of the other; but they are not separated. They are mutually dependent on each other, and neither by itself is of much value. The finest fire discipline is of little use if a large proportion of the bullets are delivered wide of the position at which the shooters are directed to aim, and the straightest individual shooting cannot, under most conditions, be very effective unless it is capable of combined action and be concentrated at will upon any object. I understand that this was exemplified in a remarkable manner during the recent Black Mountain expedition, as it certainly was in Afghanistan. The best marksmen when firing singly were seldom able to dislodge the enemy's sharpshooters, while well-aimed volleys never failed to do so.

Lord Roberts, before he resigned his Indian command, had the satisfaction of seeing the rifle meetings held in different districts of his charge increase in popularity year by year, and a marked improvement in the general standard of musketry. After ten years' strenuous preaching and labour he was able to say, The bulk of our infantry in India are now infinitely more efficient in a musketry sense than were the select marksmen of regiments at the time of the Afghan war."

At the artillery camps also he never wearied of impressing on officers and men the utmost necessity of the highest form of discipline, which trains a man to know when to obey mechanically and when to exercise his intelligence. He told the gunner what he told the infantry soldier, "Your weapon has been improved, and unless you thoroughly know how to use it you are useless." But, as with the infantry soldier, good shooting is not all that is required: "Modern teaching and experience show us that if we are to excel, or even equal, the best artilleries of Europe, we must do much more than lay each gun accurately. Good as individual excellence is, combined excellence is better, and in war concerted action of artillery is as absolutely essential to success as it is in the case of infantry or cavalry."

The following, taken from his speech at the artillery camp near Delhi so far back as 1889, is interesting and instructive when read by the light of recent events:–

Hitherto, as you doubtless know, it has been the custom when on service in this country for officers in command to rush their batteries well to the front, and then to let the subalterns and non-commissioned officers choose their own objects to fire at, and hit the enemy in their own way. This plan answered well enough with the foes we have been accustomed to fight in India, for the right way undoubtedly in dealing with Asiatics is to get to close quarters as soon as possible; moreover, we have always felt tolerably sure that our guns were better horsed and better served than those pitted against us. In the future this may not be the case our next enemy may possibly be a European one, with an artillery as well armed and as well served as our own. It behoves us, therefore, to aim at a far higher standard than has up till now been considered necessary; for with foes equally well armed, that artillery will win which can soonest find the range of its enemy, and, when found, fire with the greatest accuracy, steadiness, and rapidity.

Lord Roberts again dwelt on this point in his speech delivered at the Royal Artillery practice camp near Secunderabad, February 11, 1891. He said:–

The rough, hasty laying of guns, formerly recognised as a normal procedure, and even now, I am afraid, not altogether grown obsolete, will no longer suffice to silence the hostile fire of a well-trained artillery, nor by it will you be able to bring that heavy shower of shrapnel-bullets on the enemy's infantry, which is indispensable if you want to shake his nerves and prevent him doing such serious damage to your men and horses as may quite possibly stop your batteries from taking up a second position and continuing the fight. There must be considerably more quickness in preparing and serving the ammunition, still more accuracy in laying the guns, and, above all, better observation of fire on the part of battery commanders, without which the other points are of little avail. Intelligence must be brought to bear upon the supervision of fire, and its conduct must be regulated by method, otherwise, believe me, your individual skill and gallantry, although these may be as conspicuous as in the past, will nevertheless fail to serve you effectually.

Lord Roberts' speeches not only display the vigour and grasp of their author's mind, but they also show that amidst the incessant press of business which the office of Commander-in-Chief in India involves, he found leisure to think out the problems which may confront a general in the future. The following extract is a proof of this: "I trust that in the British army, at any rate, we shall hear no more of the 'moral effect' produced by guns, but of their destructive power; and that generals in command will readily put up with the inconvenience which long lines of guns and waggons on the march undoubtedly cause for the sake of having a superior force of well-served artillery, the possession of which would in all probability lead to victory."

Lord Roberts laboured hard to bring the army under his command into a state to take the field quickly in case of war, thoroughly prepared for a campaign. As Commander-in-Chief he was head of the Mobilisation Committee. The main object of that scheme of mobilisation was to lay down certain standards of organisation for service within or beyond the frontiers of India or beyond sea; to prepare plans of movement in various directions for a certain portion of the army which could be withdrawn for field service, and to elaborate the innumerable details which are necessary to complete a plan of this kind. Notwithstanding numerous difficulties, military and political, steady progress has been made, so that one-fourth, or say 70,000 men, of the army in India or beyond could be put in motion for field service in India or beyond it without confusion or with reasonable regularity and despatch. Twelve days after the orders were issued the mobilisation of the troops for the Chitral campaign was completed. As Commander-in-Chief he was also the head of the Defence Committee, and a great deal was done to render the harbours of India safe and secure. The position of the native soldiers was, during his tenure of office, in many ways improved. The system of granting lands to native officers was placed on a satisfactory footing, and a scheme for the employment of pensioned native soldiers was greatly developed. The condition of the British soldier also received liberal improvement. For many years before he became Commander-in-Chief, libraries, recreation-rooms, workshops, gardens, and cricket-grounds had been established, but it was not till 1887 that, at the instance and under the guidance of Lord Roberts, a further development was made by bringing together the various regimental clubs and forming them into what are now called Regimental Institutes. The aim and object of these institutes was to advance the social condition of the soldier, and to reduce intemperance by the provision of such reasonable comfort, and physical as well as mental recreation, as to make them a centre of attraction, and so lessen the habit of seeking entertainment elsewhere. The plan has been carried out in nearly every regiment stationed in India, and has proved most successful.

In 1893 Lord Roberts' splendid Indian career came to a close, and he left the land in which he had worked so long, having won the love of the soldier and sepoy, the attachment of the native chiefs, and the admiration and confidence of the European community.

On the 1st of October 1895 he was appointed Commander-in-Chief in Ireland, and carried with him his old zeal for musketry, and impressed upon the soldiers under his command, as he did in India, the value of straight shooting and the necessity of fire discipline. No man is a smarter soldier than Lord Roberts, and no man has a finer eye for a smart soldier; but modern warfare demands that the soldier shall be something more than smart. A soldier, as he well points out, need not lose any of his smartness, and a regiment need not march past with any less precision, because a certain portion of drill-time has been taken up by musketry. In the days of the old Brown Bess the object of a commanding officer was to make his battalion handy on parade, and the greater part of a soldier's life was taken up with barrack drill.

The introduction of rifled arms altered all this; but it took some time to bring about the required change in the soldier's training. Officers who had been brought up in the old school clung to drill—constant drill—as the only means by which a soldier could be made efficient; they failed to appreciate the power of the rifle, nor could they understand the necessity for more time being spent on the range to admit of their men being taught to make "bull's eyes" with tolerable certainty at a distance of half a mile or more. I must not be mistaken

about drill–drill is an essential part of discipline: it makes
the soldier understand how to obey the word of command,
but there is this difference between the drill of the past and
the present. Formerly, the idea was to make the men act
in a compact body under the immediate command of the
commanding officer, and musketry was looked upon merely
as a minor sort of adjunct. *Nowadays to keep a regiment in
close formation once the zone of fire is entered would be to
court disaster.* Men are taught to fight in loose order, and to
depend in a great degree on their own selves, and in all this
the prime mover is musketry.

Lord Roberts discovered in Ireland that the class of
officers in the army who looked upon musketry as in some
way antagonistic to, or at any rate quite apart from, drill
was not altogether extinct, and he said without hesitation
"that officers commanding districts and regiments fail in
their duty if they do not do all in their power to make the
troops serving them efficient in musketry."

His plain speaking had the desired effect. At the All-
Ireland Army Rifle Meeting held at the Curragh in July
1899 the number of entries had increased from 2714 in
the previous year to 4140–more than half as many again.
"Teams belonging to the several corps in Dublin have taken
the trouble to come to the Curragh weekly for the purpose of
practising on these excellent ranges, and a strong contingent
from almost every station in Ireland has been encamped
here for some days past for the same purpose."

In the memorandum which Lord Roberts issued at
the close of the Irish manoeuvres held the same year, he
warned artillery commanders that "good effect can seldom
be expected from artillery-fire at ranges over 4000 yards.

Such fire is apt to be dangerous to its own infantry if they are at close quarters with the opposing forces, not only on account of the difficulty of distinguishing friends from foes, but because the limit of the time-fuse has been reached."

The time was at hand when the rough school of war would show how wise Lord Roberts was in insisting upon the paramount importance of soldiers being able to shoot well, and of their being proficient in that combination of marksmanship and fire-control compressed in the term musketry. The soundness of his warning to artillery officers was made manifest at Talana Hill, where our guns opened with shrapnel at less than 2000 yards upon our infantry, and drove them with some loss off the crest which they had captured. It was the first battle in a war which began with events disastrous to England. Three months after the Irish manoeuvres the Boers determined that the question whether England was to remain the paramount power in South Africa was to be decided by the sword. On the morning of the 12th of October the Boer commandoes massed on the frontier, invaded the British colony of Natal, and plunged into a carefully prepared war with England. On the 26th of October the British soldier, in the face of a murderous fire, stormed the heights of Talana Hill, and the news filled the kingdom with pride and rejoicing. But the nation was soon unpleasantly startled to find that, though a brilliant feat of arms had been achieved, the victory was barren.

The enthusiasm of the British people was sobered when news reached London that Colonel Yule, who had succeeded to the command on the fall of that gallant soldier Penn Symons, had been compelled to abandon his wounded and retreat to Ladysmith. Two hundred of our cavalry had been taken prisoners. Grave was the anxiety as to the security and junction of Yule's detachment. On October 27 came the welcome tidings that it had reached Ladysmith—"done up," telegraphed General White, "but in good spirits, and only needs rest." Four days later came the disaster of Nicholson's Nek, and Englishmen felt humiliated on hearing that 843 British soldiers had been taken prisoners. On Tuesday, November the 2nd, the last train left Ladysmith, and that afternoon the telegraph wire was cut and all communication with the outer world broken. Thirteen thousand soldiers were shut up in a small town—situated in a hollow surrounded by hills—by a vastly superior force. Our troops were outnumbered, and our guns would have been out-ranged but for the timely arrival of four naval guns. They reached Ladysmith not three days before all communication with the outside was intercepted. On the 30th of October Sir George White telegraphed: "The enemy's guns range farther than our field-guns. I have now some naval guns, which have temporarily silenced, and I hope will permanently dominate, the enemy's best guns, with which he has been bombarding the town at a distance of over 6000 yards." The nation which allows the safety of an important province of the empire lying on the chief route to India and Australia to depend on the casual arrival of six naval guns must go to wreck. The war with the Boer was no remote and contingent danger, and it was evident that Natal, lying on the border of the Orange Free State and the Transvaal, must be exposed to the first and heaviest attack of the enemy. After the first Boer war steps should have been taken to render the frontier of Natal secure, and a vast waste of money and blood would have been avoided. It will not have been spent in vain if it teaches English statesmen to rise to an imperial conception of their duties, the first of which is to provide for the security of those portions of the earth's surface which our fathers gained at the cannon's mouth. The blow struck at Natal was a blow struck at our splendid empire, and the Canadian Dominion, Australia, and New Zealand proved to the world that they were alike interested in its safety and the fortunes of England. On the 9th of October the audacious ultimatum was issued; on the 30th the Sardinia of the Canadian line sailed with 1049 officers and men from Quebec. Ships from New Zealand and Australia also, containing the vigorous children of the mother of nations, were speeding across the sea for Cape Town to fight her cause.

On the 31st of October General Sir Redvers Buller, who had been appointed to take chief command of the British forces in South Africa, reached Cape Town. When the war broke out there were not 3000 men of regular troops and no artillery in Cape Colony. The frontier of that colony, like the frontier of Natal, had never been fortified. The importance of the natural military line of the Orange river, as a foreign critic reminds us, would have been "in more military countries emphasised by corresponding works for precaution, for defence, and for movement." The subject had, however, not been quite neglected by an Imperial Government. On the shelves of the British Museum there is a blue book on the defences of Cape Colony. About October the 25th 2500 British soldiers guarded the railway bridge which spanned the Orange river. From Cape Town the Cape Railway runs north through De Aar junction across the Orange river to Kimberley, and along the border of the Orange Free State to Mafeking and Rhodesia, north of the Transvaal. At De Aar junction, 500 miles from Cape Town, there is a branch railway to Port Elizabeth, the most important commercial centre of the colony. From Naauwpoort junction, on this branch line, runs another line, which, passing Colesberg, crosses the Orange river at Norval's Pont and proceeds in almost a straight line to Bloemfontein, Johannesburg, and Pretoria. Some sixty miles from Bloemfontein, at Springfontein, the railway from the Port of East London meets it. The lines from De Aar Junction to Port Elizabeth and from East London to Springsfontein are joined by a railway which proceeds in a curve from Port Elizabeth through Middleburg to Stormberg Junction on the East London line. About the 25th of October 800 men guarded at De Aar Junction stores estimated to be worth half a million of pounds. On the arrival of General Buller Stormberg Junction and Naauwpoort were evacuated, and the forces at De Aar Junction increased to 1500 men. He found Kimberley and Mafeking besieged by the Boers, and Ladysmith invested by the enemy. It was generally supposed that the plan of campaign would be an invasion of the Orange State by the line to Bloemfontein, which would relieve the pressure on Kimberley, Mafeking, and Ladysmith. It was determined to relieve independently and simultaneously Kimberley and Ladysmith.

On the 12th of November General Methuen, a gallant daring soldier, who had in 1885 commanded a body of irregular horse in Bechuanaland, arrived at the Orange river and proceeded to organise a column for the advance on Kimberley. On the 22nd of November he advanced with his force, numbering about 8000 men, and after three severe actions he established himself at Modder river, twenty-five miles from Kimberley. Twenty-five miles remained to be traversed, and then the heroic garrison who had made frequent sorties would be relieved. Redvers Buller, whose career had been singularly distinguished, was on his way to Ladysmith. A few days sufficed to change the whole aspect of affairs. One misfortune swiftly followed on the heels of another. On the 11th of December the following telegram from General Gatacre to the general at Cape Town was made public: "Deeply regret to inform you that I have met with serious reverse in attack this morning on Stormberg." On the 14th of December the public mind was deeply excited by the evil tidings of the repulse at Magersfontein. Seven hundred of England's best and bravest soldiers had fallen into an ambush and been swept down in five minutes by a blast of bullets. Such a disaster following on the unexpected and startling features of the first reverse struck a chill through the whole nation. The misfortunes of the times, however, were not yet over. On the morning of the 16th of December the War Office received a telegram from General Buller which began as follows: "I regret to report a serious reverse." He had the preceding morning moved with an army of over 20,000 men to force the passage of the Tugela. "There are two fordable places on the Tugela, and it was my intention to force a passage through one of them. They are about two miles apart, and my plan was to force one or the other with one brigade supported by a central brigade. General Hart was to attack the left drift, General Hildyard the right road, and General Lyttelton in the centre to support either." Early

in the morning General Hart's column was forced to retire
after the leading battalion, the Connaught Rangers, who had
displayed conspicuous gallantry, had suffered heavily. Sir
Redvers Buller then ordered General Hildyard to advance,
which he did, and his leading regiment, the East Surrey,
occupied Colenso station and the houses near the bridge. At
the moment when they were preparing to advance on the ford
Sir Redvers Buller heard that the whole of the artillery which
he had sent to support that attack–"namely, the 14th and 66th
Field Batteries and six naval 12-pounder quick-firing guns,
the whole under Colonel Long, R.A.–were out of action, as it
appears that Colonel Long in his desire to be within effective
range advanced close to the river. It proved to be full of the
enemy, who suddenly opened a galling fire at close range,
killing all their horses, and the gunners were compelled to
stand to their guns." They stuck to them manfully until the
ammunition in the limbers was exhausted, and they were
compelled to leave them in the place and retreat for shelter
to a donga. On Buller's arrival teams were harnessed and
desperate rushes made to remove the guns. But the fire was
too deadly, and only two were removed. In that gallant rush
Lieutenant Frederick Roberts, Lord Roberts' only son, was
mortally wounded, and he insisted on being left where he
fell for fear he should hamper the others. It is impossible to
conceive circumstances more honourable and glorious than
those under which Frederick Roberts lost his life in the cause
of his country. "We have retired to our camp at Chieveley,"
were the last words of General Buller's telegram.

On Saturday, December 17, over England the clouds hung
dense and black. But there was no despondency. A spirit

of fervid patriotism filled the hearts of the nation, and found responsive throbs in every corner of the vast empire. England resolved to maintain its own with its hand upon the sword, and by bonds of sympathy and ties of a common cause her far-off dependencies were welded into one, and Imperial Federation, the dream of statesmen, became a fact. From Canada, Australia, and New Zealand poured offers of further contingents, which were gratefully accepted by the Government, who promptly gave practical and effective expression to the voice of the nation. They determined that all the remaining portions of the Army Reserve should be called out at once, that the 7th Division, then in course of mobilisation, should be despatched to the seat of war without delay, as well as reinforcements of artillery, including a howitzer brigade. Nine battalions of our most ancient constitutional forces, the Militia, would be allowed to volunteer for service outside of the United Kingdom, and an equivalent additional number of Militia Battalions were to be embodied at once. The Government also appealed to the feeling of chivalry which has always spurred on our race, by resolving to send a strong force of picked volunteers from the Yeomanry and a strong contingent of Volunteers selected with care. With gallantry and noble disinterestedness men of all classes responded to the appeal. On Sunday the 17th of December it was announced that Lord Roberts would be sent to South Africa as Commander-in-Chief, and would be accompanied by Lord Kitchener as chief of the staff. The tidings called forth a general burst of approval, for men felt that the army in South Africa required the soul of a commander.

On the 23rd of December Lord Roberts, his active spirit unsubdued by sorrow or by age, left England at his country's call to again command an army in the field. Three days later he arrived at Gibraltar, where he was met by Lord Kitchener. On the 10th of January Lord Roberts landed at Cape Town. He had first to study a rare and complex problem and form a sure judgment. Methuen and Cronje were facing one another on the Modder river. General French with three cavalry regiments and one and a half battalion of infantry was holding the line from Naauwpoort to Rensberg on the road to Bloemfontein. Gatacre was with two batteries of artillery and four and a half battalions of infantry at Sterkstrom, protecting the country in its vicinity and the line to Port Elizabeth. Buller had fallen back on Chieveley to await reinforcement by the 5th Division under Lieut.-General Sir Charles Warren. On the date of Lord Roberts' arrival at the Cape Sir Redvers Buller had made his dispositions for the second attempt to relieve Ladysmith. Taking this fact into consideration, and also the distance of his headquarters from Natal, Lord Roberts determined to leave General Buller "a perfectly free hand and not to interfere with his operations." Buller, after being reinforced by the 5th Division, informed the Commander-in-Chief that "his task would not be rendered easier by a further addition to the number of his troops." Moreover, Lord Roberts had no troops to spare. "The frontier of Cape Colony was weakly held, and the attitude of a portion of the Colonials bordering the Orange Free State was in some cases doubtful, and in others disloyal." The Commander-in-Chief felt that to preserve the doubtful, to silence the discontented, to raise the spirits of all, he must strike a decisive blow. The war must be carried into the enemy's country. Two plans of campaign presented themselves to the mind of Lord Roberts. The first plan consisted in advancing from Naauwpoort junction through Colesberg direct to Bloemfontein. The country around Colesberg is, however, covered with hills and exactly suited to the tactics adopted by the Boers. They also held the points where the roads crossed the Orange river, "and it seemed certain that the bridges over that river would be destroyed if the enemy could be forced to retire to the northern bank." This plan had also the further disadvantage of being mainly dependent on a single line of railway, and the movement of an army solely by means of a line of railway is, as Lord Roberts states, most tedious and practically impossible. Lord Roberts makes the same criticism regarding the value of a railway in an operation of war that Wellington made in an unpublished minute regarding a river when it was proposed to rely solely on the use of the Indus for the transport of an army of invasion. A river or a railway, as the two great commanders state, is of the greatest assistance to an army for the conveyance of stores and supplies from the base, and it is a most valuable adjunct; but even then a certain proportion of the troops must be equipped with wheel or pack transport to enable supplies to be collected, and to render the force sufficiently mobile to deal with the many tactical difficulties which must arise.

The second plan which suggested itself, and was adopted, was to use the Cape Railway for massing troops north of the Orange River station, an excellent advance base for operations. From thence these could be forwarded to the Modder camp. At the Modder camp Lord Roberts knew he would find a large amount of supplies and transport, which would be available for any strategic movement away from the railway. His first object was the relief of Kimberley, whose flash-light told of the daily danger of surrender. It could not hold out longer, he was informed, than the 15th of February. "On the relief of Kimberley being accomplished," he wrote to the Secretary of War on the 6th of February, "I propose to leave a moderate garrison at that place, and with the remainder of the force to move eastward for the purpose of threatening Bloemfontein and seizing some point on the railway between that place and Springfontein. This operation will, I trust, cause the Boers to reduce the force which they have concentrated round Ladysmith, and enable our garrison there to be relieved before the end of February." Lord Roberts calculated that if by a strategical movement he turned the enemy's position at the Modder and relieved Kimberley, Cronje's force must break up. Two courses were then open to the Boer leader. He must retreat north and be pursued by Lord Methuen, or he might make a dash to save Bloemfontein and thus court grave disaster.

But before carrying out the concentration north of the Orange river Lord Roberts and his chief of the staff had to reform the administrative departments, on which the success of a campaign so largely depends. "No organised transport corps existed," writes Lord Roberts, "when I arrived in South Africa." Both soldiers were experienced in the wants of an army in the field, and had shown that they possessed in the highest degree the gifts of first-rate organisers. By their energy, technical knowledge, and powers of administration many practical improvements were rapidly made in the different departments, especially in that of transport, and when reinforcements arrived they were able to despatch them at once to the north of the Orange river railway station, from whence they joined the troops under Lord Methuen's command. In about three weeks 35,000 men had been collected near the Modder, and with great secrecy the cavalry division under General French was withdrawn from Colesberg to join them.

On the 26th of January the Commander-in-Chief received intelligence of Sir Redvers Buller's withdrawal from Spion Kop to Potgeiter's Drift. The second attempt to relieve Ladysmith had failed. It therefore became imperatively necessary to strike at once a decisive blow. On the 6th of February Lord Roberts left Cape Town, accompanied by Lord Kitchener, for Modder camp. On the very day of his departure the Commander-in-Chief received a telegram from Sir Redvers Buller reporting.

That he had pierced the enemy's lines, and could hold the hill which divided their position, but that to drive back the enemy on either flank, and thus give his own artillery access to the Ladysmith plain, ten miles from Sir George White's position, would cost from 2000 to 3000 men, and success was doubtful. General Buller inquired if I thought that the chance of relieving Ladysmith was worth such a risk. On the same day I replied that Ladysmith must be relieved, even at the cost anticipated. I urged Sir Redvers Buller to persevere, and desired him to point out to his troops that the honour of the Empire was in his hands, and to assure them that I had no doubt whatever of their being successful.

On the 9th February General Buller reported that he found himself not strong enough to relieve Ladysmith without reinforcements, and regarded the operation upon which he was engaged as impracticable.

As Sir Charles Warren confirms the views of Sir Redvers Buller, I have informed the latter that, though I have no wish to interfere with his dispositions, or to stop his harassing the Boers as much as possible, my original instructions must hold good.[1]

---

[1] From Field-Marshal Lord Roberts to the Secretary of State for War, Camp Jacobsdal, 16th February 1900.

Three days before his departure from Cape Town Lord Roberts ordered General Hector MacDonald with the Highland Brigade, two squadrons of the 9th Lancers, the 62nd Field Battery, and No. 7 Field Company Royal Engineers to move from the Modder camp down the left bank of the Modder river and make a show of constructing a small field redoubt commanding the Koodoosberg drift, distant about seventeen miles from the camp on the Boers' extreme right.

"The object I had in view," Lord Roberts writes, "was to threaten the enemy's lines of communication from the west of the railway to that position at Magersfontein, and also to lead the Boers to believe that I intended to turn their intrenchments from the left of the Modder camp." [1]

On the afternoon of the 6th of February MacDonald reached Koodoosberg drift and seized it. The next morning he began to erect a redoubt on the northern or right bank of the river. But the enemy had occupied in strength the *kopje* (Koodoosberg) to the north of the drift, and at 9 A.M., having established a gun on its northern end, they shelled the breastworks which MacDonald was constructing. After some desultory fighting the southern end of the *kopje* was occupied by the Black Watch, half-battalion Seaforth, one company Highland Light Infantry, and. four guns 62nd Field Battery. At the drift were seven companies Highland Light Infantry. On the left bank were the Argyll and Sutherland Highlanders, remainder of Seaforths, and two guns, the 9th Lancers observing both flanks. After firing

---

[1] From Field-Marshal Lord Roberts to the Secretary of State for war, Camp Jacobsdal, 16th February 1900.

[2] Earl Roberts' telegram, dated 8th February.

shrapnel for some time the enemy made a determined effort to drive the Highlanders from the southern end of the *kopje*. Reinforcements of three companies Highland Light Infantry and four companies Seaforth were sent up in succession, "and fighting continued throughout the day both on the summit of the hill and between it and the river." [2]

As the numbers of the enemy began to increase Mac-Donald asked for the reinforcements which had been held in readiness for him. At 11.30 A.M. on the 7th Major-General Babington and a brigade of cavalry left Modder Camp, and, marching along the northern bank of the river, arrived at Koodoosberg about 3 P.M. The fight had been renewed at dawn and had raged all day. As night began to fall the enemy gradually drew back, "being followed up by Horse Artillery and cavalry." [1] It being evident that permanently to hold the Koodoosberg drift would require a larger force than could be spared, and the troops employed there being required by this time elsewhere, the cavalry and infantry brigades were ordered to return to the Modder river camp, which they did on the 8th without molestation." [2] They were required for the daring strategic movement which Lord Roberts had conceived, and was now about to set in motion. On the 9th of February the Commander-in-Chief arrived at the Modder river, and when he was seen by the men the cries of "Bobs" followed each other lustily and rapidly, and never was the word shouted with more enthusiasm. Early the next morning he visited the camp of the Highland Brigade and spoke a few words to each battalion. He reminded the Highlanders

---

[1.] From Field-Marshal Lord Roberts to the Secretary of State for War, Camp Jacobsdal, 16th February 1900.
[2.] Ibid.

how they had fought beside him and "helped to make him" in India. He had never, he said, made a campaign without Highlanders, and he would not like to be without them now. Referring to the march from Kabul to Kandahar, he observed that the Seaforths and Gordons had made a long and arduous march with him before. This time, he told them, the march would be shorter. It would not, he said, be "a walk over," but he did not doubt it would be successful. Thus he revived the confidence and rekindled the enthusiasm of the Highlanders, who gave three loud cheers for their Chief.

On the Sunday morning, 11th February, at 3 A.M., the Cavalry Division under Lieut.-General French, with seven batteries of Horse Artillery and three field batteries, left the Modder river camp. The rumble of the artillery wheels and the tread of the horses alone betrayed the movement of the troops. When the sun rose they were far away, and Cronje's outposts were, like the Afghans at Peiwar Kotal, gazing at the standing camp they had left behind.

About midday Ramdam, which is about ten miles east of Graspan station, was reached, where the 7th Division had proceeded from the railway stations of Enslin and Graspan. At 3 A.M., Monday morning, the Cavalry Division started again due east to cross the Riet river, a tributary of the Modder, flowing from south-east to north-west.

Our goal was Waterval drift, but after pushing forward for about an hour, the darkness was so intense that the general halted the division till some daylight should pour over the adjacent *kopjes*. Then as the light rose the whole division moved on Waterval, which lay at the end of a plain bounded on both sides by the usual *kopjes*, and with a very strong frontal position on the other side of the drift. The usual advanced parties–patrols, flankers, advanced squadrons –were thrown out. It was not known whether this drift was held in force until a gun was galloped into the plain by the Boers, and opened fire immediately with such a nicety of range that the first shell just whizzed over our heads, the second burst between the general and his staff. "There are too many of us riding together," the general said, as he galloped to the top of the *kopje* to look around, and soon discovered the hill in our immediate front to be strongly held by the enemy. [1]

French then ordered Colonel Eustace, R.H.A., to engage the Boer gun. It was soon silenced and retired. Meanwhile "the general swung the whole division to the right round the *kopje*, and after a few hours crossed the Riet river at De Kiel's drift with one brigade, and before sunset with the whole division and artillery. The rapidity with which the general, after making a feint at Waterval, brought his batteries under cover of the hills and developed his attack at De Kiel's drift evidently disconcerted the Boers, for they left their strong position and galloped across to our right front in one long stream directly their rear was threatened." That evening French held both sides of the Riet river.

A few hours after French started for the Riet Lord Roberts arrived at Ramdam and sent forward the 7th Division to De Kiel's drift, its place being taken by the 6th Division under Lieut.-General Kenny, who had moved by rail to Graspan. It was late in the night when the 6th Division, with convoys of food and accompanied by Lord Kitchener and his staff, reached the Riet. "The horses were fed on the arrival of the forage, and nose-bags filled, but the sun was high in the heavens before the three brigades were massed below the ridge which ran close

---

[1] "The Cavalry Rush to Kimberley," by Captain Cecil Boyle, additional Aide to General French. The *'Nineteenth Century,'* June 1900, p. 907.

to and parallel with the river, each brigade with its artillery on its protected flank. It was nearly 10 A.M. on Tuesday morning, and the sun very hot, before all the horses had fed and the gallopers were sent off to each brigadier to order the advance. The loss of the five early hours cost the division over 100 horses, which died or failed in the march that day; but in spite of delay and all hindrances the general pushed on." Lord Roberts had ridden over that morning to watch the start, and the heart of every soldier was filled with joy at the opening of the long-delayed relief of Kimberley, and with devotion to the little man who had come to wish them God-speed.

Twenty-five miles lay between French's cavalry and Klip drift on the Modder. After marching for some hours they came to a beautiful well of water. "But this was ordered to be left for the infantry, who were to follow us on the morrow from De Kiel's drift. Men and horses, scorched with the heat and parched with thirst, rode forward. General Gordon with the left brigade led the advance. The centre brigade under General Broadwood was deployed to the right. The brigade under Colonel Alexander followed in the rear." [1] In this order they rode on through the hot day, with nothing in sight except the vast arid plain surrounded by hills. At three in the afternoon the general and his staff saw from a little stone-covered knoll the river and its green bank eight miles off. They were in sight of their goal. But men and horses were worn out by heat and thirst, and the artillery teams could scarcely drag their guns and carriages. The drift must be reached and forced before the enemy had time to gather and defend a position strong by nature. Promptly the order

---

[1] "The Cavalry Rush to Kimberley." The 'Nineteenth Century,' June 1900.

was given, "Move up the whole division." The three gallopers rode back with the orders to the brigades, which had in the meanwhile been halted. General Gordon on the left, and General Broadwood five miles to his right, started at once.

Colonel Alexander's brigade was far in the rear: he had already lost sixty horses, and the rest could but move slowly. Gordon and Broadwood pushed on their jaded horses and took the enemy by surprise. The former, after shelling it for some time, reached Roodeval drift, and crossing the river, seized the *kopjes* on the west. Meanwhile Broadwood with the 12th Lancers had rushed Blip drift, pursued the surprised foe over some *kopjes* far into the plain, until he was met by a heavy fire from a large Boer laager five miles from the Modder river towards Jacobsdal. Tired and sun-weary, the pursuit was abandoned, and that night all the brigade and most of the guns held the north bank of the Modder river with the adjacent *kopjes*.[1]

Throughout the next day, Wednesday the 14th, the Boers harassed the tired horses and men by making feints."But no attack was driven home. 'Could the Boers learn to attack they would be a most formidable foe,' the general once observed. Directly we moved out the attack failed." About midnight Lord Kitchener and his staff arrived.

"It was late at night on the 13th when the 6th Division had reached the Riet. The next day Lord Roberts informed General Kelly-Kenny how essential it was that he should join hands with General French in order to free the cavalry for a further advance. And notwithstanding the long and fatiguing march of the previous day, the 6th Division pushed on that night across the veldt and reached Klip drift before daybreak on the 15th." [2]

---

[1] "The Cavalry Rush to Kimberley." The *'Nineteenth Century,'* June 1900.

[2] From Field-Marshal Lord Roberts to the Secretary of State for War, Camp Jacobsdal, 16th February 1900.

At 9.30 A.M. French resumed his journey towards Kimberley. A few miles north of the Modder the enemy were found occupying two lines of *kopjes* through which the road to Kimberley runs. "Bringing a fire to bear upon these *kopjes* by the brigade division of Horse Artillery under command of Lieut.-Colonels Eustace and Rochfort, and escorted by the 18th Cavalry Brigade under Colonel Porter, Lieut.-General French with the 2nd and 3rd Brigades under Brigadier-Generals Broadwood and Gordon, and the brigade division Horse Artillery under Colonel Davidson, galloped through the defile in extended order." [1] "For nearly five miles in perfect order," writes an eyewitness, "they galloped on and on till the head of the plain was reached, the Carabineers and the Greys leading the main body, with the 12th Lancers and Broadwood's brigade on their left. It was a thrilling time, never to be forgotten; but our guns held the enemy on our left, and the Lancers had cleared the ground on the right. About two miles from the head of the plain the main body was halted to allow the guns from the left to rejoin us, but Broadwood's brigade continued the gallop to the very top of the pass on the left, and the 12th Lancers dismounted and held the *kopjes* in front. The right front was held by the Household Composite and Gordon's Lancers." [2]

After a brief halt, the artillery having come up, the advance began again through low brushwood and scrub and broken ground. "Just beyond the head of the plain, on some rising ground, the tall chimneys of Kimberley

[1] From Field-Marshal Lord Roberts to the Secretary of State for War, Camp Jacobsdal,16th February 1900.
[2] "The Cavalry Rush to Kimberley." The *'Nineteenth Century,'* June 1900.

and the machinery of the mines were descried. A loud cheer was raised by the men, for the day was won and Kimberley was relieved; but we had still ten miles to march. We heard the guns of Kimberley as we advanced, we saw the never-to-be-forgotten range of Magersfontein and *kopjes* grim and apparently impregnable to our left rear, and we knew then that Cronje must soon discover his false position." He had discovered it, and sent a force to intercept the advance at Benauwdheidsfontein Farm, four miles from Kimberley. But they arrived just too late to seize the commanding positions, and the centre brigade, brushing away the enemy on their front, bivouacked there for the night. The general moved the remainder of the division to the right with all his guns, and about 7 P.M. he and his staff entered Kimberley.

On the 15th of February Lord Roberts entered Jacobsdal at the head of the troops. His great strategic movement had been crowned with success. The Cavalry Division and the Horse Artillery had in four days covered a distance of ninety miles, and by a gallant rush relieved Kimberley. In four days the infantry had marched across a veldt of deep sand without water. "The men never faltered. Some fell out of the ranks from sheer exhaustion; but these, as soon as they had sufficiently recovered, seized the first opportunity to rejoin their companions. It was perhaps a finer sight than any battle to see the battalions moving through the heavy sand under a broiling sun, every man determined, persevering, and cheerful. Not a murmur was heard, and the whole force was animated by a giant faith in their commander." On Sunday morning their commander began the movement, and on Thursday night it was completed. Lord Methuen held Cronje in front at Magersfontein, and French with his Cavalry Division was in his rear. General Colvile's division was close at hand ready to move wherever required, and General Kelly-Kenny's division held the Klip and Roodeval drifts in the Modder twenty miles east of the Boer army. Cronje, who did not think an English general could leave the railway, saw that he had been completely out-manoeuvred. If he remained, he must be surrounded and starved. If he retreated north, he must, as Lord Roberts had carefully planned, be pursued by French and Methuen. The capital of the Orange Free State would be at the mercy of his opponent. He therefore determined to make a dash east to Bloemfontein, hoping to slip between French at Kimberley and Kelly-Kenny at the Klip drift.

On Friday morning, the 16th February, the outposts at Klip drift saw north of them a great cloud of dust moving eastward. It was Cronje's army with his convoy. The Mounted Infantry were promptly sent in direct pursuit, while Knox's brigade were despatched along the northern bank of the river.[1] The pursuers soon came up with the retreating army, for the Boers and their oxen were tired with the long night's march of thirty miles from Magersfontein. Turning round, they, however, stubbornly resisted every attempt to capture their waggons. A long day of rear-guard fighting ensued. When night fell Cronje had baffled his pursuers. As his horses and bullocks were exhausted and his men utterly worn out by twenty hours' marching and fighting, he rested for a few

---

[1.] Dr Conan Doyle writes, "Lord Kitchener, who was in command at Klip drift at the moment, instantly unleashed his mounted infantry." General Kelly-Kenny was senior to Lord Kitchener,. who was only acting as Lord Roberts' staff officer.

hours on the northern bank of the Modder. Before the light of morning, abandoning seventy-eight of his waggons, he started for Koodoosrand drift, intending to cross there and so reach the direct road from Jacobsdal to Bloemfontein.

Shortly after midnight French received a telegram from Lord Kitchener stating "that Cronje with 10,000 men was in full retreat from Magersfontein, with all his waggons and equipment and four guns, along the bank of the Modder river towards Bloemfontein; that he had already fought a rear-guard action with him, and if French with all available horses and guns could head him and prevent his crossing the river the infantry from Klip drift would press on and annihilate or take the whole force prisoners." At 3 A.M. on Saturday the 17th February General French with Broadwood's brigade and three batteries of artillery started for Koodoosrand drift, forty miles from Kimberley. They rode over the veldt as fast as their jaded horses could go, "and as we pressed on, large herds of buck, hares, and foxes, and numerous birds were put to flight." About 11 A.M. they caught sight in the distance of the trees lining the banks of the Modder river. The horses were ordered to water "while the general personally reconnoitred, as is his invariable custom, some rising ground afterwards called Artillery Hill. And there at about 4000 yards' distance, to our joy, we saw the long line of Cronje's convoy streaming away in the distance, with the leading waggons on the very point of dipping down into the drifts which head to the main road to Petrusberg and beyond to Bloemfontein." A galloper was immediately sent back to order up the guns. They were to come at a walk, "that no dust might betray our presence." On arriving they were quickly brought into action behind Artillery Hill, "and at 12.15 P.M. on that Saturday the first shell headed Cronje's leading waggon as it stood with its driver just ready to descend into the drift." A supreme moment. Cronje, by sacrificing his guns and teams, might have made his way across the river under the heavy fire of our guns. But that sacrifice he was not prepared to make. Wheeling his waggons to the right across the plain, he laagered opposite Woldeskrael drift, about four miles below Koodoosrand drift and four miles above Paardeberg drift. He determined to cross next morning, and he sent a large part of his force to line the river-bed down to Paardeberg in order to keep in check any force which might be coming from that quarter and interfere with his crossing. It was a fatal decision. Cronje had neglected some important factors in his calculation—the spirit of the British soldier, his eagerness to fight, and his marvellous powers of endurance. In spite of being worn by the fatigue and privation of many days' marching, Kelly-Kenny's infantry pushed on during the night to reach Paardeberg. They missed the precise point, and, tramping on, they reached and occupied the rising ground 3000 yards south of Woldeskrael drift. A few miles behind them was General Colvile's division (the 9th) and the Mounted Infantry, which had crossed from the north side. Cronje's second passage was blocked.

On Sunday morning, the 18th February, the Boers opened fire from the bed of the river on the Mounted Infantry. A stiff fight ensued, and the enemy were driven a quarter of a mile up the stream. Meanwhile Kelly-Kenny moved with the 6th Division parallel with the river, while the Highland Brigade advanced partly up the river and partly in the open. The Black

Watch were on the left of the river, then the Seaforths, and on the right the Argylls and Sutherlands touching General Knox's Brigade, which formed the centre of the long enveloping movement. The regiments comprising Knox's Brigade were the West Riding, the Buffs, the Oxfords, and the Gloucesters. The right was made up by the Essex and Welsh Regiments. In this order the infantry advanced rapidly across the level plain, supported by the 76th, 81st, and 82nd Field Batteries, posted on a slight rise about 2000 yards south-south-east of the Boer laager, and about 1600 yards from the nearest point of the river. The 71st, placed on the extreme right of the infantry, had on its right rear a *kopje* which by some accident had been vacated by our men. The Boers seized it and opened on the battery a smiting fire. At the same time there poured on them a steady hail of balls from the Vickers-Maxims. "A bombardier was killed and nearly every man in the detachment wounded. At one gun all except one man were put out of action, and he went on laying his gun as if nothing had happened." [1]

About 9 P.M. General Smith-Dorrien's brigade, except the Cornwall Light Infantry, which were kept in reserve, crossed at Paardeberg, and thence fought their way nearly a mile up the northern bank among the bushes. Finding they could go no farther owing to a bend strongly held, they retired to the north-east, and "the Shropshires and Canadians advanced by a series of short rushes in the most gallant style, the Canadians especially showing a magnificent and almost reckless courage. These two battalions and the 82nd Battery, which had been sent in support, did great execution

---

[1] The '*Times*,' weekly edition, April 6, 1900.

among the Boers in a stretch of the river-bank above the bend, where they were able to some extent to enfilade them."[1] At three o'clock the Canadians and Shropshires were unable to advance any farther. Three and a half companies of the Cornwalls were sent to support them. Taking some of the Canadians and Shropshires with them, they advanced within 800 yards of the Boer position. Then on they rushed, and the intrepid Aldworth of the Cornwalls fell and died as he was cheering on his men. A murderous fire from the Boer trenches checked them, and their desperate valour was of no avail.

At about 11 A.m. French's Horse Artillery planted itself on the rising ground north of the laager and shelled it and the river-bed. On the eastern flank the Mounted Infantry, which had occupied a *kopje* south of Koodoostrand drift, crossed the river and advanced some distance along the northern bank. An hour later the Welsh and Essex also crossed the river below Koodoostrand and worked their way down among the bushes on both sides of the river-bank. "In one of the rushes made by the Welsh twenty-four out of a party of twenty-five who attempted to storm the laager were killed or wounded." At the same time the frontal attack was continued with greater violence. General Knox was wounded in the shoulder as he led his brigade and the Yorks to the river-bank just above the bend. Hector MacDonald, who had dismounted for the advance, was shot in the foot as he was directing the movements of his Highlanders, who were struggling doggedly through the storm of the bullets towards the bushes which sheltered the enemy. The Seaforths and some of the Cornwalls drove at the point of the bayonet the

[1] The *'Times,'* weekly edition, March 23, 1900.

enemy from the bushes at the drift, and three companies of the former and three companies of the Black Watch crossed the stream. The remainder of the Highland Brigade rushed on with equal vehemence; but volleys poured into them from the bed, strongly held by Boer marksmen, checked their advance, and they could not reach the stream. Towards evening the batteries on the north and south side simultaneously opened fire. The shells, falling with remarkable precision along the river-bed, drove the enemy back until they reached the bed of the river opposite the laager, which for eight hours had been torn to pieces by lyddite and shrapnel. At sunset the firing ceased. Our men slept where they had fought, while the bearer-parties scoured the field collecting the dead and wounded. Brave men fell on both sides. Our loss amounted to 183 killed and 851 wounded.

At 4 A.M. on the 19th Lord Roberts left Jacobsdal with the 7th Division, and reached Paardeberg the following morning. On his arrival he was informed that an armistice of twenty-four hours had been granted to Cronje, who had asked for it on the plea that he desired to bury his dead. "This armistice I immediately revoked, and ordered a vigorous bombardment of the enemy's position. General Cronje knew, as we knew, that considerable reinforcements were hastening to his assistance from Natal and from the south, and his request was obviously only an expedient to gain time." Lord Roberts having found the troops in camp much exhausted by their previous marching and fighting, decided not to make a second attack on the laager, "the capture of which by a *coup de main* would have entailed a further loss of life, which did not appear to me to be warranted by the military exigencies of the situation." He determined to adopt the more bloodless course of crushing the enemy's resistance by his artillery.

On the night of the 18th a *kopje* to the south-east, which commanded the Boer intrenchments and the whole course of the stream from the Paardeberg drift upwards, was taken by surprise by the enemy. During the morning of the 20th of February it was recaptured, the enemy abandoning their defences on being threatened in the rear by the cavalry and Mounted Infantry. In the afternoon, as the Boers showed no sign of surrender, and Lord Roberts' offers of safe-conduct to the women and children had been refused, the 18th, the 62nd, and 75th Field Batteries and two naval pounders placed in position on the south bank, and the 65th (howitzer), 76th, 81st, and 82nd Field Batteries and three naval 4.7-inch guns posted on the right bank, opened fire on the Boer laager and the intrenchments surrounding it. The air shook with the roar of artillery. The lyddite shells raised great clouds of green smoke, which filled the bed of the river, while shrapnel burst along the edge of each bank. Shells searched every bush and every ravine. A Boer doctor thus describes the position of the enemy:—

Nothing could be done but crouch in the trenches and wait till dusk prevented a further attack, while waggon after waggon in the laager caught fire and burned away into a heap of scrap-iron surrounded by wood-ashes. The desolation was fearful, and it soon became impossible to make any reply. The losses inflicted upon the horses were the turning-point of the siege. So enormous a proportion (estimated by some at 75 per cent) of the horses, for which no protection could be made, were lost, that any dash for freedom by night was impossible, and the condition of that laager rapidly became so foul that that alone, apart from want of food, would have compelled an early surrender. There was no opportunity of getting rid of the vast number of dead animals; burial was impossible, and the low state of the river prevented them from sending them down stream; for several days all they could do was to drag them to leeward of their camp. Meanwhile decomposition set in, and the absolute need of clean air caused a serious rebellion in the camp, most of the 4000 men demanding that surrender should be made at once. When, Sunday the 25th, the flood brought down past our lines an unending series of dead animals, that cannot have been less than 1500 or 2000, the desperate straits of the enemy were apparent indeed.

Cronje, to appease the discontent of his men, promised them that he would surrender on the 28th. He knew that commandoes had begun to come up from the east and west to release him from his perilous situation, and he hoped by that day the English grasp would be loosened. It was a vain hope. "On the morning of the 23rd of February the 1st battalion of the Yorkshire Regiment engaged one of these parties, about 2000 strong, at the eastern end of the position south of the river, and drove off the enemy with a heavy loss, losing themselves 3 officers and 17 men wounded." Similar parties of the enemy appeared in other directions, but were beaten back without difficulty by our troops. Early on the 26th four 6-inch howitzers arrived at camp from the Modder, and the Boer laager was again shelled during the afternoon.

At 3 A.M. on the 27th of February the Royal Canadian Regiment and No. 7 Company Royal Engineers, commanded respectively by Lieut.-Colonel W. D. Otter and Lieut.-Colonel W. F. Kincaid, supported by the 1st battalion Gordon Highlanders, quitted a trench running 700 yards north from the river, which they had occupied since the day Paardeberg was fought. Covered by the darkness the Canadians in dead silence moved forward, followed by the Engineers. They advanced to within eighty yards of the enemy's defences when the trampling of the scrub betrayed their presence. A rifle was fired, and instantly there came forth from the Boer trenches a stream of fire. The Canadians proved themselves worthy descendants of the men who had fought under Montcalm. Lying down in order as if on parade, they returned the enemy's fire, guided by the flashes of the rifles of their foe. Behind them, regardless of the hail of bullets, the Engineers dug a trench from the inner edge of the bank to the crest and then for fifty or sixty yards to the north. The Canadians retired to it and waited for the dawn. "Of the three companies, foremost, and that which suffered most, was the French company under Major Pelletier." [1] "A creditable deed," writes Lord Roberts, "to all who took part in it." [2]

When dawn broke Cronje realised that he could make no further resistance. The position the Canadians occupied enfiladed securely the Boers' rifle trenches along the river and the embrasures on the north. "This apparently," as Roberts telegraphed, "clenched matters." At 6 A.M. on the day on which the Boers used to hold high festival in commemoration of their victory at Majuba Hill, Cronje sent the following letter:—

HEADQUARTER LAAGER,
MODDER RIVER, 27th February 1900.

HONOURED SIR.,—Herewith I have the honour to inform you that the council of war, which was held here last evening, resolved to surrender unconditionally with the forces here,

[1] The *Times,* weekly edition, March 23, 1900.
[2] From Field-Marshal Lord Roberts to the Secretary of State for War,Camp Paardeberg, 28th February 1900.

being compelled to do so under existing circumstances. They therefore throw themselves on the clemency of her Britannic Majesty.

As a sign of surrender a white flag will be hoisted from 6 A.M. to-day. The council of war requests that you will give immediate orders for all further hostilities to be stopped, in order that more loss of life may be prevented.—I have, &c.,

G. A. CRONJE, *General.*

Lord Roberts in his khaki uniform, without a badge of rank except his Kandahar sword, awaited the Boer general. At 8 A.M. he arrived in camp. "Commandant Cronje" was the brief introduction as the Boer dismounted from his white pony, and, answering the Field-Marshal's salute, shook hands. "I am glad to see you, I am glad to meet so brave a man," was Lord Roberts' courteous welcome. With a subtle skill had Cronje constructed and held his lines at Magersfontein, wonderfully did he effect his retreat to Paardeberg, and stubbornly did he fight, but twice in twenty-four hours he neglected "those happy occasions which in war take birth and flight at the same instant." The British soldiers treated their beaten foes with the same courtesy that Lord Roberts had shown their leader. That afternoon Cronje with the other prisoners, numbering 3919 men, exclusive of 150 wounded, were despatched to Cape Town.

Lord Roberts by his well-conceived plan, his promptness of action, and by taking the legitimate amount of risk without which no commander can gather the full harvest of success, had suddenly decided the whole fate of the campaign. Kimberley had been relieved, the lines of Magersfontein were in our possession, Cronje and his army were prisoners, the Boers had withdrawn from their positions in Cape Colony.

What Roberts had written to the Secretary of State for War on the 6th of February carne to pass: "This operation will, I trust, cause the Boers to reduce the force which they have concentrated round Ladysmith, and enable our garrison there to be relieved before the end of February." On the 27th of February Buller drove back the weakening force with which Louis Botha held the Tugela. On the 28th Ladysmith was relieved.

On the 1st of March Lord Roberts proceeded to Kimberley frontier in order to discuss with Lord Methuen the measures to be taken for the relief of Mafeking. He returned the next day to Osfontein, about five miles east of Paardeberg, where he established his headquarters. His original intention was to march towards Bloemfontein as soon as Cronje's force had surrendered; but the cavalry and artillery horses were so exhausted by their rapid march to Kimberley and back, and so weakened by the scarcity of forage, that he found it absolutely necessary to give them a week's rest. Meanwhile reports reached the Commander-in-Chief that the enemy were collecting in considerable strength to the east of Osfontein, and were intrenching themselves along a line of *kopjes* running north and south, about eight miles distant from the camp at Osfontein. "The northernmost, Leeuw *Kopje*, was to the north of and two miles distant from the river; and the southernmost cluster of *kopjes*, to which the name of the 'Seven *Kopjes*' was given, was eight miles south of the river. The front of the Boer position extended there for ten and a half miles." [1] Table Mountain, a flat-topped *kopje* which formed a salient

---

[1.] From Field-Marshal Lord Roberts to the Secretary of State for War, Government House, Bloemfontein, 15th March 1900.

to the centre of the alignment, was the key of the enemy's position. At 2 A.M. on the 7th of March Lord Roberts sent the Cavalry Division, with Alderson's and Ridley's brigades of Mounted Infantry and seven batteries of Horse Artillery, to circle round the left flank of the Boers to take their line of intrenchments in reverse, and moving eventually to the river near Poplar Grove, to cut off their line of retreat. The 6th Division, under General Kelly-Kenny, were told to follow the route taken by the cavalry to a certain point south-east of the Seven *Kopjes*, when they were to attack and to drive the Boers from them. Afterwards they were to move north in the direction of Table Mountain. To distract attention from the main attack on Table Mountain, and assist the cavalry in preventing the Boers from crossing the river at the Poplar Grove drift, the 14th Brigade of the 7th Division, with 15th Brigade Division of Field Artillery, Nesbitt's Horse, and the New South Wales and Queensland Mounted Infantry, were instructed to march eastward along the south bank of the river. The 9th Division, with three naval 12-pounders and Mounted Infantry, were ordered to operate in a similar manner on the northern bank of the river and to drive the enemy from the Leeuw *Kopje*, which formed the northern extremity of their defensive position.[1]

General French threw his Horse Artillery and cavalry entirely round the southern projection of the Boers' position. The 6th Division, however, making too wide a detour to the south, reached the Seven *Kopjes* after the Boers had been dislodged by the Horse Artillery fire in reverse and the shell-fire of the naval guns in front. The turning movement

[1] From Field-Marshal Lord Roberts to the Secretary of State for war, Camp Paardeberg, 28th February 1900.

of the cavalry and the advance of the Infantry Division north and south of the river caused the enemy to evacuate Table Mountain and Leeuw *Kopje* without offering any serious opposition. They showed great adroitness in getting away almost all their guns and waggons. Their rearguard maintained a bold front, while the rest of the force were busy inspanning. Lord Roberts writes:–

Had the cavalry, Horse Artillery, and Mounted Infantry been able to move more rapidly, they would undoubtedly have intercepted the enemy's line of retreat, and I should have had the satisfaction of capturing their guns, waggons, and supplies, as well as a large number of prisoners. The failure to effect this object was the more mortifying when I learnt the next day on good authority that the Presidents of the Orange Free State and South African Republic had been present during the engagement, and had strongly urged the Boers to continue their resistance. Their appeals to the burghers were, however, unavailing, as the Boer forces were quite broken and refused to fight any longer.[1]

On the 8th and 9th the force halted at Poplar Grove. On the 11th it again advanced in three columns on Bloemfontein. The left column under General French, consisting of Colonel Porter's cavalry brigade (18th), Alderson's mounted infantry, and General Kelly-Kenny's division (6th), advanced along the Modder. The centre column, which Lord Roberts accompanied, consisting of General Colvile's division (9th), General Pole Carew's brigade of Guards, and Colonel Broadwood's brigade (2nd) of cavalry, advanced towards Driefontein. The right column, consisting of General Tucker's division (7th), with the Gordons and the 3rd Cavalry Brigade, moved along the Petrusberg road. The

---

[1.] From Field-Marshal Lord Roberts to the Secretary of State for War, Government House, Bloemfontein, 15th March 1900.

left column found the enemy holding several large *kopjes* behind Abraham's Kraal or Driefontein, and endeavoured to turn their left flank by moving to the south. "They, however, anticipated this manoeuvre by a rapid march southward, and took up a fresh position on a ridge about four miles long, running north and south across the road, two miles east of Driefontein. Lieut.-General French followed up the enemy with the 1st Cavalry Brigade and the 6th Division, and came into contact with them about 11 A.M." [1]

The 2nd Cavalry Brigade had by this time reached Driefontein and endeavoured, in conjunction with the 1st Cavalry Brigade, to turn the rear of the Boers by operating in the plain behind the ridge which they were holding. "The enemy's guns, however, had a longer range than our field-guns, which were the only ones immediately available, and some time elapsed before the former could be silenced, especially a Creusot gun which had been placed in a commanding position on an isolated *kopje* two and a half miles east of the north end of the ridge." [2] About 2 P.M. the 6th Division reached this end of the ridge. T Battery Royal Horse Artillery prepared the way for the infantry advance, shelling the Boer centre vigorously from the south.

Here occurred an instance of the admirable coolness and splendid behaviour of our artillery. As T Battery came into action the enemy opened a heavy and accurate fire on it with their Vickers-Maxim, killing two men and several horses. The men were engaged in unhitching the gun at the time, but within

---

[1] From Field-Marshal Lord Roberts to the Secretary of State for War, Government House, Bloemfontein, 15th March 1900.
[2] Ibid.

two minutes the same gun fired the first shot, the artillerymen carrying ammunition over the bodies of their fallen comrades. U Battery, which occupied a position to the north of the Boer centre, shelled the ridges thoroughly, but on the arrival of the 76th Field Battery moved closer to T Battery. The 76th Battery then took up a position closer to the Boers, where it was able effectively to shell the ridge towards which the Welsh were moving. The gunners encountered a heavy rifle-fire, but they worked coolly and unconcernedly with great effect.[1]

All this time the infantry were advancing steadily under heavy fire, and the Boers were gradually pushed back towards the centre of the ridge, where they made an obstinate stand.

About 5 P.M. the 9th Division came up, and Lord Roberts at once ordered the Guards Brigade and the 19th Brigade to the assistance of the 6th Division. "But before these reinforcements could reach the ridge the enemy's position was stormed in the most gallant manner by the 1st battalions of the Essex and Welsh Regiments, supported by the 2nd battalion of the Buffs. The bodies of 102 Boers were afterwards found along the ridge, mainly in the position which they held to the last." Our casualties were heavy: 4 officers were killed and 20 wounded, and 60 men killed and 314 wounded. "A flagrant breach of the recognised usages of war," Lord Roberts writes, "was the cause of most of the casualties in the infantry. The enemy held up their hands and hoisted a white flag in sign of surrender, but when our troops approached they were fired on at close quarters by a number of Boers posted under cover, and had to retire until reinforced, when the position was carried at the point

[1] The 'Times,' weekly edition, March 16, 1900.

of the bayonet. The holding up their hands on the part of
the Boers was observed by me and by several officers of my
staff through telescopes." [1]

On the following day, the 11th March, the combined left
and centre columns marched to Aasvogel Kop. Lord Roberts
ordered the 3rd Cavalry Brigade, with two batteries of
Horse Artillery, to proceed from Drie Kop to Venter's Vlei.
Next morning (12th March) with the 6th and 9th Divisions
he resumed his march to Bloemfontein. The direct road
to the capital now lay due east, and a large body of Boers
under Joubert manned the heights commanding it. Our
infantry advanced towards them. A fight was expected, but
on reaching a point two miles from the enemy's fastness
the column turned abruptly to the right, leaving the Boers
alone in their position. "Throughout the day the Boers looked
down upon fifteen miles of transport passing them without
a shot being fired on either side, conscious that twelve miles
ahead, beyond all hope of check, the leading troopers of our
cavalry were sweeping a clear course before them almost
up to the gates of Bloemfontein. It was a masterly stroke,
and has succeeded to the full." [2] That evening Lord Roberts'
column halted at Venter's Vlei. The men had, on reduced
rations, marched forty miles in two days, through a desert
almost devoid of water. "But every man," writes one who was
present, "is willing to work till he drops for Lord Roberts."
Their Commander was everywhere at once, cheering the men
exhausted by fatigue and hunger, lavishing encouraging

[1.] From Field-Marshal Lord Roberts to the Secretary of State for War,
Government House, Bloemfontein, 15th March 1900.
[2.] The 'Times,' weekly edition, 15th April 1900.

words on them and appeals to duty. On reaching Venter's Vlei Lord Roberts heard that reinforcements were hourly expected at Bloemfontein. It was imperatively necessary to forestall the enemy's movements. French was ordered to push on to Brand Dam Kop, seven miles to the south-west of Bloemfontein; but his jaded horses could proceed only at a trot, and it was near midnight before he occupied two hills near the railway station, which commanded Bloemfontein. That night a gallant deed was done. Major Hunter-Weston, R.E., attached to the Cavalry Division, with a handful of Alderson's mounted infantry, broke up the railway north and south of Bloemfontein. "And this enterprising officer also succeeded in cutting the enemy's telegraph and telephone wires in both directions." [1]

An hour after noon on the 13th of March Lord Roberts at the head of his troops, moving with a smartness as if on a review-ground, entered the capital of the Orange Free State, and one of the great marches of history was brought to a close. In twenty-nine days he had, 700 miles from his base, moved 40,000 men, 20,000 horse, and a vast convoy, across a barren stretch of country where no provisions were to be found and water only once in the day. This had been done under a burning sun and in the face of a watchful enemy. It had been rapidly and successfully executed, because the Commander knew how to draw on that inexhaustible bank, the good spirits and endurance of the British soldier, and because he himself had attended to every detail in giving orders, and had

---

[1] From Field-Marshal Lord Roberts to the Secretary of State for War, Government House, Bloemfontein, 15th March 1900.

kept a close watch on the execution of his behests. But not unto himself, but his soldiers, did the General give the praise. On the 14th of March he issued the following Army Orders:–

It affords the Field-Marshal Commanding-in-Chief the greatest pleasure in congratulating the army in South Africa on the various events that have occurred during the past few weeks, and he would specially offer his sincere thanks to that portion of the army which, under his immediate command, have taken part in the operations resulting yesterday in the capture of Bloemfontein.

On the 12th February this force crossed the boundary which divided the Orange Free State from British territory. Three days later Kimberley was relieved. On the fifteenth day the bulk of the Boer army in this State, under one of their most trusted generals, were made prisoners. On the seventeenth day the news of the relief of Ladysmith was received, and on the 13th March, twenty-nine days from the commencement of the operations, the capital of the Orange Free State was occupied.

This is a record of which any army may well be proud—a record which could not have been achieved except by earnest, well-disciplined men, determined to do their duty and to surmount whatever difficulties or dangers might be encountered.

Exposed to extreme heat by day, bivouacking under heavy rain, marching long distances (not infrequently with reduced rations), the endurance, cheerfulness, and gallantry displayed by all ranks are beyond praise, and Lord Roberts feels sure that neither her Majesty the Queen nor the British nation will be unmindful of the efforts made by this force to uphold the honour of their country.

The Field-Marshal desires especially to refer to the fortitude and heroic spirit with which the wounded have borne their sufferings. Owing to the great extent of country over which modern battles have to be fought, it is not always possible to afford immediate aid to those who are struck down; many hours have, indeed, at times elapsed before some of the wounded could be attended to, but not a word of murmur or complaint has been uttered: the anxiety of all, when succour came, was that their comrades should be cared for first.

In assuring every officer and man how much he appreciates their efforts in the past, Lord Roberts is confident that in the future they will continue to show the same resolution and soldierly qualities; and to lay down their lives if need be (as so many brave men have already done) in order to ensure that the war in South Africa may be brought to a satisfactory conclusion.

As Lord Roberts states in his despatch to the Secretary of State for War dated 31st March 1900, no account of his march from Jacobsdal to Bloemfontein would be complete without special attention being drawn

to the good services performed by the splendid and highly efficient body of troops from other parts of her Majesty's empire which have, while serving under my orders, borne a distinguished share in the advance into the Orange Free State.

The various contingents from Australia, from New Zealand, and from Ceylon, the several corps which have been formed locally in the Cape Colony, and the City of London Imperial Volunteers, have vied one with the other in the performance of their duty. They have shared with the regular troops of her Majesty's army the hardships and dangers of the campaign in a manner which have gained for them the respect and admiration of all who have been associated with them. I trust that your Lordship will concur with me in considering that by their valour and endurance the soldiers and sailors serving in the force which is under my immediate command have worthily upheld the best tradition of her Majesty's army and navy.

On his entry into Bloemfontein Lord Roberts met "with a cordial reception from the inhabitants, a number of whom accompanied the troops singing 'God save the Queen' and

'Rule Britannia.'" Like all great commanders, he had now to consider the political effect of his operations. Between England and the inhabitants of the Orange Free State there had been no jealousy of conflicting interests or causes of quarrel. Their prosperous and well-governed republic had been precipitated into the horrors of war and invasion by the ambition of their President, and the attitude of the inhabitants of the capital created a belief that the bulk of the Free State farmers were tired of a struggle into which they had not entered of their own freewill. The British Commander, therefore, had every reason to hope that by a generous policy of conciliation he would make the ultimate pacification of the country more easy. He issued a proclamation warning all burghers to desist from any further hostility towards her Majesty's Government and the troops under his command, "and I undertake that any of them who may so desist, and are found staying in their homes and quietly pursuing their ordinary occupations, will not be made to suffer in their persons or their property on account of their having taken up arms in obedience to the orders of their Government." Many burghers surrendered their arms and their horses, and took an oath to abstain from further hostilities against her Majesty's Government.

Lord Roberts' advance had been so rapid and his operations so decisive that the Boer force opposed to him, crushed and overborne, retired to Kroonstad. The commandoes which were in the northern districts of Cape Colony crossed the Orange river and retreated in a northerly direction along the Basutoland border and the fertile district of Ladybrand. Had the British Commander been able to strike another blow while the Boers still reeled from those he had given them,

much good would have accrued; but his army was paralysed
by the unusual exertions it had been called upon to make.
He arrived at Bloemfontein with horses wholly starved and
men half-starved. He had to restore his men and his cattle,
he had to collect supplies from his base, for the country
itself afforded but little food, and he had to reorganise his
transport before he attempted to regain the offensive. A
long halt became imperative. The Boers, on learning the
condition of the British army, were stirred on to renewed
activity, and "they showed considerable strategical skill by
reoccupying Ladybrand and by concentrating a large force
below Brandfort and Thabanchu." [1] This gave them free
access to the south-eastern districts of the Orange Free
State. Bodies of adventurous men, nurtured in hardship and
familiar with every contour of the land, scoured the country,
cut off small parties who were engaged in distributing
the proclamation, and menaced our communications. A
large number of Free State burghers broke their oaths
and rejoined the commandoes. They conspired together
to give information. They attacked our troops. They used
their homesteads as depots for food and ammunition. Lord
Roberts' policy of conciliation had not proved a success, but
it was wise and statesmanlike. If it had succeeded it would
have solved the difficult problem of reconstruction, and
saved much misery and bloodshed.

To carefully guard the lines of railway and to collect a force
strong enough to drive the enemy north of the Brandfort
-Thabanchu line now became the British Commander's

[1.] From Field-Marshal Lord Roberts to the Secretary of State for War,
Kroonstad, 21st May 1900.

primary aim. Until that was done it was impossible for him to make the first move in his plan of campaign. To that plan of campaign he was determined if possible to adhere, "and not to be led into diverting from it for operations of subsidiary importance the troops which I required to attain my main objective—namely, to advance in adequate strength through the northern portion of the Orange Free State on Johannesburg and Pretoria." [1] An operation of subsidiary importance was the relief of Mafeking. The public mind at home had been much excited by exaggerated rumours sent by correspondents regarding the state of affairs in that city. But Lord Roberts knew that the garrison had ample supplies of food to support them till the middle of June. He promised to relieve them by the 18th of May. "History is," writes Kinglake, "replete with proof that the boldest captains have ever been those who, far from striking at random, and with half-formed notions of what they might do, have always had clear conceptions of their objects, and of the way in which they meant to succeed." Lord Roberts had a clear conception of his object and the way he meant to succeed. As the task of relieving Ladysmith had been rendered more easy by his hurling himself on Bloemfontein, so Mafeking would be released by his throwing himself on the capital of the Transvaal.

By the beginning of May Lord Roberts had all the strategical points on the south-eastern districts securely held, and he was no longer anxious for the safety of his railway. The condition of his army had materially improved.

---

[1] From Field-Marshal Lord Roberts to the Secretary of State for War, Kroonstad, 21st May 1900.

It had been increased from 40,000 men to 70,000. Six thousand horses, besides mules, had been sent up by train along a single line of railway nearly 910 miles long, every bridge of which for the last 128 miles had been destroyed by the enemy. Ammunition, food for men and horses, clothes and requirements for the sick—all, in fact, that a great army should need—were brought to Bloemfontein in five weeks. It was reckoned that 1040 tons were hauled during that time on a single track of railway—a wonderful feat of transportation, of which any country might be proud. When his supplies had been collected and the arrangements for the transport completed, Lord Roberts ordered a forward movement towards Kroonstad. On the 1st of May the 11th (Pole-Carew's) Division left Bloemfontein and marched with bands playing along the northern road. The following day the Commander-in-Chief joined them at Karu siding, twenty miles on their way to Pretoria. Two hundred and twenty remained to be traversed. "The 1st (Hutton's) Brigade of Mounted Infantry had moved to Brakpan, ten miles to the west, while Lieut.-General Tucker with the 15th (Wadell's) Brigade of the 7th Division was two miles to the east of the siding; the 14th (Maxwell's) Brigade was at Vlakfontein, five miles farther east. Beyond it was Major-General Ian Hamilton's force, at Isabellafontein, a little north of Karee, and due south of Wynberg.[1]

[1.] This consisted of the   2nd Cavalry Brigade under Brigadier-General Broadwood, the 2nd Brigade of Mounted Infantry under Brigadier-Gencral Ridley, Brigadier-General Smith-Dorrien's brigade of the 9th Division, and a newly formed brigade (21st)—composed of 1st battalion Sussex, 1st battalion Derbyshires, the 1st battalion Cameron Highlanders, and the City Imperial Volunteer battalion—under the command of Major-General Bruce Hamilton.

On the 3rd of May, the force moving forward in this order, the little town of Brandfort, ten miles north of Karee, was occupied. The following day Pole-Carew's and Tucker's divisions, with the 1st Brigade of Mounted Infantry, remained in the vicinity of Brandfort, while Ian Hamilton engaged and drove back the enemy's rear-guard about fifteen miles south of Wynberg. "On this occasion the junction of the two Boer forces was frustrated by a well-executed movement of the Household Cavalry, the 12th Lancers, and Kitchener's Horse under the command of Lieut.-Colonel the Earl of Airlie. The enemy fled after the encounter, leaving their dead and wounded on the field." [1]

On the 5th of May Lord Roberts' main column marched to within three miles of the Vet river, the north bank of which was held in considerable force.

For three hours the action was chiefly confined to artillery on both sides, our field and naval guns making excellent practice; but just before dark the Mounted Infantry executed a turning movement, crossing the river six miles west of the railway bridge, which, like other bridges over the rivers along our line of advance, had been previously destroyed by the enemy. In this affair the Canadian, New South Wales, New Zealand Mounted Infantry, and the Queensland Mounted Rifles vied with each other in their efforts to close with the enemy. We captured one Maxim gun and 26 prisoners, our losses being slight.[2]

That day Major-General Ian Hamilton captured Wynberg "after an engagement at Bobeansberg, in which the 2nd battalion Black Watch under Lieut.-Colonel Carthew-Yorstoun greatly distinguished themselves." [3]

---

[1] From Field-Marshal Lord Roberts to the Secretary of State for War, Kroonstad, 21st May 1900.
[2] Ibid.
[3] Ibid.

On the 6th of May the main force crossed the Vet river unopposed and occupied Smalldal Junction. Here it had to halt for two days owing to the difficulty in getting the baggage and supply convoys across the river. The Mounted Infantry, however, pushed on to Welgelegen, and Major-General Ian Hamilton's force moved some ten miles north of Wynberg, its place there having been taken by the Highland Brigade."[1] That day Lord Roberts galloped across country to see General Ian Hamilton. "He has made," writes a correspondent, "a most strict examination of farm-houses, with the result that Mauser and Martini rifles with abundance of ammunition were found in nearly every house." The first duty of the Commander-in-Chief, as Lord Roberts said, was to protect the army, and he was constrained to permit the destruction of those farms and properties which had been used for the purposes of war. According to the usage of war among civilised nations, if inhabitants take part directly or indirectly in hostilities, "reprisals" there must be. They are necessary evils due to that mighty scourge. To punish the zeal of the people of Shenandoah, Sheridan ravaged the rich and smiling valley, "so that a crow flying down it would have to carry his own rations." "Ten thousand barns," writes a historian of the war, "filled with wheat and hay and farming implements, and seventy mills filled with flour and wheat, were among the things destroyed." Lord Roberts permitted treachery that was proved to be punished, but he issued stringent orders to prevent the troops from plundering those who

---

[1.] From Field-Marshal Lord Roberts to the Secretary of State for War, Kroonstad, 21st May 1900.

had kept the letter of their oath. He has been accused of having refused to allow reprisals longer than was wise; but history will record that his goodness of heart made possible a reconciliation which in the hour of desperate strife seemed hopeless.

On the 8th of May Lord Roberts was joined by French with the 1st (Porter's), 3rd (Gordon's), and 4th (Dickson's) Brigades of Cavalry. The 1st and 4th Cavalry Brigades and the Mounted Infantry, marching on the left, moved on to the south bank of the Zand, opposite Dupreez' laager. "That evening a squadron of the Scots Greys succeeded in crossing the river near Verneulen's Kraal and holding the drift at that point. The 7th Division bivouacked near Merries fontein, and Major-General Ian Hamilton marched to Bloemplaatz and pushed on the 1st battalion Derbyshire Regiment to Junction Drift." [1]

On the morning of the 10th of May the enemy were seen holding the north bank of the zand in considerable strength. Their line stretched in front for twenty miles, and the ground was very favourable to them. It was a vast rolling plain studded with farmhouses and broken with *nullahs* where Boer marksmen could be cunningly hid, and small groups of hills where batteries could be planted. On the east were a series of low *kopjes* trending from the river inland. A frontal attack must lead to a grave loss of life. Lord Roberts therefore determined to try again "old Frederick's" favourite turning movement. He instructed French with the Cavalry Brigades, supported by the 1st Mounted Infantry Brigade under Major-General Hutton, to make a wide

[1] From Field-Marshal Lord Roberts to the Secretary of State for War, Kroonstad, 21st May 1900.

turning movement on the left. He directed Ross and Henry's mounted infantry-men to seize the drift near the railway bridge in the centre. Ian Hamilton was to cross by the Junction drift and attack the enemy's left. At 7.30 A.M. the 7th Division crossed the Junction drift, and as the leading corps, leaving the river, advanced on the opposite ridge, the enemy opened a heavy fire of musketry. Ian Hamilton at once sent across the river the Cavalry Brigade and the 21st and 19th Brigades to support them. General Tucker shelled on the *kopjes* in front of him, and after an hour his troops, pressing forward, found the Boers had abandoned their position. A body of them had taken up a new position on two low rocky *kopjes*, on the summit of which they had placed three guns. From these they poured their fire of shells as the Sussex Regiment, supported by the City Imperial Volunteers, advanced across the plain. "When the Sussex Regiment had approached within 500 yards, they fixed bayonets and with a cheer charged the hill in a grand rush, driving the Boers pell-mell before them. They took a few prisoners, and poured in a hot fire among the runaways."

The resistance in the centre was more stubborn. Half an hour before the 7th Division had crossed Junction drift Ross and Henry's mounted infantry battalions had seized the drift near the railway bridge, and were followed across the river by the 3rd Cavalry Brigade and the 11th Division. As the men entered the wide plain the enemy opened on them with guns posted on the hills on the right. A battery of Horse Artillery replied vigorously and checked their fire, while the 4th and 5th Mounted Infantry pushed forward on the west of the railway. A long ravine separated them from the enemy, who had five guns posted in the open on the farther side; skirmishers occupied the farm-houses and lay concealed in deep spruits. The Boers worked their guns quickly; but their shots flew beyond the Mounted Infantry, who, having dismounted, bore steadily onwards. Among them were Lumsden's Horse, consisting of young Englishmen who, deserting the counting houses of Calcutta and the tea-plantations of Assam, had answered with enthusiasm the call to defend the empire. The skirmishers moved forward, followed by the horse batteries, who as opportunity offered returned the Boer fire. When the leading line had come more closely within range a one-pounder Maxim galloped to the front and discharged showers of missiles into the enemy's guns. Quickly harnessing their teams and limbering up, the enemy dragged their guns away. The Mounted Infantry pursued them. Two hundred Boers concealed in mealy-patches suddenly opened a smiting fire, and they had to fall back on their supports. The Boers, turning round, followed their pursuers. But the Maxim again came into action and the enemy fell back. Meanwhile Lumsden's Horse had seized a *kopje* which threatened the enemy's retreat. The Boer artillerymen tried to turn them out by shells, but in vain. The shells burst right and left and all around, but the gallant band held the *kopje* till they came in touch with Hutton's brigade.[1]

At daybreak French crossed the river. His orders were to turn the Boers' flank if possible, and to reach Ventersberg station in the evening. After marching three hours he reached the diamond mines at Draksberg. The enemy were reported

---

[1.] The *'Times,'* June 25, 1900.

to be in position on low hills at Vlak Plaat. He sent the Scots Greys to cover the right and reconnoitre, while he detached his 1st Brigade, under Porter, towards Vrede Vredray to attack the Boers in front. The Carabineers and Inniskillings, belonging to Porter's brigade, rode forward, and a squadron of the latter occupied a *kopje*. Soon after the troopers on the knoll spied a huge grey mass advancing towards them. It moved slowly across the plain, and as it crept forward our men saw three columns in close order, and from the khaki dress believed they were a body of Mounted Infantry. The belief was confirmed by observing that it delivered no fire. Slowly it crept within range, and then without dismounting the Boers sent a murderous volley into the troopers on the *kopje*. Fourteen were struck down dead and many fell wounded. The survivors rushed back to their horses.

At 11.15 A.M. the Canadian Mounted Infantry and a battery were sent to the right to support the 1st Brigade. Meanwhile French continued to develop his flanking movement, and under cover of it he withdrew the 1st Brigade " and swung them to the rear of the 4th, which now retired magnificently under an artillery-fire from long-range guns which the enemy had brought to bear upon them. But the enemy's flank had been fairly turned, and their centre and left having already given way, the right fell back from before French shortly after 2 P.M." [1] The enemy, completely outmanoeuvred, retired towards Kroonstad and blew up the railway bridges and culverts as they fell back.

That evening Lord Roberts encamped with the 11th Division eight miles north of the river. The following day he marched to Geneva siding, fourteen miles from Kroonstad,

---

[1] The '*Times,*' weekly edition, June 29, 1900.

and eight miles from Boschrand, where the Boers were holding an intrenched position to cover the town. During the night they, however, evacuated their intrenchments at Boschrand and retreated northwards. On the 12th of May Lord Roberts entered Kroonstad with the 11th Division without encountering any opposition.

Another halt was now imperative, as Lord Roberts could advance no farther until the single railway upon which he was dependent for his supplies had been repaired. He had also to provide, as far as his resources would permit, for the safety of his main line of communication by occupying strategical points to the east of the railway at Wynberg, Senekal, Lindley, and Heilbron. The Commander-in-Chief calculated that as soon as Mafeking had been relieved a large proportion of the troops under the command of Lord Methuen and Sir Archibald Hunter would be available to co-operate on his left flank, and he hoped that Sir Redvers Buller would be able to assist by an advance westward to Vrede or north-westward in the Standerton direction. "But, whether these anticipations could be realised or not, I felt that the enormous advantage to be gained by striking at the enemy's capital before he had time to revive from the defeats he had already sustained, would more than counter-balance the risk of having our line of communication interfered with—a risk which had to be taken into consideration." [1]

On the 17th of May Lindley, a little south-east of Kroonstad, was occupied by General Ian Hamilton's column, and Lord Methuen, acting according to Lord Roberts' orders, reached

[1] From Field-Marshal Lord Roberts to the Secretary of State for War, Kroonstad, 21st May 1900.

Hoopstad on the south-west. "I had thought of his force taking part in the Transvaal operations, but with regard to the probability of disturbances on the line of railway I determined to place it in the neighbourhood of Kroonstad, to which place it was accordingly directed to proceed." [1]

On the 18th of May–the very day that Lord Roberts had promised succour should reach the garrison–Mafeking was relieved after a heroic defence of two hundred days. On the 17th of April the Commander-in-Chief gave orders for the formation of a flying column of mounted troops about 1100 strong, with mule transport, for the relief of the town. He placed Colonel B. T. Mahon, 8th Hussars, a young Irish officer who had made his reputation as a cavalry leader in Egypt, in command of this force. It consisted "of 900 mounted men, including the Imperial Light Horse, four Horse Artillery guns with 100 men, 100 picked infantry soldiers to guard the waggons, 52 waggons with 10 mules each, and nearly 1200 horses. The column was to take with it rations for sixteen days and forage for twelve days. Medicines and medical comforts for the Mafeking garrison were also to be taken." General Hunter was instructed to co-operate with Lord Methuen in distracting the enemy's attention until the flying column had crossed the Vaal and had obtained a good start. The day after (4th May) Lord Roberts began his advance on Kroonstad Mahon crossed the Vaal at Barkley West and moved rapidly to the north. In five days he had done 120 miles. No Boers were encountered till the column reached Koodo's Rand, where the enemy

[1] From Field-Marshal Lord Roberts to the Secretary of State for War, Pretoria, 14th August 1900.
[2] Ibid., 9th July 1900.

had arranged to dispute advances all along the main road. Mahon, however, with considerable skill deflected his line of march to the west.[2] " The Boers here had an ambush in thick scrub, which was strongly supported from Koodo's Rand (at Koodo's Rand Nek they had several guns in position); they made a determined attack, but we beat them off after forty-five minutes' fighting. All troops behaved excellently." [1]

At 5 A.M. on the 15th of May Mahon reached the river Molopo (plenty of running water) at Jan Masibi, and there met Colonel Plumer's column, which had just arrived after a night's march. It consisted of Rhodesians, and had been strengthened by C Battery of four 12-pounder guns of the Canadian Artillery under Major Enden, and a body of Queenslanders. They had formed part of General Carrington's small force which had come through Beira, and after a splendid march reached Plumer's column, hastening down from the north to the relief of Mafeking.

Mahon rested that day the men and animals who had been marching all night. At break of day, having formed his forces into two brigades (the 1st under Lieut.-Colonel Plumer and the 2nd under Lieut.-Colonel Edwardes), he advanced towards Mafeking. The force moved along the north or right bank of the Molopo in two parallel columns at half a mile interval, the convoy in the centre and slightly in rear. About 12.30 A.M. firing was heard on the left front, and Mahon, pushing forward, found the Boers posted all round him and five guns and two pom-poms in different places.

The convoy rather impeded my movements, as it was under

[1.] From Colonel B. Mahon to Lieut.-General Sir Archibald Hunter, K.C.B., commanding 10th Division.

shell-fire, and the Boers were trying to attack it from both flanks and also from the rear; so I had to strengthen both my flank—and rear-guards, at the same time I continued my advance on Mafeking, the Boers retiring from our front and keeping up with us on the flanks. Our artillery, especially the Royal Horse Artillery, were making very good practice. At 4.40 P.M. I ordered Colonel Edwardes to bring up his left and turn the Boer right flank: this movement was entirely successful. At 4.40 P.M. I had a message from Colonel Plumer to say his advance was checked on the right by a gun and pom-pom fire from the White Horse (Israel's Farm). I ordered the Royal Horse Artillery to shell the house. They soon silenced the gun, but not the pom-pom. I then sent Captain Carr with the infantry to take the house, which they did, and captured one waggon and a lot of pom-pom ammunition. It was by this time getting dark, or I think they would have got the pom-pom.[1]

At 5.45 P.M. all firing except stray shots ceased. The Boers retired, and the way to Mafeking was open. At 3.30 A.M. on the 17th of May Mahon's force entered the little town on the veldt whose gallant defence had stirred the feelings of Englishmen in every quarter of the empire. Next morning there was not a Boer near Mafeking.

On the 22nd of May Lord Roberts, with the 7th and 11th Divisions, left Kroonstad. The same day Ian Hamilton's column reached and occupied Heilbron, thus converging to the railway and main column. On the left French with the 1st and 4th Cavalry Brigades, and Hutton with the 1st Brigade of Mounted Infantry, were to the north-east of Rhenoster Kop. The next day Lord Roberts, with the main body, reached the Rhenoster river. "No opposition was met with, although the hills north of the river furnished a strong

---

[1] From Colonel B. Mahon to Lieut.-General Sir Archibald Hunter, K.C.B., commanding 10th Division.

defensive position, and all preparations had been made by the enemy to give us a warm reception. It must be concluded that they felt their line of retreat was threatened from the east by General Hamilton's column at Heilbron, and from the west by the cavalry and Mounted Infantry under Generals French and Hutton, which had effected a crossing lower down the stream." [1]

On the 24th of May Lord Roberts marched with the 11th Division to Vredefort station. The 7th bivouacked on the west of the railway four miles in rear, and the 3rd Cavalry Brigade four miles east of the station. General Ian Hamilton's column halted also to the east of the railway, but seven miles north of the station. The troops under Generals French and Hutton moved to the north-west, the 1st and 4th Cavalry crossing the Vaal at Parys and Versailles.

At Ventersberg Lord Roberts directed Ian Hamilton to move his column across the railway from the right flank of the British army to the left. "By this move the enemy were completely deceived. They had expected Hamilton's column to cross the Vaal at Engelbrecht's drift, east of the railway, and collected there in some force to oppose him.' [2]

On the 26th of May Lord Roberts marched with the 7th and 11th Divisions to Taaibosch Spruit, seven miles short of Viljoen's Drift, where Colonel Henry's mounted infantry had encamped at the spruit the preceding evening. At dawn Henry pushed forward to the railway station of Viljoen's Drift, three miles from the Vaal. "As the Oxfordshire

---

[1] From Field-Marshal Lord Roberts to the Secretary of State for War, Army Headquarters, South Africa, Pretoria, 14th August 1900.
[2] Ibid.

Mounted Infantry and the advance squadron of Loch's
Horse came within range a number of shots were fired into
them from the railway building. The Horse Battery at once
came into action, and a couple of shells sent about 200 of
the Afrikander horses streaming down towards the river."
Colonel Henry pushed on his mounted infantry across the
country, broken with the plants and shafts of coal mines, to
the drift.

Just as the first company were up to their ponies' girths in
the wash of the Vaal a great pillar of smoke went up from the
bridge. The railway bridge had gone. Then followed one of
the prettiest skirmishes of the war. The Oxford and Warwick
companies of Mounted Infantry, the Bedfordshire Yeomanry,
Lumsden's and Loch's Horse pushed over into the Transvaal
in succeeding waves. The enemy were still in the mines. For
an hour it might almost have been termed street-fighting. The
Boers held outhouses and the compound of the mine manager's
house. The Mounted Infantry dismounted, and, their horses
grouped behind mining plant, slag-refuse, and coolie huts, were
making the most of the shelter, which is plentiful in coal mines.
Groups reinforced groups. Half companies dashed from building
to building. Irresistibly the firing line was fed from the river-
bed. Section after section galloped out of the drift, cheering in
the enthusiasm of a fresh invasion. Two-horse guns dashed up
under the whip, and splashing out of the Vaal,–"Action front!"
Then all was over. Lumsden's Horse dismounted and skirmished
out into the open. The last Boer fired a parting shot and galloped
out of range of the shrapnel. A machine-gun with Compton's
Horse exhausted a belt at the scattering horsemen, and ten
minutes later the 4th Mounted Infantry were in Vereeniging. [1]

The main drift over the Vaal was won. The next morning
Lord Roberts entered the Transvaal with the 7th and
11th Divisions and 3rd Cavalry Brigade, and bivouacked

[1] The '*Times*,' June 25, 1900.

at Vereeniging. The infantry had without a halt marched ninety miles in six days. "The climate has been good, but the nights bitterly cold. The road has been the open veldt, which is not the best marching-ground now that the grass is burned and slippery. Each man with his rifle, rounds, bedding, and canteen has carried 41 lb.,–that is, has supported the load which is carried by the average native porter of the country. When I watched the infantry crossing the Vaal this morning, laughing, shaking each other by the hand at the birth of another invasion, I realised that, all said and done, the British infantry is, as it ever has been, the stay of the empire." The next morning, with only one day's supply in hand, Lord Roberts' force moved upon Johannesburg, forty-two miles distant. Headquarters with the 11th Division proceeded to Klip river station, the 7th Division to Wetkop, south of the station, the 3rd Cavalry south of the station, the 3rd Cavalry Brigade to the east, and Colonel Henry's corps of Mounted Infantry to the north. The troops under Generals French and Hutton, strengthened by the two cavalry brigades, advanced to the north-west of Johannesburg, and those under Ian Hamilton to Syperfontein, fifteen miles to the south-west of that town.

On the 29th of May Lord Roberts continued his march to Johannesburg. Colonel Henry with the 8th Mounted Infantry left Klip river at daybreak to seize Elandsfontein junction, where the main railway along which Lord Roberts was advancing meets the railway to Natal. They were supported on the right by the 3rd Cavalry Brigade, whose orders were to make a wider covering detour east of Boksburg. The 11th Division, with the 7th Division on its left, moved along the

main track. The advance-guard arrived at the Natal line
just in time to fire into the last train conveying troops to
the north. After a round, which partly destroyed the line,
the Mounted Infantry worked round to secure the main
communication to Pretoria. At midday they topped a rise
above Boksburg, from whence runs a short branch railway
to Germiston, the important junction where the line from
Johannesburg and from Cape Colony and Natal joins the
line from Pretoria. "The whole Rand lay before us, great
rolling downs similar to the Sussex downs, only desecrated
by a forest of stacks and ungainly evidences of the great
industry which indirectly is responsible for our coming."[1]
Two trains were steaming for Pretoria, and others were still
in Elandsfontein station.

It was now or never. The main body of Mounted Infantry
occupied Boksburg; the Yorkshire Mounted Infantry section
dashed for the station, and a similar party of Australians cut
the line above. The Australians now made a dash for the main
line. A shot was fired, and from every shaft-head and refuse-
mound there came a murderous volley. The Mounted Infantry
rushed for cover.

The engagement then became one of actual street-fighting. It
seemed that things would go hard with the handful of Mounted
Infantry who had made the gallant dash, and it appeared that the
enemy would recapture the train and stations. We looked over
our shoulders. A black mass was descending the southern slopes
into the Rand. It was the leading Infantry Division supporting
the Mounted Infantry which was hastening from Boksburg.
Soon the leading companies of Grenadiers extended and were
streaming through the sideway. The Germiston railway was cut
by the cavalry higher up, and Lord Roberts' grip was tightened
on this Johannesburg suburb of such vital importance.[2]

---

[1] The *'Times,'* weekly edition, June 6, 1900.
[2] Ibid.

Meanwhile Ian Hamilton, who was advancing to a point about twelve miles west of Johannesburg, found his way blocked by a considerable force of the enemy at Doornkop.

They had with them two heavy guns and several field-guns and pom-poms, and were holding a strong position on a long ridge running east and west. Hamilton decided to engage with the enemy at once. The right attack was led by the 1st battalion Gordon Highlanders, who captured the eastern end of the ridge, and, wheeling round, worked along it until after dark. The City Imperial Volunteers led on the left flank and behaved with great gallantry; but the chief share of the action and casualties fell to the Gordon Highlanders, who lost one officer killed and had nine officers wounded. The enemy, who had fought obstinately, retired during the night. Our casualties in this engagement were two officers and 24 men killed and nine officers and 106 men wounded.[1]

The progress of Ian Hamilton's column had been greatly facilitated by the movements of General French, who had before dark worked round the very extended right flank of the enemy.

On the 30th of May the great commercial and industrial capital of the Transvaal was practically in the hands of the British Commander. The 11th Division, with the heavy guns and heads, were to the south of Germiston. The 7th Division, 3rd Cavalry Brigade, and Colonel Henry's mounted infantry held the heights to the north of Johannesburg. Ian Hamilton's column was at Florida, three miles west of the town. The troops under Generals French and Hutton were a few miles north-east of the town. During the day the Boers did what they were bound to do, they agreed to surrender Johannesburg.

---

[1] From Field-Marshal Lord Roberts to the Secretary of State for War, Pretoria, 14th August 1900.

On the morning of the 31st of May Lord Roberts received
the formal surrender of the town, and entered it at noon
with the 7th and 11th Divisions, the union-jack being
hoisted with the usual salute in the main square. After
the ceremony the two divisions marched through the town.
"They made a wonderful spectacle, these battle-stained
soldiers in the streets of a modern city, with ladies on the
balconies throwing down tobacco and sweets to them. Far
into the night the great army filed through in the stern
panoply of war, looking weird and fantastic in the electrically
lighted streets." [1] Lord Roberts took up his quarters in a
small inn with the sign "Orange River," three miles north of
Johannesburg, on the Pretoria Road.

The occupation of Johannesburg marked an important
stage in Lord Roberts' great move from Bloemfontein. By his
strategy he had completely destroyed the plans of the enemy.
Botha intended with a strong force to defend Johannesburg
against French's and Hamilton's columns, but Roberts, by
throwing with extraordinary quickness his main force upon
the enemy's line of communication with the East Rand and
Pretoria, compelled the Boer commander to retire, to save the
political capital of the Transvaal. It was a well-conceived plan
of combined action, carried out with marvellous precision and
determination by the British commander and his generals.
The design required rapid movements, and success was only
possible with such soldiers as Lord Roberts commanded. His
infantry marched 130 miles in seven days, and his own alert
buoyant spirit enlivened the endurance and courage of the men.
He now determined to husband their strength by giving them

---

[1] The 'Times,' June 2, 1900.

two days' rest. During the halt news reached him which caused anxiety and suspense. The enemy were closing in behind him, and threatening the single line of railway leading to Cape Colony, upon which he was dependent for provisioning his army. "This information was the more disconcerting as, owing to our rapid advance and the extensive damage done to the railway, we had practically been living from hand to mouth, and at times had not even one day's rations to the good." [1] It was suggested to Lord Roberts that it might be prudent to halt at Johannesburg until the Orange River Colony should be thoroughly subdued and the railway from Natal opened. "But while fully recognising the danger attending a further advance, I considered the advantages of following up without delay the successes we had achieved, and not giving the enemy time to recover from their several defeats or to remove the British prisoners." And on the 3rd of June Lord Roberts went forward with a boldness marking a great commander; but he never lost sight of the danger he was incurring by exposing his communication to the attack of an active and mobile enemy. "The headquarters (Pole-Carew's) Division and Maxwell's brigade of the 7th Division halted, after a march of twelve miles, at Leeuwkop, Colonel Henry with his corps of Mounted Infantry moving to a point four miles to the north, Brigadier-General Gordon with the 3rd Cavalry Brigade six miles to the east, Lieut.-General Ian Hamilton with his column to Diepstooi, fifteen miles south of Pretoria, and the troops under Generals French and Hutton to Rooikrans, thirteen miles south-west of Pretoria. [2]

---

[1] From Field-Marshal Lord Roberts to the Secretary of State for War, Army Headquarters, South Africa, Pretoria, 14th August 1900.
[2] Ibid.

On the 4th of June Lord Roberts marched with Henry's mounted infantry, four companies Imperial Yeomanry, Pole-Carew's division, Maxwell's brigade, and the naval and siege guns to Six-Mile Spruit, both banks of which were occupied by the enemy.

The Boers were quickly dislodged from the south bank by the 'Mounted Infantry and Imperial Yeomanry, and pursued for nearly a mile, when our troops came under artillery fire. The heavy guns were at once pushed to the front, supported by Stephenson's brigade of the 11th Division, and the enemy's fire was soon silenced. They then moved to the south along a series of ridges parallel to our main line of advance with the object of turning our left flank; but in this they were checked by the Mounted Infantry and Imperial Yeomanry, supported by Maxwell's brigade. As, however, the Boers continued to press on our left flank, and thus threatened our rear, I ordered Ian Hamilton, who was moving three miles to our left, to incline to his right and close the gap between the two columns. As soon as Ian Hamilton's troops came up, and De Lisle's mounted infantry pushed well round the enemy's right flank, they fell back on Pretoria.[1]

Darkness prevented a pursuit in force, and after nearly twelve hours' marching and fighting the troops bivouacked on the ground gained during the day. "The Guards' Brigade lay near the most southern of the forts defending Pretoria, and within four miles of the town, Stephenson's next to the Guards on the west, and Ian Hamilton's column still farther to the west. French, with the 1st and 4th Cavalry Brigades and Hutton's mounted infantry towards the north of the town, Broadwood's cavalry between French and Ian Hamilton, and Gordon's cavalry to the east near

---

[1.] From Field-Marshal Lord Roberts to the Secretary of State for War, 14th August 1900.

the Irene railway station." The goal of Lord Roberts' great enterprise had been reached.

Shortly before dusk De Lisle, whose mounted infantry, chiefly consisting of Australians, had followed up the enemy to within 2000 yards of Pretoria, sent an officer under a flag of truce to demand in the name of the British Commander the surrender of the town. No answer was given. About 10 P.M., however, the military secretary to Commandant-General Botha, accompanied by a general of the Boer army, brought a letter to the Commander-in-Chief from the commandant-general, in which he proposed an armistice for the purpose of arranging the terms of capitulation. The object of this letter was to gain time to remove the rolling stock of the railway and the English prisoners. "I replied," writes Lord Roberts, "that the surrender must be unconditional, and requested an answer before five o'clock the following morning, as my troops had been ordered to advance at daybreak." [1] At five o'clock on the 5th of June Lord Roberts received an answer to this letter from Commandant-General Botha, stating "that he was not prepared further to defend the place, and that he intrusted the women, children, and property to my protection." Lord Roberts ordered Pole-Carew's division with Henry's mounted infantry to move within a mile of the town. The leading companies of the Coldstream Guards were pushed forward in extended order to occupy the hills which overlook the town, while the advanced-guard of the main body made their way

[1] From Field-Marshal Lord Roberts to the Secretary of State for War, Army Headquarters, South Africa, Pretoria, 14th August 1900.

through the country in which the brickfields lie. General Pole-Carew and his staff followed the road which looks directly upon the railway station.

As the advanced-guard appeared over this nek a train was seen to be moving in the station-yard. Although the burgo-master had surrendered the town on the previous evening, it was still necessary to advance with caution, as it was understood that Botha had agreed to the surrender of the capital with great reluctance. Thus when a movement was seen in the station-buildings a halt was made to allow the flankers to take possession of the hills immediately below the forts. This short delay lost us a train and two locomotives, for as the staff galloped down towards the station a long empty train moved out. The escort did all they could to stop it. Lieutenant Walker galloped for the signal-box. Just as he dismounted a man fired at him point-blank from the cover of some bricks. He climbed up into the box and pulled down all the levers, and a section of the guard which arrived at the double were just in time to stop a second train as it left the platform.[1]

At 9 A.M. Lord Roberts arrived at the railway station, and at 2 P.M. the Commander-in-Chief, escorted by his staff, rode into the wide square in the centre of the town. The drums and fifes of the Guards struck up the National Anthem, and the union-jack was hoisted on the Raad-zaal or Government Building. The Transvaal was once more part and parcel of the wide dominions over which that flag floats, and under which there is equal law and justice for all men. Lord Roberts rode forward and called for three cheers for the Queen. Loudly rose the warriors' shout for the gracious Sovereign who honoured her soldiers, and they loved her. For a moment there was silence, then the feelings of the men for their

---

[1.] The *'Times,'* July 9, 1900.

Commander found expression, and cheers for Lord Roberts burst forth from the ranks. His skill and courage had won their confidence, and his unselfishness their affection. The capture of the capital of the Transvaal was the crowning result of his brilliant strategy and their devotion for him.

Much hard work remained to be done by the army in South Africa. After leaving Pretoria, Botha with about 12,000 men occupied a strong position along a range of hills at Pienaar's Poort, a gap through which the railway runs. It is only fifteen miles from Pretoria, and Lord Roberts determined to drive the enemy farther away. On the 11th of June he led from the capital a force of about 16,000 or 17,000 men and 70 guns. "Pole-Carew's division, with the naval and siege guns, moved to Christinen Hall, opposite the Poort, with Ian Hamilton's column on the right and Broadwood's and Gordon's cavalry brigades still farther to the right, in touch with each other and with Hamilton's column. Henry's corps of mounted infantry was directed to close the gap in the hills at Frankpoort, to the north of Eerstefabriken railway station; while French, with Porter's and Dickson's cavalry brigades and Hutton's mounted infantry, was to work round to the north-east of the enemy's position." [1] The centre of the Boers' alignment was so strong naturally that to have assailed it by direct attack would have involved a useless loss of life. Roberts therefore determined to try again a heavy flanking movement. But the long distances to be traversed, and the defensive advantages which the nature of the ground afforded the Boers, impeded his advance. Moreover,

---

[1] From Field-Marshal Lord Roberts to the Secretary of State for War, Pretoria, 14th August 1900.

the Boers had learnt his game, and they determined to play it. Their centre was slightly held, whilst the wings of their army were so strong that French and Hutton on the left and Broadwood and Gordon on the right were just able to hold their own.

Broadwood was, indeed, at one time hardly pressed, being under a heavy artillery-fire from his front and left, whilst he was simultaneously attacked on his right rear by a commando from Heidelburg. The enemy came on with great boldness, and being intimately acquainted with the ground, were able to advance unseen so close to Q Battery Royal Horse Artillery that it was with some difficulty they were kept off, while at the same time another body made a separate attack on Broadwood's right flank. To help the guns and drive off this second body, Broadwood ordered the 12th Lancers and Household Cavalry to charge. Both charges were successful, inasmuch as they relieved the immediate pressure on the guns and Broadwood's right flank, and caused the enemy to revert to artillery and long-range rifle-fire; but I regret to say that these results were obtained at the cost of some twenty casualties, amongst them being Lieut.-Colonel the gallant Earl of Airlie, who fell at the head of his regiment, the 12th Lancers.[1]

Meanwhile Ian Hamilton's infantry pressed on as fast as it could to the assistance of the cavalry, and as each battalion caught up it deployed for attack and became hotly engaged. Lord Roberts saw that the key of the enemy's position on their flank was a high conical hill known as Diamond Hill, and from the movement of the enemy he came to the conclusion there was a chance of capturing a long low ridge in front of it. He determined, therefore, to postpone the attack on Diamond Hill till next day, when the possession

---

[1] From Field-Marshal Lord Roberts to the Secretary of State for War, Pretoria. 14th August 1900.

of the ridge would give facilities for a further advance. Before night the hills in front were occupied, and the troops along our twenty-five miles of battle-front bivouacked on the ground they held. Next morning (12th June) Hamilton, having told off Cordon's cavalry brigade with one infantry battalion to guard his rear, and Broadwood's brigade with a party of mounted infantry to contain the enemy on his right, attacked Diamond Hill with the 82nd Field Battery, the 1st battalions of the Sussex and Derbyshire Regiments, and City Imperial Volunteers battalion. "The troops," writes Lord Roberts, "advanced under artillery-fire from both flanks as well as heavy infantry-fire from the hill itself. The steadiness with which the long line moved forward, neither faltering nor hurrying, although dust from bullets and smoke from bursting shells hung thick about them, satisfied me that nothing could withstand their assaults." [1] At 2 P.M. Diamond Hill was taken. The Boers quickly occupied another position, and fighting continued till dusk. During the night the enemy withdrew towards Middelburg, and next morning Ian Hamilton took up the pursuit, his infantry moving to Elands River station, while his mounted troops pushed on towards Bronkhorst Spruit station. The enemy having been dispersed, the troops returned the next day to the neighbourhood of Pretoria, "the mounted troops requiring a large number of remounts to restore their efficacy."

When Lord Roberts determined to make a rapid advance on Pretoria in order to deal a crushing blow on the Government and main army of the Transvaal, he was aware that he would have to make the attempt at the expense of

[1] From Field-Marshal Lord Roberts to the Secretary of State for War, Pretoria, 14th August 1900.

his communications behind him. "I knew," he writes, "I was not sufficiently strong in numbers to make the railway line absolutely secure, and at the same time have a force at my disposal powerful enough to cope with the main army of the Transvaal supported by forts and guns of position." At Johannesburg, as we have noted, he heard that the enemy had dealt heavy blows on the communications. News also reached him of those errors of execution "which," as William Napier states, "all generals expect, and the experienced are most resigned, as knowing them inevitable." On May 23, owing to a failure of execution, a force of 500 Yeomanry was reduced at Lindley. On the 6th of June a disaster occurred to a post of Derbyshire Militia at Roodeval. The railway was broken in several places and valuable convoys were captured. When Pretoria was in our possession and the prisoners released immediate steps were taken by the Commander-in-Chief to strengthen the posts along the railway. The liberated prisoners were armed and equipped and despatched to stations south of the Vaal. As soon as more troops could be spared they were distributed along the lines between Pretoria. and Kroonstad. Lord Methuen was deputed to superintend these arrangements, and on the 11th of June he attacked and defeated the commando under Christian de Wet at the Rhenoster river. In a few days railway and telegraphic communications were restored between Kroonstad and Pretoria.

Lord Roberts' first objective was now to provide for the security of the railway south of the Vaal, and to capture or disperse the enemy's forces to the east of that line. His second objective was to push eastward from Pretoria towards

Komati Poort, defeating and dispersing the troops under Botha. But at the same time that portion of the Transvaal which lies west of Johannesburg had to be kept under control; the railway line from Johannesburg through Krugersdorp to Potchefstroom had to be guarded. As the Boers were north of the Delagoa railway, it would have been taking an undue risk for the British Commander to have marched eastwards against Botha until he had sufficient troops not only for the forward movement but to guard the communication with Pretoria. To obtain these troops he had to wait until the railway from Natal to Johannesburg had been restored and the military arrangements made for its protection, and the operations in the north-east of the Orange River Colony were sufficiently successful to admit of the transfer of some of the troops to the Transvaal. Considering the vast area of the country, the long distances our troops had to march, and the mobility of the enemy, untoward incidents and delay were inevitable.

After the defeat of the Boers at Diamond Hill Lord Roberts sent Ian Hamilton with a strong column to move through Heidelburg on Frankfort, and thence cooperate with Rundle, Clements, and Paget with a view of driving the enemy eastwards towards Bethlehem and surrounding them. On the 19th of June Ian Hamilton's column left Pretoria, and a few days later it occupied Heidelburg. The enemy vacated the town and were pursued by the cavalry. During the pursuit Ian Hamilton broke his collar-bone, and having to return to Pretoria, Sir Archibald Hunter, who in India and Egypt had made a reputation as a most capable general in the field, was appointed to command the column. On the 11th of July Hunter reached Bethlehem and found it had been occupied, after two days' fighting, by the force under Clements and Paget.

On the 2nd of July the two generals, having joined hands, had begun their advance on Bethlehem. Paget found the Boers in a strong position on his line of march. Four guns of the 38th R.F.A. and two guns of the City Volunteers were rapidly brought into play. The Boers, creeping up a donga, sent a volley into the battery and made a rush for the guns. Lieutenant Belcher was killed, and Captain Fitzgerald, the only other officer, was wounded. Twenty men fell, and the horses were struck down. Captain Budworth, adjutant of the City Volunteers, seeing what had taken place, charged with a troop of Australians, and drove the enemy from the guns. At this juncture the infantry, which had been carrying out a turning movement, came into action, and the Boer position was taken. The troops bivouacked fifteen miles north-east of Bethlehem. The next morning Paget moved to the north-west with the object of turning the enemy's left while Clements' troops operated on their right flank. The day's fighting was mainly an artillery duel, and sundry attempts to outflank the enemy were frustrated on both flanks. "The enemy were found on every space and hill for from six to eight miles on both right and left of the town, while the hills behind were also strongly occupied; and, in addition, on a lofty ridge in front of the town two guns were discernible. The latter position, a very strong one, was evidently the key of the situation, and its occupants were enabled to annoy and harass the infantry advancing on both sides." [1] The day wore away without any substantial result, and the infantry

---

[1] The 'Times,' weekly edition, August 15, 1900.

slept on the ground they occupied. Next morning Clements gave instructions to the colonel of the Royal Irish to storm the lofty ridge if he should think the opportunity favourable. "Extending his men to three widespread lines (H company in front), their gallant commander led them on. Without hesitation or a stop for a moment the brave fellows responded. Received with a shower of fire, to which they barely paused to reply, on they went down a long slight depression in the ridge and up the swelling slope—here and there men dropping but never stopping their comrades." [1] The Boers, on seeing the Irish pressing forward, began at once to remove their two guns. But the reverse slope was a steep rocky descent. With ropes one gun was safely hauled down the cliff. But the second overturned, and the wheel being broken, the retreating Boers abandoned it. When the gallant Irish reached the edge of the cliff they saw the enemy streaming away 200 yards off. They fired two volleys after them, and then loud rose the cheers when they found the gun fifty feet below. It was one of the 15-pounders of Stormberg.

The enemy, estimated at about 7000 strong with 20 guns, retired through the mountains to the south of Bethlehem into the Broad Water Basin, surrounded by a huge semicircular range of hills, and occupied positions of great natural strength commanding the neks or passes. Hunter's instructions were "to block the enemy into the enclosed district into which he had retired, to prevent his escape, bring him into action, and, if possible, force him to surrender." [2] To block the enemy and

---

[1] The 'Times,' weekly edition, August 15, 1900.
[2] From Lieut.-General Sir A. Hunter, K.C.B., D.S.O., commanding operations in the eastern districts of the Orange River Colony, to the Chief of the Staff, South Africa, Fouriesburg, 4th August 1900.

prevent his escape Hunter sent Bruce Hamilton to Naauwpoort
Nek and Golden Gate, at the northern extremity of the basin,
and watched Retiefs Nek himself. Paget was at Slabbert's
Nek, and Rundle was holding Commando Nek. The Boers
seemed fairly surrounded and escape impossible. But escape
is always possible to a small compact body of men who are
expert in the use of horses and transport, who have the
sympathy of the inhabitants, and who are familiar with every
bridle-path in the country, which is a network of mountains
and precipices. On the night of the 5th of September Christian
de Wet with 1500 picked Boers, each man having a horse to
carry his gear, five guns and ammunition carried on light
carts well horsed, slipped through Slabbert's Nek. It was
a mortifying incident, but about 6000 Boers remained, and
around them Hunter proceeded to draw his cordon closer.
On the 20th and 21st Bruce Hamilton attacked the enemy
holding Spitzkop, a hill nine miles south-east of Bethlehem,
and occupied it. On the 23rd of July the heights commanding
Retiefs Nek were seized by the Black Watch and Highland
Light Infantry. The same day Clements, having joined Paget,
gained a footing on the high ground to the right of the nek
by a turning movement executed by the 1st battalion Royal
Irish Regiment, the 2nd battalion Wiltshire Regiment, and
Brabant's Horse. At daybreak on the 24th of July Hunter
pressed the success he had gained the previous night, and
before sunset he had pushed through the pass to the valley
beyond. Clements having occupied Slabbert's Nek, his
mounted troops and artillery pursued the retreating enemy.
Hunter ordered Rundle to move towards Fouriesburg, to
which the Boers had retired, and on the 25th with Clements'

and Paget's troops he himself advanced towards the town. The next day on entering it he found it already occupied by a portion of Rundle's division headed by Driscoll's Scouts, who had made a march of twenty-five miles from Commando Nek. The Boers made a dash for Naauwpoort Nek and Golden Gate, but Macdonald had blocked these two entrances. On the morning of the 28th Hunter followed up the enemy beyond Fouriesburg with the available troops of the 8th Division and Clements' and Paget's brigades. Paget commanded the rear-guard, which was soon engaged with the Boers, who fought a tenacious rear - guard action throughout the day in the vicinity of Staapkranz Ridge, which was only occupied by the Scots Guards under Major Romilly, D.S.O., after midnight. On the 29th General Prinsloo asked for a four days' armistice. Hunter refused, demanding unconditional surrender, and backed up his demand by a further advance towards the enemy. At 4.30 P.M. the Boer commandant generals agreed to surrender the next day. "On the 30th July Prinsloo and Crowther, with the Ficksburg and Ladybrand commandoes, 879 strong, surrendered, other commandoes coming in later. General Olivier, with his commando, managed, however, to escape during the night through Golden Gate, though he and his men had been included by Commandant-General Prinsloo in the unconditional surrender of the Boer force. The total number of prisoners taken was 4140, with three guns, two of which belonged to U Battery Royal Horse Artillery. Over 4000 horses and ponies, a large number of rifles, and over a million rounds of small-arm ammunition, also fell into our hands." [1]

---

[1] Field-Marshal Lord Roberts to the Secretary of State for War, Pretoria, 10th August 1900.

Thus was brought to a brilliant close a series of operations "conducted by Lieut.-General Hunter," to use the words of the Commander-in-Chief, "with marked ability and judgment," and carried out by, to use the words of their general, "as fine a fighting force as ever stood to arms." "In spite of hardships there was no crime, no grumbling. Officers and men are stout-hearted, cheerful, and full of fight." On the 4th of August Macdonald occupied Harrismith, and railway communication was opened between Harrismith and Natal. Lord Roberts' first objective had been accomplished.

The time had come to carry out his second objective, to push eastward from Pretoria towards Komati Poort. But before the British Commander could move, along the Delagoa Railway he had to clear the country to the north and east of Pretoria, where the Boers, knowing that his force was crippled until his remounts arrived, had been increasing in strength and boldness. On the 28th of July, horses having reached him, and communication with Durban having been established, Lord Roberts despatched a strong column under Ian Hamilton to Hammanskraal, twenty-five miles north of Pretoria, on the Pietersburg Railway. The headquarters of the 11th Division were at Eerstefabriken, east of Pretoria, and the Guards Brigade were farther east, at Rhenosterfontein. French's force was thirty miles south-east of the capital. Ian Hamilton, acting under orders, marched on Bronkhorst Spruit, and being joined by Mahon on the way, the two columns reached Rustfontein, seven miles north of Bronkhorst Spruit. The enemy, finding their line of retreat threatened, abandoned the strong positions which they were holding in front of the

11th Division, and on the 23rd of July Stephenson's brigade advanced unopposed to Elands River station, the right flank being protected by the Mounted Infantry and cavalry under Hutton and French. The same day French, pushing on, crossed to the east of the Wilge river. On the 24th of July Lord Roberts reached Bronkhorst Spruit, which in the course of the day had been occupied by the 11th Division and Ian Hamilton's column. French and Hutton pressed forward and came in touch with the enemy six miles south of Balmoral. Colonel Alderson attacked their right, while the 1st and 4th Cavalry Brigade made a wide turning movement round their left." [1] The Boers fell back towards Middelburg. On the 25th Balmoral was occupied by Ian Hamilton's troops, and the 11th Division reached Wilge river. French and Hutton, again pushing forward, crossed Olifant's river at Naauwpoort and bivouacked on high ground, whence the enemy could be seen retreating in great disorder through Middelburg. "The next day French and Hutton entered Middelburg, and a line of outposts was established so as to cut off communications between Botha's forces and the Boer commandoes by the west and south of Pretoria." [2] So far the advance eastward along the Delagoa Bay Railway had been rapidly and successfully executed. But a long halt now became necessary. Time was required to establish the line of communication between Pretoria and Middelburg by repairing the railway bridges, which had all been destroyed. Supplies had to be collected at Middelburg. More troops than

---

[1] Field-Marshal Lord Roberts to the Secretary of State for War, Pretoria, 10th October 1900.
[2] Ibid.

were available were needed before the British Commander
could operate towards the rocky stronghold of Machadodorp,
which the Boers held in considerable force. On the 26th of
July Lord Roberts returned to Pretoria.

The chief Boer commando to the south of Pretoria was
that of Christian de Wet. After breaking away from Hunter
he had taken up his position in some extremely difficult
country round Reitzburg, seven miles south of the Vaal.
On the 4th of August Lord Kitchener left Pretoria in order
to assume command of the troops which were surrounding
his lurking-place. Again his escape from a strong force well
distributed seemed impossible; but the hills on each side of
the river furnished an effective screen to the movements of
a mobile column. On the night of the 6th August De Wet,
by a rapid dash, succeeded in crossing the Vaal by the drift
which bears his name. Instant orders were sent to Methuen,
who was at Potchefstroom, to block the drifts on the northern
side; but he reached the river too late to prevent the dashing
Boer commander from getting across. A stern chase ensued.
On the 9th Methuen engaged his rear-guard, but the Boers,
holding every *kopje*, kept off their pursuers. All night the
Boers trekked onwards, replacing some of their exhausted
horses by fresh ones from the farms which they passed. On
the 10th De Wet had crossed the railway line and left his
pursuers to the south of him. On the 12th Methuen, with
1200 mounted men of the Colonial Division and Yeomanry
and ten guns, again came in touch with and engaged the
Boer rear-guard, and captured a gun. Thirty-five miles
across the veldt the two contending forces went that day.
Before them lay the Magaliesberg range, and there were

only three passes by which De Wet could escape. Baden-Powell with his mounted troops and the 1st battalion Border Regiment held Commando Nek. Lord Methuen, leaving De Wet's direct track, took up a position six miles south of the Magato Pass. On the 15th Ian Hamilton arrived fifteen miles south-west of Olifant's Nek. "During the preceding night, however, De Wet had moved unobserved to the north of Hamilton's column, and crossing Olifant's Nek, he made for Rustenberg." De Wet had again escaped, but he could no longer threaten Lord Roberts' communications; and the troops engaged in his pursuit were available for a farther advance along the Delagoa Railway to Komati Poort.

On the 24th of August Lord Roberts made his third and final advance. Pole-Carew with the 11th Division moved along the railway line and occupied Belfast, after having encountered some opposition. Sir Redvers Buller, who had been moving up from the Natal Railway with the gallant force who had crossed the Tugela, relieved Ladysmith, and forced Laing's Nek, was fifteen miles due south of that town. French was operating on his left flank. On the 25th of August Lord Roberts arrived at Belfast. On reconnoitring the ground he saw that he was in touch with a part of the Boer main position. "This position, as far as could be ascertained, extended from the neighbourhood of Swartz *Kopje* on the north to Dalmanutha on the south, a distance of some twenty miles." [1] The Commander-in-Chief's first idea was to hold the enemy in front with the 11th Division, whilst Buller and French turned their left from the south; but on

---

[1] From Field-Marshal Lord Roberts to the Secretary of State for War, Pretoria, 10th October 1900.

consulting with General Buller he found that the ground was not favourable to a turning movement from the left, and he therefore determined to contain the enemy's front by the 18th Brigade and turn his right flank with the Guards Brigade, assisted by General French and Colonel Henry's mounted infantry. In pursuance of this plan the following day French moved from six miles south of Belfast to six miles north of it. "Pole-Carew with the 11th Division endeavoured to advance along the Lydenburg road to his support, but came under so heavy a shell and rifle fire that he made but little progress. Buller on the right had been more successful. He had pushed back the Boers, who were holding a series of strong positions to the south-east of Belfast, to within four miles of the railway between that town and Dalmanutha."[1]

On the 27th of August French advanced eight miles farther north and drove the enemy from the Swartz *Kopjes*, and from this position threatened their lines of retreat. The same morning Buller, working on the Boer left flank, advanced towards the high Bergendal ridge, which runs from Belfast on the south side of the railway. At almost the highest point of the ridge is situated Bergendal farm. "About 300 yards to the west of the farm a peculiar *kopje*, formed of a conglomeration of immense stones, covering about three acres in extent, rises suddenly from the smooth grassy slopes which prevail over the rest of the ridge. The formation is an unusual one, as, except at the *kopje* itself, which with its immense stones and rocky crevices forms a sort of natural fortress, the ground for 2000 yards round affords no shelter

---

[1] From Field-Marshal Lord Roberts to the Secretary of State for War, Pretoria, 10th October 1900.

of any sort to advancing troops. The slopes within 500 yards of the *kopje* being gentle and easy, we could see that the *kopje* was occupied in some force: we were able to locate two guns posted on the ridge to the east of it, and it was evident that several trenches had been dug, and that the ridge itself was held in considerable force." [1]

At 11 A.M. Buller's artillery began to shell the farm and rocky *kopje*. The enemy replied with a pom-pom at short range, a Long Tom, and several high velocity guns. "The bombardment," writes Sir Redvers Buller, "was much assisted by a 4.7 gun posted at Belfast, which the Commander-in-Chief, who was watching the operations, at once directed to co-operate with us." After three hours' shelling, as the enemy still clung to the *kopje*, the infantry were ordered to assault it.

General Kitchener directed Lieut.-Colonel Metcalfe to move the 1st battalion Rifle Brigade under cover of the ridge from which our guns were firing, and place his battalion across the main east and west ridge on which the *kopje* of the farm stands, and to assault in front from the west; Lieut.-Colonel Payne to move the Inniskilling Fusiliers down the face of gun ridge and to assault the flank of the position from the south; the 1st battalion Devon Regiment supporting the left centre, and the 2nd Gordon Highlanders supporting the right attack. At the moment of starting to descend gun ridge, the leading companies of the Inniskilling Fusiliers were met by a very accurate and heavy pom-pom fire which staggered them for a moment, but the men re-formed themselves and pressed onward with hardly any delay. Both regiments were admirably led by their commanding officers. The enemy stood their ground with great gallantry, and only left their positions when

---

[1] From the General Commanding the Natal Army to the Field-Marshal Commanding-in-Chief the Forces in South Africa, Machadodorp, Headquarters Natal Army, Spitzkop, Transvaal, 13th September 1900.

the Rifles were among them and the Inniskilling Fusiliers ontheir flank, between twenty and thirty of them keeping up fire until actually made prisoners. The attack, which, as I have described, was made without the assistance of any cover, was a most gallant one. The moment the *kopje* was carried, the Rifle Brigade, although they had lost their colonel, who, to our great regret, was wounded while gallantly leading the advance, at once re-formed and swept on their own initiative up the plateau, carrying all before them, supported by the Devons, who had got up on the left, and the Gordons and Inniskillings, who joined in on the right.

The honours of the assault belong to the Rifle Brigade, as they had to attack that part of the *kopje* which had been most protected from our artillery-fire; but all the troops did splendidly, and the carrying of such a position, held as it was by resolute men, will always remain present to the minds of those who witnessed it as a most gallant feat of arms.[1]

Next day Buller occupied Machadodorp almost without opposition. On the 30th of August French's cavalry, supported by the Guards Brigade, reached the neighbourhood of Nooitgedacht, and 1800 of our prisoners whom the Boers had removed from Pretoria reached our camp. On the 1st of September Lord Roberts, acting under the orders of her Majesty's Government, issued a proclamation annexing the Transvaal. The same day Buller began his movement towards Lydenburg, fifty miles north of the railway line, by moving from Helvetia to Elandspruit on the Crocodile river. Next morning his advance was opposed by the enemy, who held a strong position at Badfontein. They had with them three

---

[1] From the General Commanding the Natal Army to the Field-Marshal Commanding-in-Chief the Forces in South Africa, Spitzkop, Transvaal, 13th September 1900.

[2] From Field-Marshal Lord Roberts to the Secretary of State for War, Pretoria, 10th October 1900.

6-inch guns. "Buller described the position as resembling Laing's Nek, and I agreed with him that it would be wiser to defer his attack until I could send him assistance." [2]

Accordingly on the 3rd of September Lord Roberts sent Ian Hamilton to turn the right flank of the Boer forces in front of Buller. Two days later he occupied Zwagershoek, "thus securing the debouchement through the defile into the Lydenburg valley, so threatening the right rear of the Boer position at Badfontein." The same day Buller demonstrated strongly against the enemy's left flank, the 1st battalion Leicestershire Regiment and the 1st battalion King's Royal Rifle Corps dragging the guns of a field battery up a steep hill, when a heavy fire was brought to bear on the Boers. On the 6th of September the enemy, owing to the right flank of their position having been turned, and to the pressure on their left flank, evacuated their stronghold at Badfontein and fell back through Lydenburg. Some went to Kruger's Post, but the majority, with two 6-inch guns, took up another formidable position at Paardeplaats, in the mountains overlooking the town and seven miles to the east of it. The Boers always said they would make their last stand at Lydenburg. Ian Hamilton's force occupied the town, and on the 8th of September Buller attacked the enemy at Paardeplaats.

The Boers held a precipitous ridge 1800 feet above the valley, horse-shoe in shape and only easily approachable by paths which were completely commanded from the crest. One great feature of the attack was the skill with which the guns were pushed forward from point to point until they reached positions from which they silenced the enemy's artillery and greatly subdued the rifle-fire. Another was the dash with which the infantry pressed forward over rocks and across ravines, and other apparently impracticable ground, until they carried the ridge. A third was the simultaneous arrival of the right, left, and centre of the attack–namely, the Royal Scots, the Royal Irish, and the 1st battalion Devonshire Regiment–in the enemy's position. The Boers lost considerably, but their retreat was concealed by heavy mist. Our casualties amounted to 13 killed and 25 wounded, three of the former and 16 of the latter belonging to the Volunteer Company of the Gordon Highlanders, which came under shrapnel-fire at a distance of nearly seven miles from the enemy's guns.[1]

The next day Buller followed the beaten Boers, and on the 11th of September he had occupied the junction of the roads from the east and south near Spitzkop. That evening Paul Kruger, seeing overwhelming forces gathering around him, fled from the Transvaal. He had staked all, and all was lost. His courage, his doggedness, his power of sarcasm, his energetic vigour of language, made him a strong ruler over ignorant men. He showed no small amount of world-craft, but he was lacking in the foresight of a statesman. Had he played the game more wisely, had he spoken England fair, had he been faithful to his conventions and not sought alliances with foreign Powers, had he removed abuses and reformed his corrupt Government, he might have preserved the independence of his country. But the Boer is more cunning than wise. Paul Kruger thought that England would not fight, and if she did fight, would not win. He was fatally mistaken.

On the 13th of September French, who had been operating on the right of the railway, entered Barberton. By taking his cavalry across the mountains he completely surprised the enemy and succeeded in releasing the remaining British prisoners. Meanwhile steady progress had been made along

---

[1] Field-Marshal Lord Roberts to the Secretary of State for War, Pretoria, 10th October 1900.

the railway, and on the 19th Henry's mounted infantry and the Guards Brigade occupied Kaapmuiden, the junction where the Barberton line joins that to Lorenzo Marqucz. On the 24th of September Pole-Carew with the Guards Brigade and Henry's mounted infantry entered Komati Poort, 260 miles from Pretoria, and the Boers were driven beyond the utmost limit of their western frontier.

Advancing from the Modder river, Lord Roberts pushed before him by manoeuvres the Boer army across a continent where war would not support war, and by his combinations and marches compelled his adversaries to abandon their rocky strongholds and to desert without a serious struggle the capitals of the two republics. With the occupation of Komati Poort and the dispersal of Commandant-General Louis Botha's army, the organised resistance of the Orange Free State and the Transvaal may be said to have ceased. The Boer troops were scattered, yet to beat an army in detail the generals must be acquainted with the country and well informed of their adversary's movements. The English generals have had to fight in an unknown land, and their maps have been worse than useless—"they are a positive danger and delusion." [1] The tangled character of the country has made the handling of troops difficult, disconcerting plans and rendering engagements indecisive, since the beaten foe could always retire to some defile or ridge where cavalry could not pursue him. "Their local knowledge and power of getting over the country; their being masters of three languages in use here to our one; their sources of news from all men and women; their not wearing uniform, and so posing one moment as a peaceful farm dweller and the

---

[1] From Lieut.-General Sir A. Hunter, K.C.B., D.S.O., 4th August 1900.

next proving an active enemy; their secret supplies of arms, ammunition, and food; their hardihood and physical training; their expert and universal skill with horses and transport, with every resource of the country in their favour and denied to us,— these are some of the advantages to the Boers in this warfare."[1] Such advantages are not to be overcome in a moment, and the complete subjugation of two countries, mainly consisting of veldt, jungle, and mountains, whose united areas amount to 161,966 miles, is necessarily bound to be a long and wearisome task. But it is an imperial work and must be done.

Lord Roberts having brought his great operations in South Africa to a successful close, was summoned to England to undertake another momentous and arduous task, the creation of an effective army for the United Kingdom. On the 18th of October it was announced that "her Majesty the Queen has been pleased to approve the appointment of Field-Marshal Lord Roberts, V.C., to be Commander-in-Chief." The announcement was hailed with the deepest satisfaction not only by soldiers but also by the whole population of the empire. The war had brought home to the mind of the nation the fact that England requires a real army—an army in adequate numbers, with its appointment in sound condition, ready to take the field at home or abroad when England requires its services. It was felt that the soldier who had devoted his whole life to his profession, and knew thoroughly in all its parts and requirements the business of war, was best fitted for the creation of such an army. But being satisfied on that point, England must give him authority to carry out what is necessary without having to suit the financial ideal of a Chancellor of the Exchequer or the

---

[1] From Lieut.-General Sir A. Hunter, K.C.B., D.S.O., 4th August 1900.

varying currents of party interests.

On the 29th of November Field-Marshal Lord Roberts handed over the command in South Africa to Lord Kitchener, Chief of the Staff. The farewell address which he issued to the troops has the simple modesty, the generous glow, and the eloquent enthusiasm of the born leader who sees a hero in every private soldier:–

Being about to give up the command of the army in South Africa into the hands of Lord Kitchener, I feel that I cannot part with my comrades, with whom I have been associated for nearly a year, often under very trying circumstances, without giving expression to my profound appreciation of the noble work which they have performed for their Queen and country, and for me personally, and to my pride in the results which they have achieved by their pluck, endurance, discipline, and devotion to duty.

I greatly regret the ties which bind us are so soon to be severed, for I should like to remain with the army until it is completely broken up; but I have come to the conclusion that as Lord Kitchener has consented to take over the command, my presence is no longer required in South Africa, and that duty calls me in another direction.

I shall never forget the officers and men of this force, be they of the Royal Navy, the Colonials, the Regulars, the Militia, the Yeomanry, or the Volunteers. Their interests will always be very dear to me, and I shall continue to work for the army as long as I can work at all.

The service which the South African Force has performed is, I venture to think, unique in the annals of war, inasmuch as it has been absolutely almost incessant for a whole year, in some cases for more than a year. There have been no rest, no days off to recruit, no going into winter quarters, as in other campaigns which have extended over a long period.

For months together, in fierce heat, in biting cold, in pouring rain, you, my comrades, have marched and fought without halt, and bivouacked without shelter from the elements. You frequently have had to continue marching with your clothes in rags and your boots without soles, time being of such consequence that it was impossible for you to remain long enough in one place to refit. When not engaged in actual battle you have been continually shot at from behind *kopjes* by invisible enemies to whom every inch of the country was familiar, and who, from the peculiar nature of the country, were able to inflict severe punishment while perfectly safe themselves. You have forced your way through dense jungles, over precipitous mountains, through and over which with infinite manual labour you have had to drag heavy guns and ox-waggons. You have covered with almost incredible speed enormous distances, and that often on very short supplies of food. You have endured the sufferings inevitable in war to sick and wounded men far from the base, without a murmur and even with cheerfulness.

You have, in fact, acted up to the highest standard of patriotism, and by your conspicuous kindness and humanity to your enemies, your forbearance and good behaviour in the towns occupied, you have caused the army of Great Britain to be as highly respected as it must be henceforth feared in South Africa.

Is it any wonder that I am intensely proud of the army I have commanded, or that I regard you, my gallant and devoted comrades, with affection as well as admiration, and that I feel deeply the parting from you? Many of You, Colonials as well as British, I hope to meet again, but those I may never see more will live in my memory, and will be held in high regard to my life's end.

I have learned much during the war, and the experience I have gained will greatly help me in the work that lies before me, which is, I conceive, to make the army of the United Kingdom as perfect as it is possible for an army to be. This I shall strive to do with my best might.

And now, farewell! May God bless every member of the South African Army, and that you may be spared to return to your homes, and find those dear to you well and happy, is the earnest hope of your Commander!

ROBERTS.